CLASSIC LIBRARY

AUTOBIOGRAPHY OF A YOGI

PARAMHANSA YOGANANDA

A Wilco Book

Outstanding works of universal interest

© *Wilco* Publishing House 2018

ISBN NO. 9789386869364

AUTOBIOGRAPHY OF A YOGI
Paramhansa Yogananda
Complete and Unabridged

Cover image from Wikimedia Commons
Cover design by Haitenlo Semy

This edition published in 2020 by
Wilco International, Mumbai - India
Tel: (91-22) 2204 1420 / 2284 2574
E-mail: wilco@wilcobooks.com
Website: wilcobooks.com
          wilcopicturelibrary.com

Printed and bound in India

AUTHOR'S ACKNOWLEDGMENTS

I am deeply indebted to Miss L.V. Pratt (Tara Mata) for her long editorial labours over the manuscript of this book. My thanks are due also to Mr. C. Richard Wright for permission to use extracts from his Indian travel diary. To Dr. W.Y. Evans-Wentz I am grateful not only for his Preface, but also for suggestions and encouragement.

PARAMAHANSA YOGANANDA

October 28, 1945
Encinitas, California

Paramahansa Yogananda
(05 January, 1893 - 07 March, 1952)
A Premavatar, 'Incarnation of Love'
(see Note 21 on page 254)

**Offered unto the divine hands of
Sri Sri Swami Sri Yukteswar Giri Maharaj,
my blessed, adored,
and worshipful Gurudeva**

Sri Sri Mahavatar Babaji, guru of Sri Sri Lahiri Mahasaya

Sri Sri Lahiri Mahasaya, Guru of Sri Sri Swami Sri Yukteswar Giri

Sri Sri Swami Sri Yukteswar Giri, Guru of Sri Paramahansa Yogananda

Sri Paramahansa Yogananda

Transformation from the state of physical body to Astral body, and finally, to the blissful realm of ideas in the Casual body state.

Publisher's Note

Sri Sri Paramahansa Yogananda's *Autobiography of a Yogi* was published in 1946. It was the first ever account of life penned by any God-realized master. Universally acknowledged as a rare treasure with an unfailing message of hope for all seekers of the ultimate Truth, it is a sure source of joy, giving clear insight to the otherwise incomprehensible Infinite. Tales abound of many who were launched on the path of spirituality by merely leafing through the inspiring pages of the text that follows. In that sense this volume comes charged with powers that could potentially influence and change for ever the very life- style and thought process of the reader.

The narrative recounts the true Yogi's first-hand experiences in childhood, the revelations of growing years with attendant process of training, his inner pull to reach God, and rapid attainment of higher and higher levels of divine states through the Guru's blessings and guidance.

For a layman any scripture-like literature often makes heavy reading. Not this lively work full of subtle humour and down-to-earth approach. This easy-to-read hardbound yet lighter volume is presented in a format that is intended to be a collectors' delight.

Paramahansa Yogananda was the first yoga master of India whose mission was to live and teach in the West. In the 1920s, as he criss-crossed the United States on what he called his "spiritual campaigns," his enthusiastic audiences filled

the largest halls in America to hear him. His initial impact was truly impressive. But his lasting influence is greater still. This single volume, *Autobiography of a Yogi,* helped launch, and continues to inspire, a spiritual revolution around the world. Followers of many religious traditions recognize *Autobiography of a Yogi* as a masterpiece.

This spiritual treasure has long since crossed a million mark and been translated into more than 19 languages. To read and re-read its message of hope to all truth-seekers is to begin every time with a great adventure on an ascending path.

Wilco has been bringing out the finest Classic titles since 1958. Now the thrust of our endeavour is to extend the list and present more of these treasures to our readers, at the most affordable prices.

FOREWORD
By Swami Kriyananda
(J. Donald Walters)

I met Paramahansa Yogananda as a result of reading this book. Finding it was, I must say, a complete surprise. There it was, sitting 'innocently' on a shelf in a bookshop on Fifth Avenue in New York. I'd no idea how utterly this volume would revolutionize my life.

That was late in the summer of 1948. I was desperate to know truth. *Nothing* I'd encountered had persuaded me that people were right in what they were urging on me as my destiny. My father was a geologist working for a large oil company. My mother was respected and happy in her social milieu. Both were, in many ways, ideal parents; I'd never, for example, known them even to have an argument. Their love and respect for one another were an inspiration to their many friends.

Yet even so, I was not happy. Life *must* have more to offer, I felt, than marriage, a nice home in a nice suburb, a socially acceptable job, and 'cocktail party' friendships. I was desperately *unhappy.* I wanted God, and had no idea how to go about finding Him.

That was when I came upon this book. Reading it was the most moving experience of my life. As I launched on this literary adventure, I found myself fluctuating between tears and laughter: tears of joy, laughter of even greater joy. Here, I *knew,* I had found someone at last who had what I so urgently wanted: someone who *knew* God!

I took the next bus non-stop across the American continent: a journey of four days and four nights to Los Angeles where he lived. The first words I addressed to him would have been inconceivable to me a scant week earlier. Words such as *guru, yoga, karma,* and many others that, nowadays, are part of common parlance were utterly new to me. Yet my first words to him were, "I want to be your disciple." I knew to my core that here, before me, was my own so long-needed guide to the Infinite.

To my indescribable joy, I was accepted. His life, an epic of compassion, added further proof that day of his unfathomable kindness: He took in a callow twenty-two-year-old, wholly ignorant in spiritual matters, yet earnestly desirous of being taught. He must have realized what a Herculean task he was assuming. Yet he resolved to do what he could to mould this lump of unwieldy clay into some semblance of a yogi.

My own story, and what it meant to live with this great man of God, is related in *The Path (Autobiography of a Western Yogi)*. The present brief testimony is only an invitation to you to read the following pages.

No man, it has been said, is great in the eyes of his own valet. The saying becomes null and void in the life of Paramahansa Yogananda. He remains the greatest man I have ever known. The people closest to him were the ones who held him in the highest reverence and esteem.

There were, I confess, things in his book that I had to place mentally on a shelf – certainly not because I *disbelieved* them, for my faith in *him* was complete – yet things nevertheless for which my skeptical modern upbringing had not prepared me. The longer I lived with him, however, the more aware I became that wonders – well, why mince words? *miracles!* – were an everyday feature of his life.

Dear Reader, if you are willing to risk a complete change in your life-outlook, read this book! I promise you, it won't devastate you. Rather, you will gain from it joyful new insight into what life is *really* all about.

I met Paramahansa Yogananda fifty-six years ago. Since then I have remained his devoted disciple. And I become more certain every day that what he brought to the world was something of which the whole human race stands in desperate need.

PREFACE

By W. Y. EVANS-WENTZ, M.A. , D.Litt., D.Sc

Author and translator of many classic works on yoga and the
wisdom traditions of the East, including *Tibetan Yoga and Secret
Doctrines, Tibet's Great Yogi Milarepa,* and
The Tibetan Book of the Dead.

THE VALUE of Yogananda's Autobiography is greatly enhanced by the fact
that it is one of the few books in English about the wise men of India which
has been written, not by a journalist or foreigner, but by one of their own
race and training – in short, a book *about* yogis *by* a yogi. As an eyewitness
recountal of the extraordinary lives and powers of modern Hindu saints, the
book has importance both timely and timeless. To its illustrious author, whom
I have had the pleasure of knowing both in India and America, may every
reader render due appreciation and gratitude. His unusual life-document
is certainly one of the most revealing of the depths of the Hindu mind and
heart, and of the spiritual wealth of India, ever to be published in the West.

It has been my privilege to have met one of the sages whose life-
history is herein narrated – Sri Yukteswar Giri. A likeness of the venerable
saint appeared as part of the frontispiece of my *Tibetan Yoga and Secret
Doctrines.** It was at Puri, in Orissa, on the Bay of Bengal, that I encountered
Sri Yukteswar. He was then the head of a quiet *âshrama* near the seashore
there, and was chiefly occupied in the spiritual training of a group of youthful
disciples. He expressed keen interest in the welfare of the people of the
United States and of all the Americas, and of England, too, and questioned
me concerning the distant activities, particularly those in California, of his
chief disciple, Paramahansa Yogananda, whom he dearly loved, and whom
he had sent, in 1920, as his emissary to the West.

Sri Yukteswar was of gentle mien and voice, of pleasing presence, and
worthy of the veneration which his followers spontaneously accorded to him.
Every person who knew him, whether of his own community or not, held him
in the highest esteem. I vividly recall his tall, straight, ascetic figure, garbed
in the saffron-coloured garb of one who has renounced worldly quests, as

* Oxford University Press, 1935.

he stood at the entrance of the hermitage to give me welcome. His hair was long and somewhat curly, and his face bearded. His body was muscularly firm, but slender and well-formed, and his step energetic. He had chosen as his place of earthly abode the holy city of Puri, whither multitudes of pious Hindus, representative of every province of India, come daily on pilgrimage to the famed Temple of Jagannath, 'Lord of the World.' It was at Puri that Sri Yukteswar closed his mortal eyes, in 1936, to the scenes of this transitory state of being and passed on, knowing that his incarnation had been carried to a triumphant completion.

I am glad, indeed, to be able to record this testimony to the high character and holiness of Sri Yukteswar. Content to remain afar from the multitude, he gave himself unreservedly and in tranquillity to that ideal life which Paramahansa Yogananda, his disciple, has now described for the ages.

W. Y. EVANS-WENTZ

CONTENTS

Photo Section

PHOTO SECTION

1. *My Parents and Early Life*

THE CHARACTERISTIC FEATURES of Indian culture have long been a search for ultimate verities and the concomitant disciple-guru[1] relationship. My own path led me to a Christlike sage whose beautiful life was chiselled for the ages. He was one of the great masters who are India's sole remaining wealth. Emerging in every generation, they have bulwarked their land against the fate of ancient Egypt and Babylonia.

I find my earliest memories covering the anachronistic features of a previous incarnation. Clear recollections came to me of a distant life, a yogi[2] amidst the Himalayan snows. These glimpses of the past, by some dimensionless link, also afforded me a glimpse of the future.

The helpless humiliations of infancy are not banished from my mind. I was resentfully conscious of not being able to walk or express myself freely. Prayerful surges arose within me as I realized my bodily impotence. My strong emotional life took silent form as words in many languages. Among the inward confusion of tongues, my ear gradually accustomed itself to the circumambient Bengali syllables of my people. The beguiling scope of an infant's mind! adultly considered limited to toys and toes.

Psychological ferment and my unresponsive body brought me to many obstinate crying-spells. I recall the general family bewilderment at my distress. Happier memories, too, crowd in on me: my mother's caresses, and my first attempts at lisping phrase and toddling step. These early triumphs, usually forgotten quickly, are yet a natural basis of self-confidence.

My far-reaching memories are not unique. Many yogis are known to have retained their self-consciousness without interruption by the dramatic transition to and from 'life' and 'death.' If man be solely a body, its loss indeed places the final period to identity. But if prophets down the millenniums spake with truth, man is essentially a soul, incorporeal and omnipresent. The persistent core of human egoity is only temporarily allied with sense perception.

Although odd, clear memories of infancy are not extremely rare. During travels in numerous lands, I have listened to early recollections from the lips of veracious men and women.

I was born in the last decade of the nineteenth century, and passed my first eight years at Gorakhpur. This was my birthplace in the United Provinces of north-eastern India. We were eight children: four boys and

1 Spiritual teacher; (from Sanskrit root *gur*, to raise, to uplift).
2 A practitioner of yoga, 'union,' ancient Indian science of meditation on God.

four girls. I, Mukunda Lal Ghosh,[3] was the second son and the fourth child.

Father and Mother were Bengalis, of the *Kshatriya* caste.[4] Both were blessed with saintly nature. Their mutual love, tranquil and dignified, never expressed itself frivolously. A perfect parental harmony was the calm centre for the revolving tumult of eight young lives.

Father, Bhagabati Charan Ghosh, was kind, grave, at times stern. Loving him dearly, we children yet observed a certain reverential distance. An outstanding mathematician and logician, he was guided principally by his intellect. But Mother was a queen of hearts, and taught us only through love. After her death, Father displayed more of his inner tenderness. I noticed then that his gaze often metamorphosed into my mother's gaze.

In Mother's presence we tasted our earliest bittersweet acquaintance with the scriptures. Tales from the *Mahabharata* and *Ramayana*[5] were resourcefully summoned to meet the exigencies of discipline. Instruction and chastisement went hand in hand.

A daily gesture of respect to Father was given by Mother's dressing us carefully in the afternoons to welcome him home from the office. His position was similar to that of a vice-president, in the Bengal-Nagpur Railway, one of India's large companies. His work involved travelling, and our family lived in several cities during my childhood.

Mother held an open hand toward the needy. Father was also kindly disposed, but his respect for law and order extended to the budget. One fortnight Mother spent, in feeding the poor, more than Father's monthly income.

"All I ask, please, is to keep your charities within a reasonable limit." Even a gentle rebuke from her husband was grievous to Mother. She ordered a hackney carriage, not hinting to the children at any disagreement.

"Good-by; I am going away to my mother's home." Ancient ultimatum!

We broke into astounded lamentations. Our maternal uncle arrived opportunely; he whispered to Father some sage counsel, garnered no doubt from the ages. After Father had made a few conciliatory remarks, Mother happily dismissed the cab. Thus ended the only trouble I ever noticed between my parents. But I recall a characteristic discussion.

"Please give me ten rupees for a hapless woman who has just arrived at the house." Mother's smile had its own persuasion.

3 My name was changed to Yogananda when I entered the ancient monastic Swami Order in 1915. My guru bestowed the religious title of *Paramahansa* on me in 1935. (See Chap. 42).

4 Traditionally, the second caste of warriors and rulers.

5 These ancient epics are the hoard of India's history, mythology, and philosophy. An 'Everyman's Library' volume, *Ramayana and Mahabharata*, is a condensation in English verse by Romesh Dutt (New York: E. P. Dutton).

"Why ten rupees? One is enough." Father added a justification: "When my father and grandparents died suddenly, I had my first taste of poverty. My only breakfast, before walking miles to my school, was a small banana. Later, at the university, I was in such need that I applied to a wealthy judge for aid of one rupee per month. He declined, remarking that even a rupee is important."

"How bitterly you recall the denial of that rupee!" Mother's heart had an instant logic. "Do you want this woman also to remember painfully your refusal of ten rupees which she needs urgently?"

"You win!" With the immemorial gesture of vanquished husbands, he opened his wallet. "Here is a ten-rupee note. Give it to her with my good will."

Father tended to first say "No" to any new proposal. His attitude toward the strange woman who so readily enlisted Mother's sympathy was an example of his customary caution. Aversion to instant acceptance – typical of the French mind in the West – is really only honouring the principle of 'due reflection.' I always found Father reasonable and evenly balanced in his judgments. If I could bolster up my numerous requests with one or two good arguments, he invariably put the coveted goal within my reach, whether it were a vacation trip or a new motorcycle.

Father was a strict disciplinarian to his children in their early years, but his attitude toward himself was truly Spartan. He never visited the theater, for instance, but sought his recreation in various spiritual practices and in reading the *Bhagavad Gita.*[6] Shunning all luxuries, he would cling to one old pair of shoes until they were useless. His sons bought automobiles after they came into popular use, but Father was always content with the trolley car for his daily ride to the office. The accumulation of money for the sake of power was alien to his nature. Once, after organizing the Calcutta Urban Bank, he refused to benefit himself by holding any of its shares. He had simply wished to perform a civic duty in his spare time.

Several years after Father had retired on a pension, an English accountant arrived to examine the books of the Bengal-Nagpur Railway Company. The amazed investigator discovered that Father had never applied for overdue bonuses.

"He did the work of three men!" the accountant told the company. "He has rupees 125,000 (about $41,250) owing to him as back compensation." The officials presented Father with a check for this amount. He thought so little about it that he overlooked any mention to the family. Much later he was questioned by my youngest brother Bishnu, who noticed the large deposit on a bank statement.

6 This noble Sanskrit poem, which occurs as part of the *Mahabharata* epic, is the Hindu Bible. The most poetical English translation is Edwin Arnold's *The Song Celestial.*

"Why be elated by material profit?" Father replied. "The one who pursues a goal of even mindedness is neither jubilant with gain nor depressed by loss. He knows that man arrives penniless in this world, and departs without a single rupee."

Early in their married life, my parents became disciples of a great master, Lahiri Mahasaya of Benares. This contact strengthened Father's naturally ascetical temperament. Mother made a remarkable admission to my eldest sister Roma: "Your father and myself live together as man and wife only once a year, for the purpose of having children."

Father first met Lahiri Mahasaya through Abinash Babu,[7] an employee in the Gorakhpur office of the Bengal-Nagpur Railway. Abinash instructed my young ears with engrossing tales of many Indian saints. He invariably concluded with a tribute to the superior glories of his own guru.

"Did you ever hear of the extraordinary circumstances under which your father became a disciple of Lahiri Mahasaya?"

It was on a lazy summer afternoon, as Abinash and I sat together in the compound of my home, that he put this intriguing question. I shook my head with a smile of anticipation.

"Years ago, before you were born, I asked my superior officer – your father – to give me a week's leave from my Gorakhpur duties in order to visit my guru in Benares. Your father ridiculed my plan.

" 'Are you going to become a religious fanatic?' he inquired. 'Concentrate on your office work if you want to forge ahead.'

"Sadly walking home along a woodland path that day, I met your father in a palanquin. He dismissed his servants and conveyance, and fell into step beside me. Seeking to console me, he pointed out the advantages of striving for worldly success. But I heard him listlessly. My heart was repeating: 'Lahiri Mahasaya! I cannot live without seeing you!'

"Our path took us to the edge of a tranquil field, where the rays of the late afternoon sun were still crowning the tall ripple of the wild grass. We paused in admiration. There in the field, only a few yards from us, the form of my great guru suddenly appeared![8]

" 'Bhagabati, you are too hard on your employee!' His voice was resonant in our astounded ears. He vanished as mysteriously as he had come. On my knees I was exclaiming, 'Lahiri Mahasaya! Lahiri Mahasaya!' Your father was motionless with stupefaction for a few moments.

" 'Abinash, not only do I give *you* leave, but I give *myself* leave to start for Benares tomorrow. I must know this great Lahiri Mahasaya, who is able to materialize himself at will in order to intercede for you! I will take my wife and ask this master to initiate us in his spiritual path. Will you guide us to him?'

" 'Of course.' Joy filled me at the miraculous answer to my prayer, and the quick, favourable turn of events.

"The next evening your parents and I entrained for Benares. We took a horse cart the following day, and then had to walk through narrow lanes to my guru's secluded home. Entering his little parlour, we bowed before the master, enlocked in his habitual lotus posture. He blinked his piercing eyes and levelled them on your father.

" 'Bhagabati, you are too hard on your employee!' His words were the same as those he had used two days before in the Gorakhpur field. He added, 'I am glad that you have allowed Abinash to visit me, and that you and your wife have accompanied him.'

"To their joy, he initiated your parents in the spiritual practice of *Kriya Yoga*.[9] Your father and I, as brother disciples, have been close friends since the memorable day of the vision. Lahiri Mahasaya took a definite interest in your own birth. Your life shall surely be linked with his own: the master's blessing never fails."

Lahiri Mahasaya left this world shortly after I had entered it. His picture, in an ornate frame, always graced our family altar in the various cities to which Father was transferred by his office. Many a morning and evening found Mother and me meditating before an improvised shrine, offering flowers dipped in fragrant sandalwood paste. With frankincense and myrrh as well as our united devotions, we honoured the divinity which had found full expression in Lahiri Mahasaya.

His picture had a surpassing influence over my life. As I grew, the thought of the master grew with me. In meditation I would often see his photographic image emerge from its small frame and, taking a living form, sit before me. When I attempted to touch the feet of his luminous body, it would change and again become the picture. As childhood slipped into boyhood, I found Lahiri Mahasaya transformed in my mind from a little image, cribbed in a frame, to a living, enlightening presence. I frequently prayed to him in moments of trial or confusion, finding within me his solacing direction. At first I grieved because he was no longer physically living. As I began to discover his secret omnipresence, I lamented no more. He had often written to those of his disciples who were over-anxious to see him: "Why come to view my bones and flesh, when I am ever within range of your *kutastha* (spiritual sight)?"

[9] A yogic technique whereby the sensory tumult is stilled, permitting its practitioner to achieve an ever-increasing identity with cosmic consciousness. (See chap.26).

I was blessed, about the age of eight, with a wonderful healing through the photograph of Lahiri Mahasaya. This experience gave intensification to my love. While at our family estate in Icchapur, Bengal, I was stricken with Asiatic cholera. My life was despaired of; the doctors could do nothing. At my bedside, Mother frantically motioned me to look at Lahiri Mahasaya's picture on the wall above my head.

"Bow to him mentally!" She knew I was too feeble even to lift my hands in salutation. "If you really show your devotion and inwardly kneel before him, your life will be spared!"

I gazed at his photograph and saw there a blinding light, enveloping my body and the entire room. My nausea and other uncontrollable symptoms disappeared; I was well. At once I felt strong enough to bend over and touch Mother's feet in appreciation of her immeasurable faith in her guru. Mother pressed her head repeatedly against the little picture.

"O Omnipresent Master, I thank thee that thy light hath healed my son!"

I realized that she too had witnessed the luminous blaze through which I had instantly recovered from a usually fatal disease.

One of my most precious possessions is that same photograph. Given to Father by Lahiri Mahasaya himself, it carries a holy vibration. The picture had a miraculous origin. I heard the story from Father's brother disciple, Kali Kumar Roy.

It appears that the master had an aversion to being photo-graphed. Over his protest, a group picture was once taken of him and a cluster of devotees, including Kali Kumar Roy. It was an amazed photographer who discovered that the plate, which had clear images of all the disciples, revealed nothing more than a blank space in the centre where he had reasonably expected to find the outlines of Lahiri Mahasaya. The phenomenon was widely discussed.

A certain student and expert photographer, Ganga Dhar Babu, boasted that the fugitive figure would not escape him. The next morning, as the guru sat in lotus posture on a wooden bench with a screen behind him, Ganga Dhar Babu arrived with his equipment. Taking every precaution for success, he greedily exposed twelve plates. On each one he soon found the imprint of the wooden bench and screen, but once again the master's form was missing.

With tears and shattered pride, Ganga Dhar Babu sought out his guru. It was many hours before Lahiri Mahasaya broke his silence with a pregnant comment:

"I am Spirit. Can the camera reflect the omnipresent Invisible?"

"I see it cannot! But, Holy Sir, I lovingly desire a picture of the bodily temple where alone, to my narrow vision, that Spirit appears fully to dwell."

"Come, then, tomorrow morning. I will pose for you."

Again the photographer focused his camera. This time the sacred figure, not cloaked with mysterious imperceptibility, was sharp on the plate. The master never posed for another picture; at least, I have seen none.

The photograph appears in the photo section of this book. Lahiri Mahasaya's fair features, of a universal cast, hardly suggest to what race he belonged. His intense joy of God-communion is slightly revealed in a somewhat enigmatic smile. His eyes, half open to denote a nominal direction on the outer world, are half closed also. Completely oblivious to the poor lures of the earth, he was fully awake at all times to the spiritual problems of seekers who approached for his bounty.

Shortly after my healing through the potency of the guru's picture, I had an influential spiritual vision. Sitting on my bed one morning, I fell into a deep reverie.

"What is behind the darkness of closed eyes?" This probing thought came into my mind. An immense flash of light at once manifested to my inward gaze. Divine shapes of saints, sitting in meditation posture in mountain caves, formed like miniature cinema pictures on the large screen of radiance within my forehead.

"Who are you?" I spoke aloud.

"We are the Himalayan yogis." The celestial response is difficult to describe; my heart was thrilled.

"Ah, I long to go to the Himalayas and become like you!" The vision vanished, but the silvery beams expanded in ever-widening circles to infinity.

"What is this wondrous glow?"

"I am Iswara.[10] I am Light." The voice was as murmuring clouds.

"I want to be one with Thee!"

Out of the slow dwindling of my divine ecstasy, I salvaged a permanent legacy of inspiration to seek God. "He is eternal, ever-new Joy!" This memory persisted long after the day of rapture.

Another early recollection is outstanding; and literally so, for I bear the scar to this day. My elder sister Uma and I were seated in the early morning under a *neem* tree in our Gorakhpur compound. She was helping me with a Bengali primer, what time I could spare my gaze from the near-by parrots eating ripe margosa fruit. Uma complained of a boil on her leg, and fetched a jar of ointment. I smeared a bit of the salve on my forearm.

10 Sanskrit for God as Ruler of the universe. from the root is, to rule. There are thousands of names for God in the Hindu scriptures, each one carrying a different shade of philosophical meaning.

"Why do you use medicine on a healthy arm?"

"Well, Sis, I feel I am going to have a boil tomorrow. I am testing your ointment on the spot where the boil will appear."

"You little liar!"

"Sis, don't call me a liar until you see what happens in the morning." Indignation filled me.

Uma was unimpressed, and thrice repeated her taunt. An adamant resolution sounded in my voice as I made slow reply.

"By the power of will in me, I say that tomorrow I shall have a fairly large boil in this exact place on my arm; and your boil shall swell to twice its present size!"

Morning found me with a stalwart boil on the indicated spot; the dimensions of Uma's boil had doubled. With a shriek, my sister rushed to Mother. "Mukunda has become a necromancer!" Gravely, Mother instructed me never to use the power of words for doing harm. I have always remembered her counsel, and followed it.

My boil was surgically treated. A noticeable scar, left by the doctor's incision, is present today. On my right forearm is a constant reminder of the power in man's sheer word.

Those simple and apparently harmless phrases to Uma, spoken with deep concentration, had possessed sufficient hidden force to explode like bombs and produce definite, though injurious, effects. I understood, later, that the explosive vibratory power in speech could be wisely directed to free one's life from difficulties, and thus operate without scar or rebuke.[11]

Our family then moved to Lahore in the Punjab. There I acquired a picture of the Divine Mother in the form of the Goddess Kali.[12] It sanctified a small informal shrine on our balcony. An unequivocal conviction came over me that fulfillment would crown any of my prayers uttered in that sacred spot. Standing there with Uma one day, I watched two kites flying over the roofs of the buildings on the opposite side of the very narrow lane.

"Why are you so quiet?" Uma pushed me playfully.

11 The infinite potencies of sound derive from the Creative Word, *Aum*, the cosmic vibratory power behind all atomic energies. Any word spoken with clear realization and deep concentration has a materializing value. Loud or silent repetition of inspiring words has been found effective in Couéism and similar systems of psychotherapy; the secret lies in the stepping-up of the mind's vibratory rate. The poet Tennyson has left us, in his *Memoirs*, an account of his repetitious device for passing beyond the conscious mind into superconsciousness:

'A kind of waking trance – this for lack of a better word – I have frequently had, quite up from boyhood, when I have been all alone,' Tennyson wrote. 'This has come upon me through *repeating* my own name to myself silently, till all at once, as it were out of the intensity of the consciousness of individuality, individuality itself seemed to dissolve and fade away into boundless being, and this not a confused state but the clearest, the surest of the surest, utterly beyond words – where death was an almost laughable impossibility – the loss of personality (if so it were) seeming no extinction, but the only true life.' He wrote further: 'It is no nebulous ecstasy, but a state of transcendent wonder, associated with absolute clearness of mind.'

"I am just thinking how wonderful it is that Divine Mother gives me whatever I ask."

"I suppose She would give you those two kites!" My sister laughed derisively.

"Why not?" I began silent prayers for their possession.

Matches are played in India with kites whose strings are covered with glue and ground glass. The players attempt to sever the string of his opponent. A freed kite sails over the roofs; there is great fun in catching it. Inasmuch as Uma and I were on the roofed and recessted balcony, it seemed impossible that any loosed kite could come into our hands; its string would naturally dangle over the roof.

The players across the lane began their match. One string was cut; immediately the kite floated in my direction. It was stationary for a moment, through sudden abatement of breeze, which sufficed to firmly entangle the string with a cactus plant on top of the opposite house. A perfect loop was formed for my seizure. I handed the prize to Uma.

"It was just an extraordinary accident, and not an answer to your prayer. If the other kite comes to you, then I shall believe." Sister's dark eyes conveyed more amazement than her words.

I continued my prayers with a crescendo intensity. A forcible tug by the other player resulted in the abrupt loss of his kite. It headed toward me, dancing in the wind. My helpful assistant, the cactus plant, again secured the kite string in the necessary loop by which I could grasp it. I presented my second trophy to Uma.

"Indeed, Divine Mother listens to you! This is all too uncanny for me!" Sister bolted away like a frightened fawn.

2. *My Mother's Death and the Mystic Amulet*

MY MOTHER'S GREATEST desire was the marriage of my elder brother. "Ah, when I behold the face of Ananta's wife, I shall find heaven on this earth!" I frequently heard Mother express in these words her strong Indian sentiment for family continuity.

I was about eleven years old at the time of Ananta's betrothal. Mother was in Calcutta, joyously supervising the wedding preparations. Father and I alone remained at our home in Bareilly in northern India, whence Father had been transferred after two years at Lahore.

I had previously witnessed the splendour of nuptial rites for my two elder sisters, Roma and Uma; but for Ananta, as the eldest son, plans were

12 Kali is a symbol of God in the aspect of eternal Mother Nature.

truly elaborate. Mother was welcoming numerous relatives, daily arriving in Calcutta from distant homes. She lodged them comfortably in a large, newly acquired house at 50, Amherst Street. Everything was in readiness – the banquet delicacies, the gay throne on which Brother was to be carried to the home of the bride-to-be, the rows of colourful lights, the mammoth cardboard elephants and camels, the English, Scottish and Indian orchestras, the professional entertainers, the priests for the ancient rituals.

Father and I, in gala spirits, were planning to join the family in time for the ceremony. Shortly before the great day, however, I had an ominous vision.

It was in Bareilly on a midnight. As I slept beside Father on the piazza of our bungalow, I was awakened by a peculiar flutter of the mosquito netting over the bed. The flimsy curtains parted and I saw the beloved form of my mother.

"Awaken your father!" Her voice was only a whisper. "Take the first available train, at four o'clock this morning. Rush to Calcutta if you would see me!" The wraith-like figure vanished.

"Father, Father! Mother is dying!" The terror in my tone aroused him instantly. I sobbed out the fatal tidings.

"Never mind that hallucination of yours." Father gave his characteristic negation to a new situation. "Your mother is in excellent health. If we get any bad news, we shall leave tomorrow."

"You shall never forgive yourself for not starting now!" Anguish caused me to add bitterly, "Nor shall I ever forgive you!"

The melancholy morning came with explicit words: "Mother dangerously ill; marriage postponed; come at once."

Father and I left distractedly. One of my uncles met us en route at a transfer point. A train thundered toward us, looming with telescopic increase. From my inner tumult, an abrupt determination arose to hurl myself on the railroad tracks. Already bereft, I felt, of my mother, I could not endure a world suddenly barren to the bone. I loved Mother as my dearest friend on earth. Her solacing black eyes had been my surest refuge in the trifling tragedies of childhood.

"Does she yet live?" I stopped for one last question to my uncle.

"Of course she is alive!" He was not slow to interpret the desperation in my face. But I scarcely believed him.

When we reached our Calcutta home, it was only to confront the stunning mystery of death. I collapsed into an almost lifeless state. Years passed before any reconciliation entered my heart. Storming the very gates of heaven, my cries at last summoned the Divine Mother. Her words brought final healing to my suppurating wounds:

"It is I who have watched over thee, life after life, in the tenderness of many mothers! See in My gaze the two black eyes, the lost beautiful eyes, thou seekest!"

Father and I returned to Bareilly soon after the crematory rites for the well-beloved. Early every morning I made a pathetic memorial-pilgrimage to a large *sheoli* tree which shaded the smooth, green-gold lawn before our bungalow. In poetical moments, I thought that the white *sheoli* flowers were strewing themselves with a willing devotion over the grassy altar. Mingling tears with the dew, I often observed a strange other-worldly light emerging from the dawn. Intense pangs of longing for God assailed me. I felt powerfully drawn to the Himalayas.

One of my cousins, fresh from a period of travel in the holy hills, visited us in Bareilly. I listened eagerly to his tales about the high mountain abode of yogis and swamis.[1]

"Let us run away to the Himalayas." My suggestion one day to Dwarka Prasad, the young son of our landlord in Bareilly, fell on unsympathetic ears. He revealed my plan to my elder brother, who had just arrived to see Father. Instead of laughing lightly over this impractical scheme of a small boy, Ananta made it a definite point to ridicule me.

"Where is your orange robe? You can't be a swami without that!"

But I was inexplicably thrilled by his words. They brought a clear picture of myself roaming about India as a monk. Perhaps they awakened memories of a past life; in any case, I began to see with what natural ease I would wear the garb of that anciently-founded monastic order.

Chatting one morning with Dwarka, I felt a love for God descending with avalanchic force. My companion was only partly attentive to the ensuing eloquence, but I was whole-heartedly listening to myself.

I fled that afternoon toward Nainital in the Himalayan foothills. Ananta gave determined chase; I was forced to return sadly to Bareilly. The only pilgrimage permitted me was the customary one at dawn to the *sheoli* tree. My heart wept for the lost Mothers, human and divine.

The rent left in the family fabric by Mother's death was irreparable. Father never remarried during his forty remaining years. Assuming the difficult role of Father-Mother to his little flock, he grew noticeably more tender, more approachable. With calmness and insight, he solved various family problems. After office hours he retired like a hermit to the cell of his room, practicing Kriya Yoga in a sweet serenity. Long after Mother's death, I attempted to engage an English nurse to attend to details that would make my parent's life more comfortable. But Father shook his head.

"Service to me ended with your mother." His eyes were remote with a lifelong devotion. "I will not accept ministrations from any other woman."

1 Sanskrit root-meaning of *swami* is 'he who is one with his Self (*Swa*).' Applied to a member of the Indian order of monks, the title has the formal respect of 'the reverend.'

Fourteen months after Mother's passing, I learned that she had left me a momentous message. Ananta was present at her death bed and had recorded her words. Although she had asked that the disclosure be made to me in one year, my brother delayed. He was soon to leave Bareilly for Calcutta, to marry the girl Mother had chosen for him.[2] One evening he summoned me to his side.

"Mukunda, I have been reluctant to give you strange tidings." Ananta's tone held a note of resignation. "My fear was to inflame your desire to leave home. But in any case you are bristling with divine ardour. When I captured you recently on your way to the Himalayas, I came to a definite resolve. I must not further postpone the fulfillment of my solemn promise." My brother handed me a small box, and delivered Mother's message.

"Let these words be my final blessing, my beloved son Mukunda!" Mother had said. "The hour is here when I must relate a number of phenomenal events following your birth. I first knew your destined path when you were but a babe in my arms. I carried you then to the home of my guru in Benares. Almost hidden behind a throng of disciples, I could barely see Lahiri Mahasaya as he sat in deep meditation.

"While I patted you, I was praying that the great guru take notice and bestow a blessing. As my silent devotional demand grew in intensity, he opened his eyes and beckoned me to approach. The others made a way for me; I bowed at the sacred feet. My master seated you on his lap, placing his hand on your forehead by way of spiritually baptizing you.

" 'Little mother, thy son will be a yogi. As a spiritual engine, he will carry many souls to God's kingdom.'

"My heart leaped with joy to find my secret prayer granted by the omniscient guru. Shortly before your birth, he had told me you would follow his path.

"Later, my son, your vision of the Great Light was known to me and your sister Roma, as from the next room we observed you motionless on the bed. Your little face was illuminated; your voice rang with iron resolve as you spoke of going to the Himalayas in quest of the Divine.

"In these ways, dear son, I came to know that your road lies far from worldly ambitions. The most singular event in my life brought further confirmation – an event which now impels my death bed message.

"It was an interview with a sage in the Punjab. While our family was living in Lahore, one morning the servant came precipitantly into my room.

" 'Mistress, a strange *sadhu*[3] is here. He insists that he "see the mother of Mukunda." ' "

2 The Indian custom of choosing the life-partner for their child, has resisted the blunt assaults of time. The percentage is high of thus arranged happy Indian marriages.

"These simple words struck a profound chord within me; I went at once to greet the visitor. Bowing at his feet, I sensed that before me was a true man of God.

" 'Mother,' he said, 'the great masters wish you to know that your stay on earth will not be long. Your next illness shall prove to be your last.'[4] There was a silence, during which I felt no alarm but only a vibration of great peace. Finally he addressed me again:

" 'You are to be the custodian of a certain silver amulet. I will not give it to you today; to demonstrate the truth in my words, the talisman shall materialize in your hands tomorrow as you meditate. On your death bed, you must instruct your eldest son Ananta to keep the amulet for one year and then to hand it over to your second son. Mukunda will understand the meaning of the talisman from the great ones. He should receive it about the time he is ready to renounce all worldly hopes and start his vital search for God. When he has retained the amulet for some years, and when it has served its purpose, it shall vanish. Even if kept in the most secret spot, it shall return whence it came.'

"I proffered alms[5] to the saint, and bowed before him in great reverence. Not taking the offering, he departed with a blessing. The next evening, as I sat with folded hands in meditation, a silver amulet materialized between my palms, even as the *sadhu* had promised. It made itself known by a cold, smooth touch. I have jealously guarded it for more than two years, and now leave it in Ananta's keeping. Do not grieve for me, as I shall have been ushered by my great guru into the arms of the Infinite. Farewell, my child; the Cosmic Mother will protect you."

A blaze of illumination came over me with possession of the amulet; many dormant memories awakened. The talisman, round and anciently quaint, was covered with Sanskrit characters. I understood that it came from teachers of past lives, who were invisibly guiding my steps. A further significance there was, indeed; but one does not reveal fully the heart of an amulet.[6]

How the talisman finally vanished amidst deeply unhappy circumstances of my life; and how its loss was a herald of my gain of a guru, cannot be told in this chapter.

But the small boy, thwarted in his attempts to reach the Himalayas, daily travelled far on the wings of his amulet.

3 An anchorite; one who pursues a *sadhana* or path of spiritual discipline.
4 When I discovered by these words that Mother had possessed secret knowledge of a short life, I understood for the first time why she had been insistent on hastening the plans for Ananta's marriage. Though she died before the wedding, her natural maternal wish had been to witness the rites.
5 A customary gesture of respect to *sadhus*.
6 The amulet was an astrally produced object. Structurally evanescent, such objects must finally disappear from our earth. (See chapter 43).

3. *The Saint with Two Bodies*

FATHER, IF I PROMISE to return home without coercion, may I take a sight-seeing trip to Benares?"

My keen love of travel was seldom hindered by Father. He permitted me, even as a mere boy, to visit many cities and pilgrimage spots. Usually one or more of my friends accom-panied me; we would travel comfortably on first-class passes provided by Father. His position as a railroad official was fully satisfactory to the nomads in the family.

Father promised to give my request due consideration. The next day he summoned me and held out a round-trip pass from Bareilly to Benares, a number of rupee notes, and two letters.

"I have a business matter to propose to a Benares friend, Kedar Nath Babu. Unfortunately I have lost his address. But I believe you will be able to get this letter to him through our common friend, Swami Pranabananda. The swami, my brother disciple, has attained an exalted spiritual stature. You will benefit by his company; this second note will serve as your introduction."

Father's eyes twinkled as he added, "Mind, no more flights from home!"

I set forth with the zest of my twelve years (though time has never dimmed my delight in new scenes and strange faces). Reaching Benares, I proceeded immediately to the swami's residence. The front door was open; I made my way to a long, hall-like room on the second floor. A rather stout man, wearing only a loincloth, was seated in lotus posture on a slightly raised platform. His head and unwrinkled face were clean-shaven; a beatific smile played about his lips. To dispel my thought that I had intruded, he greeted me as an old friend.

"*Baba anand* (bliss to my dear one)." His welcome was given heartily in a childlike voice. I knelt and touched his feet.

"Are you Swami Pranabananda?"

He nodded. "Are you Bhagabati's son?" His words were out before I had had time to get Father's letter from my pocket. In astonishment, I handed him the note of introduction, which now seemed superfluous.

"Of course I will locate Kedar Nath Babu for you." The saint again surprised me by his clairvoyance. He glanced at the letter, and made a few affectionate references to my parent.

"You know, I am enjoying two pensions. One is by the recommendation of your father, for whom I once worked in the railroad office. The other is by the recommendation of my Heavenly Father, for whom I have conscientiously finished my earthly duties in life."

I found this remark very obscure. "What kind of pension, sir, do you receive from the Heavenly Father? Does He drop money in your lap?"

He laughed. "I mean a pension of fathomless peace – a reward for many years of deep meditation. I never crave money now. My few material needs are amply provided for. Later you will understand the significance of a second pension."

Abruptly terminating our conversation, the saint became gravely motionless. A sphinx-like air enveloped him. At first his eyes sparkled, as if observing something of interest, then grew dull. I felt abashed at his pauciloquy; he had not yet told me how I could meet Father's friend. A trifle restlessly, I looked about me in the bare room, empty except for us two. My idle gaze took in his wooden sandals, lying under the platform seat.

"Little sir,[1] don't get worried. The man you wish to see will be with you in half an hour." The yogi was reading my mind – a feat not too difficult at the moment!

Again he fell into inscrutable silence. My watch informed me that thirty minutes had elapsed.

The swami aroused himself. "I think Kedar Nath Babu is nearing the door." he said.

I heard somebody coming up the stairs. An amazed incompre-hension arose suddenly; my thoughts raced in confusion: "How is it possible that Father's friend has been summoned to this place without the help of a messenger? The swami has spoken to no one but myself since my arrival!"

Abruptly I quitted the room and descended the steps. Halfway down I met a thin, fair-skinned man of medium height. He appeared to be in a hurry.

"Are you Kedar Nath Babu?" Excitement coloured my voice.

"Yes. Are you not Bhagabati's son who has been waiting here to meet me?" He smiled in friendly fashion.

"Sir, how do you happen to come here?" I felt baffled resentment over his inexplicable presence.

"Everything is mysterious today! Less than an hour ago I had just finished my bath in the Ganges when Swami Pranabananda approached me. I have no idea how he knew I was there at that time.

" 'Bhagabati's son is waiting for you in my apartment,' he said. 'Will you come with me?' I gladly agreed. As we proceeded hand in hand, the swami in his wooden sandals was strangely able to outpace me, though I wore these stout walking shoes.

" 'How long will it take you to reach my place?' Pranabanandaji suddenly halted to ask me this question.

---

1 *Choto Mahasaya* is the term by which a number of Indian saints addressed me. It translates "little sir."

" 'About half an hour.'

" 'I have something else to do at present.' He gave me an enigmatical glance. 'I must leave you behind. You can join me in my house, where Bhagabati's son and I will be awaiting you.'

"Before I could remonstrate, he dashed swiftly past me and disappeared in the crowd. I walked here as fast as possible."

This explanation only increased my bewilderment. I inquired how long he had known the swami.

"We met a few times last year, but not recently. I was very glad to see him again today at the bathing *ghat*."

"I cannot believe my ears! Am I losing my mind? Did you meet him in a vision, or did you actually see him, touch his hand, and hear the sound of his feet?"

"I don't know what you're driving at!" He flushed angrily. "I am not lying to you. Can't you understand that only through the swami could I have known you were waiting at this place for me?"

"Why, that man, Swami Pranabananda, has not left my sight a moment since I first came about an hour ago." I blurted out the whole story.

His eyes opened widely. "Are we living in this material age, or are we dreaming? I never expected to witness such a miracle in my life! I thought this swami was just an ordinary man, and now I find he can materialize an extra body and work through it!" Together we entered the saint's room.

"Look, those are the very sandals he was wearing at the *ghat*," Kedar Nath Babu whispered. "He was clad only in a loincloth, just as I see him now."

As the visitor bowed before him, the saint turned to me with a quizzical smile.

"Why are you stupefied at all this? The subtle unity of the phenomenal world is not hidden from true yogis. I instantly see and converse with my disciples in distant Calcutta. They can similarly transcend at will every obstacle of gross matter."

It was probably in an effort to stir spiritual ardour in my young breast that the swami had condescended to tell me of his powers of astral radio and television.[2] But instead of enthusiasm, I experienced only an awe-stricken fear. Inasmuch as I was destined to undertake my divine search

2. In its own way, physical science is affirming the validity of laws discovered by yogis through mental science. For example, a demonstration that man has televisional powers was given on Nov. 26, 1934 at the Royal University of Rome. Dr. Giuseppe Calligaris, professor of neuro-psychology, pressed certain points of a subject's body and the subject responded with minute descriptions of other persons and objects on the opposite side of a wall. Dr. Calligaris told the other professors that if certain areas on the skin are agitated, the subject is given super-sensorial impressions enabling him to see objects that he could not otherwise perceive. To enable his subject to discern things on the other side of a wall, Professor Calligaris pressed on a spot to the right of the thorax for fifteen minutes. Dr. Calligaris said that if other spots of the body were agitated, the subjects could see objects at any distance, regardless of whether they had ever before seen those objects.

through one particular guru – Sri Yukteswar, whom I had not yet met – I felt no inclination to accept Pranabananda as my teacher. I glanced at him doubtfully, wondering if it were he or his counterpart before me.

The master sought to banish my disquietude by bestowing a soul-awakening gaze, and by some inspiring words about his guru.

"Lahiri Mahasaya was the greatest yogi I ever knew. He was Divinity Itself in the form of flesh."

If a disciple, I reflected, could materialize an extra fleshly form at will, what miracles indeed could be barred to his master?

"I will tell you how priceless is a guru's help. I used to meditate with another disciple for eight hours every night. We had to work at the railroad office during the day. Finding difficulty in carrying on my clerical duties, I desired to devote my whole time to God. For eight years I persevered, meditating half the night. I had wonderful results; tremendous spiritual perceptions illumined my mind. But a little veil always remained between the Infinite and me. Even with superhuman earnestness, I found the final irrevocable union to be denied me. One evening I paid a visit to Lahiri Mahasaya and pleaded for his divine intercession. My importunities continued during the entire night.

" 'Angelic Guru, my spiritual anguish is such that I can no longer bear my life without meeting the Great Beloved face to face!'

" 'What can I do? You must meditate more profoundly.'

" 'I am appealing to Thee, O God my Master! I see Thee materialized before me in a physical body; bless me that I may perceive Thee in Thine infinite form!'

"Lahiri Mahasaya extended his hand in a benign gesture. 'You may go now and meditate. I have interceded for you with Brahma.'[3]

"Immeasurably uplifted, I returned to my home. In meditation that night, the burning Goal of my life was achieved. Now I ceaselessly enjoy the spiritual pension. Never from that day has the Blissful Creator remained hidden from my eyes behind any screen of delusion."

Pranabananda's face was suffused with divine light. The peace of another world entered my heart; all fear had fled. The saint made a further confidence.

"Some months later I returned to Lahiri Mahasaya and tried to thank him for his bestowal of the infinite gift. Then I mentioned another matter.

" 'Divine Guru, I can no longer work in the office. Please release me. Brahma keeps me continuously intoxicated.'

" 'Apply for a pension from your company.'

3 God in His aspect of Creator: from Sanskrit root *brih*, to expand. When Emerson's poem *Brahma* appeared in the *Atlantic Monthly* in 1857, most of the readers were bewildered. Emerson chuckled. "Tell them," he said, "to say 'Jehovah' instead of 'Brahma' and they will not feel any perplexity."

" 'What reason shall I give, so early in my service?'

" 'Say what you feel.'

"The next day I made my application. The doctor inquired the grounds for my premature request.

" 'At work, I find an overpowering sensation rising in my spine.[4] It permeates my whole body, unfitting me for the performance of my duties.'

"Without further questioning the physician recommended me highly for a pension, which I soon received. I know the divine will of Lahiri Mahasaya worked through the doctor and the railroad officials, including your father. Automatically they obeyed the great guru's spiritual direction, and freed me for a life of unbroken communion with the Beloved."[5]

After this extraordinary revelation, Swami Pranabananda retired into one of his long silences. As I was taking leave, touching his feet reverently, he gave me his blessing:

"Your life belongs to the path of renunciation and yoga. I shall see you again, with your father, later on." The years brought fulfillment to both these predictions.[6]

Kedar Nath Babu walked by my side in the gathering darkness. I delivered Father's letter, which my companion read under a street lamp.

"Your father suggests that I take a position in the Calcutta office of his railroad company. How pleasant to look forward to at least one of the pensions that Swami Pranabananda enjoys! But it is impossible; I cannot leave Benares. Alas, two bodies are not yet for me!"

4. *My interrupted Flight toward the Himalayas*

"LEAVE YOUR CLASSROOM on some trifling pretext, and engage a hackney carriage. Stop in the lane where no one in my house can see you."

These were my final instructions to Amar Mitter, a high school friend who planned to accompany me to the Himalayas. We had chosen the following day for our flight. Precautions were necessary, as Ananta exercised a vigilant eye. He was determined to foil the plans of escape which he suspected were uppermost in my mind. The amulet, like a spiritual yeast, was silently at work within me. Amidst the Himalayan snows, I hoped to find the master whose face often appeared to me in visions.

---

4 In deep meditation, the first experience of Spirit is on the altar of the spine, and then in the brain. The torrential bliss is overwhelming, but the yogi learns to control its outward manifestations.

5 After his retirement, Pranabananda wrote one of the most profound commentaries on the *Bhagavad Gita,* available in Bengali and Hindi. At the time of our meeting, Pranabananda was, indeed, a fully illumined master.

6 See Chapter 27.

The family was living now in Calcutta, where Father had been permanently transferred. Following the patriarchal Indian custom, Ananta had brought his bride to live in our home, now at 4, Gurpar Road. There in a small attic room I engaged in daily meditations and prepared my mind for the divine search.

The memorable morning arrived with inauspicious rain. Hearing the wheels of Amar's carriage in the road, I hastily tied together a blanket, a pair of sandals, Lahiri Mahasaya's picture, a copy of the *Bhagavad Gita,* a string of prayer beads, and two loincloths. This bundle I threw from my third-story window. I ran down the steps and passed my uncle, buying fish at the door.

"What is the excitement?" His gaze roved suspiciously over my person.

I gave him a noncommittal smile and walked to the lane. Retrieving my bundle, I joined Amar with conspiratorial caution. We drove to Chandni Chauk, a merchandise centre. For months we had been saving our Tiffin money to buy English clothes. Knowing that my clever brother could easily play the part of a detective, we thought to outwit him by European garb.

On the way to the station, we stopped for my cousin, Jotin Ghosh, whom I called Jatinda. He was a new convert, longing for a guru in the Himalayas. He donned the new suit we had in readiness. Well-camouflaged, we hoped! A deep elation possessed our hearts.

"All we need now are canvas shoes." I led my companions to a shop displaying rubber-soled footwear. "Articles of leather, gotten only through the slaughter of animals, must be absent on this holy trip." I halted on the street to remove the leather cover from my *Bhagavad Gita*, and the leather straps from my English-made *sola topee* (helmet).

At the station we bought tickets to Burdwan, where we planned to transfer for Hardwar in the Himalayan foothills. As soon as the train, like ourselves, was in flight, I gave utterance to a few of my glorious anticipations.

"Just imagine!" I ejaculated. "We shall be initiated by the masters and experience the trance of cosmic consciousness. Our flesh will be charged with such magnetism that wild animals of the Himalayas will come tamely near us. Tigers will be no more than meek house cats awaiting our caresses!"

This remark – picturing a prospect I considered entrancing, both metaphorically and literally – brought an enthusiastic smile from Amar. But Jatinda averted his gaze, directing it through the window at the scampering landscape.

"Let the money be divided in three portions." Jatinda broke a long silence with this suggestion. "Each of us should buy his own ticket at Burdwan. Thus no one at the station will surmise that we are running away together."

I unsuspectingly agreed. At dusk our train stopped at Burdwan. Jatinda entered the ticket office; Amar and I sat on the platform. We waited fifteen minutes, then made unavailing inquiries. Searching in all directions, we shouted Jatinda's name with the urgency of fright. But he had faded into the dark unknown surrounding the little station.

I was completely unnerved, shocked to a peculiar numbness. That God would countenance this depressing episode! The romantic occasion of my first carefully-planned flight after Him was cruelly marred.

"Amar, we must return home." I was weeping like a child. "Jatinda's callous departure is an ill omen. This trip is doomed to failure."

"Is this your love for the Lord? Can't you stand the little test of a treacherous companion?"

Through Amar's suggestion of a divine test, my heart steadied itself. We refreshed ourselves with famous Burdwan sweetmeats, *sitabhog* (food for the goddess) and *motichur* (nuggets of sweet pearl). In a few hours, we entrained for Hardwar, via Bareilly. Changing trains at Moghul Serai, we discussed a vital matter as we waited on the platform.

"Amar, we may soon be closely questioned by railroad officials. I am not underrating my brother's ingenuity! No matter what the outcome, I will not speak untruth."

"All I ask of you, Mukunda, is to keep still. Don't laugh or grin while I am talking."

At this moment, a European station agent accosted me. He waved a telegram whose import I immediately grasped.

"Are you running away from home in anger?"

"No!" I was glad his choice of words permitted me to make emphatic reply. Not anger but 'divinest melancholy' was responsible, I knew, for my unconventional behaviour.

The official then turned to Amar. The duel of wits that followed hardly permitted me to maintain the counseled stoic gravity.

"Where is the third boy?" The man injected a full ring of authority into his voice. "Come on; speak the truth!"

"Sir, I notice you are wearing eyeglasses. Can't you see that we are only two?" Amar smiled impudently. "I am not a magician; I can't conjure up a third companion."

The official, noticeably disconcerted by this impertinence, sought a new field of attack.

"What is your name?"

"I am called Thomas. I am the son of an English mother and a converted Christian Indian father."

"What is your friend's name?"

"I call him Thompson."

By this time my inward mirth had reached a zenith; I unceremoniously made for the train, whistling for departure. Amar followed with the official, who was credulous and obliging enough to put us into a European compartment. It evidently pained him to think of two half-English boys travelling in the section allotted to natives. After his polite exit, I lay back on the seat and laughed uncontrollably. My friend wore an expression of blithe satisfaction at having outwitted a veteran European official.

On the platform I had contrived to read the telegram. From my brother, it went thus: "Three Bengali boys in English clothes running away from home toward Hardwar via Moghul Serai. Please detain them until my arrival. Ample reward for your services."

"Amar, I told you not to leave marked timetables in your home." My glance was reproachful. "Brother must have found one there."

My friend sheepishly acknowledged the thrust. We halted briefly in Bareilly, where Dwarka Prasad (mentined on page 14) awaited us with a telegram from Ananta. My old friend tried valiantly to detain us; I convinced him that our flight had not been undertaken lightly. As on a previous occasion, Dwarka refused my invitation to set forth to the Himalayas.

While our train stood in a station that night, and I was half asleep, Amar was awakened by another questioning official. He, too, fell a victim to the hybrid charms of 'Thomas' and 'Thompson.' The train bore us triumphantly into a dawn arrival at Hardwar. The majestic mountains loomed invitingly in the distance. We dashed through the station and entered the freedom of city crowds. Our first act was to change into native costume, as Ananta had somehow penetrated our European disguise. A premonition of capture weighed on my mind.

Deeming it advisable to leave Hardwar at once, we bought tickets to proceed north to Rishikesh, a soil long hallowed by feet of many masters. I had already boarded the train, while Amar lagged on the platform. He was brought to an abrupt halt by a shout from a policeman. Our unwelcome guardian escorted us to a station bungalow and took charge of our money. He explained courteously that it was his duty to hold us until my elder brother arrived.

Learning that the truants' destination had been the Himalayas, the officer related a strange story.

"I see you are crazy about saints! You will never meet a greater man of God than the one I saw only yesterday. My brother officer and I first encountered him five days ago. We were patrolling by the Ganges, on a sharp lookout for a certain murderer. Our instructions were to capture him, alive or dead. He was known to be masquerading as a *sadhu* in order to rob pilgrims. A short way before us, we spied a figure which resembled the description of the criminal. He ignored our command to stop; we ran to overpower him. Approaching his back, I wielded my axe with tremendous force; the man's right arm was severed almost completely from his body.

"Without outcry or any glance at the ghastly wound, the stranger astonishingly continued his swift pace. As we jumped in front of him, he spoke quietly.

" 'I am not the murderer you are seeking.'

"I was deeply mortified to see I had injured the person of a divine-looking sage. Prostrating myself at his feet, I implored his pardon, and offered my turban-cloth to staunch the heavy spurts of blood.

" 'Son, that was just an understandable mistake on your part.' The saint regarded me kindly. 'Run along, and don't reproach yourself. The Beloved Mother is taking care of me.' He pushed his dangling arm into its stump and lo! it adhered; the blood inexplicably ceased to flow.

" 'Come to me under yonder tree in three days and you will find me fully healed. Thus you will feel no remorse.'

"Yesterday my brother officer and I went eagerly to the designated spot. The *sadhu* was there and allowed us to examine his arm. It bore no scar or trace of hurt!

" 'I am going via Rishikesh to the Himalayan solitudes.' He blessed us as he departed quickly. I feel that my life has been uplifted through his sanctity."

The officer concluded with a pious ejaculation; his experience had obviously moved him beyond his usual depths. With an impressive gesture, he handed me a printed clipping about the miracle. In the usual garbled manner of the sensational type of newspaper (not missing, alas! even in India), the reporter's version was slightly exaggerated: it indicated that the *sadhu* had been almost decapitated!

Amar and I lamented that we had missed the great yogi who could forgive his persecutor in such a Christ-like way. India, materially poor for the last two centuries, yet has an inexhaustible fund of divine wealth; spiritual 'skyscrapers' may occasionally be encountered by the wayside, even by worldly men like this policeman.

We thanked the officer for relieving our tedium with his marvellous story. He was probably intimating that he was more fortunate than we: he had met an illumined saint without effort; our earnest search had ended, not at the feet of a master, but in a coarse police station!

So near the Himalayas and yet, in our captivity, so far, I told Amar I felt doubly impelled to seek freedom.

"Let us slip away when opportunity offers. We can go on foot to holy Rishikesh." I smiled encouragingly.

But my companion had turned pessimist as soon as the stalwart prop of our money had been taken from us.

"If we started a trek over such dangerous jungle land, we should finish, not in the city of saints, but in the stomachs of tigers!"

Ananta and Amar's brother arrived after three days. Amar greeted his relative with affectionate relief. I was un-reconciled; Ananta got no more from me than a severe upbraiding.

"I understand how you feel." My brother spoke soothingly. "All I ask of you is to accompany me to Benares to meet a certain saint, and go on to Calcutta to visit your grieving father for a few days. Then you can resume your search here for a master."

Amar entered the conversation at this point to disclaim any intention of returning to Hardwar. He was enjoying the familial warmth. But I knew I would never abandon the quest for my guru.

Our party entrained for Benares. There I had a singular and instant response to my prayers.

A clever scheme had been prearranged by Ananta. Before seeing me at Hardwar, he had stopped in Benares to ask a certain scriptural authority to interview me later. Both the pundit and his son had promised to undertake my dissuasion from the path of a *sannyasi*.[1]

Ananta took me to their home. The son, a young man of ebullient manner, greeted me in the courtyard. He engaged me in a lengthy philosophic discourse. Professing to have a clairvoyant knowledge of my future, he discountenanced my idea of being a monk.

"You will meet continual misfortune, and be unable to find God, if you insist on deserting your ordinary responsibilities! You cannot work out your past karma[2] without worldly experiences."

Krishna's immortal words rose to my lips in reply: " 'Even he with the worst of karma who ceaselessly meditates on Me quickly loses the effects of his past bad actions. Becoming a high-souled being, he soon attains perennial peace. Arjuna, know this for certain: the devotee who puts his trust in Me never perishes!' "[3]

---

1 Literally, 'renunciant.' From Sanskrit verb roots, 'to cast aside.'

2 Effects of past actions, in this or a former life; from Sanskrit *kri*, 'to do.'

3 *Bhagavad Gita*, IX, 30-31. Krishna was the greatest prophet of India; Arjuna was his foremost disciple.

But the forceful prognostications of the young man had slightly shaken my confidence. With all the fervor of my heart I prayed silently to God:

"Please solve my bewilderment and answer me, right here and now, if Thou dost desire me to lead the life of a renunciate or a worldly man!"

I noticed a *sadhu* of noble countenance standing just outside the compound of the pundit's house. Evidently he had overheard the spirited conversation between the self-styled clairvoyant and myself, for the stranger called me to his side. I felt a tremendous power flowing from his calm eyes.

"Son, don't listen to that ignoramus. In response to your prayer, the Lord tells me to assure you that your sole path in this life is that of the renunciant."

With astonishment as well as gratitude, I smiled happily at this decisive message.

"Come away from that man!" The 'ignoramus' was calling me from the courtyard. My saintly guide raised his hand in blessing and slowly departed.

"That *sadhu* is just as crazy as you are." It was the hoary-headed pundit who made this charming observation. He and his son were gazing at me lugubriously. "I heard that he too has left his home in a vague search for God."

I turned away. To Ananta I remarked that I would not engage in further discussion with our hosts. My brother agreed to an immediate departure; we soon entrained for Calcutta.

"Mr. Detective, how did you discover I had fled with two companions?" I vented my lively curiosity to Ananta during our homeward journey. He smiled mischievously.

"At your school, I found that Amar had left his classroom and had not returned. I went to his home the next morning and unearthed a marked timetable. Amar's father was just leaving by carriage and was talking to the coachman.

" 'My son will not ride with me to his school this morning. He has disappeared!' the father moaned.

" 'I heard from a brother coachman that your son and two others, dressed in European suits, boarded the train at Howrah Station,' the man stated. 'They made a present of their leather shoes to the cab driver.'

"Thus I had three clues – the timetable, the trio of boys, and the English clothing."

I was listening to Ananta's disclosures with mingled mirth and vexation. Our generosity to the coachman had been slightly misplaced!

"Of course I rushed to send telegrams to station officials in all the cities which Amar had underlined in the timetable. He had checked Bareilly, so I wired your friend Dwarka there. After inquiries in our Calcutta neighborhood, I learned that cousin Jatinda had been absent one night but had arrived home the following morning in European garb. I sought him out and invited him to dinner. He accepted, quite disarmed by my friendly manner. On the way I led him unsuspectingly to a police station. He was surrounded by several officers whom I had previously selected for their ferocious appearance. Under their formidable gaze, Jatinda agreed to account for his mysterious conduct.

" 'I started for the Himalayas in a buoyant spiritual mood,' he explained. 'Inspiration filled me at the prospect of meeting the masters. But as soon as Mukunda said, "During our ecstasies in the Himalayan caves, tigers will be spellbound and sit around us like tame pussies," my spirits froze; beads of perspiration formed on my brow. "What then?" I thought. "If the vicious nature of the tigers be not changed through the power of our spiritual trance, shall they treat us with the kindness of house cats?" In my mind's eye, I already saw myself the compulsory inmate of some tiger's stomach – entering there not at once with the whole body, but by installments of its several parts!' "

My anger at Jatinda's vanishment was evaporated in laughter. The hilarious sequel on the train was worth all the anguish he had caused me. I must confess to a slight feeling of satisfaction: Jatinda too had not escaped an encounter with the police!

"Ananta,[4] you are a born sleuthhound!" My glance of amusement was not without some exasperation. "And I shall tell Jatinda I am glad he was prompted by no mood of treachery, as it appeared, but only by the prudent instinct of self-preservation!"

At home in Calcutta, Father touchingly requested me to curb my roving feet until, at least, the completion of my high school studies. In my absence, he had lovingly hatched a plot by arranging for a saintly pundit, Swami Kebalananda,[5] to come regularly to the house.

"The sage will be your Sanskrit tutor," my parent announced confidently.

Father hoped to satisfy my religious yearnings by instructions from a learned philosopher. But the tables were subtly turned: my new teacher, far from offering intellectual aridities, fanned the embers of my God-aspiration. Unknown to Father, Swami Kebalananda was an exalted disciple of Lahiri Mahasaya. The peerless guru had possessed thousands of disciples, silently drawn to him by the irresistibility of his divine magnetism. I learned later that Lahiri Mahasaya had often characterized Kebalananda as *rishi* or illumined sage.

4 I always addressed him as Ananta-da. *Da* or *Dada* is a respectful suffix which the eldest brother in an Indian family receives from junior brothers and sisters.
5 At the time of our meeting, Kebalananda had not yet joined the Swami Order and was generally called 'Shastri Mahasaya.' To avoid confusion with the name of Lahiri Mahasaya and of Master Mahasaya (chapter 9), I am referring to my Sanskrit tutor only by his later monastic name of Swami Kebalananda. His biography has been recently published in Bengali. Born in the Khulna district of Bengal in 1863, Kebalananda gave up his body in Benares at the age of sixty-eight. His family name was Ashutosh Chatterji.

Luxuriant curls framed my tutor's handsome face. His dark eyes were guileless, with the transparency of a child's. All the movements of his slight body were marked by a restful deliberation. Ever gentle and loving, he was firmly established in the infinite consciousness. Many of our happy hours together were spent in deep *Kriya* meditation.

Kebalananda was a noted authority on the ancient *shastras* or sacred books: his erudition had earned him the title of 'Shastri Mahasaya,' by which he was usually addressed. But my progress in Sanskrit scholarship was un-noteworthy. I sought every opportunity to forsake prosaic grammar and to talk of yoga and Lahiri Mahasaya. My tutor obliged me one day by telling me something of his own life with the master.

"Rarely fortunate, I was able to remain near Lahiri Mahasaya for ten years. His Benares home was my nightly goal of pilgrimage. The guru was always present in a small front parlour on the first floor. As he sat in lotus posture on a backless wooden seat, his disciples garlanded him in a semicircle. His eyes sparkled and danced with the joy of the Divine. They were ever half closed, peering through the inner telescopic orb into a sphere of eternal bliss. He seldom spoke at length. Occasionally his gaze would focus on a student in need of help; healing words poured then like an avalanche of light.

"An indescribable peace blossomed within me at the master's glance. I was permeated with his fragrance, as though from a lotus of infinity. To be with him, even without exchanging a word for days, was experience which changed my entire being. If any invisible barrier rose in the path of my concentration, I would meditate at the guru's feet. There the most tenuous states came easily within my grasp. Such perceptions eluded me in the presence of lesser teachers. The master was a living temple of God whose secret doors were open to all disciples through devotion.

"Lahiri Mahasaya was no bookish interpreter of the scriptures. Effortlessly he dipped into the 'divine library.' Foam of words and spray of thoughts gushed from the fountain of his omniscience. He had the wondrous clavis which unlocked the profound philosophical science embedded ages ago in the *Vedas*.[6] If asked to explain the different planes of consciousness mentioned in the ancient texts, he would smilingly assent.

" 'I will undergo those states, and presently tell you what I perceive.' He was thus diametrically unlike the teachers who commit scripture to memory

6 The ancient four *Vedas* comprise over 100 extant canonical books. Emerson paid the following tribute in his Journal to Vedic thought: "It is sublime as heat and night and a breathless ocean. It contains every religious sentiment, all the grand ethics which visit in turn each noble poetic mind. . . . It is of no use to put away the book; if I trust myself in the woods or in a boat upon the pond, Nature makes a *Brahmin* of me presently: eternal necessity, eternal compensation, un-fathomable power, unbroken silence. . . . This is her creed. Peace, she saith to me, and purity and absolute abandonment – these panaceas expiate all sin and bring you to the beatitude of the Eight Gods." (See also N.7 on page 52).

and then give forth unrealized abstractions.

" 'Please expound the holy stanzas as the meaning occurs to you.' The taciturn guru often gave this instruction to a nearby disciple. 'I will guide your thoughts, that the right interpretation be uttered.' In this way many of Lahiri Mahasaya's perceptions came to be recorded, with voluminous commentaries by various students.

"The master never counseled slavish belief. 'Words are only shells,' he said. 'Win conviction of God's presence through your own joyous contact in meditation.'

"No matter what the disciple's problem, the guru advised *Kriya Yoga* for its solution.

" 'The yogic key will not lose its efficiency when I am no longer present in the body to guide you. This technique cannot be bound, filed, and forgotten, in the manner of theoretical inspirations. Continue ceaselessly on your path to liberation through *Kriya,* whose power lies in practice.'

"I myself consider *Kriya* the most effective device of salvation through self-effort ever to be evolved in man's search for the Infinite." Kebalananda concluded with this earnest testimony. "Through its use, the omnipotent God, hidden in all men, became visibly incarnated in the flesh of Lahiri Mahasaya and a number of his disciples."

A Christlike miracle by Lahiri Mahasaya took place in Kebalananda's presence. My saintly tutor recounted the story one day, his eyes remote from the Sanskrit texts before us.

"A blind disciple, Ramu, aroused my active pity. Should he have no light in his eyes, when he faithfully served our master, in whom the Divine was fully blazing? One morning I sought to speak to Ramu, but he sat for patient hours fanning the guru with a hand-made palm-leaf *punkha*. When the devotee finally left the room, I followed him.

" 'Ramu, how long have you been blind?'

" 'From my birth, sir! Never have my eyes been blessed with a glimpse of the sun.'

" 'Our omnipotent guru can help you. Please make a supplication.'

"The following day Ramu diffidently approached Lahiri Mahasaya. The disciple felt almost ashamed to ask that physical wealth be added to his spiritual superabundance.

" 'Master, the Illuminator of the cosmos is in you. I pray you to bring His light into my eyes, that I perceive the sun's lesser glow.'

" 'Ramu, someone has connived to put me in a difficult position. I have no healing power.'

" 'Sir, the Infinite One within you can certainly heal.'

" 'That is indeed different, Ramu. God's limit is nowhere! He who ignites the stars and the cells of flesh with mysterious life-effulgence can surely bring lustre of vision into your eyes.'

"The master touched Ramu's forehead at the point between the eyebrows.[7]

" 'Keep your mind concentrated there, and frequently chant the name of the prophet Rama[8] for seven days. The splendour of the sun shall have a special dawn for you.'

"Lo! in one week it was so. For the first time, Ramu beheld the fair face of nature. The Omniscient One had unerringly directed his disciple to repeat the name of Rama, adored by him above all other saints. Ramu's faith was the devotionally ploughed soil in which the guru's powerful seed of permanent healing sprouted." Kebalananda was silent for a moment, then paid a further tribute to his guru.

"It was evident in all miracles performed by Lahiri Mahasaya that he never allowed the ego-principle[9] to consider itself a causative force. By perfection of resistless surrender, the master enabled the Prime Healing Power to flow freely through him.

"The numerous bodies which were spectacularly healed through Lahiri Mahasaya eventually had to feed the flames of cremation. But the silent spiritual awakenings he effected, the Christ-like disciples he fashioned, are his imperishable miracles."

I never became a Sanskrit scholar; Kebalananda taught me a diviner syntax.

5. A 'Perfume Saint' displays his Wonders

To EVERY THING there is a season, and a time to every purpose under the heaven."

I did not have this wisdom of Solomon to comfort me; I gazed searchingly about me, on any excursion from home, for the face of my destined guru. But my path did not cross his own until after the completion of my high school studies.

Two years elapsed between my flight with Amar toward the Himalayas, and the great day of Sri Yukteswar's arrival into my life. During that interim I met a number of sages – the 'Perfume Saint,' the 'Tiger Swami,' Nagendra Nath Bhaduri, Master Mahasaya, and the famous Bengali scientist, Jagadis Chandra Bose.

7 The seat of the 'single' or spiritual eye. At death the consciousness of man is usually drawn to this holy spot, accounting for the upraised eyes found in the dead.
8 The central sacred figure of the Sanskrit epic *Ramayana*.
9 *Ahankara*: egoism; literally, 'I do.' The root cause of dualism or illusion of *maya*, whereby the subject (ego) appears as object; the creatures imagine themselves to be creators.

My encounter with the 'Perfume Saint' had two preambles, one harmonious and the other humorous.

"God is simple. Everything else is complex. Do not seek absolute values in the relative world of nature."

These philosophical finalities gently entered my ear as I stood silently before a temple image of Kali.[1] Turning, I confronted a tall man whose garb, or lack of it, revealed him a wandering *sadhu*.

"You have indeed penetrated the bewilderment of my thoughts!" I smiled gratefully. "The confusion of benign and terrible aspects in nature, as symbolized by Kali, has puzzled wiser heads than mine!"

"Few there be who solve her mystery! Good and evil is the challenging riddle which life places sphinxlike before every intelligence. Attempting no solution, most men pay forfeit with their lives, penalty now even as in the days of Thebes. Here and there, a towering lonely figure never cries defeat. From the *maya*[2] of duality he plucks the cleaveless truth of unity."

"You speak with conviction, sir."

"I have long exercised an honest introspection, the exquisitely painful approach to wisdom. Self-scrutiny, relentless observance of one's thoughts, is a stark and shattering experience. It pulverizes the stoutest ego. But true self-analysis mathematically operates to produce seers. The way of 'self-expression,' individual acknowledgments, results in egotists, sure of the right to their private interpretations of God and the universe."

"Truth humbly retires, no doubt, before such arrogant originality." I was enjoying the discussion.

"Man can understand no eternal verity until he has freed himself from pretensions. The human mind, bared to a centuried slime, is teeming with repulsive life of countless world-delusions. Struggles of the battlefields pale into insignificance here, when man first contends with inward enemies! No mortal foes these, to be overcome by harrowing array of might! Omnipresent, unresting, pursuing man even in sleep, subtly equipped with miasmic weapons, these soldiers of ignorant lusts seek to slay us all. Thoughtless is the man who buries his ideals, surrendering to the common fate. Can he seem other than impotent, wooden, ignominious?"

"Respected Sir, have you no sympathy for the bewildered masses?"

1 Kali represents the eternal principle in nature. She is traditionally pictured as a four-armed woman, standing on the form of the God Shiva or the Infinite, because nature or the phenomenal world is rooted in the Noumenon (that which is apprehended by thought). The four arms symbolize cardinal attributes, two beneficent, two destructive, indicating the essential duality of matter or creation.
2 Cosmic illusion; literally, 'the measurer.' *Maya* is the magical power in creation by which limitations and divisions are apparently present in the Immeasurable and Inseparable.
Emerson wrote the following poem, to which he gave the title of *Maya:*

    Illusion works impenetrable, Weaving webs innumerable,
    Her gay pictures never fail, Crowd each other, veil on veil,
    Charmer who will be believed, By man who thirsts to be deceived.

The sage was silent for a moment, then answered obliquely.

"To love both the invisible God, Repository of All Virtues, and visible man, apparently possessed of none, is often baffling! But ingenuity is equal to the maze. Inner research soon exposes a unity in all human minds – the stalwart kinship of selfish motive. In one sense at least, the brotherhood of man stands revealed. An aghast humility follows this levelling discovery. It ripens into compassion for one's fellows, blind to the healing potencies of the soul awaiting exploration."

"The saints of every age, sir, have felt like yourself for the sorrows of the world."

"Only the shallow man loses responsiveness to the woes of others' lives, as he sinks into narrow suffering of his own." The *sadhu's* austere face was noticeably softened. "The one who practices a scalpel self-dissection will know an expansion of universal pity. Release is given him from the deafening demands of his ego. The love of God flowers on such soil. The creature finally turns to his Creator, if for no other reason than to ask in anguish: 'Why, Lord, why?' By ignoble whips of pain, man is driven at last into the Infinite Presence, whose beauty alone should lure him."

The sage and I were present in Calcutta's Kalighat Temple, whither I had gone to view its famed magnificence. With a sweeping gesture, my chance companion dismissed the ornate dignity.

"Bricks and mortar sing us no audible tune; the heart opens only to the human chant of being."

We strolled to the inviting sunshine at the entrance, where throngs of devotees were passing to and fro.

"You are young." The sage surveyed me thoughtfully. "India too is young. The ancient *rishis*[3] laid down ineradicable patterns of spiritual living. Their hoary dictums suffice for this day and land. Not outmoded, not unsophisticated against the guiles of materialism, the disciplinary precepts mould India still. By millenniums – more than embarrassed scholars care to compute! – the skeptic Time has validated Vedic worth. Take it for your heritage."

As I was reverently bidding farewell to the eloquent *sadhu,* he revealed a clairvoyant perception:

"After you leave here today, an unusual experience will come your way."

I quitted the temple precincts and wandered along aimlessly. Turning a corner, I ran into an old acquaintance – one of those long-winded fellows whose conversational powers ignore time and embrace eternity.

"I will let you go in a very short while, if you will tell me all that has happened during the six years of our separation."

3 The *rishis*, literally 'seers,' were the authors of the *Vedas* in an indeterminable antiquity.

"What a paradox! I must leave you now."

But he held me by the hand, forcing out tidbits of information. He was like a ravenous wolf, I thought in amusement; the longer I spoke, the more hungrily he sniffed for news. Inwardly I petitioned the Goddess Kali to devise a graceful means of escape.

My companion left me abruptly. I sighed with relief and doubled my pace, dreading any relapse into the garrulous fever. Hearing rapid footsteps behind me, I quickened my speed. I dared not look back. But with a bound, the youth rejoined me, jovially clasping my shoulder.

"I forgot to tell you of Gandha Baba (Perfume Saint), who is gracing yonder house." He pointed to a dwelling a few yards distant. "Do meet him; he is interesting. You may have an unusual experience. Good-by," and he actually left me.

The similarly worded prediction of the *sadhu* at Kalighat Temple flashed to my mind. Definitely intrigued, I entered the house and was ushered into a commodious parlour. A crowd of people were sitting, Orientwise, here and there on a thick orange-coloured carpet. An awed whisper reached my ear:

"Behold Gandha Baba on the leopard skin. He can give the natural perfume of any flower to a scentless one, or revive a wilted blossom, or make a person's skin exude delightful fragrance."

I looked directly at the saint; his quick gaze rested on mine. He was plump and bearded, with dark skin and large, gleaming eyes.

"Son, I am glad to see you. Say what you want. Would you like some perfume?"

"What for?" I thought his remark rather childish.

"To experience the miraculous way of enjoying perfumes."

"Harnessing God to make odours?"

"What of it? God makes perfume anyway."

"Yes, but He fashions frail bottles of petals for fresh use and discard. Can you materialize flowers?"

"I materialize perfumes, little friend."

"Then scent factories will go out of business."

"I will permit them to keep their trade! My own purpose is to demonstrate the power of God."

"Sir, is it necessary to prove God? Isn't He performing miracles in everything, everywhere?"

"Yes, but we too should manifest some of His infinite creative variety."

"How long did it take to master your art?"

"Twelve years."

"For manufacturing scents by astral means! It seems, my honoured saint, you have been wasting a dozen years for fragrances which you can obtain with a few rupees from a florist's shop."

"Perfumes fade with flowers."

"Perfumes fade with death. Why should I desire that which pleases the body only?"

"Mr. Philosopher, you please my mind. Now, stretch forth your right hand." He made a gesture of blessing.

I was a few feet away from Gandha Baba; no one else was near enough to contact my body. I extended my hand, which the yogi did not touch.

"What perfume do you want?"

"Rose."

"Be it so."

To my great surprise, the charming fragrance of rose was wafted strongly from the centre of my palm. I smilingly took a large white scentless flower from a near-by vase.

"Can this odourless blossom be permeated with jasmine?"

"Be it so."

A jasmine fragrance instantly shot from the petals. I thanked the wonder-worker and seated myself by one of his students. He informed me that Gandha Baba, whose proper name was Vishudhananda, had learned many astonishing yoga secrets from a master in Tibet. The Tibetan yogi, I was assured, had attained the age of over a thousand years.

"His disciple Gandha Baba does not always perform his perfume-feats in the simple verbal manner you have just witnessed." The student spoke with obvious pride in his master. "His procedure differs widely, to accord with diversity in temperaments. He is marvellous! Many members of the Calcutta intelligentsia are among his followers."

I inwardly resolved not to add myself to their number. A guru too literally 'marvellous' was not to my liking. With polite thanks to Gandha Baba, I departed. Sauntering home, I reflected on the three varied encounters the day had brought forth.

My sister Uma met me as I entered our Gurpar Road door.

"You are getting quite stylish, using perfumes!"

Without a word, I motioned her to smell my hand.

"What an attractive rose fragrance! It is unusually strong!"

Thinking it was 'strongly unusual,' I silently placed the astrally scented blossom under her nostrils.

"Oh, I love jasmine!" She seized the flower. A ludicrous bafflement passed over her face as she repeatedly sniffed the odour of jasmine from a type of flower she well knew to be scentless. Her reactions disarmed my suspicion that Gandha Baba had induced an auto-suggestive state whereby I alone could detect the fragrances.

Later I heard from a friend, Alakananda, that the 'Perfume Saint' had a power which I wish were possessed by the starving millions of Asia and, today, of Europe as well.

"I was present with a hundred other guests at Gandha Baba's home in Burdwan," Alakananda told me. "It was a gala occasion. Because the yogi was reputed to have the power of extracting objects out of thin air, I laughingly requested him to materialize some out-of-season tangerines. Immediately the *luchis*[4] which were present on all the banana-leaf plates became puffed up. Each of the bread-envelopes proved to contain a peeled tangerine. I bit into my own with some trepidation, but found it delicious."

Years later I understood by inner realization how Gandha Baba accomplished his materializations. The method, alas! is beyond the reach of the world's hungry hordes.

The different sensory stimuli to which man reacts – tactual, visual, gustatory, auditory, and olfactory – are produced by vibratory variations in electrons and protons. The vibrations in turn are regulated by 'lifetrons,' subtle life forces or finer-than-atomic energies intelligently charged with the five distinctive sensory idea-substances.

Gandha Baba, tuning himself with the cosmic force by certain yogic practices, was able to guide the lifetrons to rearrange their vibratory structure and objectivize the desired result. His perfume, fruit and other miracles were actual materializations of mundane vibrations, and not inner sensations hypnotically produced.[5]

Performances of miracles such as shown by the 'Perfume Saint' are spectacular but spiritually useless. Having little purpose beyond entertainment, they are digressions from a serious search for God.

Hypnotism has been used by physicians in minor operations as a sort of

4 Flat, round Indian home-cooked bread.

5 Laymen scarcely realize the vast strides of twentieth-century science. Transmutation of metals and other alchemical dreams are seeing fulfillment every day in centres of scientific research over the world. The eminent French chemist, M. Georges Claude performed 'miracles' at Fontainebleau in 1928 before a scientific assemblage through his chemical knowledge of oxygen transformations. His 'magician's wand' was simple oxygen, bubbling in a tube on a table. The scientist 'turned' a handful of sand into precious stones, iron into a state resembling melted chocolate and, after depriving flowers of their tints, turned them into the consistency of glass.

M. Claude explained how the sea could be turned by oxygen transformations into many millions of pounds of horsepower; how water which boils is not necessarily burning; how little mounds of sand, by a single whiff of the oxygen blowpipe, could be changed into sapphires, rubies, and topazes; and he predicted the time when it will be possible for men to walk on the bottom of the ocean minus the diver's equipment. Finally the scientist amazed his onlookers by turning their faces black by taking the red out of the sun's rays. This noted French scientist has produced liquid air by an expansion method in which he has been able to separate the various gases of the air, and has discovered various means of mechanical utilization of differences of temperature in sea water.

psychical chloroform for persons who might be endangered by an anesthetic. But a hypnotic state is harmful to those often subjected to it; a negative psychological effect ensues which in time deranges the brain cells. Hypnotism is trespass into the territory of another's consciousness. Its temporary phenomena have nothing in common with the miracles performed by men of divine realization. Awake in God, true saints effect changes in this dream-world by means of a will harmoniously attuned to the Creative Cosmic Dreamer.

Ostentatious display of unusual powers are decried by masters. The Persian mystic, Abu Said, once laughed at certain *fakirs* who were proud of their miraculous powers over water, air, and space.

"A frog is also at home in the water!" Abu Said pointed out in gentle scorn. "The crow and the vulture easily fly in the air; the Devil is simultaneously present in the East and in the West! A true man is he who dwells in righteousness among his fellow men, who buys and sells, yet is never for a single instant forgetful of God!"[6] On another occasion the great Persian teacher gave his views on the religious life thus: "To lay aside what you have in your head (selfish desires and ambitions); to freely bestow what you have in your hand; and never to flinch from the blows of adversity!"

Neither the impartial sage at Kalighat Temple nor the Tibetan-trained yogi had satisfied my yearning for a guru. My heart needed no tutor for its recognitions, and cried its own "Bravos!" the more resoundingly because unoften summoned from silence. When I finally met my master, he taught me by sublimity of example alone the measure of a true man.

6. *The Tiger Swami*

"I HAVE DISCOVERED the Tiger Swami's address. Let us visit him tomorrow."

This welcome suggestion came from Chandi, one of my high school friends. I was eager to meet the saint who, in his premonastic life, had caught and fought tigers with his naked hands. A boyish enthusiasm over such remarkable feats was strong within me.

The next day dawned wintry cold, but Chandi and I sallied forth gaily. After much vain hunting in Bhowanipur, outside Calcutta, we arrived at the right house. The door held two iron rings, which I sounded piercingly. Notwithstanding the clamour, a servant approached with leisurely gait. His

---

6 'To buy and sell, yet never to forget God!' The ideal is that hand and heart work harmoniously together. Certain Western writers claim that Hindu goal is one of timid 'escape' of inactivity and antisocial withdrawal. The four-fold Vedic plan for man's life, however, is a well-balanced one for the masses, allotting half the span to study and householder duties; the second half to contemplation and meditational practices. (See Note 1 on page 194).

ironical smile implied that visitors, despite their noise, were powerless to disturb the calmness of a saint's home.

Feeling the silent rebuke, my companion and I were thankful to be invited into the parlour. Our long wait there caused uncomfortable misgivings. India's unwritten law for the truth seeker is patience; a master may purposely make a test of one's eagerness to meet him. This psychological ruse is freely employed in the West by doctors and dentists!

Finally summoned by the servant, Chandi and I entered a sleeping apartment. The famous Sohong[1] Swami was seated on his bed. The sight of his tremendous body affected us strangely. With bulging eyes, we stood speechless. We had never before seen such a chest or such football-like biceps. On an immense neck, the swami's fierce yet calm face was adorned with flowing locks, beard and moustache. A hint of dovelike and tigerlike qualities shone in his dark eyes. He was unclothed, save for a tiger skin about his muscular waist.

Finding our voices, my friend and I greeted the monk, expressing our admiration for his prowess in the extraordinary feline arena.

"Will you not tell us, please, how it is possible to subdue with bare fists the most ferocious of jungle beasts, the royal Bengals?"

"My sons, it is nothing to me to fight tigers. I could do it today if necessary." He gave a childlike laugh. "You look upon tigers as tigers; I know them as pussycats."

"Swamiji, I think I could impress my subconsciousness with the thought that tigers are pussycats, but could I make tigers believe it?"

"Of course strength also is necessary! One cannot expect victory from a baby who imagines a tiger to be a house cat! Powerful hands are my sufficient weapon."

He asked us to follow him to the patio, where he struck the edge of a wall. A brick crashed to the floor; the sky peered boldly through the gaping lost tooth of the wall. I fairly staggered in astonishment; he who can remove mortared bricks from a solid wall with one blow, I thought, must surely be able to displace the teeth of tigers!

"A number of men have physical power such as mine, but still lack in cool confidence. Those who are bodily but not mentally stalwart may find themselves fainting at mere sight of a wild beast bounding freely in the jungle. The tiger in its natural ferocity and habitat is vastly different from the opium-fed circus animal!

1 Sohong was his monastic name. He was popularly known as the 'Tiger Swami.'

"Many a man with Herculean strength has nonetheless been terrorized into abject helplessness before the onslaught of a royal Bengal. Thus the tiger has converted the man, in his own mind, to a state as nerveless as the pussycat's. It is possible for a man, owning a fairly strong body and an immensely strong determination, to turn the tables on the tiger, and force it to a conviction of pussycat defenselessness. How often I have done just that!"

I was quite willing to believe that the titan before me was able to perform the tiger-pussycat metamorphosis. He seemed in a didactic mood; Chandi and I listened respectfully.

"Mind is the wielder of muscles. The force of a hammer blow depends on the energy applied; the power expressed by a man's bodily instrument depends on his aggressive will and courage. The body is literally manufactured and sustained by mind. Through pressure of instincts from past lives, strengths or weaknesses percolate gradually into human consciousness. They express as habits, which in turn ossify into a desirable or an undesirable body. Outward frailty has mental origin; in a vicious circle, the habit-bound body thwarts the mind. If the master allows himself to be commanded by a servant, the latter becomes autocratic; the mind is similarly enslaved by submitting to bodily dictation."

At our entreaty, the impressive swami consented to tell us something of his own life.

"My earliest ambition was to fight tigers. My will was mighty, but my body was feeble."

An ejaculation of surprise broke from me. It appeared incredible that this man, now 'with Atlantean shoulders, fit to bear,' could ever have known weakness.

"It was by indomitable persistency in thoughts of health and strength that I overcame my handicap. I have every reason to extol the compelling mental vigor which I found to be the real subduer of royal Bengals."

"Do you think, revered swami, that I could ever fight tigers?" This was the first, and the last, time that the bizarre ambition ever visited my mind!

"Yes." He was smiling. "But there are many kinds of tigers; some roam in jungles of human desires. No spiritual benefit accrues by knocking beasts unconscious. Rather be victor over the inner prowlers."

"May we hear, sir, how you changed from a tamer of wild tigers to a tamer of wild passions?"

The Tiger Swami fell into silence. Remoteness came into his gaze, summoning visions of bygone years. I discerned his slight mental struggle to decide whether to grant my request. Finally he smiled in acquiescence.

"When my fame reached a zenith, it brought the intoxication of pride.

I decided not only to fight tigers but to display them in various tricks. My ambition was to force savage beasts to behave like domesticated ones. I began to perform my feats publicly, with gratifying success.

"One evening my father entered my room in pensive mood.

" 'Son, I have words of warning. I would save you from coming ills, produced by the grinding wheels of cause and effect.'

" 'Are you a fatalist, Father? Should superstition be allowed to discolour the powerful waters of my activities?'

" 'I am no fatalist, son. But I believe in the just law of retribution, as taught in the holy scriptures. There is resentment against you in the jungle family; sometime it may act to your cost.'

" 'Father, you astonish me! You well know what tigers are – beautiful but merciless! Even immediately after an enormous meal of some hapless creature, a tiger is fired with fresh lust at sight of new prey. It may be a joyous gazelle, frisking over the jungle grass. Capturing it and biting an opening in the soft throat, the malevolent beast tastes only a little of the mutely crying blood, and goes its wanton way.

" 'Tigers are the most contemptible of the jungle breed! Who knows? my blows may inject some slight sanity of consideration into their thick heads. I am headmaster in a forest finishing school, to teach them gentle manners!

" 'Please, Father, think of me as tiger tamer and never as tiger killer. How could my good actions bring ill upon me? I beg you not to impose any command that I change my way of life.' "

Chandi and I were all attention, understanding the past dilemma. In India a child does not lightly disobey his parents' wishes.

"In stoic silence Father listened to my explanation. He followed it with a disclosure which he uttered gravely.

" 'Son, you compel me to relate an ominous prediction from the lips of a saint. He approached me yesterday as I sat on the veranda in my daily meditation.

" 'Dear friend, I come with a message for your belligerent son. Let him cease his savage activities. Otherwise, his next tiger-encounter shall result in his severe wounds, followed by six months of deathly sickness. He shall then forsake his former ways and become a monk.' "

"This tale did not impress me. I considered that Father had been the credulous victim of a deluded fanatic."

The Tiger Swami made this confession with an impatient gesture, as though at some stupidity. Grimly silent for a long time, he seemed oblivious of our presence. When he took up the dangling thread of his narrative, it was suddenly, with subdued voice.

"Not long after Father's warning, I visited the capital city of Cooch Behar. The picturesque territory was new to me, and I expected a restful change. As usual everywhere, a curious crowd followed me on the streets. I would catch bits of whispered comment:

" 'This is the man who fights wild tigers.'

" 'Has he legs, or tree-trunks?'

" 'Look at his face! He must be an incarnation of the king of tigers himself!'

"You know how village urchins function like final editions of a newspaper! With what speed do the even later speech-bulletins of the women circulate from house to house! Within a few hours, the whole city was in a state of excitement over my presence.

"I was relaxing quietly in the evening, when I heard the hoof beats of galloping horses. They stopped in front of my dwelling place. In came a number of tall, turbaned policemen.

"I was taken aback. 'All things are possible unto these creatures of human law,' I thought. 'I wonder if they are going to take me to task about matters utterly unknown to me.' But the officers bowed with unwonted courtesy.

" 'Honoured Sir, we are sent to welcome you on behalf of the Prince of Cooch Behar. He is pleased to invite you to his palace tomorrow morning.'

"I speculated awhile on the prospect. For some obscure reason I felt sharp regret at this interruption in my quiet trip. But the suppliant manner of the policemen moved me; I agreed to go.

"I was bewildered the next day to be obsequiously escorted from my door into a magnificent coach drawn by four horses. A servant held an ornate umbrella to protect me from the scorching sunlight. I enjoyed the pleasant ride through the city and its woodland outskirts. The royal scion himself was at the palace door to welcome me. He proffered his own gold-brocaded seat, smilingly placing himself in a chair of simpler design.

" 'All this politeness is certainly going to cost me something!' I thought in mounting astonishment. The prince's motive emerged after a few casual remarks.

" 'My city is filled with the rumour that you can fight wild tigers with nothing more than your naked hands. Is it a fact?'

" 'It is quite true.'

" 'I can scarcely believe it! You are a Calcutta Bengali, nurtured on the white rice of city folk. Be frank, please; have you not been fighting only spineless, opium-fed animals?' His voice was loud and sarcastic, tinged with provincial accent.

"I vouchsafed no reply to his insulting question.

" 'I challenge you to fight my newly-caught tiger, Raja Begum.[2] If you can successfully resist him, bind him with a chain, and leave his cage in a conscious state, you shall have this royal Bengal! Several thousand rupees and many other gifts shall also be bestowed. If you refuse to meet him in combat, I shall blazon your name throughout the state as an impostor!'

"His insolent words struck me like a volley of bullets. I shot an angry acceptance. Half risen from the chair in his excitement, the prince sank back with a sadistic smile. I was reminded of the Roman emperors who delighted in setting Christians in bestial arenas.

" 'The match will be set for a week hence. I regret that I cannot give you permission to view the tiger in advance.'

"Whether the prince feared I might seek to hypnotize the beast, or secretly feed him opium, I know not!

"I left the palace, noting with amusement that the royal umbrella and panoplied coach were now missing.

"The following week I methodically prepared my mind and body for the coming ordeal. Through my servant I learned of fantastic tales. The saint's direful prediction to my father had somehow got abroad, enlarging as it ran. Many simple villagers believed that an evil spirit, cursed by the gods, had reincarnated as a tiger which took various demoniac forms at night, but remained a striped animal during the day. This demon-tiger was supposed to be the one sent to humble me.

"Another imaginative version was that animal prayers to Tiger Heaven had achieved a response in the shape of Raja Begum. He was to be the instrument to punish me – the audacious biped, so insulting to the entire tiger species! A furless, fangless man daring to challenge a claw-armed, sturdy-limbed tiger! The concentrated venom of all humiliated tigers – the villagers declared – had gathered momentum sufficient to operate hidden laws and bring about the fall of the proud tiger tamer.

"My servant further apprised me that the prince was in his element as manager of the bout between man and beast. He had supervised the erection of a storm-proof pavilion, designed to accommodate thousands. Its centre held Raja Begum in an enormous iron cage, surrounded by an outer safety room. The captive emitted a ceaseless series of blood-curdling roars. He was fed sparingly, to kindle a wrathful appetite. Perhaps the prince expected me to be the meal of reward!

"Crowds from the city and suburbs bought tickets eagerly in response to the beat of drums announcing the unique contest. The day of battle saw hundreds turned away for lack of seats. Many men broke through the tent

2 'Prince Princess' so named to indicate that this beast possessed the combined ferocity of tiger and tigress.

openings, or crowded any space below the galleries."

As the Tiger Swami's story approached a climax, my excitement mounted with it; Chandi also was raptly mute.

"Amidst piercing sound-explosions from Raja Begum, and the hubbub of the somewhat terrified crowd, I quietly made my appearance. Scantily clad around the waist, I was otherwise unprotected by clothing. I opened the bolt on the door of the safety room and calmly locked it behind me. The tiger sensed blood. Leaping with a thunderous crash on his bars, he sent forth a fearsome welcome. The audience was hushed with pitiful fear; I seemed a meek lamb before the raging beast.

"In a trice I was within the cage; but as I slammed the door, Raja Begum was headlong upon me. My right hand was desperately torn. Human blood, the greatest treat a tiger can know, fell in appalling streams. The prophecy of the saint seemed about to be fulfilled.

"I rallied instantly from the shock of the first serious injury I had ever received. Banishing the sight of my gory fingers by thrusting them beneath my waistcloth, I swung my left arm in a bone-cracking blow. The beast reeled back, swirled around the rear of the cage, and sprang forward convulsively. My famous fistic punishment rained on his head.

"But Raja Begum's taste of blood had acted like the maddening first sip of wine to a dipsomaniac long-deprived. Punctuated by deafening roar, the brute's assaults grew in fury. My inadequate defense of only one hand left me vulnerable before claws and fangs. But I dealt out dazing retribution. Mutually ensanguined, we struggled as to the death. The cage was pandemonium, as blood splashed in all directions, and blasts of pain and lethal lust came from the bestial throat.

" 'Shoot him!' 'Kill the tiger!' Shrieks arose from the audience. So fast did man and beast move, that a guard's bullet went amiss. I mustered all my will force, bellowed fiercely, and landed a final concussive blow. The tiger collapsed and lay quietly.

"Like a pussycat!" I interjected.

The swami laughed in hearty appreciation, then continued the engrossing tale.

"Raja Begum was vanquished at last. His royal pride was further humbled: with my lacerated hands, I audaciously forced open his jaws. For a dramatic moment, I held my head within the yawning deathtrap. I looked around for a chain. Pulling one from a pile on the floor, I bound the tiger by his neck to the cage bars. In triumph I moved toward the door.

"But that fiend incarnate, Raja Begum, had stamina worthy of his supposed demoniac origin. With an incredible lunge, he snapped the chain and leaped on my back. My shoulder fast in his jaws, I fell violently. But in a trice I had him pinned beneath me. Under merciless blows, the treacherous animal sank into semiconsciousness. This time I secured him more carefully. Slowly I left the cage.

"I found myself in a new uproar, this time one of delight. The crowd's cheer broke as though from a single gigantic throat. Disastrously mauled, I had yet fulfilled the three conditions of the fight – stunning the tiger, binding him with a chain, and leaving him without requiring assistance for myself. In addition, I had so drastically injured and frightened the aggressive beast that he had been content to overlook the opportune prize of my head in his mouth!

"After my wounds were treated, I was honoured and garlanded; hundreds of gold pieces showered at my feet. The whole city entered a holiday period. Endless discussions were heard on all sides about my victory over one of the largest and most savage tigers ever seen. Raja Begum was presented to me, as promised, but I felt no elation. A spiritual change had entered my heart. It seemed that with my final exit from the cage I had also closed the door on my worldly ambitions.

"A woeful period followed. For six months I lay near death from blood poisoning. As soon as I was well enough to leave Cooch Behar, I returned to my native town.

" 'I know now that my teacher is the holy man who gave the wise warning.' I humbly made this confession to my father. 'Oh, if I could only find him!' My longing was sincere, for one day the saint arrived unheralded.

" 'Enough of tiger taming.' He spoke with calm assurance. 'Come with me; I will teach you to subdue the beasts of ignorance roaming in jungles of the human mind. You are used to an audience: let it be a galaxy of angels, entertained by your thrilling mastery of yoga!'

"I was initiated into the spiritual path by my saintly guru. He opened my soul-doors, rusty and resistant with long disuse. Hand in hand, we soon set out for my training in the Himalayas."

Chandi and I bowed at the swami's feet, grateful for his vivid outline of a life truly cyclonic. I felt amply repaid for the long probationary wait in the cold parlour!

7. *The Levitating Saint*

"I saw a yogi remain in the air, several feet above the ground, last night at a group meeting." My friend, Upendra Mohun Chowdhury, spoke impressively.

I gave him an enthusiastic smile. "Perhaps I can guess his name. Was it Bhaduri Mahasaya, of Upper Circular Road?"

Upendra nodded, a little crestfallen not to be a news-bearer. My inquisitiveness about saints was well-known among my friends; they delighted in setting me on a fresh track.

"The yogi lives so close to my home that I often visit him." My words brought keen interest to Upendra's face, and I made a further confidence.

"I have seen him in remarkable feats. He has expertly mastered the various *pranayamas*[1] of the ancient eightfold yoga outlined by Patanjali.[2] Once Bhaduri Mahasaya performed the *Bhastrika Pranayama* before me with such amazing force that it seemed an actual storm had arisen in the room! Then he extinguished the thundering breath and remained motionless in a high state of superconsciousness.[3] The aura of peace after the storm was vivid beyond forgetting."

"I heard that the saint never leaves his home." Upendra's tone was a trifle incredulous.

"Indeed it is true! He has lived indoors for the past twenty years. He slightly relaxes his self-imposed rule at the times of our holy festivals, when he goes as far as his front sidewalk! The beggars gather there, because Saint Bhaduri is known for his tender heart."

"How does he remain in the air, defying the law of gravitation?"

"A yogi's body loses its grossness after use of certain *pranayamas*. Then it will levitate or hop about like a leaping frog. Even saints who do not practice a formal yoga[4] have been known to levitate during a state of intense devotion to God."

"I would like to know more of this sage. Do you attend his evening meetings?" Upendra's eyes were sparkling with curiosity.

"Yes, I go often. I am vastly entertained by the wit in his wisdom. Occasionally my prolonged laughter mars the solemnity of his gatherings. The saint is not displeased, but his disciples look daggers!"

On my way home from school that afternoon, I passed Bhaduri Mahasaya's cloister and decided on a visit. The yogi was inaccessible to the general public. A lone disciple, occupying the ground floor, guarded his master's privacy. The student was something of a martinet; he now inquired formally if I had an 'engagement.' His guru put in an appearance just in time to save me from summary ejection.

---

1 Methods of controlling life-force through regulation of breath.

2 The foremost ancient exponent of yoga (BC 500-200).

3 French professors were the first to scientifically investigate the possibilities of the superconscious mind. Professor Jules-Bois, member of the L'Ecole de Psychologic of the Sorbonne, lectured in America in 1928; he told his audiences that French scientists have accorded recognition to the superconsciousness, "which is the exact opposite of Freud's subconscious mind and is the faculty which makes man really man and not just a super-animal." M. Jules-Bois explained that the awakening of the higher consciousness "was not to be confused with Couéism or hypnotism. The existence of a superconscious mind has long been recognized philosophically, being in reality the Oversoul spoken of by Emerson, but only recently has it been recognized scientifically." The French scientist pointed out that from the superconsciousness come inspiration, genius, moral values. "Belief in this is not mysticism though it recognized and valued the qualities which mystics preached."

4 St. Theresa of Avila of Spain and other Christian saints were often observed in a state of levitation.

"Let Mukunda come when he will." The sage's eyes twinkled. "My rule of seclusion is not for my own comfort, but for that of others. Worldly people do not like the candour which shatters their delusions. Saints are not only rare but disconcerting. Even in scripture, they are often found embarrassing!"

I followed Bhaduri Mahasaya to his austere quarters on the top floor, from which he seldom stirred. Masters often ignore the panorama of the world's ado, out of focus till centred in the ages. The contemporaries of a sage are not only those of the narrow present.

"Maharishi,[5] you are the first yogi I have known who always stays indoors."

"God plants his saints sometimes in unexpected soil, lest we think we may reduce Him to a rule!"

The sage locked his vibrant body in the lotus posture. In his seventies, he displayed no unpleasing signs of age or sedentary life. Stalwart and straight, he was ideal in every respect. His face was that of a *rishi,* as described in the ancient texts. Noble-headed, abundantly bearded, he always sat firmly upright, his quiet eyes fixed on Omnipresence.

The saint and I entered the meditative state. After an hour, his gentle voice roused me.

"You go often into the silence, but have you developed *anubhava*?"[6] He was reminding me to love God more than meditation. "Do not mistake the technique for the Goal."

He offered me some mangoes. With that good-humoured wit that I found so delightful in his grave nature, he remarked, "People in general are more fond of *Jala Yoga* (union with drink and food) than of *Dhyana Yoga* (union with God)."

His yogic pun affected me uproariously.

"What a laugh you have!" An affectionate gleam came into his gaze. His own face was always serious, yet touched with an ecstatic smile. His large, lotus eyes held a hidden divine laughter.

"Those letters come from far-off America." The sage indicated several thick envelopes on a table. "I correspond with a few societies there whose members are interested in yoga. They are discovering India anew, with a better sense of direction than Columbus! I am glad to help them. The knowledge of yoga is free to all who will receive it, like the ungarnishable daylight.

"What *rishis* perceived as essential for human salvation need not be diluted for the West. Alike in soul though diverse in outer experience, neither West nor East will flourish if some form of disciplinary yoga be not practiced."

The saint held me with his tranquil eyes. I did not realize that his speech was a veiled prophetic guidance. It is only now, as I write these words, that

5 'Great sage.'   6 Actual perception of God.

I understand the full meaning in the casual intimations he often gave me that someday I would carry India's teachings to America.

"Maharishi, I wish you would write a book on yoga for the benefit of the world."

"I am training disciples. They and their students will be living volumes, proof against the natural disintegrations of time and the unnatural interpretations of the critics." Bhaduri's wit put me into another gale of laughter.

I remained alone with the yogi until his disciples arrived in the evening. Bhaduri Mahasaya entered one of his inimitable discourses. Like a peaceful flood, he swept away the mental debris of his listeners, floating them Godward. His striking parables were expressed in a flawless Bengali.

This evening Bhaduri expounded various philosophical points connected with the life of Mirabai, a medieval Rajputani princess who abandoned her court life to seek the company of sadhus. One great sannyasi refused to receive her because she was a woman; her reply brought him humbly to her feet.

"Tell the master," she had said, "that I did not know there was any Male in the universe save God; are we all not females before Him?" (A scriptural conception of the Lord as the only Positive Creative Principle, His creation being naught but a passive *maya*.)

Mirabai composed many ecstatic songs which are still treasured in India; I translate one of them here:

> "If by bathing daily God could be realized
> Sooner would I be a whale in the deep;
> If by eating roots and fruits He could be known
> Gladly would I choose the form of a goat;
> If the counting of rosaries uncovered Him
> I would say my prayers on mammoth beads;
> If bowing before stone images unveiled Him
> A flinty mountain I would humbly worship;
> If by drinking milk the Lord could be imbibed
> Many calves and children would know Him;
> If abandoning one's wife would summon God
> Would not thousands be eunuchs?
> Mirabai knows that to find the Divine One
> The only indispensable is Love."

Several students put rupees in Bhaduri's slippers which lay by his side as he sat in yoga posture. This respectful offering, customary in India, indicates that the disciple places his material goods at the guru's feet. Grateful friends are only the Lord in disguise, looking after His own.

"Master, you are wonderful!" A student, taking his leave, gazed ardently at the patriarchal sage. "You have renounced riches and comforts to seek God and teach us wisdom!" It was well known that Bhaduri Mahasaya had forsaken great family wealth in his early childhood, when single-mindedly he entered the yogic path.

"You are reversing the case!" The saint's face held a mild rebuke. "I have left a few paltry rupees, a few petty pleasures, for a cosmic empire of endless bliss. How then have I denied myself anything? I know the joy of sharing the treasure. Is that a sacrifice? The shortsighted worldly folk are verily the real renunciates! They relinquish an unparalleled divine possession for a poor handful of earthly toys!"

I chuckled over this paradoxical view of renunciation – one which puts the cap of Croesus[7] on any saintly beggar, whilst transforming all proud millionaires into unconscious martyrs.

"The divine order arranges our future more wisely than any insurance company." The master's concluding words were the realized creed of his faith. "The world is full of uneasy believers in an outward security. Their bitter thoughts are like scars on their foreheads. The One who gave us air and milk from our first breath knows how to provide day by day for His devotees."

I continued my after-school pilgrimages to the saint's door. With silent zeal he aided me to attain *anubhava*. One day he moved to Ram Mohan Roy Road, away from the neighborhood of my Gurpar Road home. His loving disciples had built him a new hermitage, known as 'Nagendra Math.'[8] (on the Upper Circular road.)

Although it throws me ahead of my story by a number of years, I will recount here the last words given to me by Bhaduri Mahasaya.[9] Shortly before I embarked for the West, I sought him out and humbly knelt for his farewell blessing:

"Son, go to America. Take the dignity of hoary India for your shield. Victory is written on your brow; the noble distant people will well receive you."

---

7 6th century wealthy Lydian King who branded Gold as the most precious metal

8 The saint's full name was Nagendranath Bhaduri. *Math* means hermitage or *ashram*.

9 Among 'levitating saints' of the Christian world was the 17th-century St. Joseph of Cupertino. His feats received ample attestation from eyewitnesses. St. Joseph exhibited a worldly absentmindedness that was really a divine recollectedness. His monastery brothers could not permit him to serve at the common table, lest he ascend to the ceiling with the crockery. The saint, indeed, was uniquely disqualified for earthly duties by his inability to remain, for any long period, on the earth! Often the sight of a holy statue was enough to exalt St. Joseph in vertical flight; the two saints, one of stone, and the other of flesh, would be seen circling together in the upper air.

St. Teresa of Avila, she of the great elevation of soul, found physical elevation very disconcerting. Charged with heavy organizational duties, she vainly tried to prevent her 'uplifting' experiences. 'But little precautions are unavailing,' she wrote, 'when the Lord will have it otherwise.' The body of St. Teresa, which lies in a church in Alba in Spain, has for four centuries manifested incorruptibility, accompanied by a perfume of flowers. The site has witnessed innumerable miracles.

8. *India's Great Scientist, J.C.Bose*

"JAGADIS CHANDRA BOSE'S wireless inventions antedated those of Marconi."

Overhearing this provocative remark, I walked closer to a sidewalk group of professors engaged in scientific discussion. If my motive in joining them was racial pride, I regret it. I cannot deny my keen interest in evidence that India can play a leading part in physics, and not metaphysics alone.

"What do you mean, sir?"

The professor obligingly explained. "Bose was the first one to invent a wireless coherer (radio signal detector) and an instrument for indicating the refraction of electric waves. But the Indian scientist did not exploit his inventions commercially. He soon turned his attention from the inorganic to the organic world. His revolutionary discoveries as a plant physiologist are outpacing even his radical achievements as a physicist."

I politely thanked my mentor. He added, "The great scientist is one of my brother professors at Presidency College."

I paid a visit the next day to the sage at his home, which was close to mine on Gurpar Road. I had long admired him from a respectful distance. The grave and retiring botanist greeted me graciously. He was a handsome, robust man in his fifties, with thick hair, broad forehead, and the abstracted eyes of a dreamer. The precision in his tones revealed the lifelong scientific habit.

"I have recently returned from an expedition to scientific societies of the West. Their members exhibited intense interest in delicate instruments of my invention which demonstrate the indivisible unity of all life.[1] The Bose crescograph has the enormity of ten million magnifications. The microscope enlarges only a few thousand times; yet it brought vital impetus to biological science. The crescograph[2] opens incalculable vistas."

"You have done much, sir, to hasten the embrace of East and West in the impersonal arms of science."

"I was educated at Cambridge. How admirable is the Western method of submitting all theory to scrupulous experimental verification! That empirical procedure has gone hand in hand with the gift for introspection which is my Eastern heritage. Together they have enabled me to sunder the silences of natural realms long uncommunicative. The telltale charts of my crescograph are evidence for the most skeptical that plants have a sensitive nervous system and a varied

1 'All science is transcendental or else passes away. Botany is now acquiring the right theory – the *avataras* of Brahma will be the text books of Natural History in the future.' – *Emerson.*

2 From the Latin *crescere,* to increase. For his crescograph and other inventions, Bose was knighted in 1917.

3 The lotus flower is an ancient divine symbol in India; its unfolding petals suggest the expansion of the soul; the growth of its pure beauty from the mud of its origin holds a benign spiritual promise.

emotional life. Love, hate, joy, fear, pleasure, pain, excitability, stupor, and countless appropriate responses to stimuli are as universal in plants as in animals."

"The unique throb of life in all creation could seem only poetic imagery before your advent, Professor! A saint I once knew would never pluck flowers. 'Shall I rob the rosebush of its pride in beauty? Shall I cruelly affront its dignity by my rude divestment?' His sympathetic words are verified literally through your discoveries!"

"The poet is intimate with truth, while the scientist approaches awkwardly. Come someday to my laboratory and see the unequivocal testimony of the crescograph."

Gratefully I accepted the invitation, and took my departure. I heard later that the botanist had left Presidency College, and was planning a research centre in Calcutta.

When the Bose Institute was opened, I attended the dedicatory services. Enthusiastic hundreds strolled over the premises. I was charmed with the artistry and spiritual symbolism of the new home of science. Its front gate, I noted, was a centuried relic from a distant shrine. Behind the lotus[3] fountain, a sculptured female figure with a torch conveyed the Indian respect for woman as the immortal light-bearer. The garden held a small temple consecrated to the Noumenon beyond phenomena. Thought of the divine incorporeity was suggested by absence of any altar-image.

Bose's speech on this great occasion might have issued from the lips of one of the inspired ancient *rishis*.

"I dedicate today this Institute as not merely a laboratory but a temple." His reverent solemnity stole like an unseen cloak over the crowded auditorium. "In the pursuit of my investigations I was unconsciously led into the border region of physics and physiology. To my amazement, I found boundary lines vanishing, and points of contact emerging, between the realms of the living and the non-living. Inorganic matter was perceived as anything but inert; it was a thrill under the action of multitudinous forces.

"A universal reaction seemed to bring metal, plant and animal under a common law. They all exhibited essentially the same phenomena of fatigue and depression, with possibilities of recovery and of exaltation, as well as the permanent irresponsiveness associated with death. Filled with awe at this stupendous generalization, it was with great hope that I announced my results before the Royal Society – results demonstrated by experiments. But the physiologists present advised me to confine myself to physical investigations, in which my success had been assured, rather than encroach on their preserves. I had unwittingly strayed into the domain of an unfamiliar caste system and so offended its etiquette.

"An unconscious theological bias was also present, which confounds ignorance with faith. It is often forgotten that He who surrounded us with this ever-evolving mystery of creation has also implanted in us the desire to question and understand. Through many years of miscomprehension, I came to know that the life of a devotee of science is inevitably filled with unending struggle. It is for him to cast his life as an ardent offering – regarding gain and loss, success and failure, as one.

"In time the leading scientific societies of the world accepted my theories and results, and recognized the importance of the Indian contribution to science.[4] Can anything small or circumscribed ever satisfy the mind of India? By a continuous living tradition, and a vital power of rejuvenescence, this land has readjusted itself through unnumbered transformations. Indians have always arisen who, discarding the immediate and absorbing prize of the hour, have sought for the realization of the highest ideals in life – not through passive renunciation, but through active struggle. The weakling who has refused the conflict, acquiring nothing, has had nothing to renounce. He alone who has striven and won can enrich the world by bestowing the fruits of his victorious experience.

"The work already carried out in the Bose laboratory on the response of matter, and the unexpected revelations in plant life, have opened out very extended regions of inquiry in physics, in physiology, in medicine, in agriculture, and even in psychology. Problems hitherto regarded as insoluble have now been brought within the sphere of experimental investigation.

"But high success is not to be obtained without rigid exactitude. Hence the long battery of super-sensitive instruments and apparatus of my design, which stand before you today in their cases in the entrance hall. They tell you of the protracted efforts to get behind the deceptive seeming into the reality that remains unseen, of the continuous toil and persistence and resourcefulness called forth to overcome human limitations. All creative scientists know that the true laboratory is the mind, where behind illusions they uncover the laws of truth.

"The lectures given here will not be mere repetitions of second-hand knowledge. They will announce new discoveries, demonstrated for the first time in these halls. Through regular publication of the work of the Institute, these Indian contributions will reach the whole world. They will become

---

4 'At present, only the sheerest accident brings India into the purview of the American college student. Eight universities (Harvard, Yale, Columbia, Princeton, Johns Hopkins, Pennsylvania, Chicago, and California) have chairs of Indology or Sanskrit, but India is virtually unrepresented in history, philosophy, fine arts, political science, sociology, or any of the departments of intellectual experience in which India has made great contributions . . . We believe that no department of study, particularly in the humanities, can be fully equipped without a properly trained specialist in the Indic phases of its discipline. We believe, too, that every college which aims to prepare its graduates for intelligent work in the world which is to be theirs to live in, must engage a scholar competent in Indian civilization.' – From an article by Prof. W. Norman Brown, Pennsylvania University.

public property. No patents will ever be taken. The spirit of our national culture demands that we should forever be free from the desecration of utilizing knowledge only for personal gain.

"It is my further wish that the facilities of this Institute be available, so far as possible, to workers from all countries. In this I am attempting to carry on the traditions of my country. So far back as twenty-five centuries, India welcomed to its ancient univer-sities, at Nalanda and Taxila, scholars from all parts of the world.

"Although science is neither of the East nor of the West but rather international in its universality, yet India is specially fitted to make great contributions.[5] The burning Indian imagination, which can extort new order out of a mass of apparently contradictory facts, is held in check by the habit of concentration. This restraint confers the power to hold the mind to the pursuit of truth with an infinite patience."

Tears stood in my eyes at the scientist's concluding words. Is 'patience' not indeed a synonym of India, confounding Time and the historians alike?

I visited the research centre again, soon after the day of opening. The great botanist, mindful of his promise, took me to his quiet laboratory.

"I will attach the crescograph to this fern; the magnification is tremendous. If a snail's crawl were enlarged in the same proportion, the creature would appear to be travelling like an express train!"

My gaze was fixed eagerly on the screen which reflected the magnified fern-shadow. Minute life-movements were now clearly perceptible; the plant was growing very slowly before my fascinated eyes. The scientist touched the

5 The atomic structure of matter was well-known to the ancient Hindus. One of the six systems of Indian philosophy is *Vaisesika*, from the Sanskrit root *visesas*, 'atomic individuality.' One of the foremost *Vaisesika* expounders was Aulukya, also called Kanada, 'the atom-eater,' born about 2800 years ago.

In an article in *East-West,* April, 1934, a summary of *Vaisesika* scientific knowledge was given as follows: "Though the modern 'atomic theory' is generally considered a new advance of science, it was brilliantly expounded long ago by Kanada, 'the atom-eater.' The Sanskrit 'anoo' can be properly translated as 'atom' in the latter's literal Greek sense of 'uncut' or indivisible. Other scientific expositions of *Vaisesika* treatises of the B.C. era include (1) the movement of needles toward magnets, (2) the circulation of water in plants, (3) *akash* or ether, inert and structureless, as a basis for transmitting subtle forces, (4) the solar fire as the cause of all other forms of heat, (5) heat as the cause of molecular change, (6) the law of gravitation as caused by the quality that inheres in earth-atoms to give them their attractive power or downward pull, (7) the kinetic nature of all energy; causation as always rooted in an expenditure of energy or a redistribution of motion, (8) universal dissolution through the disintegration of atoms, (9) the radiation of heat and light rays, infinitely small particles, darting forth in all directions with inconceivable speed (the modern 'cosmic rays' theory), (10) the relativity of time and space.

Vaisesika assigned the origin of the world to atoms, eternal in their nature, i.e., their ultimate peculiarities. These atoms were regarded as possessing an incessant vibratory motion. The recent discovery that an atom is a miniature solar system would be no news to the old *Vaisesika* philosophers, who also reduced time to its furthest mathematical concept by describing the smallest unit of time (*kaal*) as the period taken by an atom to traverse its own unit of space.

tip of the fern with a small metal bar. The developing pantomime came to an abrupt halt, resuming the eloquent rhythms as soon as the rod was withdrawn.

"You saw how any slight outside interference is detrimental to the sensitive tissues," Bose remarked. "Watch; I will now administer chloroform, and then give an antidote."

The effect of the chloroform discontinued all growth; the antidote was revivifying. The evolutionary gestures on the screen held me more raptly than a 'movie' plot. My companion (here in the role of villain) thrust a sharp instrument through a part of the fern; pain was indicated by spasmodic flutters. When he passed a razor partially through the stem, the shadow was violently agitated, then stilled itself with the final punctuation of death.

"By first chloroforming a huge tree, I achieved a successful transplantation. Usually, such monarchs of the forest die very quickly after being moved." Jagadis smiled happily as he recounted the life-saving manoeuvre. "Graphs of my delicate apparatus have proved that trees possess a circulatory system; their sap movements correspond to the blood pressure of animal bodies. The ascent of sap is not explicable on the mechanical grounds ordinarily advanced, such as capillary attraction. The phenomenon has been solved through the crescograph as the activity of living cells. Peristaltic waves issue from a cylindrical tube which extends down a tree and serves as an actual heart! The more deeply we perceive the more striking becomes the evidence that a uniform plan links every form in manifold nature."

The great scientist pointed to another Bose instrument.

"I will show you experiments on a piece of tin. The life-force in metals responds adversely or beneficially to stimuli. Ink markings will register the various reactions."

Deeply engrossed, I watched the graph which recorded the characteristic waves of atomic structure. When the professor applied chloroform to the tin, the vibratory writings stopped. They recommenced as the metal slowly regained its normal state. My companion dispensed a poisonous chemical. Simultaneous with the quivering end of the tin, the needle dramatically wrote on the chart a death-notice.

"Bose instruments have demonstrated that metals, such as the steel used in scissors and machinery, are subject to fatigue, and regain efficiency by periodic rest. The life-pulse in metals is seriously harmed or even extinguished through the application of electric currents or heavy pressure."

I looked around the room at the numerous inventions, eloquent testimony of a tireless ingenuity.

"Sir, it is lamentable that mass agricultural development is not speeded by fuller use of your marvellous mechanisms. Would it not be easily possible to employ some of them in quick laboratory experiments to indicate the influence of various types of fertilizers on plant growth?"

"You are right. Countless uses of Bose instruments will be made by future generations. The scientist seldom knows contemporaneous reward; enough is the joy of creative service."

With expressions of unreserved gratitude to the indefatigable sage, I took my leave. "Can the astonishing fertility of his genius ever be exhausted?" I thought.

No diminution came with the years. Inventing an intricate instrument, the 'Resonant Cardiograph,' Bose then pursued extensive researches on innumerable Indian plants. An enormous unsuspected pharmacopoeia of useful drugs was revealed. The cardiograph is constructed with an unerring accuracy by which a one-hundredth part of a second is indicated on a graph. Resonant records measure infinitesimal pulsations in plant, animal and human structure. The great botanist predicted that use of his cardiograph will lead to vivisection on plants instead of animals.

"Side-by-side recordings of the effects of a medicine given simultaneously to a plant and an animal have shown astounding unanimity in result," he pointed out. "Everything in man has been foreshadowed in the plant. Experimentation on vegetation will contribute to lessening of human suffering."

Years later Bose's pioneer plant findings were substantiated by other scientists. Work done in 1938 at Columbia University was reported by *The New York Times* as follows:

> It is determined that when the nerves transmit messages between the brain and other parts of the body, tiny electrical impulses are being generated. These impulses have been measured by delicate galvanometers and magnified millions of times by modern amplifying apparatus. Until now no satisfactory method had been found to study the passages of the impulses along the nerve fibers in living animals or man because of the great speed with which these impulses travel.

> Drs. K. S. Cole and H. J. Curtis reported having discovered that the long single cells of the fresh-water plant nitella, used frequently in goldfish bowls, are virtually identical with those of single nerve fibers. Furthermore, they found that nitella fibers, on being excited,

propagate electrical waves that are similar in every way, except velocity, to those of the nerve fibers in animals and man. The electrical nerve impulses in the plant were found to be much slower than those in animals. This discovery was therefore seized upon by the Columbia workers as a means for taking slow motion pictures of the passage of the electrical impulses in nerves. The nitella plant thus may become a sort of Rosetta stone for deciphering the closely guarded secrets close to the very borderland of mind and matter.

The poet Rabindranath Tagore was a stalwart friend of India's idealistic scientist. To him, the sweet Bengali singer addressed the following lines:[6]

> O Hermit, call thou in the authentic words
> Of that old hymn called *Sama*;[7] "Rise! Awake!"
> Call to the man who boasts his *shastric* lore
> From vain pedantic wranglings profitless,
> Call to that foolish braggart to come forth
> Out on the face of nature, this broad earth,
> Send forth this call unto thy scholar band;
> Together round thy sacrifice of fire
> Let them all gather. So may our India,
> Our ancient land unto herself return
> O once again return to steadfast work,
> To duty and devotion, to her trance
> Of earnest meditation; let her sit
> Once more unruffled, greedless, strifeless, pure,
> O once again upon her lofty seat
> And platform, teacher of all lands.

6 Translated from the Bengali of Rabindranath Tagore, by Manmohan Ghosh, in Viswa-Bharati.

7 *Sama, Rig, Yajur* and *Atharva* are four Vedas. These sacred texts expound the nature of Brahma; God the Creator, whose expression in the individual man is termed *atma*, soul. The verb root of Brahma is *brih*, 'to expand,' conveying the Vedic concept of the divine power of spontaneous growth, of bursting forth into creative activity. The cosmos, like a spiders web, is said to evolve (*vikurute*) out of His being. The conscious fusion of *atma* with Brahma, soul with Spirit, is the whole import of the Vedas.

The *Vedanta* summaries in Vedas have inspired many great Western thinkers. The French historian, Victor Cousin, said: "When we read the philosophy of the Orient – above all that of India – we discover many a truth so profound.... that we are humbled to see in this cradle of human race, the highest philosophy." Schlegel observed that even the loftiest European philosophy and the Greek idealism of reason.... appears a feeble Promethean spark against a full flood of the sunlight of the Oriental vigour of thought.

In the immense literature of India the Vedas (root *vid*, to know) are the only texts to which no author is ascribed. Divinely revealed from age to age to the rishis, 'seers,' the Vedas are said to possess *nityatva*, 'timeless finality.' The 100,000 couplets of the Vedas were directly heard by the rishis, who, for millenniums, transmitted them orally to Brahmin priests, acknowledging the superiority of mind over matter. By observing the particular order (*anupurvi*) in which the Vedic words occur, and with the aid of phonological rules (*sandhi*), and relation of letters (*santana*), the Brahmins have uniquely preserved, from dim antiquity, the original purity of the Vedas. Each syllable (*akshra*) of a Vedic word is endowed with significance and efficacy. (See Chap 35.).

9. *The Blissful Devotee and his Cosmic Romance*

"LITTLE SIR, please be seated. I am talking to my Divine Mother."

Silently I had entered the room in great awe. The angelic appearance of Master Mahasaya fairly dazzled me. With silky white beard and large lustrous eyes, he seemed an incarnation of purity. His upraised chin and folded hands apprized me that my first visit had disturbed him in the midst of his devotions.

His simple words of greeting produced the most violent effect my nature had so far experienced. The bitter separation of my mother's death I had thought the measure of all anguish. Now an agony at separation from my Divine Mother was an indescribable torture of the spirit. I fell moaning to the floor.

"Little sir, quiet yourself!" The saint was sympathetically distressed.

Abandoned in some oceanic desolation, I clutched his feet as the sole raft of my rescue.

"Holy sir, thy intercession! Ask Divine Mother if I find any favour in Her sight!"

The sacred promise of intercession is one not easily bestowed; the master was constrained to silence.

Beyond reach of doubt, I was convinced that Master Mahasaya was in intimate converse with the Universal Mother. It was deep humiliation to realize that my eyes were blind to Her who even at this moment was perceptible to the faultless gaze of the saint. Shamelessly gripping his feet, deaf to his gentle remonstrances, I besought him again and again for his intervening grace.

"I will make your plea to the Beloved." The master's capitulation came with a slow, compassionate smile.

What power in those few words, that my being should know release from its stormy exile?

"Sir, remember your pledge! I shall return soon for Her message!" Joyful anticipation rang in my voice that only a moment ago had been sobbing in sorrow.

Descending the long stairway, I was overwhelmed by memories. This house at 50 Amherst Street, now the residence of Master Mahasaya, had once been my family home, scene of my mother's death. Here my human heart had broken for the vanished mother; and here today my spirit had been as though crucified by absence of the Divine Mother. Hallowed walls, silent witness of my grievous hurts and final healing!

My steps were eager as I returned to my Gurpar Road home. Seeking the seclusion of my small attic, I remained in meditation until ten o'clock. The darkness of the warm Indian night was suddenly lit with a wondrous vision.

Haloed in splendour, the Divine Mother stood before me. Her face, tenderly smiling, was beauty itself.

"Always have I loved thee! Ever shall I love thee!"

The celestial tones still ringing in the air, She disappeared.

The sun on the following morning had hardly risen to an angle of decorum when I paid my second visit to Master Mahasaya. Climbing the staircase in the house of poignant memories, I reached his fourth-floor room. The knob of the closed door was wrapped around with a cloth; a hint, I felt, that the saint desired privacy. As I stood irresolutely on the landing, the door was opened by the master's welcoming hand. I knelt at his holy feet. In a playful mood, I wore a solemn mask over my face, hiding the divine elation.

"Sir, I have come – very early, I confess! – for your message. Did the Beloved Mother say anything about me?"

"Mischievous little sir!"

Not another remark would he make. Apparently my assumed gravity was unimpressive.

"Why so mysterious, so evasive? Do saints never speak plainly?" Perhaps I was a little provoked.

"Must you test me?" His calm eyes were full of understanding. "Could I add a single word this morning to the assurance you received last night at ten o'clock from the Beautiful Mother Herself?"

Master Mahasaya possessed control over the flood-gates of my soul: again I plunged prostrate at his feet. But this time my tears welled from a bliss, and not a pain, past bearing.

"Think you that your devotion did not touch the Infinite Mercy? The Motherhood of God, that you have worshiped in forms both human and divine, could never fail to answer your forsaken cry."

Who was this simple saint, whose least request to the Universal Spirit met with sweet acquiescence? His role in the world was humble, as befitted the greatest man of humility I ever knew. In this Amherst Street house, Master Mahasaya[1] conducted a small high school for boys. No words of chastisement passed his lips; no rule and ferule maintained his discipline. Higher mathematics indeed were taught in these modest classrooms, and a chemistry of love absent from the textbooks. He spread his wisdom by spiritual contagion rather than impermeable precept. Consumed by an unsophisticated passion for the Divine Mother, the saint no more demanded the outward forms of respect than a child.

1 These are respectful titles by which he was customarily addressed. His name was Mahendra Nath Gupta; he signed his literary works simply with *M*.

"I am not your guru; he shall come a little later," he told me. "Through his guidance, your experiences of the Divine in terms of love and devotion shall be translated into his terms of fathomless wisdom."

Every late afternoon, I betook myself to Amherst Street. I sought Master Mahasaya's divine cup, so full that its drops daily overflowed on my being. Never before had I bowed in utter reverence; now I felt it an immeasurable privilege even to tread the same ground which Master Mahasaya sanctified.

"Sir, please wear this champak garland I have fashioned especially for you." I arrived one evening, holding my chain of flowers. But shyly he drew away, repeatedly refusing the honour. Perceiving my hurt, he finally smiled consent.

"Since we are both devotees of the Mother, you may put the garland on this bodily temple, as offering to Her who dwells within." His vast nature lacked space in which any egotistical consideration could gain foothold.

"Let us go tomorrow to the Dakshineswar Temple, forever hallowed by my guru." Master Mahasaya was a disciple of a Christ-like master, Sri Ramakrishna Paramahansa.

The four-mile journey on the following morning was taken by boat on the River Ganges. We entered the nine-domed Temple of Kali, where the figures of the Divine Mother and Shiva rest on a burnished silver lotus, its thousand petals meticulously chiselled. Master Mahasaya beamed in enchantment. He was engaged in his inexhaustible romance with the Beloved. As he chanted Her name, my enraptured heart seemed shattered into a thousand pieces.

We strolled later through the sacred precincts, halting in a tamarisk grove. The manna characteristically exuded by this tree was symbolic of the heavenly food Master Mahasaya was bestowing. His divine invocations continued. I sat rigidly motionless on the grass amid the pink feathery tamarisk flowers. Temporarily absent from the body, I soared in a supernal visit.

This was the first of many pilgrimages to Dakshineswar with the holy teacher. From him I learned the sweetness of God in the aspect of Mother, or Divine Mercy. The childlike saint found little appeal in the Father aspect, or Divine Justice. Stern, exacting, mathematical judgment was alien to his gentle nature.

"He can serve as an earthly prototype for the very angels of heaven!" I thought fondly, watching him one day at his prayers. Without a breath of censure or criticism, he surveyed the world with eyes long familiar with the Primal Purity. His body, mind, speech, and actions were effortlessly harmonized with his soul's simplicity.

"My Master told me so." Shrinking from personal assertion, the saint ended any sage counsel with this invariable tribute. So deep was his identity with Sri Ramakrishna that Master Mahasaya no longer considered his thoughts as his own.

Hand-in-hand, the saint and I walked one evening on the block of his school. My joy was dimmed by the arrival of a conceited acquaintance who burdened us with a lengthy discourse.

"I see this man doesn't please you." The saint's whisper to me was unheard by the egotist, spellbound by his own monologue. "I have spoken to Divine Mother about it; She realizes our sad predicament. As soon as we get to yonder red house, She has promised to remind him of more urgent business."

My eyes were glued to the site of salvation. Reaching its red gate, the man unaccountably turned and departed, neither finishing his sentence nor saying good-by. The assaulted air was comforted with peace.

Another day found me walking alone near the Howrah railway station. I stood for a moment by a temple, silently criticizing a small group of men with drum and cymbals who were violently reciting a chant.

"How undevotionally they use the Lord's divine name in mechanical repetition," I reflected. My gaze was astonished by the rapid approach of Master Mahasaya. "Sir, how come you here?"

The saint, ignoring my question, answered my thought. "Isn't it true, little sir, that the Beloved's name sounds sweet from all lips, ignorant or wise?" He passed his arm around me affectionately; I found myself carried on his magic carpet to the Merciful Presence.

"Would you like to see some bioscopes?" This question one afternoon from Master Mahasaya was mystifying; the term was then used in India to signify motion pictures. I agreed, glad to be in his company in any circumstances. A brisk walk brought us to the garden fronting Calcutta University. My companion indicated a bench near the *goldighi* or pond.

"Let us sit here for a few minutes. My Master always asked me to meditate whenever I saw an expanse of water. Here its placidity reminds us of the vast calmness of God. As all things can be reflected in water, so the whole universe is mirrored in the lake of the Cosmic Mind. So my *gurudeva* often said."

Soon we entered a university hall where a lecture was in progress. It proved abysmally dull, though varied occasionally by lantern slide illustrations, equally uninteresting.

"So this is the kind of bioscope the master wanted me to see!"

My thought was impatient, yet I would not hurt the saint with boredom on my face. But he leaned toward me confidentially.

"I see, little sir, that you don't like this bioscope. I have mentioned it to Divine Mother; She is in full sympathy with us both. She tells me that the electric lights will now go out, and won't be relit until we have a chance to leave the room."

As his whisper ended, the hall was plunged into darkness. The professor's strident voice was stilled in astonishment, then remarked, "The electrical system of this hall appears to be defective." By this time, Master Mahasaya and I were safely across the threshold. Glancing back from the corridor, I saw that the scene of our martyrdom had again become illuminated.

"Little sir, you were disappointed in that bioscope,[2] but I think you will like a different one." The saint and I were standing on the sidewalk in front of the university building. He gently slapped my chest over the heart.

A transforming silence ensued. Just as the modern 'talkies' become inaudible motion pictures when the sound apparatus goes out of order, so the Divine Hand, by some strange miracle, stifled the earthly bustle. The pedestrians as well as the passing trolley cars, automobiles, bullock carts, and iron-wheeled hackney carriages were all in noiseless transit. As though possessing an omnipresent eye, I beheld the scenes which were behind me, and to each side, as easily as those in front. The whole spectacle of activity in that small section of Calcutta passed before me without a sound. Like a glow of fire dimly seen beneath a thin coat of ashes, a mellow luminescence permeated the panoramic view.

My own body seemed nothing more than one of the many shadows, though it was motionless, while the others flitted mutely to and fro. Several boys, friends of mine, approached and passed on; though they had looked directly at me, it was without recognition.

The unique pantomime brought me an inexpressible ecstasy. I drank deep from some blissful fount. Suddenly my chest received another soft blow from Master Mahasaya. The pandemonium of the world burst upon my unwilling ears. I staggered, as though harshly awakened from a gossamer dream. The transcendental wine removed beyond my reach.

"Little sir, I see you found the second bioscope to your liking." The saint was smiling; I started to drop in gratitude on the ground before him. "You can't do that to me now; you know God is in your temple also! I won't let Divine Mother touch my feet through your hands!"

2 The Oxford English Dictionary gives, as rare, this definition of *bioscope:* A view of life; (or) that which gives such a view. Master Mahasaya's choice of a word was, then, peculiarly justified.

If anyone observed the unpretentious master and myself as we walked away from the crowded pavement, the onlooker surely suspected us of intoxication. I felt that the falling shades of evening were sympathetically drunk with God. When darkness recovered from its nightly swoon, I faced the new morning bereft of my ecstatic mood. But ever enshrined in memory is the seraphic son of Divine Mother – Master Mahasaya!

Trying with poor words to do justice to his benignity, I wonder if Master Mahasaya, and others among the deep-visioned saints whose paths crossed mine, knew that years later, in a Western land, I would be writing about their lives as divine devotees. Their foreknowledge would not surprise me nor, I hope, my readers, who have come thus far with me.

Saints of all religions have attained God-realization through the simple concept of the Cosmic Beloved. Because the Absolute is *nirguna*, 'without qualities,' and *acintya*, 'inconceivable,' human thought and yearning have ever personalized It as the Universal Mother. A combination of personal theism and the philosophy of the Absolute is an ancient achievement of Hindu thought, expounded in the Vedas and the *Bhagavad Gita*. This 'reconciliation of opportunities' satisfies heart and head; *bhakti* (devotion) and *jnana* (wisdom) are essentially one. *Prapatti*, 'taking refuge' in God, and *sharanagati*, 'flinging oneself on the Divine Compassion,' are really paths of the highest knowledge.

The humility of Master Mahasaya and other saints springs from a recognition of their total dependence (*seshatva*) on the Lord as the sole Life and Judge. Because the very nature of God is Bliss, the man in attunement with Him experiences a native boundless joy. 'The first of the passions of the soul and the will is joy.'[3]

Devotes of all ages, approaching the Mother in a childlike spirit, testify that they find Her ever at play with them. In Master Mahasaya's life the manifestations of divine play occurred on occasions important and unimportant. In God's eyes nothing is large or small. Were it not for His perfect nicety in constructing the tiny atom, could the skies wear the proud structures of Vega, Arcturus? Distinctions of 'important' and 'unimportant' are surely known to the Lord, lest, for want of a pin, the cosmos collapse!

3 St. John of the Cross. The body of this loveable Christian saint, who died in 1591, was exhumed in 1859 and found to be in a state of incorruptibility.

Sir Francis Younghusband (*Atlantic Monthly*, 12/36) tells of cosmic joy: "...far more than elation or exhilaration, I was beside myself with an intensity of joy, and with this, came a revelation of the essential goodness of the world. I was convinced that men at heart were good, that the evil in them was superficial.

10. *I meet my Master, Sri Yukteswar*

"FAITH IN GOD can produce any miracle except one – passing an examination without study." Distastefully I closed the book I had picked up in an idle moment.

"The writer's exception shows his complete lack of faith," I thought. "Poor chap, he has great respect for the midnight oil!"

My promise to Father had been that I would complete my high school studies. I cannot pretend to diligence. The passing months found me less frequently in the classroom than in secluded spots along the Calcutta bathing *ghats*. The adjoining crematory grounds, especially gruesome at night, are considered highly attractive by the yogi. He who would find the Deathless Essence must not be dismayed by a few unadorned skulls. Human inadequacy becomes clear in the gloomy abode of miscellaneous bones. My midnight vigils were thus of a different nature from the scholar's.

The week of final examinations at the Hindu High School was fast approaching. This interrogatory period, like the sepulchral haunts, inspires a well-known terror. My mind was nevertheless at peace. Braving the ghouls, I was exhuming a knowledge not found in lecture halls. But it lacked the art of Swami Pranabananda, who easily appeared in two places at one time. My educational dilemma was plainly a matter for the Infinite Ingenuity. This was my reasoning, (though to many, alas, it seems illogic) was that the Lord would notice my dilemma and would extricate me from it. The devotee's irrationality springs from a thousand inexplicable demonstrations of God's instancy in trouble.

"Hello, Mukunda! I catch hardly a glimpse of you these days!" A classmate accosted me one afternoon on Gurpar Road.

"Hello, Nantu! My invisibility at school has actually placed me there in a decidedly awkward position." I unburdened myself under his friendly gaze.

Nantu, who was a brilliant student, laughed heartily; my predicament was not without a comic aspect.

"You are utterly unprepared for the finals! I suppose it is up to me to help you!"

The simple words conveyed divine promise to my ears; with alacrity I visited my friend's home. He kindly outlined the solutions to various problems he considered likely to be set by the instructors.

"These questions are the bait which will catch many trusting boys in the examination trap. Remember my answers, and you will escape without injury."

The night was far gone when I departed. Bursting with unseasoned erudition, I devoutly prayed it would remain for the next few critical days. Nantu had coached me in my various subjects but, under press of time, had forgotten my course in Sanskrit. Fervently I reminded God of the oversight.

I set out on a short walk the next morning, assimilating my new knowledge to the rhythm of swinging footsteps. As I took a short cut through the weeds of a corner lot, my eye fell on a few loose printed sheets. A triumphant pounce proved them to be Sanskrit verse. I sought out a pundit for aid in my stumbling interpretation. His rich voice filled the air with the edgeless, honeyed beauty of the ancient tongue.[1]

"These exceptional stanzas cannot possibly be of aid in your Sanskrit test." The scholar dismissed them skeptically.

But familiarity with that particular poem enabled me on the following day to pass the Sanskrit examination. Through the discerning help Nantu had given, I also attained the minimum grade for success in all my other subjects.

Father was pleased that I had kept my word and concluded my secondary school course. My gratitude sped to the Lord, whose sole guidance I perceived in my visit to Nantu and my walk by the un-habitual route of the debris-filled lot. Playfully He had given a dual expression to His timely design for my rescue.

I came across the discarded book whose author had denied God precedence in the examination halls. I could not restrain a chuckle at my own silent comment:

"It would only add to this fellow's confusion, if I were to tell him that divine meditation among the cadavers is a short cut to a high school diploma!"

In my new dignity, I was now openly planning to leave home. Together with a young friend, Jitendra Mazumdar,[2] I decided to join a Mahamandal hermitage in Benares, and receive its spiritual discipline.

A desolation fell over me one morning at thought of separation from my family. Since Mother's death, my affection had grown especially tender for my two younger brothers, Sananda and Bishnu, and my youngest sister Thamu. I rushed to my retreat, the little attic which had witnessed so many scenes in my turbulent *sadhana*.[3] After a two-hour flood of tears, I felt

---

1 *Sanskrita:* polished or complete. Sanskrit is the eldest sister of all Indo-European tongues. Its alphabetical script is *Devanagari,* literally 'divine abode.' "Who knows my grammar knows God!" Panini, great philologist of ancient India, paid this tribute to the mathematical and psychological perfection in Sanskrit. He who would track language to its lair must indeed end as omniscient.

2 He was not Jatin-da (Jotin Ghosh), who will be remembered for his timely aversion to tigers!

3 Path or preliminary road to God.

singularly transformed, as by some alchemical cleanser. All attachment[4] disappeared; my resolution to seek God as the Friend of friends set like granite within me. I quickly completed my travel preparations.

"I make one last plea." Father was distressed as I stood before him for final blessing. "Do not forsake me and your grieving brothers and sisters."

"Revered Father, how can I tell my love for you! But even greater is my love for the Heavenly Father, who has given me the gift of a perfect father on earth. Let me go, that I someday return with a more divine understanding."

With reluctant parental consent, I set out to join Jitendra, already in Benares at the hermitage. On my arrival the young head swami, Dayananda, greeted me cordially. Tall and thin, of thoughtful mien, he impressed me favourably. His fair face had a Buddhalike composure.

I was pleased that my new home possessed an attic, where I managed to spend the dawn and morning hours. The ashram members, knowing little of meditation practices, thought I should employ my whole time in organizational duties. They gave me praise for my afternoon work in their office.

"Don't try to catch God so soon!" This ridicule from a fellow resident accompanied one of my early departures toward the attic. I went to Dayananda, busy in his small sanctum overlooking the Ganges.

"Swamiji,[5] I don't understand what is required of me here. I am seeking direct perception of God. Without Him, I cannot be satisfied with affiliation or creed or performance of good works."

The orange-robed ecclesiastic gave me an affectionate pat. Staging a mock rebuke, he admonished a few near-by disciples. "Don't bother Mukunda. He will learn our ways."

I politely concealed my doubt. The students left the room, not overly bent with their chastisement. Dayananda*ji* had further words for me.

"Mukunda, I see your father is regularly sending you money. Please return it to him; you require none here. A second injunction for your discipline concerns food. Even when you feel hunger, do not mention it."

Whether famishment gleamed in my eye, I knew not. That I was hungry, I knew only too well. The invariable hour for the first hermitage meal was twelve noon. I had been accustomed in my own home to a large breakfast at nine o'clock.

The three-hour gap became daily more interminable. Gone were the Calcutta years when I could rebuke the cook for a ten-minute delay. Now

---

4 Hindu scriptures teach that family attachment is delusive if it prevents the devotee from seeking the Giver of all boons, including the one of loving relatives, not to mention life itself. Jesus similarly taught: "Who is my mother? and who are my brethren?" and, "He that loveth father or mother more than me is not worthy of me." – *Matthew* 12: 48, and 10: 37. (From the *Books of Bible*. See Note on page 97).

5 *Ji* is a customary respectful suffix. *e.g.* "swamiji," "guruji," "Sri Yukteswarji," "Paramahansaji."

I tried to control my appetite; one day I undertook a twenty-four-hour fast. With double zest I awaited the following midday.

"Dayananda*ji*'s train is late; we are not going to eat until he arrives." Jitendra brought me this devastating news. As gesture of welcome to the swami, who had been absent for two weeks, many delicacies were in readiness. An appetizing aroma filled the air. Nothing else offering, what else could be swallowed except pride over yesterday's achievement of a fast?

"Lord hasten the train!" The Heavenly Provider, I thought, was hardly included in the interdiction with which Dayananda*ji* had silenced me. Divine Attention was elsewhere, however; the plodding clock covered the hours. Darkness was descending as our leader entered the door. My greeting was one of unfeigned joy.

"Dayanandaji will bathe and meditate before we can serve food." Jitendra approached me again as a bird of ill omen.

I was in near-collapse. My young stomach, new to deprivation, protested with gnawing vigor. Pictures I had seen of famine victims passed wraithlike before me.

"The next Benares death from starvation is due at once in this hermitage," I thought. Impending doom averted at nine o'clock. Ambrosial summons! In memory that meal is vivid as one of life's perfect hours.

Intense absorption yet permitted me to observe that Dayanandaji ate absentmindedly. He was apparently above my gross pleasures.

"Swamiji, weren't you hungry?" Happily surfeited, I was alone with the leader in his study.

"O yes! I have spent the last four days without food or drink. I never eat on trains, filled with the heterogenous vibrations of worldly people. Strictly I observe the *shastric*[6] rules for monks of my particular order.

"Certain organizational problems lie on my mind. Tonight at home I neglected my dinner. What's the hurry? Tomorrow I'll make it a point to have a proper meal." He laughed merrily.

Shame spread within me like a suffocation. But the past day of my torture was not easily forgotten; I ventured a further remark.

"Swamiji, I am puzzled. Following your instruction, suppose I never asked for food, and nobody gives me any. I should starve to death."

"Die, then!" This alarming counsel split the air. "Die if you must, Mukunda! Never admit that you live by the power of food and not by the power of God! He

6 Pertaining to the *shastras,* literally, 'sacred books,' comprising four classes of scripture: the *shruti, smriti, purana,* and *tantra.* These comprehensive treatises cover every aspect of religious and social life, and the fields of law, medicine, architecture, art, etc. The *shrutis* are the 'directly heard' or 'revealed' scriptures, the *Vedas.* The *smritis* or 'remembered' lore was finally written down in a remote past as the world's longest epic poems, the *Mahabharata* and the *Ramayana. Puranas* are literally 'ancient' allegories; *tantras* literally mean 'rites' or 'rituals'; these treatises convey profound truths under a veil of detailed symbolism.

who has created every form of nourishment, He who has bestowed appetite, will certainly see that His devotee is sustained! Do not imagine that rice maintains you, or that money or men support you! Could they aid if the Lord withdraws your life-breath? They are His indirect instruments merely. Is it by any skill of yours that food digests in your stomach? Use the sword of your discrimination, Mukunda! Cut through the chains of agency and perceive the Single Cause!"

I found his incisive words entering some deep marrow. Gone was an age-old delusion by which bodily imperatives outwit the soul. There and then I tasted the Spirit's all-sufficiency. In how many strange cities, in my later life of ceaseless travel, did occasion arise to prove the serviceability of this lesson in a Benares hermitage!

The sole treasure which had accompanied me from Calcutta was the *sadhu's* silver amulet bequeathed to me by Mother. Guarding it for years, I now had it carefully hidden in my ashram room. To renew my joy in the talismanic testimony, one morning I opened the locked box. The sealed covering untouched, lo! the amulet was gone. Mournfully I tore open its envelope and made unmistakably sure. It had vanished, in accordance with the *sadhu's* prediction, into the ether whence he had summoned it.

My relationship with Dayananda's followers grew steadily worse. The household was alienated, hurt by my determined aloofness. My strict adherence to meditation on the very Ideal for which I had left home and all worldly ambitions called forth shallow criticism on all sides.

Torn by spiritual anguish, I entered the attic one dawn, resolved to pray until answer was vouchsafed.

"Merciful Mother of the Universe, teach me Thyself through visions, or through a guru sent by Thee!"

The passing hours found my sobbing pleas without response. Suddenly I felt lifted as though bodily to a sphere un-circumscribed.

"Thy Master cometh today!" A divine womanly voice came from everywhere and nowhere.

This supernal experience was pierced by a shout from a definite locale. A young priest nicknamed Habu was calling me from the downstairs kitchen.

"Mukunda, enough of meditation! You are needed for an errand."

Another day I might have replied impatiently; now I wiped my tear-swollen face and meekly obeyed the summons. Together Habu and I set out for a distant market place in the Bengali section of Benares. The ungentle Indian sun was not yet at zenith as we made our purchases in the bazaars. We pushed our way through the colourful medley of housewives, guides, priests, simply-clad widows, dignified Brahmins, and the ubiquitous holy bulls. Passing an inconspicuous lane, I turned my head and surveyed the narrow length.

A Christlike man in the ochre robes of a swami stood motion-less at the end of the road. Instantly and anciently familiar he seemed; my gaze fed hungrily for a trice. Then doubt assailed me.

"You are confusing this wandering monk with someone known to you," I thought. "Dreamer, walk on."

After ten minutes, I felt heavy numbness in my feet. As though turned to stone, they were unable to carry me farther. Laboriously I turned around; my feet regained normalcy. I faced the opposite direction; again the curious weight oppressed me.

"The saint is magnetically drawing me to him!" With this thought, I heaped my parcels into the arms of Habu. He had been observing my erratic footwork with amazement, and now burst into laughter.

"What ails you? Are you crazy?"

My tumultuous emotion prevented any retort; I sped silently away.

Retracing my steps as though wing-shod, I reached the narrow lane. My quick glance revealed the quiet figure, steadily gazing in my direction. A few eager steps and I was at his feet.

"Gurudeva!"[7] The divine face was none other than he of my thousand visions. These halcyon eyes, in leonine head with pointed beard and flowing locks, had oft peered through gloom of my nocturnal reveries, holding a promise I had not fully understood.

"O my own, you have come to me!" My guru uttered the words again and again in Bengali, his voice tremulous with joy. "How many years I have waited for you!"

We entered a oneness of silence; words seemed the rankest superfluities. Eloquence flowed in soundless chant from heart of master to disciple. With an antenna of irrefragable insight I sensed that my guru knew God, and would lead me to Him. The obscuration of this life disappeared in a fragile dawn of prenatal memories. Dramatic time! Past, present, and future are its cycling scenes. This was not the first sun to find me at these holy feet!

My hand in his, my guru led me to his temporary residence in the Rana Mahal section of the city. His athletic figure moved with firm tread. Tall, erect, about fifty-five at this time, he was active and vigorous as a young man. His dark eyes were large, beautiful with plumbless wisdom. Slightly curly hair softened a face of striking power. Strength mingled subtly with gentleness.

As we made our way to the stone balcony of a house overlooking the Ganges, he said affectionately:

"I will give you my hermitages and all I possess."

---

7 'Divine teacher,' the Sanskrit term for one's spiritual preceptor. I have rendered it simply as 'Master.'

"Sir, I come for wisdom and God-contact. Those are your treasure-troves I am after!"

The swift Indian twilight had dropped its half-curtain before my master spoke again. His eyes held unfathomable tenderness.

"I give you my unconditional love."

Precious words! A quarter-century elapsed before I had another auricular proof of his love. His lips were strange to ardour; silence became his oceanic heart.

"Will you give me the same unconditional love?" He gazed at me with childlike trust.

"I will love you eternally, Gurudeva!"

"Ordinary love is selfish, darkly rooted in desires and satisfactions. Divine love is without condition, without boundary, without change. The flux of the human heart is gone forever at the transfixing touch of pure love." He added humbly, "If ever you find me falling from a state of God-realization, please promise to put my head on your lap and help to bring me back to the Cosmic Beloved we both worship."

He rose then in the gathering darkness and guided me to an inner room. As we ate mangoes and almond sweetmeats, he unobtrusively wove into his conversation an intimate knowledge of my nature. I was awe-struck at the grandeur of his wisdom, exquisitely blended with an innate humility.

"Do not grieve for your amulet. It has served its purpose." Like a divine mirror, my guru apparently had caught a reflection of my whole life.

"The living reality of your presence, is joy beyond any symbol."

"It is time for a change, inasmuch as you are unhappily situated in the ashram."

I had made no references to my life; they now seemed superfluous! By his natural, unemphatic manner, I understood that he wished no astonished ejaculations at his clairvoyance.

"You should go back to Calcutta. Why exclude relatives from your love of humanity?"

His suggestion dismayed me. My family was predicting my return, though I had been unresponsive to many pleas by letter. "Let the young bird fly in the metaphysical skies," Ananta had remarked. "His wings will tire in the heavy atmosphere. We shall yet see him swoop toward home, fold his pinions, and humbly rest in our family nest." This discouraging simile fresh in my mind, I was determined to do no 'swooping' in the direction of Calcutta.

8 Shankaracharya, India's greatest philosopher wrote his famous commentary on a treatise *Mandukya Karika* by his guru's guru Gaudapada, in which he interpreted Vedanta philosophy in a monistic (*advaita*) spirit. He also composed poems of devotional love. His *Prayer to the Divine Mother for Forgiveness of Sins* bears the refrain: 'Though bad sons are many, never has there been a bad mother!'

"Sir, I am not returning home. But I will follow you anywhere. Please give me your address, and your name."

"Swami Sri Yukteswar Giri. My chief hermitage is in Serampore, on Rai Ghat Lane. I am visiting my mother here for only a few days."

I wondered at God's intricate play with His devotees. Serampore is but twelve miles from Calcutta, yet in those regions I had never caught a glimpse of my guru. We had had to travel for our meeting to the ancient city of Kasi (Benares), hallowed by memories of Lahiri Mahasaya. Here too the feet of Buddha, Shankaracharya[8] and other Yogi-Christs had blessed the soil.

"You will come to me in four weeks." For the first time, Sri Yukteswar's voice was stern. "Now that I have told you of my eternal affection, and have shown my happiness at finding you – that is why you disregard my request. The next time we meet, you will have to reawaken my interest: I won't accept you as a disciple easily. There must be complete surrender by obedience to my strict training."

I remained obstinately silent. My guru easily sensed my difficulty.

"Do you think your relatives will laugh at you?"

"I will not return."

"You will return in thirty days."

"Never."

Bowing reverently at his feet, I departed without lightening the controversial tension. As I made my way in the midnight darkness, I wondered why the miraculous meeting had ended on an inharmonious note. The dual scales of *maya*, that balance every joy with a grief! My young heart was not yet malleable to the transforming fingers of my guru.

The next morning I noticed increased hostility in the attitude of the hermitage members. My days became spiked with invariable rudeness. In three weeks, Dayananda left the ashram to attend a conference in Bombay; pandemonium broke over my hapless head.

"Mukunda is a parasite, accepting hermitage hospitality without making proper return." Overhearing this remark, I regretted for the first time that I had obeyed the request to send back my money to Father. With heavy heart, I sought out my sole friend, Jitendra.

"I am leaving. Please convey my respectful regrets to Dayanandaji when he returns."

"I will leave also! My attempts to meditate here meet with no more favour than your own." Jitendra spoke with determination.

"I have met a Christ-like saint. Let us visit him in Serampore."

And so the 'bird' prepared to 'swoop' perilously close to Calcutta!

11. *Two Penniless Boys in Brindaban*

"IT WOULD SERVE you right if Father disinherited you, Mukunda! How foolishly you are throwing away your life!" An elder-brother sermon was assaulting my ears.

Jitendra and I, fresh from the train (a figure of speech merely; we were covered with dust), had just arrived at the home of Ananta, recently transferred from Calcutta to the ancient city of Agra. Brother was a supervising accountant for the Public Works Department of the Government.

"You well know, Ananta, I seek my inheritance from the Heavenly Father."

"Money first; God can come later! Who knows? Life may be too long."

"God first; money is His slave! Who can tell? Life may be too short."

My retort was summoned by the exigencies of the moment, and held no presentiment. Yet the leaves of time unfolded to early finality for Ananta; a few years later[1] he entered the land where bank notes avail neither first nor last.

"Wisdom from the hermitage, I suppose! But I see you have left Benares." Ananta's eyes gleamed with satisfaction; he yet hoped to secure my pinions in the family nest.

"My sojourn in Benares was not in vain! I found there everything my heart had been longing for! You may be sure it was not your pundit or his son!"

Ananta joined me in reminiscent laughter; he had had to admit that the Benares 'clairvoyant' he selected was a shortsighted one.

"What are your plans, my wandering brother?"

"Jitendra persuaded me to Agra. We shall view the beauties of the Taj Mahal[2] here," I explained. "Then we are going to my newly-found guru, who has a hermitage in Serampore."

Ananta hospitably arranged for our comfort. Several times during the evening I noticed his eyes fixed on me reflectively.

"I know that look!" I thought. "A plot is brewing!"

The denouement took place during our early breakfast.

"So you feel quite independent of Father's wealth." Ananta's gaze was innocent as he resumed the barbs of yesterday's conversation.

"I am conscious of my dependence on God."

"Words are cheap! Life has shielded you thus far! What a plight if you were forced to look to the Invisible Hand for your food and shelter! You would soon be begging on the streets!"

"Never! I would not put faith in passers-by rather than God! He can devise for His devotee a thousand resources besides the begging-bowl!"

1 See chapter 25.   2 The world-famous mausoleum.

"More rhetoric! Suppose I suggest that your vaunted philosophy be put to a test in this tangible world?"

"I would agree! Do you confine God to a speculative world?"

"We shall see; today you shall have opportunity either to enlarge or to confirm my own views!" Ananta paused for a dramatic moment; then spoke slowly and seriously.

"I propose that I send you and your fellow disciple Jitendra this morning to the nearby city of Brindaban. You must not take a single rupee; you must not beg, either for food or money; you must not reveal your predicament to anyone; you must not go without your meals; and you must not be stranded in Brindaban. If you return to my bungalow here before twelve o'clock tonight, without having broken any rule of the test, I shall be the most astonished man in Agra!"

"I accept the challenge." No hesitation was in my words or in my heart. Grateful memories flashed of the Instant Beneficence: my healing of deadly cholera through appeal to Lahiri Mahasaya's picture; the playful gift of the two kites on the Lahore roof with Uma; the opportune amulet amidst my discouragement; the decisive message through the unknown Benares *sadhu* outside the compound of the pundit's home; the vision of Divine Mother and Her majestic words of love; Her swift heed through Master Mahasaya to my trifling embarrassments; the last-minute guidance which materialized my high school diploma; and the ultimate boon, my living Master from the mist of lifelong dreams. Never could I admit my 'philosophy' unequal to any tussle on the world's harsh proving grounds!

"Your willingness does you credit. I'll escort you to the train at once." Ananta turned to the openmouthed Jitendra. "You must go along as a witness and, very likely, a fellow victim!"

A half-hour later Jitendra and I were in possession of one-way tickets for our impromptu trip. We submitted, in a secluded corner of the station, to a search of our persons. Ananta was quickly satisfied that we were carrying no hidden hoard; our simple *dhotis*[3] concealed nothing more than was necessary.

As faith invaded the serious realms of finance, my friend spoke protestingly. "Ananta, give me one or two rupees as a safeguard. Then I can telegraph you in case of misfortune."

"Jitendra!" My ejaculation was sharply reproachful. "I will not proceed with the test if you take any money as final security."

"There is something reassuring about the clink of coins." Jitendra said no more as I regarded him sternly.

"Mukunda, I am not heartless." A hint of humility had crept into Ananta's voice. It may be that his conscience was smiting him; perhaps for sending two insolvent boys to a strange city; perhaps for his own religious skepticism. "If by any chance or grace you pass successfully through the Brindaban ordeal, I shall ask you to initiate me as your disciple."

This promise had a certain irregularity, in keeping with the unconventional occasion. The eldest brother in an Indian family seldom bows before his juniors; he receives respect and obedience second only to a father. But no time remained for my comment; our train was at point of departure.

Jitendra maintained a lugubrious silence as our train covered the miles. Finally he bestirred himself; leaning over, he pinched me painfully at an awkward spot.

"I see no sign that God is going to supply our next meal!"

"Be quiet, doubting Thomas; the Lord is working with us."

"Can you also arrange that He hurry? Already I am famished merely at the prospect before us. I left Benares to view the Taj's mausoleum, not to enter my own!"

"Cheer up, Jitendra! Are we not to have our first glimpse of the sacred wonders of Brindaban?[4] I am in deep joy at thought of treading the ground hallowed by feet of Lord Krishna."

The door of our compartment opened; two men seated themselves. The next train stop would be the last.

"Young lads, do you have friends in Brindaban?" The stranger opposite me was taking a surprising interest.

"None of your business!" Rudely I averted my gaze.

"You are probably flying away from your families under the enchantment of the Stealer of Hearts.[5] I am of devotional temperament myself. I will make it my positive duty to see that you receive food, and shelter from this overpowering heat."

"No, sir, let us alone. You are very kind; but you are mistaken in judging us to be truants from home."

No further conversation ensued; the train came to a halt. As Jitendra and I descended to the platform, our chance companions linked arms with us and summoned a horse cab.

We alighted before a stately hermitage, set amidst the ever-green trees of well-kept grounds. Our benefactors were evidently known here; a smiling lad led us without comment to a parlour. We were soon joined by an elderly woman of dignified bearing.

3 A *dhoti*-cloth is knotted around the waist and also covers the legs.

"Gauri Ma, the princes could not come." One of the men addressed the ashram hostess. "At the last moment their plans went awry; they send deep regrets. But we have brought two other guests. As soon as we met on the train, I felt drawn to them as devotees of Lord Krishna."

"Good-by, young friends." Our two acquaintances walked to the door. "We shall meet again, if God be willing."

"You are welcome here." Gauri Ma smiled in motherly fashion on her two unexpected charges. "You could not have come on a better day. I was expecting two royal patrons of this hermitage. What a shame if my cooking had found none to appreciate it!"

These appetizing words had disastrous effect on Jitendra: he burst into tears. The 'prospect' he had feared in Brindaban was turning out as royal entertainment; his sudden mental adjustment proved too much for him. Our hostess looked at him with curiosity, but without remark; perhaps she was familiar with adolescent quirks.

Lunch was announced; Gauri Ma led the way to a dining patio, spicy with savory odours. She vanished into an adjoining kitchen.

I had been premeditating this moment. Selecting the appropriate spot on Jitendra's anatomy, I administered a pinch as resounding as the one he had given me on the train.

"Doubting Thomas, the Lord works – in a hurry, too!"

The hostess reentered with a *punkha*. She steadily fanned us in the Oriental fashion as we squatted on ornate blanket-seats. Ashram disciples passed to and fro with some thirty courses. Rather than 'meal,' the description can only be 'sumptuous repast.' Since arriving on this planet, Jitendra and I had never before tasted such delicacies.

"Dishes fit for princes indeed, Honoured Mother! What your royal patrons could have found more urgent than attending this banquet, I cannot imagine! You have given us a memory for a lifetime!"

Silenced as we were by Ananta's requirement, we could not explain to the gracious lady that our thanks held a double significance. Our sincerity at least was patent. We departed with her blessing and an attractive invitation to revisit the hermitage.

The heat outdoors was merciless. My friend and I made for the shelter of a lordly cadamba tree at the ashram gate. Sharp words followed; once again Jitendra was beset with misgivings.

"A fine mess you have got me into! Our luncheon was only accidental good fortune! How can we see the sights of this city, without a single pice (1/192 of a rupee) between us? And how on earth are you going to take me back to Ananta's place?"

"You forget God quickly, now that your stomach is filled." My words, not bitter, were accusatory. How short is human memory for divine favours! No man lives who has not seen certain of his prayers granted.

"I am not likely to forget my folly in venturing out with a madcap like you!"

"Be quiet, Jitendra! The same Lord who fed us will show us Brindaban, and return us to Agra."

A slight young man of pleasing countenance approached at rapid pace. Halting under our tree, he bowed before me.

"Dear friend, you and your companion must be strangers here. Permit me to be your host and guide."

It is scarcely possible for an Indian to pale, but Jitendra's face was suddenly sickly. I politely declined the offer.

"You are surely not banishing me?" The stranger's alarm would have been comic in any other circumstances.

"Why not?"

"You are my guru." His eyes sought mine trustfully. "During my mid-day devotions, the blessed Lord Krishna appeared in a vision. He showed me two forsaken figures under this very tree. One face was yours, my master! Often have I seen it in meditation! What joy if you accept my humble services!"

"I too am glad you have found me. Neither God nor man has forsaken us!" Though I was motionless, smiling at the eager face before me, an inward obeisance cast me at the Divine Feet.

"Dear friends, will you not honour my home for a visit?"

"You are kind; but the plan is unfeasible. Already we are guests of my brother in Agra."

"At least give me memories of touring Brindaban with you."

I gladly consented. The young man, who said his name was Pratap Chatterji, hailed a horse carriage. We visited Madanamohana Temple and other Krishna shrines. Night descended while we were at our temple devotions.

"Excuse me while I get *sandesh*."[6] Pratap entered a shop near the railroad station. Jitendra and I sauntered along the wide street, crowded now in the comparative coolness. Our friend was absent for some time, but finally returned with gifts of many sweetmeats.

"Please allow me to gain this religious merit." Pratap smiled pleadingly as he held out a bundle of rupee notes and two tickets, just purchased, to Agra.

6 An exotic Bengali sweetmeat.

The reverence of my acceptance was for the Invisible Hand. Scoffed at by Ananta, had Its bounty not far exceeded necessity?

We sought out a secluded spot near the station.

"Pratap, I will instruct you in the *Kriya* of Lahiri Mahasaya, the greatest yogi of modern times. His technique will be your guru."

The initiation was concluded in a half hour. "*Kriya* is your *chintamani*,"[7] I told the new student. "The technique, which as you see is simple, embodies the art of quickening man's spiritual evolution. Hindu scriptures teach that the incarnating ego requires a million years to obtain liberation from *maya*. This natural period is greatly shortened through *Kriya Yoga*. Just as Jagadis Chandra Bose has demonstrated that plant growth can be accelerated far beyond its normal rate, so man's psychological development can be also speeded by an inner science. Be faithful in your practice; you will approach the Guru of all gurus."

"I am transported to find this yogic key, long sought!" Pratap spoke thoughtfully. "Its unshackling effect on my sensory bonds will free me for higher spheres. The vision today of Lord Krishna could only mean my highest good."

We sat awhile in silent understanding, then walked slowly to the station. Joy was within me as I boarded the train, but this was Jitendra's day for tears. My affectionate farewell to Pratap had been punctuated by stifled sobs from both my companions. The journey once more found Jitendra in a welter of grief. Not for himself this time, but against himself.

"How shallow my trust! My heart has been stone! Never in future shall I doubt God's protection!"

Midnight was approaching. The two 'Cinderellas,' sent forth penniless, entered Ananta's bedroom. His face, as he had promised, was a study in astonishment. Silently I showered the table with rupees.

"Jitendra, the truth!" Ananta's tone was jocular. "Has not this youngster been staging a holdup?"

But as the tale was unfolded, my brother turned sober, then solemn.

"The law of demand and supply reaches into subtler realms than I had supposed." Ananta spoke with a spiritual enthusiasm never before noticeable. "I understand for the first time your indifference to the vaults and vulgar accumulations of the world."

Late as it was, my brother insisted that he receive *diksha*[8] into *Kriya Yoga*. The 'guru' Mukunda had to shoulder the responsibility of two unsought disciples in one day.

Breakfast the following morning was eaten in a harmony absent the day before. I smiled at Jitendra.

7 A mythological gem with power to grant desires, also the name of God.
8 Spiritual initiation; from the Sanskrit root *diksh:* to dedicate oneself.

"You shall not be cheated of the Taj. Let us view it before starting for Serampore."

Bidding farewell to Ananta, my friend and I were soon before the glory of Agra, the Taj Mahal. White marble dazzling in the sun, it stands a vision of pure symmetry. The perfect setting is dark cypress, glossy lawn, and tranquil lagoon. The interior is exquisite with lacelike carvings inlaid with semiprecious stones. Delicate wreaths and scrolls emerge intricately from marbles, brown and violet. Illumination from the dome falls on the cenotaphs of Emperor Shah-Jahan and Mumtaz Mahal, queen of his realm and his heart.

Enough of sight-seeing! I was longing for my guru. Jitendra and I were shortly travelling south by train toward Bengal.

"Mukunda, I have not seen my family in months. I have changed my mind; perhaps later I shall visit your master in Serampore."

My friend, who may mildly be described as vacillating in temperament, left me in Calcutta. By local train I soon reached Serampore, twelve miles to the north.

A throb of wonderment stole over me as I realized that twenty-eight days had elapsed since the Benares meeting with my guru. "You will come to me in four weeks!" Here I was, heart pounding, standing within his courtyard on quiet Rai Ghat Lane. I entered for the first time the hermitage where I was to spend the best part of the next ten years with India's *Jyanavatar*, 'incarnation of wisdom.'

12. *Years in my Master's Hermitage*

"YOU HAVE COME." Sri Yukteswar greeted me from a tiger skin on the floor of a balconied sitting room. His voice was cold, his manner unemotional.

"Yes, dear Master, I am here to follow you." Kneeling, I touched his feet.

"How can that be? You ignore my wishes."

"No longer, Guruji! Your wish shall be my law!"

"That is better! Now I can assume responsibility for your life."

"I willingly transfer the burden, Master."

"My first request, then, is that you return home to your family. I want you to enter college in Calcutta. Your education should be continued."

"Very well, sir." I hid my consternation. Would importunate books pursue me down the years? First Father, now Sri Yukteswar!

"Someday you will go to the West. Its people will lend ears more receptive to India's ancient wisdom if the strange Hindu teacher has a university degree."

"You know best, Guruji." My gloom departed. The reference to the
West I found puzzling, remote; but my opportunity to please Master by
obedience was vitally immediate.

"You will be near in Calcutta; come here whenever you find time."

"Every day if possible, Master! Gratefully I accept your authority in
every detail of my life – on one condition."

"Yes?"

"That you promise to reveal God to me!"

An hour-long verbal tussle ensued. A master's word cannot be
falsified; it is not lightly given. The implications in the pledge open out
vast metaphysical vistas. A guru must be on intimate terms indeed with
the Creator before he can obligate Him to appear! I sensed Sri Yukteswar's
divine unity, and was determined, as his disciple, to press my advantage.

"You are of exacting disposition!" Then Master's consent rang out with
compassionate finality:

"Let your wish be my wish."

A lifelong shadow lifted from my heart; the vague search, hither and yon,
was over. I had found eternal shelter in a true guru.

"Come; I will show you the hermitage." Master rose from his tiger
mat. I glanced about me; my gaze fell with astonishment on a wall picture,
garlanded with a spray of jasmine.

"Lahiri Mahasaya!" I said in astonishment.

"Yes, my divine guru." Sri Yukteswar's tone was reverently vibrant.
"Greater he was, as man and yogi, than any other teacher whose life came
within the range of my investigations."

Silently I bowed before the familiar picture. Soul-homage sped to the
peerless master who, blessing my infancy, had guided my steps to this hour.

Led by my guru, I strolled over the house and its grounds. Large, ancient
and well-built, the hermitage was surrounded by a massive-pillared courtyard.
Outer walls were moss-covered; pigeons fluttered over the flat gray roof,
unceremoniously sharing the ashram quarters. A rear garden was pleasant with
jackfruit, mango, and plantain trees. Balustraded balconies of upper rooms
in the two-storied building faced the courtyard from three sides. A spacious
ground-floor hall, with high ceiling supported by colonnades, was used, Master
said, chiefly during the annual festivities of *Durgapuja*.[1] A narrow stairway
led to Sri Yukteswar's sitting room, whose small balcony overlooked the
street. The ashram was plainly furnished; everything was simple, clean, and

---

1 Worship of Durga. This is the chief festival of the Bengali year, and lasts for nine days around the end of September.
Immediately following is the ten-day festival of *Dashahara* ('the One who removes ten sins' – three of body,
three of mind, four of speech). Both *pujas* are sacred to Durga, literally 'the Inaccessible,' an aspect of Divine
Mother Shakti, the female creative force personified.

utilitarian. Several Western-styled chairs, benches, and tables were in evidence.

Master invited me to stay overnight. A supper of vegetable curry was served by two young disciples who were receiving hermitage training.

"Guruji, please tell me something of your life." I was squatting on a straw mat near his tiger skin. The friendly stars were very close, it seemed, beyond the balcony.

"My family name was Priya Nath Karar. I was born[2] here in Serampore, where Father was a wealthy businessman. He left me this ancestral mansion, now my hermitage. My formal schooling was little; I found it slow and shallow. In early manhood, I undertook the responsibilities of a householder, and have one daughter, now married. My middle life was blessed with the guidance of Lahiri Mahasaya. After my wife died, I joined the Swami Order and received the new name of Sri Yukteswar Giri.[3] Such are my simple annals."

Master smiled at my eager face. Like all biographical sketches, his words had given the outward facts without revealing the inner man.

" 'Guruji, I would like to hear some stories of your childhood."

"I will tell you a few – each one with a moral!" Sri Yukteswar's eyes twinkled with his warning. "My mother once tried to frighten me with an appalling story of a ghost in a dark chamber. I went there immediately, and expressed my disappointment at having missed the ghost. Mother never told me another horror-tale. Moral: Look fear in the face and it will cease to trouble you.

"Another early memory is my wish for an ugly dog belonging to a neighbor. I kept my household in turmoil for weeks to get that dog. My ears were deaf to offers of pets with more prepossessing appearance. Moral: Attachment is blinding; it lends an imaginary halo of attractiveness to the object of desire.

"A third story concerns the plasticity of the youthful mind. I heard my mother remark occasionally: 'A man who accepts a job under anyone is a slave.' That impression became so indelibly fixed that even after my marriage I refused all positions. I met expenses by investing my family endowment in land. Moral: Good and positive suggestions should instruct the sensitive ears of children. Their early ideas long remain sharply etched."

Master fell into tranquil silence. Around midnight he led me to a narrow cot. Sleep was sound and sweet the first night under my guru's roof.

Sri Yukteswar chose the following morning to grant me his *Kriya Yoga* initiation. The technique I had already received from two disciples of Lahiri

2 Sri Yukteswar was born on May 10, 1855.

3 *Yukteswar* means 'united to God.' *Giri* is a classificatory distinction of one of the ten ancient Swami branches. *Sri* means 'holy'; it is not a name but a title of respect.

Mahasaya – Father and my tutor, Swami Kebalananda – but in Master's presence I felt transforming power. At his touch, a great light broke upon my being, like glory of countless suns blazing together. A flood of ineffable bliss, overwhelming my heart to an innermost core, continued during the following day. It was late that afternoon before I could bring myself to leave the hermitage.

"You will return in thirty days." As I reached my Calcutta home, the fulfillment of Master's prediction entered with me. None of my relatives made the pointed remarks I had feared about the reappearance of the 'soaring bird.'

I climbed to my little attic and bestowed affectionate glances, as though on a living presence. "You have witnessed my meditations, and the tears and storms of my *sadhana.* Now I have reached the harbour of my divine teacher."

"Son, I am happy for us both." Father and I sat together in the evening calm. "You have found your guru, as in miraculous fashion I once found my own. The holy hand of Lahiri Mahasaya is guarding our lives. Your master has proved no inaccessible Himalayan saint, but one near-by. My prayers have been answered: you have not in your search for God been permanently removed from my sight."

Father was also pleased that my formal studies would be resumed; he made suitable arrangements. I was enrolled the following day at the Scottish Church College in Calcutta.

Happy months sped by. My readers have doubtless made the perspicacious surmise that I was little seen in the college classrooms. The Serampore hermitage held a lure too irresistible. Master accepted my ubiquitous presence without comment. To my relief, he seldom referred to the halls of learning. Though it was plain to all that I was never cut out for a scholar, I managed to attain minimum passing grades from time to time.

Daily life at the ashram flowed smoothly, infrequently varied. My guru awoke before dawn. Lying down, or sometimes sitting on the bed, he entered a state of *samadhi.*[4] It was simplicity itself to discover when Master had awakened: abrupt halt of stupendous snores.[5] A sigh or two; perhaps a bodily movement. Then a soundless state of breathlessness: he was in deep yogic joy.

Breakfast did not follow; first came a long walk by the Ganges. Those morning strolls with my guru – how real and vivid still! In the easy resurrection of memory, I often find myself by his side: the early sun is warming the river. His voice rings out, rich with the authenticity of wisdom.

A bath; then the midday meal. Its preparation, according to Master's daily directions, had been the careful task of young disciples. My guru

4 Literally 'to direct together.' *Samadhi* is a superconscious state of ecstasy in which the yogi perceives the identity of soul and Spirit.
5 Snoring, according to physiologists, is an indication of utter relaxation (to the oblivious practitioner, solely).

was a vegetarian. Before embracing monkhood, however, he had eaten
eggs and fish. His advice to students was to follow any simple diet which
proved suited to one's constitution.

Master ate little; often rice, coloured with turmeric or juice of beets or
spinach and lightly sprinkled with buffalo *ghee* or melted butter. Another
day he might have lentil-*dhal* or *channa*[6] curry with vegetables. For dessert,
mangoes or oranges with rice pudding, or jackfruit juice.

Visitors appeared in the afternoons. A steady stream poured from the
world into the hermitage tranquillity. Everyone found in Master an equal
courtesy and kindness. To a man who has realized himself as a soul, not the
body or the ego, the rest of humanity assumes a striking similarity of aspect.

The impartiality of saints is rooted in wisdom. Masters have escaped
maya; its alternating faces of intellect and idiocy no longer cast an influential
glance. Sri Yukteswar showed no special consideration to those who
happened to be powerful or accomplished; neither did he slight others for
their poverty or illiteracy. He would listen respectfully to words of truth
from a child, and openly ignore a conceited pundit.

Eight o'clock was the supper hour, and sometimes found lingering guests.
My guru would not excuse himself to eat alone; none left his ashram hungry or
dissatisfied. Sri Yukteswar was never at a loss, never dismayed by unexpected
visitors; scanty food would emerge a banquet under his resourceful direction.
Yet he was economical; his modest funds went far. "Be comfortable within
your purse," he often said. "Extravagance will buy you discomfort." Whether
in the details of hermitage entertainment, or his building and repair work, or
other practical concerns, Master manifested the originality of a creative spirit.

Quiet evening hours often brought one of my guru's discourses,
treasures against time. His every utterance was measured and chiselled by
wisdom. A sublime self-assurance marked his mode of expression: it was
unique. He spoke as none other in my experience ever spoke.

His thoughts were weighed in a delicate balance of discrimination before
he permitted them an outward garb. The essence of truth, all-pervasive with
even a physiological aspect, came from him like a fragrant exudation of the
soul. I was conscious always that I was in the presence of a living manifestation
of God. The weight of his divinity automatically bowed my head before him.

If late guests detected that Sri Yukteswar was becoming engrossed with
the Infinite, he quickly engaged them in conversation. He was incapable of
striking a pose, or of flaunting his inner withdrawal. Always one with the

6 *Dhal* is a thick soup made from split peas or other pulses. *Channa* is a cheese of fresh curdled
milk, cut into squares and curried with potatoes.

Lord, he needed no separate time for communion. A self-realized master has already left behind the steppingstone of meditation. "The flower falls when the fruit appears." But saints often cling to spiritual forms for the encouragement of disciples.

As midnight approached, my guru might fall into a doze with the naturalness of a child. There was no fuss about bedding. He often lay down, without even a pillow, on a narrow davenport which was the background for his customary tiger-skin seat.

A night-long philosophical discussion was not rare; any disciple could summon it by intensity of interest. I felt no tiredness then, no desire for sleep; Master's living words were sufficient. "Oh, it is dawn! Let us walk by the Ganges." So ended many of my periods of nocturnal edification.

My early months with Sri Yukteswar culminated in a useful lesson – "How to Outwit a Mosquito." At home my family always used protective curtains at night. I was dismayed to discover that in the Serampore hermitage this prudent custom was honoured in the breach. Yet the insects were in full residency; I was bitten from head to foot. My guru took pity on me.

"Buy yourself a curtain, and also one for me." He laughed and added, "If you buy only one, for yourself, all mosquitoes will concentrate on me!"

I was more than thankful to comply. Every night that I spent in Serampore, my guru would ask me to arrange the bedtime curtains.

The mosquitoes one evening were especially virulent. But Master failed to issue his usual instructions. I listened nervously to the anticipatory hum of the insects. Getting into bed, I threw a propitiatory prayer in their general direction. A half hour later, I coughed pretentiously to attract my guru's attention. I thought I would go mad with the bites and especially the singing drone as the mosquitoes celebrated blood-thirsty rites.

No responsive stir from Master; I approached him cautiously. He was not breathing. This was my first observation of him in the yogic trance; it filled me with fright.

"His heart must have failed!" I placed a mirror under his nose; no breath-vapor appeared. To make doubly certain, for minutes I closed his mouth and nostrils with my fingers. His body was cold and motionless. In a daze, I turned toward the door to summon help.

"So! A budding experimentalist! My poor nose!" Master's voice was shaky with laughter. "Why don't you go to bed? Is the whole world going to change for you? Change yourself: be rid of the mosquito consciousness."

Meekly I returned to my bed. Not one insect ventured near. I realized that my guru had previously agreed to the curtains only to please me; he had no fear of mosquitoes. His yogic power was such that he either could will them not to bite, or could escape to an inner invulnerability.

"He was giving me a demonstration," I thought. "That is the yogic state I must strive to attain." A yogi must be able to pass into, and continue in, the superconsciousness, regardless of multitudinous distractions never absent from this earth. Whether in the buzz of insects or the pervasive glare of daylight, the testimony of the senses must be barred. Sound and sight come then indeed, but to worlds fairer than the pristine Eden.[7]

The instructive mosquitoes served for another early lesson at the ashram. It was the gentle hour of dusk. My guru was matchlessly interpreting the ancient texts. At his feet, I was in perfect peace. A rude mosquito entered the idyl and competed for my attention. As it dug a poisonous hypodermic needle into my thigh, I automatically raised an avenging hand. Reprieve from impending execution! An opportune memory came to me of one of Patanjali's yoga aphorisms – that on *ahimsa* (non-violence).

"Why didn't you finish the job?"

"Master! Do you advocate taking life?"

"No; but the deathblow already had been struck in your mind."

"I don't understand."

"Patanjali's meaning was the removal of *desire* to kill." Sri Yukteswar had found my mental processes an open book. "This world is inconveniently arranged for a literal practice of *ahimsa*. Man may be compelled to exterminate harmful creatures. He is not under similar compulsion to feel anger or animosity. All forms of life have equal right to the air of *maya*. The saint who uncovers the secret of creation will be in harmony with its countless bewildering expressions. All men may approach that understanding who curb the inner passion for destruction."

"Guruji, should one offer himself a sacrifice rather than kill a wild beast?"

"No; man's body is precious. It has the highest evolutionary value because of unique brain and spinal centres. These enable the advanced devotee to fully grasp and express the loftiest aspects of divinity. No lower form is so equipped. It is true that one incurs the debt of a minor sin if he is forced to kill an animal or any living thing. But the *Vedas* teach that wanton loss of a human body is a serious transgression against the karmic law."

I sighed in relief; scriptural reinforcement of one's natural instincts is not always forthcoming.

---

7 The omnipresent powers of a yogi, whereby he sees, hears, tastes, smells, and feels his oneness in creation without the use of sensory organs, have been described as follows in the *Taittiriya Aranyaka:* "The blind man pierced the pearl; the fingerless put a thread into it; the neckless wore it; and the tongueless praised it."

It so happened that I never saw Master at close quarters with a leopard or a tiger. But a deadly cobra once confronted him, only to be conquered by my guru's love. This variety of snake is much feared in India, where it causes more than five thousand deaths annually. The dangerous encounter took place at Puri, where Sri Yukteswar had a second hermitage, charmingly situated near the Bay of Bengal. Prafulla, a young disciple of later years, was with Master on this occasion.

"We were seated outdoors near the ashram," Prafulla told me. "A cobra appeared near-by, a four-foot length of sheer terror. Its hood was angrily expanded as it raced toward us. My guru gave a welcoming chuckle, as though to a child. I was beside myself with consternation to see Master engage in a rhythmical clapping of hands.[8] He was entertaining the dreaded visitor! I remained absolutely quiet, inwardly ejaculating what fervent prayers I could muster. The serpent, very close to my guru, was now motionless, seemingly magnetized by his caressing attitude. The frightful hood gradually contracted; the snake slithered between Master's feet and disappeared into the bushes.

"Why my guru would move his hands, and why the cobra would not strike them, were inexplicable to me then," Prafulla concluded. "I have since come to realize that my divine master is beyond fear of hurt from any living creature."

One afternoon during my early months at the ashram, I found Sri Yukteswar's eyes fixed on me piercingly.

"You are too thin, Mukunda."

His remark struck a sensitive point. That my sunken eyes and emaciated appearance were far from my liking was testified to by rows of tonics in my room at Calcutta. Nothing availed; chronic dyspepsia had pursued me since childhood. My despair reached an occasional zenith when I asked myself if it were worth-while to carry on this life with a body so unsound.

"Medicines have limitations; the creative life-force has none. Believe that: you shall be well and strong."

Sri Yukteswar's words aroused a conviction of personally-applicable truth which no other healer – and I had tried many! – had been able to summon within me such profound faith.

Day by day, behold! I waxed. Two weeks after Master's hidden blessing, I had accumulated the invigorating weight which eluded me in the past. My persistent stomach ailments vanished with a lifelong permanency. On later occasions I witnessed my guru's instantaneous divine healings of

---

8 The cobra swiftly strikes at any moving object within its range. Complete immobility is usually one's sole hope of safety.

persons suffering from ominous disease – tuberculosis, diabetes, epilepsy, or paralysis. Not one could have been more grateful for his cure than I was at sudden freedom from my cadaverous aspect.

"Years ago, I too was anxious to put on weight," Sri Yukteswar told me. "During convalescence after a severe illness, I visited Lahiri Mahasaya in Benares.

" 'Sir, I have been very sick and lost many pounds.'

" 'I see, Yukteswar,'[9] you made yourself unwell, and now you think you are thin.'

"This reply was far from the one I had expected; my guru, however, added encouragingly:

" 'Let me see; I am sure you ought to feel better tomorrow.'

"Taking his words as a gesture of secret healing toward my receptive mind, I was not surprised the next morning at a welcome accession of strength. I sought out my master and exclaimed exultingly, 'Sir, I feel much better today.'

" 'Indeed! Today you invigorate yourself.'

" 'No, master!' I protested. 'It was you who helped me; this is the first time in weeks that I have had any energy.'

" 'O yes! Your malady has been quite serious. Your body is frail yet; who can say how it will be tomorrow?'

"The thought of possible return of my weakness brought me a shudder of cold fear. The following morning I could hardly drag myself to Lahiri Mahasaya's home.

" 'Sir, I am ailing again.'

"My guru's glance was quizzical. 'So! Once more you indispose yourself.'

" 'Gurudeva, I realize now that day by day you have been ridiculing me.' My patience was exhausted. 'I don't understand why you disbelieve my truthful reports.'

" 'Really, it has been your thoughts that have made you feel alternately weak and strong.' My master looked at me affectionately. 'You have seen how your health has exactly followed your expectations. Thought is a force, even as electricity or gravitation. The human mind is a spark of the almighty consciousness of God. I could show you that whatever your powerful mind believes very intensely would instantly come to pass.'

9 Lahiri Mahasaya actually said 'Priya' (first or given name), not 'Yukteswar' (monastic name, not received by my guru during Lahiri Mahasaya's lifetime. See chap. 12). 'Yukteswar' is substituted here, and in a few other places in this book, in order to avoid the confusion, to reader, of two names.

"Knowing that Lahiri Mahasaya never spoke idly, I addressed him with great awe and gratitude: 'Master, if I think I am well and have regained my former weight, shall that happen?'

" 'It is so, even at this moment.' My guru spoke gravely, his gaze concentrated on my eyes.

"Lo! I felt an increase not alone of strength but of weight. Lahiri Mahasaya retreated into silence. After a few hours at his feet, I returned to my mother's home, where I stayed during my visits to Benares.

" 'My son! What is the matter? Are you swelling with dropsy?' Mother could hardly believe her eyes. My body was now of the same robust dimensions it had possessed before my illness.

"I weighed myself and found that in one day I had gained fifty pounds; they remained with me permanently. Friends and acquaintances who had seen my thin figure were aghast with wonderment. A number of them changed their mode of life and became disciples of Lahiri Mahasaya as a result of this miracle.

"My guru, awake in God, knew this world to be nothing but an objectivized dream of the Creator. Because he was completely aware of his unity with the Divine Dreamer, Lahiri Mahasaya could materialize or dematerialize or make any change he wished in the cosmic vision.[10]

"All creation is governed by law," Sri Yukteswar concluded. "The ones which manifest in the outer universe, discoverable by scientists, are called natural laws. But there are subtler laws ruling the realms of consciousness which can be known only through the inner science of yoga. The hidden spiritual planes also have their natural and lawful principles of operation. It is not the physical scientist but the fully self-realized master who comprehends the true nature of matter. Thus Christ was able to restore the servant's ear after it had been severed by one of the disciples."[11]

Sri Yukteswar was a peerless interpreter of the scriptures. Many of my happiest memories are centred in his discourses. But his jewelled thoughts were not cast into ashes of heedlessness or stupidity. One restless movement of my body, or my slight lapse into absent-mindedness, sufficed to put an abrupt period to Master's exposition.

"You are not here." Master interrupted himself one afternoon with this disclosure. As usual, he was keeping track of my attention with a devastating immediacy.

10 'Therefore I say unto you, What things soever ye desire, when ye pray, believe that ye receive them, and ye shall have them.' – *Mark* 11: 24. Masters who possess the Divine Vision are fully able to transfer their realizations to advanced disciples, as Lahiri Mahasaya did for Sri Yukteswar on this occasion.

11 'And one of them smote the servant of the high priest, and cut off his right ear. And Jesus answered and said, Suffer ye thus far. And he touched his ear and healed him.' – *Luke* 22: 50-51.

"Guruji!" My tone was a protest. "I have not stirred; my eyelids have not moved; I can repeat each word you have uttered!"

"Nevertheless you were not fully with me. Your objection forces me to remark that in your mental background you were creating three institutions. One was a sylvan retreat on a plain, another on a hilltop, a third by the ocean."

Those vaguely formulated thoughts had indeed been present almost subconsciously. I glanced at him apologetically.

"What can I do with such a master, who penetrates my random musings?"

"You have given me that right. The subtle truths I am expounding cannot be grasped without your complete concentration. Unless necessary I do not invade the seclusion of others' minds. Man has the natural privilege of roaming secretly among his thoughts. The unbidden Lord does not enter there; neither do I venture intrusion."

"You are ever welcome, Master!"

"Your architectural dreams will materialize later. Now is the time for study!"

Thus incidentally my guru revealed in his simple way the coming of three great events in my life. Since early youth I had had enigmatic glimpses of three buildings, each in a different setting. In the exact sequence Sri Yukteswar had indicated, these visions took ultimate form. First came my founding of a boys' yoga school on a Ranchi plain, then my American headquarters on a Los Angeles hilltop, finally a hermitage in southern California by the vast Pacific.

Master never arrogantly asserted: "I prophesy that such and such an event shall occur!" He would rather hint: "Don't you think it may happen?" But his simple speech hid vatic power. There was no recanting; never did his slightly veiled words prove false.

Sri Yukteswar was reserved and matter-of-fact in demeanor. There was naught of the vague or daft visionary about him. His feet were firm on the earth, his head in the haven of heaven. Practical people aroused his admiration. "Saintliness is not dumbness! Divine perceptions are not incapacitating!" he would say. "The active expression of virtue gives rise to the keenest intelligence."

In Master's life I fully discovered the cleavage between spiritual realism and the obscure mysticism that spuriously passes as a counterpart. My guru was reluctant to discuss the super-physical realms. His only 'marvellous' aura was one of perfect simplicity. In conversation he avoided startling references; in action he was freely expressive. Others talked of miracles but could manifest nothing; Sri Yukteswar seldom mentioned the subtle laws but secretly operated them at will.

"A man of realization does not perform any miracle until he receives an inward sanction," Master explained. "God does not wish the secrets of His creation revealed promiscuously.[12] Also, every individual in the world has inalienable right to his free will. A saint will not encroach upon that independence."

The silence habitual to Sri Yukteswar was caused by his deep perceptions of the Infinite. No time remained for the interminable "revelations" that occupy the days of teachers without self-realization. "In shallow men the fish of little thoughts cause much commotion. In oceanic minds the whales of inspiration make hardly a ruffle." This observation from the Hindu scriptures is not without discerning humour.

Because of my guru's unspectacular guise, only a few of his contemporaries recognized him as a superman. The popular adage: "He is a fool that cannot conceal his wisdom," could never be applied to Sri Yukteswar. Though born a mortal like all others, Master had achieved identity with the Ruler of time and space. In his life I perceived a godlike unity. He had not found any insuperable obstacle to mergence of human with Divine. No such barrier exists, I came to understand, save in man's spiritual un-adventurousness.

I always thrilled at the touch of Sri Yukteswar's holy feet. Yogis teach that a disciple is spiritually magnetized by reverent contact with a master; a subtle current is generated. The devotee's undesirable habit-mechanisms in the brain are often cauterized; the groove of his worldly tendencies beneficially disturbed. Momentarily at least he may find the secret veils of *maya* lifting, and glimpse the reality of bliss. My whole body responded with a liberating glow whenever I knelt in the Indian fashion before my guru.

"Even when Lahiri Mahasaya was silent," Master told me, "or when he conversed on other than strictly religious topics, I discovered that nonetheless he had transmitted to me ineffable knowledge."

Sri Yukteswar affected me similarly. If I entered the hermitage in a worried or indifferent frame of mind, my attitude imperceptibly changed. A healing calm descended at mere sight of my guru. Every day with him was a new experience in joy, peace, and wisdom. Never did I find him deluded or intoxicated with greed or emotion or anger or any human attachment.

"The darkness of *maya* is silently approaching. Let us hie homeward within." With these words at dusk Master constantly reminded his disciples of their need for *Kriya Yoga*. A new student occasionally expressed doubts regarding his own worthiness to engage in yoga practice.

"Forget the past," Sri Yukteswar would console him. "The vanished lives of all men are dark with many shames. Human conduct is ever unreliable until anchored in the Divine. Everything in future will improve if you are making a spiritual effort now."

12 'Give not that which is holy unto the dogs, neither cast ye your pearls before swine, lest they trample them under their feet, and turn again and rend you.' – *Matthew* 7: 6.

Master always had young *chelas*[13] in his hermitage. Their spiritual and intellectual education was his lifelong interest: even shortly before he passed on, he accepted for training two six-year-old boys and one youth of sixteen. He directed their minds and lives with that careful discipline in which the word 'disciple' is etymologically rooted. The ashram residents loved and revered their guru; a slight clap of his hands sufficed to bring them eagerly to his side. When his mood was silent and withdrawn, no one ventured to speak; when his laugh rang jovially, children looked upon him as their own.

Master seldom asked others to render him a personal service, nor would he accept help from a student unless the willingness were sincere. My guru quietly washed his clothes if the disciples overlooked that privileged task. Sri Yukteswar wore the traditional ochre-coloured swami robe; his lace-less shoes, in accordance with yogi custom, were of tiger or deerskin.

Master spoke fluent English, French, Hindi, and Bengali; his Sanskrit was fair. He patiently instructed his young disciples by certain short cuts which he had ingeniously devised for the study of English and Sanskrit.

Master was cautious of his body, while withholding solicitous attachment. The Infinite, he pointed out, properly manifests through physical and mental soundness. He discountenanced any extremes. A disciple once started a long fast. My guru only laughed: "Why not throw the dog a bone?"

Sri Yukteswar's health was excellent; I never saw him unwell.[14] He permitted students to consult doctors if it seemed advisable. His purpose was to give respect to the worldly custom: "Physicians must carry on their work of healing through God's laws as applied to matter." But he extolled the superiority of mental therapy, and often repeated: "Wisdom is the greatest cleanser."

"The body is a treacherous friend. Give it its due; no more," he said. "Pain and pleasure are transitory; endure all dualities with calmness, while trying at the same time to remove their hold. Imagination is the door through which disease as well as healing enters. Disbelieve in the reality of sickness even when you are ill; an unrecognized visitor will flee!"

Master numbered many doctors among his disciples. "Those who have ferreted out the physical laws can easily investigate the science of the soul," he told them. "A subtle spiritual mechanism is hidden just behind the bodily structure."[15]

13 Disciples; from Sanskrit verb root 'to serve.'
14 He was once ill in Kashmir, when I was away from him. (See page 145).
15 A courageous medical man, Charles Robert Richet, awarded the Nobel Prize in physiology, wrote as follows: 'Metaphysics is not yet officially a science, recognized as such. But it is going to be . . . At Edinburgh, I was able to affirm before 100 physiologists that our five senses are not our only means of knowledge and that a fragment of reality sometimes reaches the intelligence in other ways. . . . Because a fact is rare is no reason that it does not exist. Because a study is difficult, is that a reason for not understanding it? . . . Those who have railed at metaphysics as an occult science will be as ashamed of themselves as those who railed at chemistry on the ground that pursuit of the philosopher's stone was illusory. . . . In the matter of principles there are only those of Lavoisier, Claude Bernard, and Pasteur – the *experimental* everywhere and always. Greetings, then, to the new science which is going to change the orientation of human thought.'

Sri Yukteswar counselled his students to be living liaisons of Western and Eastern virtues. Himself an executive Occidental in outer habits, inwardly he was the spiritual Oriental. He praised the progressive, resourceful and hygienic habits of the West, and the religious ideals which give a centuried halo to the East.

Discipline had not been unknown to me: at home Father was strict, Ananta often severe. But Sri Yukteswar's training cannot be described as other than drastic. A perfectionist, my guru was hypercritical of his disciples, whether in matters of moment or in the subtle nuances of behaviour.

"Good manners without sincerity are like a beautiful dead lady," he remarked on suitable occasion. "Straightforwardness without civility is like a surgeon's knife, effective but unpleasant. Candour with courtesy is helpful and admirable."

Master was apparently satisfied with my spiritual progress, for he seldom referred to it; in other matters my ears were no strangers to reproof. My chief offenses were absentmindedness, intermittent indulgence in sad moods, non-observance of certain rules of etiquette, and occasional unmethodical ways.

"Observe how the activities of your father Bhagabati are well-organized and balanced in every way," my guru pointed out. The two disciples of Lahiri Mahasaya had met, soon after I began my pilgrimages to Serampore. Father and Sri Yukteswar admiringly evaluated the other's worth. Both had built an inner life of spiritual granite, insoluble against the ages.

From transient teachers of my earlier life I had imbibed a few erroneous lessons. A *chela*, I was told, need not concern himself strenuously over worldly duties; when I had neglected or carelessly performed my tasks, I was not chastised. Human nature finds such instruction very easy of assimilation. Under Master's unsparing rod, however, I soon recovered from the agreeable delusions of irresponsibility.

"Those who are too good for this world are adorning some other," Sri Yukteswar remarked. "So long as you breathe the free air of earth, you are under obligation to render grateful service. He alone who has fully mastered the breathless state[16] is freed from cosmic imperatives. I will not fail to let you know when you have attained the final perfection."

My guru could never be bribed, even by love. He showed no leniency to anyone who, like myself, willingly offered to be his disciple. Whether Master and I were surrounded by his students or by strangers, or were alone together, he always spoke plainly and upbraided sharply. No trifling lapse into

16 *Samadhi:* perfect union of the individualized soul with the Infinite Spirit.

shallowness or inconsistency escaped his rebuke. This flattening treatment was hard to endure, but my resolve was to allow Sri Yukteswar to iron out each of my psychological kinks. As he laboured at this titanic transformation, I shook many times under the weight of his disciplinary hammer.

"If you don't like my words, you are at liberty to leave at any time," Master assured me. "I want nothing from you but your own improvement. Stay only if you feel benefited."

For every humbling blow he dealt my vanity, for every tooth in my metaphorical jaw he knocked loose with stunning aim, I am grateful beyond any facility of expression. The hard core of human egotism is hardly to be dislodged except rudely. With its departure, the Divine finds at last an unobstructed channel. In vain It seeks to percolate through flinty hearts of selfishness.

Sri Yukteswar's wisdom was so penetrating that, heedless of remarks, he often replied to one's unspoken observation. "What a person imagines he hears, and what the speaker has really implied, may be poles apart," he said. "Try to feel the thoughts behind the confusion of men's verbiage."

But divine insight is painful to worldly ears; Master was not popular with superficial students. The wise, always few in number, deeply revered him. I daresay Sri Yukteswar would have been the most sought-after guru in India had his words not been so candid and so censorious.

"I am hard on those who come for my training," he admitted to me. "That is my way; take it or leave it. I will never compromise. But you will be much kinder to your disciples; that is your way. I try to purify only in the fires of severity, searing beyond the average toleration. The gentle approach of love is also transfiguring. The inflexible and the yielding methods are equally effective if applied with wisdom. You will go to foreign lands, where blunt assaults on the ego are not appreciated. A teacher could not spread India's message in the West without an ample fund of accommodative patience and forbearance." I refuse to say how often, in America, I have remembered Master's words!

Though Sri Yukteswar's un-dissembling speech prevented a large following during his years on earth, nevertheless his living spirit manifests today over the world, through sincere students of his *Kriya Yoga* and other teachings. Worriors like Alexander the Great seek sovereignty over the soil; masters like Sri Yukteswar win a farther dominion – in men's souls.

My father arrived one day to pay his respects to Sri Yukteswar. My parent expected, very likely, to hear some words in my praise. He was shocked to be given a long account of my imperfections. It was Master's practice to recount simple, negligible short-comings with an air of portentous gravity. Father rushed to see me. "From your guru's remarks I thought to find you a complete wreck!" My parent was between tears and laughter.

The only cause of Sri Yukteswar's displeasure at the time was that I had been trying, against his gentle hint, to convert a certain man to the spiritual path.

With indignant speed I sought out my guru. He received me with downcast eyes, as though conscious of guilt. It was the only time I ever saw the divine lion meek before me. The unique moment was savored to the full.

"Sir, why did you judge me so mercilessly before my astounded father? Was that just?"

"I will not do it again." Master's tone was apologetic.

Instantly I was disarmed. How readily the great man admitted his fault! Though he never again upset Father's peace of mind, Master relentlessly continued to dissect me whenever and wherever he chose.

New disciples often joined Sri Yukteswar in exhaustive criticism of others. Wise like the guru! Models of flawless discrimination! But he who takes the offensive must not be defenseless. The same carping students fled precipitantly as soon as Master publicly unloosed in their direction a few shafts from his analytical quiver.

"Tender inner weaknesses, revolting at mild touches of censure, are like diseased parts of the body, recoiling before even delicate handling." This was Sri Yukteswar's amused comment on the flighty ones.

There are disciples who seek a guru made in their own image. Such students often complained that they did not understand Sri Yukteswar.

"Neither do you comprehend God!" I retorted on one occasion. "When a saint is clear to you, you will be one." Among the trillion mysteries, breathing every second the inexplicable air, who may venture to ask that the fathomless nature of a master be instantly grasped?

Students came, and generally went. Those who craved a path of oily sympathy and comfortable recognitions did not find it at the hermitage. Master offered shelter and shepherding for the aeons, but many disciples miserly demanded ego-balm as well. They departed, preferring life's countless humiliations before any humility. Master's blazing rays, the open penetrating sunshine of his wisdom, were too powerful for their spiritual sickness. They sought some lesser teacher who, shading them with flattery, permitted the fitful sleep of ignorance.

During my early months with Master, I had experienced a sensitive fear of his reprimands. These were reserved, I soon saw, for disciples who had asked for his verbal vivisection. If any writhing student made a protest, Sri Yukteswar would become un-offendedly silent. His words were never wrathful, but impersonal with wisdom.

Master's insight was not for the unprepared ears of casual visitors; he seldom remarked on their defects, even if conspicuous. But toward students who sought his counsel, Sri Yukteswar felt a serious responsibility. Brave indeed is the guru who undertakes to transform the crude ore of ego-permeated humanity! A saint's courage roots in his compassion for the stumbling eyeless of this world.

When I had abandoned underlying resentment, I found a marked decrease in my chastisement. In a very subtle way, Master melted into comparative clemency. In time I demolished every wall of rationalization and subconscious reservation behind which the human personality generally shields itself.[17] The reward was an effortless harmony with my guru. I discovered him then to be trusting, considerate, and silently loving. Undemonstrative, however, he bestowed no word of affection.

My own temperament is principally devotional. It was disconcerting at first to find that my guru, saturated with *jnana* but seemingly dry of *bhakti*,[18] expressed himself only in terms of cold spiritual mathematics. But as I tuned myself to his nature, I discovered no diminution but rather increase in my devotional approach to God. A self-realized master is fully able to guide his various disciples along natural lines of their essential bias.

My relationship with Sri Yukteswar, somewhat inarticulate, nonetheless possessed all eloquence. Often I found his silent signature on my thoughts, rendering speech inutile. Quietly sitting beside him, I felt his bounty pouring peacefully over my being.

Sri Yukteswar's impartial justice was notably demonstrated during the summer vacation of my first college year. I welcomed the opportunity to spend uninterrupted months at Serampore with my guru.

"You may be in charge of the hermitage." Master was pleased over my enthusiastic arrival. "Your duties will be the reception of guests, and supervision of the work of the other disciples."

17 The subconsciously guided rationalizations of the mind are utterly different from the infallible guidance of truth of the superconsciousness. Led by French scientists of the Sorbonne, Western thinkers are beginning to investigate the possibility of divine perception in man.

'For the past twenty years, students of psychology, influenced by Freud, gave all their time to searching the subconscious realms,' Rabbi Israel H. Levinthal pointed out in 1929. 'It is true that the subconscious reveals much of the mystery that can explain human actions, but not all of our actions. It can explain the abnormal, but not deeds that are above the normal. The latest psychology, sponsored by the French schools, has discovered a new region in man, which it terms the superconscious. In contrast to the subconscious which represents the submerged currents of our nature, it reveals the heights to which our nature can reach. Man represents a triple, not a double, personality; our conscious and subconscious being is crowned by a superconsciousness. Many years ago the English psychologist, F. W. H. Myers, suggested that 'hidden in the deep of our being is a rubbish heap as well as a treasure house.' In contrast to the psychology that centers all its researches on the subconscious in man's nature, this new psychology of the superconscious focuses its attention upon the treasure-house, the region that alone can explain the great, unselfish, heroic deeds of men.'

18 *Jnana:* wisdom, and *bhakti:* devotion; two main paths to realize God.

Kumar, a young villager from east Bengal, was accepted a fortnight later for hermitage training. Remarkably intelligent, he quickly won Sri Yukteswar's affection. For some unfathomable reason, Master was very lenient to the new resident.

"Mukunda, let Kumar assume your duties. Employ your own time in sweeping and cooking." Master issued these instructions after the new boy had been with us for a month.

Exalted to leadership, Kumar exercised a petty household tyranny. In silent mutiny, the other disciples continued to seek me out for daily counsel.

"Mukunda is impossible! You made me supervisor, yet the others go to him and obey him." Three weeks later Kumar was complaining to our guru. I overheard him from an adjoining room.

"That's why I assigned him to the kitchen and you to the parlour." Sri Yukteswar's withering tones were new to Kumar. "In this way you have come to realize that a worthy leader has the desire to serve, and not to dominate. You wanted Mukunda's position, but could not maintain it by merit. Return now to your earlier work as cook's assistant."

After this humbling incident, Master resumed toward Kumar a former attitude of unwonted indulgence. Who can solve the mystery of attraction? In Kumar our guru discovered a charming fount which did not spurt for the fellow disciples. Though the new boy was obviously Sri Yukteswar's favourite, I felt no dismay. Personal idiosyncrasies, possessed even by masters, lend a rich complexity to the pattern of life. My nature is seldom commandeered by a detail; I was seeking from Sri Yukteswar a more inaccessible benefit than an outward praise.

Kumar spoke venomously to me one day without reason; I was deeply hurt.

"Your head is swelling to the bursting point!" I added a warning whose truth I felt intuitively: "Unless you mend your ways, someday you will be asked to leave this ashram."

Laughing sarcastically, Kumar repeated my remark to our guru, who had just entered the room. Fully expecting to be scolded, I retired meekly to a corner.

"Maybe Mukunda is right." Master's reply to the boy came with unusual coldness. I escaped without castigation.

A year later, Kumar set out for a visit to his childhood home. He ignored the quiet disapproval of Sri Yukteswar, who never authoritatively controlled his disciples' movements. On the boy's return to Serampore in a few months, a change was unpleasantly apparent. Gone was the stately

Kumar with serenely glowing face. Only an undistinguished peasant stood before us, one who had lately acquired a number of evil habits.

Master summoned me and brokenheartedly discussed the fact that the boy was now unsuited to the monastic hermitage life.

"Mukunda, I will leave it to you to instruct Kumar to leave the ashram tomorrow; I can't do it!" Tears stood in Sri Yukteswar's eyes, but he controlled himself quickly. "The boy would never have fallen to these depths had he listened to me and not gone away to mix with undesirable companions. He has rejected my protection; the callous world must be his guru still."

Kumar's departure brought me no elation; sadly I wondered how one with power to win a master's love could ever respond to cheaper allures. Enjoyment of wine and sex are rooted in the natural man, and require no delicacies of perception for their appreciation. Sense wiles are comparable to the evergreen oleander, fragrant with its multicoloured flowers: every part of the plant is poisonous. The land of healing lies within, radiant with that happiness blindly sought in a thousand misdirections.[19]

"Keen intelligence is two-edged," Master once remarked in reference to Kumar's brilliant mind. "It may be used constructively or destructively like a knife, either to cut the boil of ignorance, or to decapitate one's self. Intelligence is rightly guided only after the mind has acknowledged the inescapability of spiritual law."

My guru mixed freely with men and women disciples, treating all as his children. Perceiving their soul equality, he showed no distinction or partiality.

"In sleep, you do not know whether you are a man or a woman," he said. "Just as a man, impersonating a woman, does not become one, so the soul, impersonating both man and woman, has no sex. The soul is the pure, changeless image of God."

Sri Yukteswar never avoided or blamed women as the cause of 'man's downfall'. Men, he said, were also a temptation to women. I once inquired of my guru why a great ancient saint had called women 'the door to hell.'

"A girl must have proved very troublesome to his peace of mind in his early life," my guru answered causticly. "Otherwise he would have denounced, not woman, but some imperfection in his own self-control."

If a visitor dared to relate a suggestive story in the hermitage, Master would maintain an unresponsive silence. "Do not allow yourself to be thrashed

19 Shankara, the great Vedantist writes: 'Man in his waking state puts forth innumerable efforts for experiencing sensual pleasures; when the entire group of sensory organs is fatigued, he forgets even the pleasure on hand and goes to sleep in order to enjoy rest in the soul, his own nature.' Ultra-sensual bliss is thus extremely easy of attainment and is far superior to sense delights which always end in disgust.

by the provoking whip of a beautiful face," he told the disciples. "How can sense-slaves enjoy the world? Its subtle flavours escape them while they grovel in primal mud. All nice discriminations are lost to the man of elemental lusts."

Students seeking to escape from the dualistic *maya* delusion received from Sri Yukteswar patient and understanding counsel.

"Just as the purpose of eating is to satisfy hunger, not greed, so the sex instinct is designed for the propagation of the species according to natural law, never for the kindling of insatiable longings," he said. "Destroy wrong desires now; otherwise they will follow you after the astral body is torn from its physical casing. Even when the flesh is weak, the mind should be constantly resistant. If temptation assails you with cruel force, overcome it by impersonal analysis and indomitable will. Every natural passion can be mastered.

"Conserve your powers. Be like the capacious ocean, absorbing within all the tributary rivers of the senses. Small yearnings are openings in the reservoir of your inner peace, permitting healing waters to be wasted in the desert soil of materialism. The forceful activating impulse of wrong desire is the greatest enemy to the happiness of man. Roam in the world as a lion of self-control; see that the frogs of weakness don't kick you around."

A true devotee is finally freed from all instinctive compulsions. He transforms his need for human affection into aspiration for God alone, a love solitary because omnipresent.

Sri Yukteswar's mother lived in the Rana Mahal district of Benares where I had first visited my guru. Gracious and kindly, she was yet a woman of very decided opinions. I stood on her balcony one day and watched mother and son talking together. In his quiet, sensible way, Master was trying to convince her about something. He was apparently unsuccessful, for she shook her head with great vigor.

"Nay, nay, my son, go away now! Your wise words are not for me! I am not your disciple!"

Sri Yukteswar backed away without further argument, like a scolded child. I was touched at his great respect for his mother even in her unreasonable moods. She saw him only as her little boy, not as a sage. There was a charm about the trifling incident; it supplied a sidelight on my guru's unusual nature, inwardly humble and outwardly unbendable.

The monastic regulations do not allow a swami to retain connection with worldly ties after their formal severance. He cannot perform the ceremonial family rites which are obligatory on the householder. Yet Shankara, the ancient founder of the Swami Order, disregarded the injunctions. At the death of his beloved mother, he cremated her body with heavenly fire which he caused to spurt from his upraised hand.

Sri Yukteswar also ignored the restrictions, in a fashion less spectacular. When his mother passed on, he arranged the crematory services by the holy Ganges in Benares, and fed many Brahmins in conformance with age-old custom.

The *shastric* prohibitions were intended to help swamis overcome narrow identifications. Shankara and Sri Yukteswar had wholly merged their beings in the Impersonal Spirit; they needed no rescue by rule. Sometimes, too, a master purposely ignores a canon in order to uphold its principle as superior to and independent of form. Thus Jesus plucked ears of corn on the day of rest. To the inevitable critics he said: "The Sabbath was made for man, and not man for the Sabbath."[20]

Outside of the scriptures, seldom was a book honoured by Sri Yukteswar's perusal. Yet he was invariably acquainted with the latest scientific discoveries and other advancements of knowledge.[21] A brilliant conversationalist, he enjoyed an exchange of views on countless topics with his guests. My guru's ready wit and rollicking laugh enlivened every discussion. Often grave, Master was never gloomy. "To seek the Lord, one need not disfigure his face," he would remark. "Remember that finding God will mean the funeral of all sorrows."

Among the philosophers, professors, lawyers and scientists who came to the hermitage, a number arrived for their first visit with the expectation of meeting an orthodox religionist. A supercilious smile or a glance of amused tolerance occasionally betrayed that the newcomers anticipated nothing more than a few pious platitudes. Yet their reluctant departure would bring an expressed conviction that Sri Yukteswar had shown precise insight into their specialized fields.

My guru ordinarily was gentle and affable to guests; his welcome was given with charming cordiality. Yet inveterate egotists sometimes suffered an invigorating shock. They confronted in Master either a frigid indifference or a formidable opposition: ice or iron!

A noted chemist once crossed swords with Sri Yukteswar. The visitor would not admit the existence of God, inasmuch as science has devised no means of detecting Him.

"So you have inexplicably failed to isolate the Supreme Power in your test tubes!" Master's gaze was stern. "I recommend an unheard-of experiment. Examine your thoughts unremittingly for twenty-four hours. Then wonder no longer at God's absence."

20 *Mark* 2: 27.
21 The Master could instantly attune himself to any person in consonance with the *Yoga Sutras* of Patanjali.

A celebrated pundit received a similar jolt. With ostentatious zeal, the scholar shook the ashram rafters with scriptural lore. Resounding passages poured from the *Mahabharata*, the *Upanishads*,[22] the *bhasyas*[23] of Shankara.

"I am waiting to hear you." Sri Yukteswar's tone was inquiring, as though utter silence had reigned. The pundit was puzzled.

"Quotations there have been, in superabundance." Master's words convulsed me with mirth, as I squatted in my corner, at a respectful distance from the visitor. "But what original commentary can you supply, from the uniqueness of your particular life? What holy text have you absorbed and made your own? In what ways have these timeless truths renovated your nature? Are you content to be a hollow victrola (a branded phono-graph), mechanically repeating the words of other men?"

"I give up!" The scholar's chagrin was comical. "I have no inner realization."

For the first time, perhaps, he understood that discerning placement of the comma does not atone for a spiritual coma.

"These bloodless pedants smell unduly of the lamp," my guru remarked after the departure of the chastened one. "They prefer philosophy to be a gentle intellectual setting-up exercise. Their elevated thoughts are carefully unrelated either to the crudity of outward action or to any scourging inner discipline!"

Master stressed on other occasions the futility of mere book learning.

"Do not confuse understanding with a larger vocabulary," he remarked. "Sacred writings are beneficial in stimulating desire for inward realization, if one stanza at a time is slowly assimilated. Continual intellectual study results in vanity and the false satisfaction of an undigested knowledge."

Sri Yukteswar related one of his own experiences in scriptural edification. The scene was a forest hermitage in eastern Bengal, where he observed the procedure of a renowned teacher, Dabru Ballav. His method, at once simple and difficult, was common in ancient India.

Dabru Ballav had gathered his disciples around him in the sylvan solitudes. The holy *Bhagavad Gita* was open before them. Steadfastly they looked at one passage for half an hour, then closed their eyes. Another half hour slipped away. The master gave a brief comment. Motionless, they meditated again for an hour. Finally the guru spoke.

22 The *Upanishads* or *Vedanta* (literally, 'end of the Vedas'), occur in certain parts of the *Vedas* as essential summaries. The *Upanishads* furnish the doctrinal basis of the Hindu religion. They received the following tribute from Schopenhauer: 'How entirely does the *Upanishad* breathe throughout the holy spirit of the *Vedas!* How is everyone who has become familiar with that incomparable book stirred by that spirit to the very depths of his soul! From every sentence deep, original, and sublime thoughts arise, and the whole is pervaded by a high and holy and earnest spirit. . . . The access to the *Vedas* by means of the *Upanishads* is in my eyes the greatest privilege this century may claim before all previous centuries.'

23 Commentaries. Shankara peerlessly expounded the *Upanishads*.

"Have you understood?"

"Yes, sir." One in the group ventured this assertion.

"No; not fully. Seek the spiritual vitality that has given these words the power to rejuvenate India century after century." Another hour disappeared in silence. The master dismissed the students, and turned to Sri Yukteswar.

"Do you know the *Bhagavad Gita*?"

"No, sir, not really; though my eyes and mind have run through its pages many times."

"Hundreds have replied to me differently!" The great sage smiled at Master in blessing. "If one busies himself with an outer display of scriptural wealth, what time is left for silent inward diving after the priceless pearls?"

Sri Yukteswar directed the study of his own disciples by the same intensive method of one-pointedness. "Wisdom is not assimilated with the eyes, but with the atoms," he said. "When your conviction of a truth is not merely in your brain but in your being, you may diffidently vouch for its meaning." He discouraged any tendency a student might have to construe book-knowledge as a necessary step to spiritual realization.

"The *rishis* wrote in one sentence profundities that commentating scholars busy themselves over for generations," he remarked. "Endless literary controversy is for sluggard minds. What more liberating thought than 'God is' – nay, 'God'?"

But man does not easily return to simplicity. It is seldom 'God' for him, but rather learned pomposities. His ego is pleased, that he can grasp such erudition.

Men who were pridefully conscious of high worldly position were likely, in Master's presence, to add humility to their other possessions. A local magistrate once arrived for an interview at the seaside hermitage in Puri. The man, who held a reputation for ruthlessness, had it well within his power to oust us from the ashram. I cautioned my guru about the despotic possibilities. But he seated himself with an uncompromising air, and did not rise to greet the visitor. Slightly nervous, I squatted near the door. The man had to content himself with a wooden box; my guru did not request me to fetch a chair. There was no fulfillment of the magistrate's obvious expectation that his importance would be ceremoniously acknowledged.

A metaphysical discussion ensued. The guest blundered through misinterpretations of the scriptures. As his accuracy sank, his ire rose.

"Do you know that I stood first in the M. A. examination?" Reason had forsaken him, but he could still shout.

"Mr. Magistrate, you forget that this is not your courtroom," Master replied evenly. "From your childish remarks I would have surmised that your college career was unremarkable. A university degree, in any case, is not remotely related to Vedic realization. Saints are not produced in batches every semester like accountants."

After a stunned silence, the visitor laughed heartily.

"This is my first encounter with a heavenly magistrate," he said. Later he made a formal request, couched in the legal terms which were evidently part and parcel of his being, to be accepted as a 'probationary' disciple.

My guru personally attended to the details connected with the management of his property. Unscrupulous persons on various occasions attempted to secure possession of Master's ancestral land. With determination and even by instigating lawsuits, Sri Yukteswar outwitted every opponent. He under-went these painful experiences from a desire never to be a begging guru, or a burden on his disciples.

His financial independence was one reason why my alarmingly outspoken Master was innocent of the cunnings of diplomacy. Unlike those teachers who have to flatter their supporters, my guru was impervious to the influences, open or subtle, of others' wealth. Never did I hear him ask or even hint for money for any purpose. His hermitage training was given free and freely to all disciples.

An insolent court deputy arrived one day at the Serampore ashram to serve Sri Yukteswar with a legal summons. A disciple named Kanai and myself were also present. The officer's attitude toward Master was offensive.

"It will do you good to leave the shadows of your hermitage and breathe the honest air of a courtroom." The deputy grinned contemptuously. I could not contain myself.

"Another word of your impudence and you will be on the floor!" I advanced threateningly.

"You wretch!" Kanai's shout was simultaneous with my own. "Dare you bring your blasphemies into this sacred ashram?"

But Master stood protectively in front of his abuser. "Don't get excited over nothing. This man is only doing his rightful duty."

The officer, dazed at his varying reception, respectfully offered a word of apology and sped away.

Amazing it was to find that a master with such a fiery will could be so calm within. He fitted the Vedic definition of a man of God: "Softer than the flower, where kindness is concerned; stronger than the thunder, where principles are at stake."

There are always those in this world who, in Browning's words, "endure no light, being themselves obscure." An outsider occasionally berated Sri Yukteswar for an imaginary grievance. My imperturbable guru listened politely, analyzing himself to see if any shred of truth lay within the denunciation. These scenes would bring to my mind one of Master's inimitable observations: "Some people try to be tall by cutting off the heads of others!"

The unfailing composure of a saint is impressive beyond any sermon. "He that is slow to anger is better than the mighty; and he that ruleth his spirit than he that taketh a city."[24]

I often reflected that my majestic Master could easily have been an emperor or world-shaking warrior had his mind been centred on fame or worldly achievement. He had chosen instead to storm those inner citadels of wrath and egotism whose fall is the height of a man.

13. *The Sleepless Saint*

"PLEASE PERMIT ME to go to the Himalayas. I hope in unbroken solitude to achieve continuous divine communion."

I actually once addressed these ungrateful words to my Master. Seized by one of the unpredictable delusions which occasionally assail the devotee, I felt a growing impatience with hermitage duties and college studies. A feebly extenuating circumstance is that my proposal was made when I had been only six months with Sri Yukteswar. Not yet had I fully surveyed his towering stature.

"Many hillmen live in the Himalayas, yet possess no God-perception." My guru's answer came slowly and simply. "Wisdom is better sought from a man of realization than from an inert mountain."

---

24 *Proverbs* 16: 32 (Bible).

[THE BOOKS OF BIBLE: Paramahansa Yoganandaji quotes extensively from the Holy Scripture Bible which is a collection of sacred writings of the Jewish and Christian religions, comprising the Old and New Testaments; the former of Judaism which was the faith of the ancient Hebrews, and the latter of Christianity.

The Old Testament, also called the Hebrew Bible or Tanakh, is an account of God's dealings with his chosen peoples. The Books of Old Testament (*Proverbs, Genesis Psalms, Kings, Chronicles, Isaiah,* etc.) vary in their content according to religious tradition. The Jewish, Roman Catholic, and Protestant canons differ from each other on the adoption of these Books. The Books, more of which have since been added to the original 24, are divided in three sections: the *Law,* the *Prophets,* and the *Writings.*

The Christians see the New Testament as the fulfillment of the promise of the Old Testament, for it recounts the life and ministry of Jesus; focusing on the covenants (the promises that God extended to humankind *e.g.* that given to Noah never to flood the earth, or to Abraham that his tribe will multiply and inherit the land of Israel) between God and the followers of Jesus. There are 27 Books in the New Testament: (*Matthew, Mark, Luke, John, Acts, Romans,* I & II *Corinthians, Timothy, James, Revelations* etc.) They comprise the four sections of the *Gospels* (orig. god-spells or good news), the *Acts* of the apostles, *epistles* or advisory letters to early Christians, and the Book of *Revelation* describing the coming of apocalypse (the upheaval preceding the end of the world).

Paramahansa Yoganandaji also draws a remarkable parallel in the core teachings between the Bible and the Hindu scriptures, as an effective tool to introduce the tenets of Hindu philosophy and to highlight Indian Spirituality to his Western followers. – *Ed.*]

Ignoring Master's plain hint that he, and not a hill, was my teacher, I repeated my plea. Sri Yukteswar vouchsafed no reply. I took his silence for consent, a precarious interpretation readily accepted at one's convenience.

In my Calcutta home that evening, I busied myself with travel preparations. Tying a few articles inside a blanket, I remembered a similar bundle, surreptitiously dropped from my attic window a few years earlier. I wondered if this were to be another ill-starred flight toward the Himalayas. The first time my spiritual elation had been high; tonight conscience smote heavily at thought of leaving my guru.

The following morning I sought out Behari Pundit, my Sanskrit professor at Scottish Church College.

"Sir, you have told me of your friendship with a great disciple of Lahiri Mahasaya. Please give me his address."

"You mean Ram Gopal Muzumdar. I call him the 'sleepless saint.' He is always awake in an ecstatic consciousness. His home is at Ranbajpur, near Tarakeswar."

I thanked the pundit, and entrained immediately for Tarakeswar. I hoped to silence my misgivings by wringing a sanction from the 'sleepless saint' to engage myself in lonely Himalayan meditation. Behari's friend, I heard, had received illumination after many years of *Kriya Yoga* practice in isolated caves in Bengal.

At Tarakeswar I approached a famous shrine. Hindus regard it with the same veneration that Catholics give to the Lourdes sanctuary in France. Innumerable healing miracles have occurred at Tarakeswar, including one for a member of my family.

"I sat in the temple there for a week," my eldest aunt once told me. "Observing a complete fast, I prayed for the recovery of your Uncle Sarada from a chronic malady. On the seventh day I found a herb materialized in my hand! I made a brew from the leaves, and gave it to your uncle. His disease vanished at once, and has never reappeared."

I entered the sacred Tarakeswar shrine; the altar contains nothing but a round stone. Its circumference, beginningless and endless, makes it aptly significant of the Infinite. Cosmic abstractions are not alien even to the humblest Indian peasant; he has been accused by Westerners, in fact, of living on abstractions!

My own mood at the moment was so austere that I felt disinclined to bow before the stone symbol. God should be sought, I reflected, only within the soul.

I left the temple without genuflection and walked briskly toward the outlying village of Ranbajpur. My appeal to a passerby for guidance caused him to sink into long cogitation.

"When you come to a crossroad, turn right and keep going," he finally pronounced oracularly.

Obeying the directions, I wended my way alongside the banks of a canal. Darkness fell; the outskirts of the jungle village were alive with winking fireflies and the howls of nearby jackals. The moonlight was too faint to supply any reassurance; I stumbled on for two hours.

Welcome clang of a cowbell! My repeated shouts eventually brought a peasant to my side.

"I am looking for Ram Gopal Babu."

"No such person lives in our village." The man's tone was surly. "You are probably a lying detective."

Hoping to allay suspicion in his politically troubled mind, I touchingly explained my predicament. He took me to his home and offered a hospitable welcome.

"Ranbajpur is far from here," he remarked. "At the crossroad, you should have turned left, not right."

My earlier informant, I thought sadly, was a distinct menace to travellers. After a relishable meal of coarse rice, lentil-*dhal*, and curry of potatoes with raw bananas, I retired to a small hut adjoining the courtyard. In the distance, villagers were singing to the loud accompaniment of *mridangas*[1] and cymbals. Sleep was inconsiderable that night; I prayed deeply to be directed to the secret yogi, Ram Gopal.

As the first streaks of dawn penetrated the fissures of my dark room, I set out for Ranbajpur. Crossing rough paddy fields, I trudged over sickled stumps of the prickly plant and mounds of dried clay. An occasionally-met peasant would inform me, invariably, that my destination was 'only a *krosha* (two miles).' In six hours the sun travelled victoriously from horizon to meridian, but I began to feel that I would ever be distant from Ranbajpur by one *krosha*.

At midafternoon my world was still an endless paddy field. Heat pouring from the avoidless sky was bringing me to near-collapse. As a man approached at leisurely pace, I hardly dared utter my usual question, lest it summon the monotonous: 'Just a *krosha*.'

The stranger halted beside me. Short and slight, he was physically unimpressive save for an extraordinary pair of piercing dark eyes.

"I was planning to leave Ranbajpur, but your purpose was good, so I awaited you." He shook his finger in my astounded face. "Aren't you clever to think that, unannounced, you could pounce on me? That professor Behari had no right to give you my address."

---

1 Hand-played drums, used exclusively for devotional music, religious ceremonies and processions.

Considering that introduction of myself would be mere verbosity in the presence of this master, I stood speechless, somewhat hurt at my reception. His next remark was abruptly put.

"Tell me; where do you think God is?"

"Why, He is within me and everywhere." I doubtless looked as bewildered as I felt.

"All-pervading, eh?" The saint chuckled. "Then why, young sir, did you fail to bow before the Infinite in the stone symbol at the Tarakeswar temple yesterday?[2] Your pride caused you the punishment of being misdirected by the passer-by who was not bothered by fine distinctions of left and right. Today, too, you have had a fairly uncomfortable time of it!"

I agreed wholeheartedly, wonder-struck that an omniscient eye hid within the unremarkable body before me. Healing strength emanated from the yogi; I was instantly refreshed in the scorching field.

"The devotee inclines to think his path to God is the only way," he said. "Yoga, through which divinity is found within, is doubtless the highest road: so Lahiri Mahasaya has told us. But discovering the Lord within, we soon perceive Him without. Holy shrines at Tarakeswar and elsewhere are rightly venerated as nuclear centres of spiritual power."

The saint's censorious attitude vanished; his eyes became compassionately soft. He patted my shoulder.

"Young yogi, I see you are running away from your master. He has everything you need; you must return to him. Mountains cannot be your guru." Ram Gopal was repeating the same thought which Sri Yukteswar had expressed at our last meeting.

"Masters are under no cosmic compulsion to limit their residence." My companion glanced at me quizzically. "The Himalayas in India and Tibet have no monopoly on saints. What one does not trouble to find within will not be discovered by transporting the body hither and yon. As soon as the devotee is *willing* to go even to the ends of the earth for spiritual enlightenment, his guru appears near-by."

I silently agreed, recalling my prayer in the Benares hermitage, followed by the meeting with Sri Yukteswar in a crowded lane.

"Are you able to have a little room where you can close the door and be alone?"

"Yes." I reflected that this saint descended from the general to the particular with disconcerting speed.

"That is your cave." The yogi bestowed on me a gaze of illumination

2 One is reminded here of Dostoevsky's observation in his work: *The Possessed*: 'A man who bows down to nothing can never bear the burden of himself.'

which I have never forgotten. "That is your sacred mountain. That is where you will find the kingdom of God."

His simple words instantaneously banished my lifelong obsession for the Himalayas. In a burning paddy field I awoke from the dreams of mountains and eternal snows.

"Young sir, your divine thirst is laudable. I feel great love for you." Ram Gopal took my hand and led me to a quaint hamlet. The adobe houses were covered with coconut leaves and rustically adorned over their entrances with fresh tropical flowers.

The saint seated me on the umbrageous bamboo platform of his small cottage. After giving me sweetened limejuice and a piece of rock candy, he entered his patio and assumed the lotus posture. In about four hours I opened my meditative eyes and saw that the moonlit figure of the yogi was still motionless. As I was sternly reminding my stomach that man does not live by bread alone, Ram Gopal approached me.

"I see you are famished; food will be ready soon."

A fire was kindled under a clay oven on the patio: rice and *dhal* were quickly served on large banana leaves. My host courteously refused my aid in all cooking chores. 'The guest is God,' a Hindu proverb, has commanded devout observance from time immemorial. In my later world travels, I was charmed to see that a similar respect for visitors is manifested in rural sections of many countries. The city dweller finds the keen edge of hospitality blunted by superabundance of strange faces.

The marts of men seemed remotely dim as I squatted by the yogi in the isolation of the tiny jungle village. The cottage room was mysterious with a mellow light. Ram Gopal arranged some torn blankets on the floor for my bed, and seated himself on a straw mat. Overwhelmed by his spiritual magnetism, I ventured a request.

"Sir, why don't you grant me a *samadhi*?"

"Dear one, I would be glad to convey the divine contact, but it is not my place to do so." The saint looked at me with half-closed eyes. "Your master will bestow that experience shortly. Your body is not tuned just yet. As a small lamp cannot withstand excessive electrical voltage, so your nerves are unready for the cosmic current. If I gave you the infinite ecstasy right now, you would burn as if every cell were on fire.

"You are asking illumination from me," the yogi continued musingly, "while I am wondering – inconsiderable as I am, and with the little meditation I have done – if I have succeeded in pleasing God, and what worth I may find in His eyes at the final reckoning."

"Sir, have you not been single heartedly seeking God for a long time?"

"I have not done much. Behari must have told you something of my life. For twenty years I occupied a secret grotto, meditating eighteen hours a day. Then I moved to a more inaccessible cave and remained there for twenty-five years, entering the yoga union for twenty hours daily. I did not need sleep, for I was ever with God. My body was more rested in the complete calmness of the superconsciousness than it could be by the partial peace of the ordinary subconscious state.

"The muscles relax during sleep, but the heart, lungs, and circulatory system are constantly at work; they get no rest. In superconsciousness, the internal organs remain in a state of suspended animation, electrified by the cosmic energy. By such means I have found it unnecessary to sleep for years. The time will come when you too will dispense with sleep."

"My goodness, you have meditated for so long and yet are unsure of the Lord's favour!" I gazed at him in astonishment. "Then what about us poor mortals?"

"Well, don't you see, my dear boy, that God is Eternity Itself? To assume that one can fully know Him by forty-five years of meditation is rather a preposterous expectation. Babaji assures us, however, that even a little meditation saves one from the dire fear of death and after-death states. Do not fix your spiritual ideal on a small mountain, but hitch it to the star of unqualified divine attainment. If you work hard, you will get there."

Enthralled by the prospect, I asked him for further enlightening words. He related a wondrous story of his first meeting with Lahiri Mahasaya's guru, Babaji.[3] Around midnight Ram Gopal fell into silence, and I lay down on my blankets. Closing my eyes, I saw flashes of lightning; the vast space within me was a chamber of molten light. I opened my eyes and observed the same dazzling radiance. The room became a part of that infinite vault which I beheld with interior vision.

"Why don't you go to sleep?" the yogi said.

"Sir, how can I sleep in the presence of lightning, blazing whether my eyes are shut or open?"

"You are blessed to have this experience; the spiritual radiations are not easily seen." The saint added a few words of affection.

At dawn Ram Gopal gave me rock candies and said I must depart. I felt such reluctance to bid him farewell that tears coursed down my cheeks.

"I will not let you go empty-handed." The yogi spoke tenderly. "I will do something for you."

3 See chapter 33.

He smiled and looked at me steadfastly. I stood rooted to the ground, peace rushing like a mighty flood through the gates of my eyes. I was instantaneously healed of a pain in my back, which had troubled me intermittently for years. Renewed, bathed in a sea of luminous joy, I wept no more. After touching the saint's feet, I sauntered into the jungle, making my way through its tropical tangle until I reached Tarakeswar.

There I made a second pilgrimage to the famous shrine, and prostrated myself fully before the altar. The round stone enlarged before my inner vision until it became the cosmical spheres, ring within ring, zone after zone, all dowered with divinity.

I entrained happily an hour later for Calcutta. My travels ended, not in the lofty mountains, but in the Himalayan presence of my Master.

14. *An Experience in Cosmic Consciousness*

"I AM HERE, Guruji." My shamefacedness spoke more eloquently for me.

"Let us go to the kitchen and find something to eat." Sri Yukteswar's manner was as natural as if hours and not days had separated us.

"Master, I must have disappointed you by my abrupt departure from my duties here; I thought you might be angry with me."

"No, of course not! Wrath springs only from thwarted desires. I do not expect anything from others, so their actions cannot be in opposition to wishes of mine. I would not use you for my own ends; I am happy only in your own true happiness."

"Sir, one hears of divine love in a vague way, but for the first time I am having a concrete example in your angelic self! In the world, even a father does not easily forgive his son if he leaves his parent's business without warning. But you show not the slightest vexation, though you must have been put to great inconvenience by the many unfinished tasks I left behind."

We looked into each other's eyes, where tears were shining. A blissful wave engulfed me; I was conscious that the Lord, in the form of my guru, was expanding the small ardours of my heart into the incompressible reaches of cosmic love.

A few mornings later I made my way to Master's empty sitting room. I planned to meditate, but my laudable purpose was unshared by disobedient thoughts. They scattered like birds before the hunter.

"Mukunda!" Sri Yukteswar's voice sounded from a distant inner balcony.

I felt as rebellious as my thoughts. "Master always urges me to meditate," I muttered to myself. "He should not disturb me when he knows why I came to his room."

He summoned me again; I remained obstinately silent. The third time his tone held rebuke.

"Sir, I am meditating," I shouted protestingly.

"I know how you are meditating," my guru called out, "with your mind distributed like leaves in a storm! Come here to me."

Thwarted and exposed, I made my way sadly to his side.

"Poor boy, the mountains couldn't give what you wanted." Master spoke caressively, comfortingly. His calm gaze was unfathomable. "Your heart's desire shall be fulfilled."

Sri Yukteswar seldom indulged in riddles; I was bewildered. He struck gently on my chest above the heart.

My body became immovably rooted; breath was drawn out of my lungs as if by some huge magnet. Soul and mind instantly lost their physical bondage, and streamed out like a fluid piercing light from my every pore. The flesh was as though dead, yet in my intense awareness I knew that never before had I been fully alive. My sense of identity was no longer narrowly confined to a body, but embraced the circumambient atoms. People on distant streets seemed to be moving gently over my own remote periphery. The roots of plants and trees appeared through a dim transparency of the soil; I discerned the inward flow of their sap.

The whole vicinity lay bare before me. My ordinary frontal vision was now changed to a vast spherical sight, simultaneously all-perceptive. Through the back of my head I saw men strolling far down Rai Ghat Road, and noticed also a white cow who was leisurely approaching. When she reached the space in front of the open ashram gate, I observed her with my two physical eyes. As she passed by, behind the brick wall, I saw her clearly still.

All objects within my panoramic gaze trembled and vibrated like quick motion pictures. My body, Master's, the pillared courtyard, the furniture and floor, the trees and sunshine, occasionally became violently agitated, until all melted into a luminescent sea; even as sugar crystals, thrown into a glass of water, dissolve after being shaken. The unifying light alternated with materializations of form, the metamorphoses revealing the law of cause and effect in creation.

An oceanic joy broke upon calm endless shores of my soul. The Spirit of God, I realized, is exhaustless Bliss; His body is countless tissues of light. A swelling glory within me began to envelop towns, continents, the earth, solar and stellar systems, tenuous nebulae, and floating universes. The entire cosmos, gently luminous, like a city seen afar at night, glimmered within the infinitude of my being. The sharply etched global outlines faded somewhat at the farthest edges; there I could see a mellow radiance, ever-undiminished. It was indescribably subtle; the planetary pictures were formed of a grosser light.

The divine dispersion of rays poured from an Eternal Source, blazing into galaxies, transfigured with ineffable auras. Again and again I saw the creative beams condense into constellations, then resolve into sheets of transparent flame. By rhythmic reversion, sextillion worlds passed into diaphanous lustre; fire became firmament.

I cognized the centre of the empyrean as a point of intuitive perception in my heart. Irradiating splendor issued from my nucleus to every part of the universal structure. Blissful *amrita,* the nectar of immortality, pulsed through me with a quicksilver-like fluidity. The creative voice of God I heard resounding as *Aum,*[1] the vibration of the Cosmic Motor.

Suddenly the breath returned to my lungs. With a disappointment almost unbearable, I realized that my infinite immensity was lost. Once more I was limited to the humiliating cage of a body, not easily accommodative to the Spirit. Like a prodigal child, I had run away from my macrocosmic home and imprisoned myself in a narrow microcosm.

My guru was standing motionless before me; I started to drop at his holy feet in gratitude for the experience in cosmic consciousness which I had long passionately sought. He held me upright, and spoke calmly, unpretentiously.

"You must not get overdrunk with ecstasy. Much work yet remains for you in the world. Come; let us sweep the balcony floor; then we shall walk by the Ganges."

I fetched a broom; Master, I knew, was teaching me the secret of balanced living. The soul must stretch over the cosmogonic abysses, while the body performs its daily duties. When we set out later for a stroll, I was still entranced in unspeakable rapture. I saw our bodies as two astral pictures, moving over a road by the river whose essence was sheer light.

'It is the Spirit of God that actively sustains every form and force in the universe; yet He is transcendental and aloof in the blissful uncreated void beyond the worlds of vibratory phenomena,"[2] Master explained. "Saints

---

1 'In the beginning was the Word, and the Word was with God, and the Word was God.' – *John* 1: 1.

2 'For, the Father judgeth no man, but hath committed all judgment unto the Son.' – *John* 5: 22. 'No man hath seen God at any time; the only begotten Son, which is in the bosom of the Father, he hath declared him.' – *John* 1: 18. 'Verily, verily, I say unto you, he that believeth on me, the works that I do shall he do also; and greater works than these shall he do; because I go unto my Father.' – *John* 14: 12. 'But the Comforter, which is the Holy Ghost, whom the Father will send in my name, he shall teach you all things, and bring all things to your remembrance, whatsoever I have said to *you*.' – *John* 14: 26.

These Biblical words refer to the threefold nature of God as Father, Son, Holy Ghost (*Sat, Tat, Aum* in the Hindu scriptures). God the Father is the Absolute, Unmanifested, existing *beyond* vibratory creation. God the Son is the Christ Consciousness (Brahma or *Kutastha Chaitanya*) existing *within* vibratory creation; this Christ Consciousness is the 'only begotten' or sole reflection of the Uncreated Infinite. Its outward manifestation or 'witness' is *Aum* or Holy Ghost, the divine, creative, invisible power which structures all creation through vibration. *Aum* the blissful Comforter is heard in meditation and reveals to the devotee the ultimate Truth, bringing 'all things to.... remembrance.'

who realize their divinity even while in the flesh know a similar twofold existence. Conscientiously engaging in earthly work, they yet remain immersed in an inward beatitude. The Lord has created all men from the limitless joy of His being. Though they are painfully cramped by the body, God nevertheless expects that souls made in His image shall ultimately rise above all sense identifications and reunite with Him."

The cosmic vision left many permanent lessons. By daily stilling my thoughts, I could win release from the delusive conviction that my body was a mass of flesh and bones, traversing the hard soil of matter. The breath and the restless mind, I saw, were like storms which lashed the ocean of light into waves of material forms – earth, sky, human beings, animals, birds, trees. No perception of the Infinite as One Light could be had except by calming those storms. As often as I silenced the two natural tumults, I beheld the multitudinous waves of creation melt into one lucent sea, even as the waves of the ocean, their tempests subsiding, serenely dissolve into unity.

A master bestows the divine experience of cosmic consciousness when his disciple, by meditation, has strengthened his mind to a degree where the vast vistas would not overwhelm him. The experience can never be given through one's mere intellectual willingness or open-mindedness. Only adequate enlargement by yoga practice and devotional *bhakti* can prepare the mind to absorb the liberating shock of omnipresence. It comes with a natural inevitability to the sincere devotee. His intense craving begins to pull at God with an irresistible force. The Lord, as the Cosmic Vision, is drawn by the seeker's magnetic ardour into his range of consciousness.

I wrote, in my later years, the following poem, 'Samadhi,' endeavoring to convey the glory of its cosmic state:

> Vanished the veils of light and shade,
> Lifted every vapor of sorrow,
> Sailed away all dawns of fleeting joy,
> Gone the dim sensory mirage.
> Love, hate, health, disease, life, death,
> Perished these false shadows on the screen of duality.
> Waves of laughter, scyllas of sarcasm, melancholic whirlpools,
> Melting in the vast sea of bliss.
> The storm of *maya* stilled
> By magic wand of intuition deep.
> The universe, forgotten dream, subconsciously lurks,
> Ready to invade my newly-wakened memory divine.

I live without the cosmic shadow,
But it is not, bereft of me;
As the sea exists without the waves,
But they breathe not without the sea.
Dreams, wakings, states of deep *turia*,[3] sleep,
Present, past, future, no more for me,
But ever-present, all-flowing I, I, everywhere.
Planets, stars, Stardust, earth,
Volcanic bursts of doomsday cataclysms,
Creation's moulding furnace,
Glaciers of silent x-rays, burning electron floods,
Thoughts of all men, past, present, to come,
Every blade of grass, myself, mankind,
Each particle of universal dust,
Anger, greed, good, bad, salvation, lust,
I swallowed, transmuted all
    into a vast ocean of blood of my own one Being!
Smoldering joy, oft-puffed by meditation
Blinding my tearful eyes,
Burst into immortal flames of bliss,
Consumed my tears, my frame, my all.
Thou art I, I am Thou,
Knowing, Knower, Known, as One!
Tranquilled, unbroken thrill, eternally living, ever-new peace!
Enjoyable beyond imagination of expectancy, *samadhi* bliss!
Not an unconscious state
    or mental chloroform without wilful return,
Samadhi but extends my conscious realm
    beyond limits of the mortal frame
To farthest boundary of eternity
    where I, the Cosmic Sea,
Watch the little ego floating in Me.
The sparrow, each grain of sand, fall not without My sight.
All space floats like an iceberg in My mental sea.
Colossal Container, I, of all things made.
By deeper, longer, thirsty, guru-given meditation
    comes this celestial *samadhi*.
Mobile murmurs of atoms are heard,
The dark earth, mountains, vales, lo! molten liquid!

3 The last stage of *Samadhi*.

Flowing seas change into vapors of nebulae!
Aum blows upon vapors, opening wondrously their veils,
Oceans stand revealed, shining electrons,
Till, at last sound of the cosmic drum,[4]
Vanish the grosser lights into eternal rays
    of all-pervading bliss.
From joy I came, for joy I live, in sacred joy I melt.
Ocean of mind, I drink all creation's waves.
Four veils of solid, liquid, vapor, light
    lift aright.
Myself, in everything, enters the Great Myself.
Gone forever, fitful, flickering shadows of mortal memory.
Spotless is my mental sky, below, ahead, and high above.
Eternity and I, one united ray.
A tiny bubble of laughter, I
    am become the Sea of Mirth Itself.

Sri Yukteswar taught me how to summon the blessed experience at
will, and also how to transmit it to others[5] if their intuitive channels were
developed. For months I entered the ecstatic union, comprehending why
the *Upanishads* say God is *rasa*, 'the most relishable.' One day, however,
I took a problem to Master.

"I want to know, sir – when shall I find God?"

"You have found Him."

"O no, sir, I don't think so!"

My guru was smiling. "I am sure you aren't expecting a venerable
Personage, adorning a throne in some antiseptic corner of the cosmos! I see,
however, that you are imagining that the possession of miraculous powers
is knowledge of God. One might have the whole universe, and find the
Lord elusive still! Spiritual advancement is not measured by one's outward
powers, but only by the depth of his bliss in meditation.

"*Ever-new Joy is God.* He is inexhaustible; as you continue your meditations
during the years, He will beguile you with an infinite ingenuity. Devotees like
yourself who have found the way to God never dream of exchanging Him for
any other happiness; He is seductive beyond thought of competition.

"How quickly we weary of earthly pleasures! Desire for material things is
endless; man is never satisfied completely, and pursues one goal after another.
The 'something else' he seeks is the Lord, who alone can grant lasting joy.

4 *Aum*, the creative vibration that externalizes all creations.
5 I have transmitted the Cosmic Vision to many *Kriya Yogis* in East and West. One of them, Mr. James
    J. Lynn, is shown in a *samadhi* in a picture in this book. (on pg. 184).

"Outward longings drive us from the Eden within; they offer false pleasures which only impersonate soul-happiness. The lost paradise is quickly regained through divine meditation. As God is un-anticipatory Ever-Newness, we never tire of Him. Can we be surfeited with bliss, delightfully varied throughout eternity?"

"I understand now, sir, why saints call the Lord unfathomable. Even everlasting life could not suffice to appraise Him."

"That is true; but He is also near and dear. After the mind has been cleared by *Kriya Yoga* of sensory obstacles, meditation furnishes a twofold proof of God. Ever-new joy is evidence of His existence, convincing to our very atoms. Also, in meditation one finds His instant guidance, His adequate response to every difficulty."

"I see, Guruji; you have solved my problem." I smiled gratefully. "I do realize now that I have found God, for whenever the joy of meditation has returned subconsciously during my active hours, I have been subtly directed to adopt the right course in everything, even details."

"Human life is beset with sorrow until we know how to tune in with the Divine Will, whose 'right course' is often baffling to the egoistic intelligence. God bears the burden of the cosmos; He alone can give unerring counsel; who but Him bears the burden of the Cosmos?"

15. *The Cauliflower Robbery*

'MASTER, a gift for you! These six huge cauliflowers were planted with my hands; I have watched over their growth with the tender care of a mother nursing her child." I presented the basket of vegetables with a ceremonial flourish.

"Thank you!" Sri Yukteswar's smile was warm with appreciation. "Please keep them in your room; I shall need them tomorrow for a special dinner."

I had just arrived in Puri[1] to spend my college summer vacation with my guru at his seaside hermitage. Built by Master and his disciples, the cheerful little two-storied retreat fronts on the Bay of Bengal.

I awoke early the following morning, refreshed by the salty sea breezes and the charm of my surroundings. Sri Yukteswar's melodious voice was calling; I took a look at my cherished cauliflowers and stowed them neatly under my bed.

---

1 Puri, about 310 miles south of Calcutta, is a famous pilgrimage city for devotees of Krishna; His worship is celebrated there with two immense annual festivals, *Snanayatra* and *Rathayatra*. Lord Krishna is called here as *Jagannath*.

"Come, let us go to the beach." Master led the way; several young disciples and myself followed in a scattered group. Our guru surveyed us in mild criticism.

"When our Western brothers walk, they usually take pride in unison. Now, please march in two rows; keep rhythmic step with one another." Sri Yukteswar watched as we obeyed; he began to sing: "Boys go to and fro, in a pretty little row." I could not but admire the ease with which Master was able to match the brisk pace of his young students.

"Halt!" My guru's eyes sought mine. "Did you remember to lock the back door of the hermitage?"

"I think so, sir."

Sri Yukteswar was silent for a few minutes, a half-suppressed smile on his lips. "No, you forgot," he said finally. "Divine contemplation must not be made an excuse for material carelessness. You have neglected your duty in safeguarding the ashram; you must be punished."

I thought he was obscurely joking when he added: "Your six cauliflowers will soon be only five."

We turned around at Master's orders and marched back until we were close to the hermitage.

"Rest awhile. Mukunda, look across the compound on our left; observe the road beyond. A certain man will arrive there presently; he will be the means of your chastisement."

I concealed my vexation at these incomprehensible remarks. A peasant soon appeared on the road; he was dancing grotesquely and flinging his arms about with meaningless gestures. Almost paralyzed with curiosity, I glued my eyes on the hilarious spectacle. As the man reached a point in the road where he would vanish from our view, Sri Yukteswar said, "Now, he will return."

The peasant at once changed his direction and made for the rear of the ashram. Crossing a sandy tract, he entered the building by the back door. I had left it unlocked, even as my guru had said. The man emerged shortly, holding one of my prized cauliflowers. He now strode along respectably, invested with the dignity of possession.

The unfolding farce, in which my role appeared to be that of bewildered victim, was not so disconcerting that I failed in indignant pursuit. I was halfway to the road when Master recalled me. He was shaking from head to foot with laughter.

"That poor crazy man has been longing for a cauliflower," he explained between outbursts of mirth. "I thought it would be a good idea if he got one of yours, so ill-guarded!"

I dashed to my room, where I found that the thief, evidently one with a vegetable fixation, had left untouched my gold rings, watch, and money, all lying openly on the blanket. He had crawled instead under the bed where, completely hidden from casual sight, one of my cauliflowers had aroused his single-hearted desire.

I asked Sri Yukteswar that evening to explain the incident which had, I thought, a few baffling features.

My guru shook his head slowly. "You will understand it someday. Science will soon discover a few of these hidden laws."

When the wonders of radio burst some years later on an astounded world, I remembered Master's prediction. Age-old concepts of time and space were annihilated; no peasant's home so narrow that London or Calcutta could not enter! The dullest intelligence enlarged before indisputable proof of one aspect of man's omnipresence.

The 'plot' of the cauliflower comedy can be best understood by a radio analogy. Sri Yukteswar was a perfect human radio. Thoughts are no more than very gentle vibrations moving in the ether. Just as a sensitized radio picks up a desired musical number out of thousands of other programs from every direction, so my guru had been able to catch the thought of the half-witted man who hankered for a cauliflower, out of the countless thoughts of broadcasting human wills in the world.[2]

By his powerful will, Master was also a human broadcasting station, and had successfully directed the peasant to reverse his steps and go to a certain room for a single cauliflower.

Intuition[3] is soul guidance, appearing naturally in man during those instants when his mind is calm. Nearly everyone has had the experience of an inexplicably correct 'hunch,' or has transferred his thoughts effectively to another person.

2 The 1939 discovery of a radio microscope revealed a new world of hitherto unknown rays. 'Man himself as well as all kinds of supposedly inert matter constantly emits the rays that this instrument *sees*,' reported the *Associated Press*. 'Those who believe in telepathy, second sight, and clairvoyance, have in this announcement the first scientific proof of the existence of invisible rays which really travel from one person to another. The radio device actually is a radio frequency spectroscope. It does the same thing for cool, nonglowing matter that the spectroscope does when it discloses the kinds of atoms that make the stars. The existence of such rays coming from man and all living things has been suspected by scientists for many years. Today is the first experimental proof of their existence. The discovery shows that every atom and every molecule in nature is a continuous radio broadcasting station. . . . Thus even after death the substance that was a man continues to send out its delicate rays. The wave lengths of these rays range from shorter than anything now used in broadcasting to the longest kind of radio waves. The jumble of these rays is almost inconceivable. There are millions of them. A single very large molecule may give off 1,000,000 different wave lengths at the same time. The longer wave lengths of this sort travel with the ease and speed of radio waves. . . . There is one amazing difference between the new radio rays and familiar rays like light. This is the prolonged time, amounting to thousands of years, which these radio waves will keep on emitting from undisturbed matter.'

3 One hesitates to use 'intuition'; Hitler has almost ruined the word along with more ambitious devastations. The Latin root meaning of *intuition* is 'inner protection.' The Sanskrit word *agama* means intuitional knowledge born of direct soul-perception; hence certain ancient treatises by the rishis were called *agamas*.

The human mind, free from the static of restlessness, can perform through its antenna of intuition all the functions of complicated radio mechanisms – sending and receiving thoughts, and tuning out undesirable ones. As the power of a radio depends on the amount of electrical current it can utilize, so the human radio is energized according to the power of will possessed by each individual.

All thoughts vibrate eternally in the cosmos. By deep concentration, a master is able to detect the thoughts of any mind, living or dead. Thoughts are universally and not individually rooted; a truth cannot be created, but only perceived. The erroneous thoughts of man result from imperfections in his discernment. The goal of yoga science is to calm the mind, that without distortion it may mirror the divine vision in the universe.

Radio and television have brought the instantaneous sound and sight of remote persons to the firesides of millions: the first faint scientific intimations that man is an all-pervading spirit. Not a body confined to a point in space, but the vast soul, which the ego in most barbaric modes conspires in vain to cramp.

"Very strange, very wonderful, seemingly very improbable phenomena may yet appear which, when once established, will not astonish us more than we are now astonished at all that science has taught us during the last century," Charles Robert Richet, Nobel laureate in physiology, has declared. "It is assumed that the phenomena which we now accept without surprise, do not excite our astonishment because they are understood. But this is not the case. If they do not surprise us it is not because they are understood, it is because they are familiar; for if that which is not understood ought to surprise us, we should be surprised at everything – the fall of a stone thrown into the air, the acorn which becomes an oak, mercury which expands when it is heated, iron attracted by a magnet, phosphorus which burns when it is rubbed. . . . The science of today is a light matter; the revolutions and evolutions which it will experience in a hundred thousand years will far exceed the most daring anticipations. The truths – those surprising, amazing, unforeseen truths – which our descendants will discover, are even now all around us, staring us in the eyes, so to speak, and yet we do not see them. But it is not enough to say that we do not see them; we do not wish to see them; for as soon as an unexpected and unfamiliar fact appears, we try to fit it into the framework of the commonplaces of acquired knowledge, and we are indignant that anyone should dare to experiment further."

A humorous occurrence took place a few days after I had been so implausibly robbed of a cauliflower. A certain kerosene lamp could not be found. Having so lately witnessed my guru's omniscient insight, I thought he would demonstrate that it was child's play to locate the lamp.

Master perceived my expectation. With exaggerated gravity he questioned all ashram residents. A young disciple confessed that he had used the lamp to go to the well in the back yard.

Sri Yukteswar gave the solemn counsel: "Seek the lamp near the well."

I rushed there; no lamp! Crestfallen, I returned to my guru. He was now laughing heartily, without compunction for my disillusionment.

"Too bad I couldn't direct you to the vanished lamp; I am not a fortune teller!" With twinkling eyes, he added, "I am not even a satisfactory Sherlock Holmes!"

I realized that Master would never display his powers when challenged, or for a triviality.

Delightful weeks sped by. Sri Yukteswar was planning a religious procession. He asked me to lead the disciples over the town and beach of Puri. The festive day dawned as one of the hottest of the summer.

"Guruji, how can I take the barefooted students over the fiery sands?" I spoke despairingly.

"I will tell you a secret," Master responded. "The Lord will send an umbrella of clouds; you all shall walk in comfort."

I happily organized the procession; our group started from the ashram with a *Sat-Sanga*[4] banner. Designed by Sri Yukteswar, it bore the symbol of the single[5] eye, the telescopic gaze of intuition.

No sooner had we left the hermitage than the part of the sky which was overhead became filled with clouds as though by magic. To the accompaniment of astonished ejaculations from all sides, a very light shower fell, cooling the city streets and the burning seashore. The soothing drops descended during the two hours of the parade. The exact instant at which our group returned to the ashram, the clouds and rain passed away tracelessly.

"You see how God feels for us," Master replied after I had expressed my gratitude. "The Lord responds to all and works for all. Just as He sent rain at my plea, so He fulfills any sincere desire of the devotee. Seldom do men realize how often God heeds their prayers. He is not partial to a few, but listens to everyone who approaches Him trustingly. His children should ever have implicit faith in the loving-kindness of their Omnipresent Father."[6]

4 *Sat* is literally 'being,' hence 'essence; reality.' *Sanga* is 'association.' Sri Yukteswar called his hermitage organization *Sat-Sanga*, 'fellowship with truth.'

5 'If therefore thine eye be single, thy whole body shall be full of light.' – *Matthew* 6: 22. During deep meditation, the single or spiritual eye becomes visible within the central part of the forehead. This omniscient eye is variously referred to in scriptures as the third eye, the star of the East, the inner eye, the dove descending from heaven, the eye of Shiva, the eye of intuition, etc.

6 'He that planted the ear, shall he not hear? he that formed the eye, shall he not see? . . . he that teacheth man knowledge, shall he not know?' – *Psalms* 94: 9-10.

Sri Yukteswar sponsored four yearly festivals, at the equinoxes and solstices, when his students gathered from far and near. The winter solstice celebration was held in Serampore; the first one I attended left me with a permanent blessing.

The festivities started in the morning with a barefoot procession along the streets. The voices of a hundred students rang out with sweet religious songs; a few musicians played the flute and *khol kartal* (drums and cymbals). Enthusiastic townspeople strewed the path with flowers, glad to be summoned from prosaic tasks by our resounding praise of the Lord's blessed name. The long tour ended in the courtyard of the hermitage. There we encircled our guru, while students on upper balconies showered us with marigold blossoms.

Many guests went upstairs to receive a pudding of *channa* and oranges. I made my way to a group of brother disciples who were serving today as cooks. Food for such large gatherings had to be cooked outdoors in huge cauldrons. The improvised wood-burning brick stoves were smoky and tear provoking, but we laughed merrily at our work. Religious festivals in India are never considered troublesome; each one does his part, supplying money, rice, vegetables, or his personal services.

Master was soon in our midst, supervising the details of the feast. Busy every moment, he kept pace with the most energetic young student.

A *sankirtan* (group chanting), accompanied by the harmonium and hand-played Indian drums, was in progress on the second floor. Sri Yukteswar listened appreciatively; his musical sense was acutely perfect.

"They are off key!" Master left the cooks and joined the artists. The melody was heard again, this time correctly rendered.

In India, music as well as painting and the drama is considered a divine art. Brahma, Vishnu, and Shiva – the Eternal Trinity – were the first musicians. The Divine Dancer Shiva is scripturally represented as having worked out the infinite modes of rhythm in His cosmic dance of universal creation, preservation, and dissolution, while Brahma accentuated the time-beat with the clanging cymbals, and Vishnu sounded the holy *mridanga* or drum. Krishna, an incarnation of Vishnu, is always shown in Hindu art with a flute, on which he plays the enrapturing song that recalls to their true home the human souls wandering in *maya*-delusion. Saraswati, goddess of wisdom, is symbolized as performing on the *vina*, mother of all stringed instruments. The *Sama Veda* of India contains the world's earliest writings on musical science.

The foundation stone of Hindu music is the *ragas* or fixed melodic scales. The six basic *ragas* branch out into 126 derivative *raginis* (wives) and *putras* (sons). Each *raga* has a minimum of five notes: a leading note (*vadi* or king), a secondary note (*samavadi* or prime minister), helping notes (*anuvadi*, attendants), and a dissonant note (*vivadi*, the enemy).

Each one of the six basic *ragas* has a natural correspondence with a certain hour of the day, season of the year, and a presiding deity who bestows a particular potency. Thus, (1) the *Hindole Raga* is heard only at dawn in the spring, to evoke the mood of universal love; (2) *Deepaka Raga* is played during the evening in summer, to arouse compassion; (3) *Megha Raga* is a melody for midday in the rainy season, to summon courage; (4) *Bhairava Raga* is played in the mornings of August, September, October, to achieve tranquillity; (5) *Sri Raga* is reserved for autumn twilights, to attain pure love; (6) *Malkounsa Raga* is heard at midnights in winter, for valour.

The ancient rishis discovered these laws of sound alliance between nature and man. Because nature is an objectification of *Aum*, the Primal Sound or Vibratory Word, man can obtain control over all natural manifestations through the use of certain *mantras* or chants.[7] Historical documents tell of the remarkable powers possessed by Miyan Tansen, sixteenth century court musician for Akbar the Great. Commanded by the Emperor to sing a night *raga* while the sun was overhead, Tansen intoned a *mantra* which instantly caused the whole palace precincts to become enveloped in darkness.

Indian music divides the octave into 22 *srutis* or demi-semitones. These microtonal intervals permit fine shades of musical expression unattainable by the Western chromatic scale of 12 semitones. Each one of the seven basic notes of the octave is associated in Hindu mythology with a colour, and the natural cry of a bird or beast – *Do* with green, and the peacock; *Re* with red, and the skylark; *Mi* with golden, and the goat; *Fa* with yellowish white, and the heron; *Sol* with black, and the nightingale; *La* with yellow, and the horse; *Si* with a combination of all colours, and the elephant.

Three scales – major, harmonic minor, melodic minor – are the only ones which Occidental music employs, but Indian music outlines 72 *thatas* or scales. The musician has a creative scope for endless improvisation around the fixed traditional melody or *raga;* he concentrates on the sentiment or

---

7 Folklore of all peoples contains references to incantations with power over nature. The American Indians are well-known to have developed sound rituals for rain and wind. Tansen, the great Hindu musician, was able to quench fire by the power of his song. Charles Kellogg, the California naturalist, gave a demonstration of the effect of tonal vibration on fire in 1926 before a group of New York firemen. 'Passing a bow, like an enlarged violin bow, swiftly across an aluminum tuning fork, he produced a screech like intense radio static. Instantly the yellow gas flame, two feet high, leaping inside a hollow glass tube, subsided to a height of six inches and became a sputtering blue flare. Another attempt with the bow, and another screech of vibration, extinguished it.'

definitive mood of the structural theme and then embroiders it to the limits of his own originality. The Hindu musician does not read set notes; he clothes anew at each playing the bare skeleton of the *raga*, often confining himself to a single melodic sequence, stressing by repetition all its subtle microtonal and rhythmic variations. Bach, among Western composers, had an understanding of the charm and power of repetitious sound slightly differentiated in a hundred complex ways.

Ancient Sanskrit literature describes 120 *talas* or time-measures. The traditional founder of Hindu music, Bharata, is said to have isolated 32 kinds of *tala* in the song of a lark. The origin of *tala* or rhythm is rooted in human movements – the double time of walking, and the triple time of respiration in sleep, when inhalation is twice the length of exhalation. India has always recognized the human voice as the most perfect instrument of sound. Hindu music therefore largely confines itself to the voice range of three octaves. For the same reason, melody (relation of successive notes) is stressed, rather than harmony (relation of simultaneous notes).

The deeper aim of the early rishi-musicians was to blend the singer with the Cosmic Song which can be heard through awakening of man's occult spinal centres.[8] Indian music is a subjective, spiritual, and individualistic art, aiming not at symphonic brilliance but at personal harmony with the Over-Soul. The Sanskrit word for musician is *bhagavathar*, "he who sings the praises of God." The *sankirtans* or musical gatherings are an effective form of yoga or spiritual discipline, necessitating deep concentration, intense absorption in the seed thought and sound. Because man himself is an expression of the Creative Word, sound has the most potent and immediate effect on him, offering a way to remembrance of his divine origin.

The *sankirtan* issuing from Sri Yukteswar's second-story sitting room on the day of the festival was inspiring to the cooks amidst the steaming pots. My brother disciples and I joyously sang the refrains, beating time with our hands.

By sunset we had served our hundreds of visitors with *khichuri* (rice and lentils), vegetable curry, and rice pudding. We laid cotton blankets over the courtyard; soon the assemblage was squatting under the starry vault, quietly attentive to the wisdom pouring from Sri Yukteswar's lips. His public

8 The awakening of the occult cerebrospinal centres (*chakras,* astral lotuses) is the sacred goal of the yogi. There are seven lotuses ('trap doors') of light, in the cerebrospinal axis through which the yogi exits by scientific meditation to escape from the bodily prison, and resumes his true identity as Spirit. (see chapter 26). The seventh centre, the 'thousand-petaled lotus' in the brain, is the throne of the Infinite Conciousness. In Divine illumination the yogi percives God as *Padmaja* 'the One born of the Lotus'.

speeches emphasized the value of *Kriya Yoga*, and a life of self-respect, calmness, determination, simple diet, and regular exercise.

A group of very young disciples then chanted a few sacred hymns; the meeting concluded with *sankirtan*. From ten o'clock until midnight, the ashram residents washed pots and pans, and cleared the courtyard. My guru called me to his side.

"I am pleased over your cheerful labours today and during the past week of preparations. I want you with me; you may sleep in my bed tonight."

This was a privilege I had never thought would fall to my lot. We sat awhile in a state of intense divine tranquillity. Hardly ten minutes after we had gotten into bed, Master rose and began to dress.

"What is the matter, sir?" I felt a tinge of unreality in the unexpected joy of sleeping beside my guru.

"I think that a few students who missed their proper train connections will be here soon. Let us have some food ready."

"Guruji, no one would come at one o'clock in the morning!"

"Stay in bed; you have been working very hard. But I am going to cook."

At Sri Yukteswar's resolute tone, I jumped up and followed him to the small daily-used kitchen adjacent to the second-floor inner balcony. Rice and *dhal* were soon boiling.

My guru smiled affectionately. "Tonight you have conquered fatigue and fear of hard work; you shall never be bothered by them in the future."

As he uttered this lifelong blessing, footsteps sounded in the courtyard. I ran downstairs and admitted a group of students.

"Dear brother, how reluctant we are to disturb Master at this hour!" One man addressed me apologetically. "We made a mistake about train schedules, but felt we could not return home without a glimpse of our guru."

"He has been expecting you and is now preparing your food."

Sri Yukteswar's welcoming voice rang out; I led the astonished visitors to the kitchen. Master turned to me with twinkling eyes.

"Now that you have finished comparing notes, no doubt you are satisfied that our guests really did miss their train!"

I followed him to his bedroom a half hour later, realizing fully that I was about to sleep beside a godlike guru.

* * *

16. *Outwitting the Stars*

"MUKUNDA, why don't you get an astrological armlet?"

"Should I, Master? I don't believe in astrology."

"It is never a question of *belief;* the only scientific attitude one can take on any subject is whether it is *true.* The law of gravitation worked as efficiently before Newton as after him. The cosmos would be fairly chaotic if its laws could not operate without the sanction of human belief.

"Charlatans have brought the stellar science to its present state of disrepute. Astrology is too vast, both mathematically[1] and philosophically, to be rightly grasped except by men of profound understanding. If ignoramuses misread the heavens, and see there a scrawl instead of a script, that is to be expected in this imperfect world. One should not dismiss the wisdom with the 'wise.'

"All parts of creation are linked together and interchange their influences. The balanced rhythm of the universe is rooted in reciprocity," my guru continued. "Man, in his human aspect, has to combat two sets of forces – first, the tumults within his being, caused by the admixture of earth, water, fire, air, and ethereal elements; second, the outer disintegrating powers of nature. So long as man struggles with his mortality, he is affected by the myriad mutations of heaven and earth.

"Astrology is the study of man's response to planetary stimuli. The stars have no conscious benevolence or animosity; they merely send forth positive and negative radiations. Of themselves, these do not help or harm humanity, but offer a lawful channel for the outward operation of cause-effect equilibriums which each man has set into motion in the past.

"A child is born on that day and at that hour when the celestial rays are in mathematical harmony with his individual karma. His horoscope is a challenging portrait, revealing his unalterable past and its probable future results. But the natal chart can be rightly interpreted only by men of intuitive wisdom: these are few.

1 From astronomical references in ancient Hindu scriptures, scholars have been able to correctly ascertain the dates of the authors. The scientific knowledge of the rishis was very great; in the *Kaushitaki Brahmana* we find precise astronomical passages which show that in 3100 B.C. the Hindus were far advanced in astronomy, which had a practical value in determining the auspicious times for astrological ceremonies. In an article in *East-West,* February, 1934, the following summary is given of the *Jyotish* or body of Vedic astronomical treatises: 'It contains the scientific lore which kept India at the forefront of all ancient nations and made her the mecca of seekers after knowledge. The very ancient *Brahmagupta,* one of the *Jyotish* works, is an astronomical treatise dealing with such matters as the heliocentric motion of the planetary bodies in our solar system, the obliquity of the ecliptic, the earth's spherical form, the reflected light of the moon, the earth's daily axial revolution, the presence of fixed stars in the Milky Way, the law of gravitation, and other scientific facts which did not dawn in the Western world until the time of Copernicus and Newton.'

It is now well-known that the so-called 'Arabic numerals,' without whose symbols advanced mathematics is difficult, came to Europe in the 9th century, via the Arabs, from India, where that system of notation had been anciently formulated. Further light on India's vast scientific heritage will be found in Dr. P. C. Ray's *History of Hindu Chemistry,* and in Dr. B. N. Seal's *Positive Sciences of the Ancient Hindus.*

"The message boldly blazoned across the heavens at the moment of birth is not meant to emphasize fate – the result of past good and evil – but to arouse man's will to escape from his universal thralldom. What he has done, he can undo. None other than himself was the instigator of the causes of whatever effects are now prevalent in his life. He can overcome any limitation, because he created it by his own actions in the first place, and because he has spiritual resources which are not subject to planetary pressure.

"Superstitious awe of astrology makes one an automaton, slavishly dependent on mechanical guidance. The wise man defeats his planets – which is to say, his past – by transferring his allegiance from the creation to the Creator. The more he realizes his unity with Spirit, the less he can be dominated by matter. The soul is ever free; it is deathless because birthless. It cannot be regimented by stars.

"Man *is* a soul, and *has* a body. When he properly places his sense of identity, he leaves behind all compulsive patterns. So long as he remains confused in his ordinary state of spiritual amnesia, he will know the subtle fetters of environmental law.

"God is harmony; the devotee who attunes himself will never perform any action amiss. His activities will be correctly and naturally timed to accord with astrological law. After deep prayer and meditation he is in touch with his divine consciousness; there is no greater power than that inward protection."

"Then, dear Master, why do you want me to wear an astro-logical bangle?" I ventured this question after a long silence, during which I had tried to assimilate Sri Yukteswar's noble exposition.

"It is only when a traveller has reached his goal that he is justified in discarding his maps. During the journey, he takes advantage of any convenient short cut. The ancient rishis discovered many ways to curtail the period of man's exile in delusion. There are certain mechanical features in the law of karma which can be skillfully adjusted by the fingers of wisdom.

"All human ills arise from some transgression of universal law. The scriptures point out that man must satisfy the laws of nature, while not discrediting the divine omnipotence. He should say: 'Lord, I trust in Thee, and know Thou canst help me, but I too will do my best to undo any wrong I have done.' By a number of means – by prayer, by will-power, by yoga meditation, by consultation with saints, by use of astrological bangles – the adverse effects of past wrongs can be minimized or nullified.

"Just as a house can be fitted with a copper rod to absorb the shock of lightning, so the bodily temple can be benefited by various protective measures. Ages ago our yogis discovered that pure metals emit an astral light which is powerfully counteractive to negative pulls of the planets. Subtle electrical and magnetic radiations are constantly circulating in the universe; when a man's body is being aided, he does not know it; when it is being disintegrated, he is still in ignorance. Can he do anything about it?

"This problem received attention from our rishis; they found helpful not only a combination of metals, but also of plants and – most effective of all – faultless jewels of not less than two carats. The preventive uses of astrology have seldom been seriously studied outside of India. One little-known fact is that the proper jewels, metals, or plant preparations are valueless unless the required weight is secured, and unless these remedial agents are worn next to the skin."

"Sir, of course I shall take your advice and get a bangle. I am intrigued at the thought of outwitting a planet!"

"For general purposes I counsel the use of an armlet made of gold, silver, and copper. But for a specific purpose I want you to get one of silver and lead." Sri Yukteswar added careful directions.

"Guruji, what 'specific purpose' do you mean?"

"The stars are about to take an unfriendly interest in you, Mukunda. Fear not; you shall be protected. In about a month your liver will cause you much trouble. The illness is scheduled to last for six months, but your use of an astrological armlet will shorten the period to twenty-four days."

I sought out a jeweler the next day, and was soon wearing the bangle. My health was excellent; Master's prediction slipped from my mind. He left Serampore to visit Benares. Thirty days after our conversation, I felt a sudden pain in the region of my liver. The following weeks were a nightmare of excruciating pain. Reluctant to disturb my guru, I thought I would bravely endure my trial alone.

But twenty-three days of torture weakened my resolution; I entrained for Benares. There Sri Yukteswar greeted me with unusual warmth, but gave me no opportunity to tell him my woes in private. Many devotees visited Master that day, just for a *darshan*.[2] Ill and neglected, I sat in a corner. It was not until after the evening meal that all guests had departed. My guru summoned me to the octagonal balcony of the house.

"You must have come about your liver disorder." Sri Yukteswar's gaze was averted; he walked to and fro, occasionally intercepting the moonlight. "Let me see; you have been ailing for twenty-four days, haven't you?"

"Yes, sir."

"Please do the stomach exercise I have taught you."

2 The blessing which flows from the mere sight of a saint.

"If you knew the extent of my suffering, Master, you would not ask me to exercise." Nevertheless I made a feeble attempt to obey him.

"You say you have pain; I say you have none. How can such contradictions exist?" My guru looked at me inquiringly.

I was dazed and then overcome with joyful relief. No longer could I feel the continuous torment that had kept me nearly sleepless for weeks; at Sri Yukteswar's words the agony vanished as though it had never been.

I started to kneel at his feet in gratitude, but he quickly prevented me.

"Don't be childish. Get up and enjoy the beauty of the moon over the Ganges." But Master's eyes were twinkling happily as I stood in silence beside him. I understood by his attitude that he wanted me to feel that not he, but God, had been the Healer.

I wear even now the heavy silver and lead bangle, a memento of that day – long-past, ever-cherished – when I found anew that I was living with a personage indeed superhuman. On later occasions, when I brought my friends to Sri Yukteswar for healing, he invariably recommended jewels or the bangle, extolling their use as an act of astrological wisdom.

I had been prejudiced against astrology from my childhood, partly because I observed that many people are sequaciously attached to it, and partly because of a prediction made by our family astrologer: "You will marry three times, being twice a widower." I brooded over the matter, feeling like a goat awaiting sacrifice before the temple of triple matrimony.

"You may as well be resigned to your fate," my brother Ananta had remarked. "Your written horoscope has correctly stated that you would fly from home toward the Himalayas during your early years, but would be forcibly returned. The forecast of your marriages is also bound to be true."

A clear intuition came to me one night that the prophecy was wholly false. I set fire to the horoscope scroll, placing the ashes in a paper bag on which I wrote: "Seeds of past karma cannot germinate if they are roasted in the divine fires of wisdom." I put the bag in a conspicuous spot; Ananta immediately read my defiant comment.

"You cannot destroy truth as easily as you have burnt this paper scroll." My brother laughed scornfully.

It is a fact that on three occasions before I reached manhood, my family tried to arrange my betrothal. Each time I refused to fall in with the plans,[3] knowing that my love for God was more overwhelming than any astrological persuasion from the past.

3 One of the girls whom my family selected as a possible bride for me, afterwards married my cousin, Prabhas Chandra Ghosh. (Sri Ghosh later became Vice-President of YSS of India. He passed away on January 24, 1975).

"The deeper the self-realization of a man, the more he influences the whole universe by his subtle spiritual vibrations, and the less he himself is affected by the phenomenal flux." These words of Master's often returned inspiringly to my mind.

Occasionally I told astrologers to select my worst periods, according to planetary indications, and I would still accomplish whatever task I set myself. It is true that my success at such times has been accompanied by extraordinary difficulties. But my conviction has always been justified: faith in the divine protection, and the right use of man's God-given will, are forces more formidable than are influences flowing from the heavens.

The starry inscription at one's birth, I came to understand, is not that man is a puppet of his past. Its message is rather a prod to pride; the very heavens seek to arouse man's determination to be free from every limitation. God created each man as a soul, dowered with individuality, hence essential to the universal structure, whether in the temporary role of pillar or parasite. His freedom is final and immediate, if he so wills; it depends not on outer but inner victories.

Sri Yukteswar discovered the mathematical application of a 24,000-year equinoctial cycle to our present age.[4] The cycle is divided into an Ascending Arc and a Descending Arc, each of 12,000 years. Within each Arc fall four *Yugas* or Ages, called *Kali, Dwapara, Treta,* and *Satya,* corresponding to the Greek ideas of Iron, Bronze, Silver, and Golden Ages.

My guru determined by various calculations that the last *Kali Yuga* or Iron Age, of the Ascending Arc, started about AD. 500. The Iron Age, 1200 years in duration, is a span of materialism; it ended about A.D. 1700. That year ushered in *Dwapara Yuga,* a 2400-year period of electrical and atomic-energy developments, the age of telegraph, radio, airplanes, and other space-annihilators.

The 3600-year period of *Treta Yuga* will start in A.D. 4100; its age will be marked by common knowledge of telepathic communications and other time-annihilators. During the 4800 years of *Satya Yuga*, final age in an ascending arc, the intelligence of a man will be completely developed; he will work in harmony with the divine plan.

A descending arc of 12,000 years, starting with a descending Golden Age of 4800 years, then begins[5] for the world; man gradually sinks into ignorance. These cycles are the eternal rounds of *maya*, the contrasts and

4 A series of thirteen articles on the historical verification of Sri Yukteswar's *Yuga* theory appeared in the magazine *East-West* (Los Angeles) from September, 1932, to September, 1933.
5 In the year 12,500 A.D.

relativities of the phenomenal universe,[6] Man, one by one, escapes from creation's prison of duality as he awakens to consciousness of his inseverable divine unity with the Creator.

Master enlarged my understanding not only of astrology but of the world's scriptures. Placing the holy texts on the spotless table of his mind, he was able to dissect them with the scalpel of intuitive reasoning, and to separate errors and interpolations of scholars from the truths as originally expressed by the prophets.

"Fix one's vision on the end of the nose." This inaccurate interpretation of a *Bhagavad Gita* stanza,[7] widely accepted by Eastern pundits and Western translators, used to arouse Master's droll criticism.

"The path of a yogi is singular enough as it is," he remarked. "Why counsel him that he must also make himself cross-eyed? The true meaning of *nasikagram* is 'origin of the nose,' not 'end of the nose.' The nose begins at the point between the two eyebrows, the seat of spiritual vision."[8]

Because of one *Sankhya*[9] aphorism, *"Iswar-ashidha,"* – "A Lord of Creation cannot be deduced" or "God is not proved,"[10] – many scholars call the whole philosophy atheistical.

"The verse is not atheistical," Sri Yukteswar explained. "It merely signifies that to the unenlightened man, dependent on his senses for all final judgments, proof of God must remain unknown and therefore non-existent. True *Sankhya* followers, with unshakable insight born of meditation, understand that the Lord is both existent and knowable."

Master expounded the Christian Bible with a beautiful clarity. It was from my Hindu guru, unknown to the roll call of Christian membership, that

6 The Hindu scriptures place the present world-age as occurring within the *Kali Yuga* of a much longer universal cycle than the simple 24,000-year equinoctial cycle with which Sri Yukteswar was concerned. The universal cycle of the scriptures is 4,300,560,000 years in extent, and measures out a Day of Creation or the length of life assigned to our planetary system in its present form. This vast figure given by the rishis is based on a relationship between the length of the solar year and a multiple of Pi (3.1416, the ratio of the circumference to the diameter of a circle).

The life span for a whole universe, according to the ancient seers, is 314,159,000,000,000 solar years, or 'One Age of Brahma.' Scientists estimate the present age of the earth to be about two billion years, basing their conclusions on a study of lead pockets left as a result of radioactivity in rocks. The Hindu scriptures declare that an earth such as ours is dissolved for one of two reasons: the inhabitants as a whole become either completely good or completely evil. The world-mind thus generates a power which releases the captive atoms held together as an earth.

Dire pronouncements are occasionally published regarding an imminent 'end of the world.' The latest prediction of doom was given by Rev. Chas. G. Long of Pasadena, who publicly set the 'Day of Judgment' for Sept. 21, 1945. *United Press* reporters asked my opinion; I explained that world cycles follow an orderly progression according to a divine plan. No earthly dissolution is in sight; two billion years of ascending and descending equinoctial cycles are yet in store for our planet in its present form. The figures given by the rishis for the various world ages deserve careful study in the West; the magazine *Time* (Dec. 17, 1945, page 6) called them 'reassuring statistics.'

7. *Bhagavad Gita* Chapter VI: 13.

8 The light of the body is the eye: therefore when thine eye is single, thy whole body also is full of light; but when thine eye is evil, thy body also is full of darkness. Take heed therefore that the light which is in thee be not darkness – *Luke* 11: 34-35.

9 One of the six systems of Hindu philosophy. *Sankhya* teaches final emancipation through knowledge of twenty-five principles, starting with *prakriti* or nature and ending with *purusha* or soul.

10 *Sankhya Aphorisms*, I: 92.

I learned to perceive the deathless essence of the Bible, and to understand the truth in Christ's assertion – surely the most thrillingly intransigent ever uttered: "Heaven and earth shall pass away, but my words shall not pass away."[11]

The great masters of India mould their lives by the same godly ideals which animated Jesus; these men are his proclaimed kin: "Whosoever shall do the will of my Father which is in heaven, the same is my brother, and sister, and mother."[12] "If ye continue in my word," Christ pointed out, "then are ye my disciples indeed; and ye shall know the truth, and the truth shall make you free."[13] Freemen all, lords of themselves, the Yogi-Christs of India are part of the immortal fraternity: those who have attained a liberating knowledge of the One Father.

"The Adam and Eve story is incomprehensible to me!" I observed with considerable heat one day in my early struggles with the allegory. "Why did God punish not only the guilty pair, but also the innocent unborn generations?"

Master was more amused by my vehemence than my ignorance. "*Genesis* is deeply symbolic, and cannot be grasped by a literal interpretation," he explained. "Its 'tree of life' is the human body. The spinal cord is like an upturned tree, with man's hair as its roots, and afferent and efferent nerves as branches. The tree of the nervous system bears many enjoyable fruits, or sensations of sight, sound, smell, taste, and touch. In these, man may rightfully indulge; but he was forbidden the experience of sex, the 'apple' at the centre of the bodily garden.[14]

"The 'serpent' is the coiled-up spinal energy which stimulates the sex nerves. 'Adam' is reason, and 'Eve' is feeling. When the emotion or Eve-consciousness in human beings is overpowered by the sex impulse, his reason or Adam also succumbs.[15]

"God created the human species by materializing the bodies of man and woman through the force of His will; He endowed the new species with the power to create children in a similar 'immaculate' or divine manner.[16] Because His manifestation in the individualized soul had hitherto been limited to animals, instinct-bound and lacking the potentialities of full

---

11 *Matthew* 24: 35.   12 *Matthew* 12: 50.

13 *John* 8: 31-32. St. John testified: "But as many as received him, to them gave he power to become the sons of God, even to them that believe on his name (even to them who are established in the Christ Consciousness)." – *John* 1: 12.

14 We may eat of the fruit of the trees of the garden: but of the fruit of the tree which is in the midst of the garden, God hath said, Ye shall not eat of it, neither shall ye touch it, lest ye die." – *Genesis* 3: 2-3.

15 'The woman whom thou gavest to be with me, she gave me of the tree, and I did eat. The woman said, The serpent beguiled me, and *I did* eat.' – *Genesis* 3: 12-13.

16 'So God created man *in his* own image, in the image of God created he him; male and female created he them. And God blessed them, and God said unto them, Be fruitful and multiply, and replenish the earth, and subdue it.' – *Genesis* 1: 27-28.

reason, God made the first human bodies; symbolically called Adam and Eve. To these, for advantageous upward evolution, He transferred the souls or divine essence of two animals.[17] In Adam or man, reason predominated; in Eve or woman, feeling was ascendant. Thus was expressed the duality or polarity which underlies the phenomenal worlds. Reason and feeling remain in a heaven of cooperative joy so long as the human mind is not tricked by the serpentine energy of animal propensities.

"The human body was therefore not solely a result of evolution from beasts, but was produced by an act of special creation by God. The animal forms were too crude to express full divinity; the human being was uniquely given a tremendous mental capacity – the 'thousand-petaled lotus' of the brain – as well as acutely awakened occult centres in the spine.

"God, or the Divine Consciousness present within the first created pair, counseled them to enjoy all human sensibilities, but not to put their concentration on touch sensations.[18] These were banned in order to avoid the development of the sex organs, which would enmesh humanity in the inferior animal method of propagation. The warning not to revive subconsciously-present bestial memories was not heeded. Resuming the way of brute procreation, Adam and Eve fell from the state of heavenly joy natural to the original perfect man.

"Knowledge of 'good and evil' refers to the cosmic dualistic compulsion. Falling under the sway of *maya* through misuse of his feeling and reason, or Eve – and Adam – consciousness, man relinquishes his right to enter the heavenly garden of divine self-sufficiency.[19] The personal responsibility of every human being is to restore his 'parents' or dual nature to a unified harmony or Eden."

As Sri Yukteswar ended his discourse, I glanced with new respect at the pages of *Genesis*.

"Dear Master," I said, "for the first time I feel a proper filial obligation toward Adam and Eve!"[20]

---

17 'And the Lord God formed man of the dust of the ground, and breathed into his nostrils the breath of life; and man became a living soul.' – *Genesis* 2: 7.

18 'Now the serpent (sex force) was more subtil than any beast of the field,' (any other sense of the body). – *Genesis* 3: 1.

19 'And the Lord God planted a garden eastward in Eden; and there he put the man whom he had formed.' – *Genesis* 2: 8. 'Therefore the Lord God sent him forth from the garden of Eden, to till the ground from whence he was taken.' – *Genesis* 3: 23. The divine man first made by God had his consciousness centred in the omnipotent single eye in the forehead (eastward). The all-creative powers of his will, focused at that spot, were lost to man when he began to 'till the ground' of his physical nature.

20 Understanding karma and its corollary reincarnation appears in numerous Biblical passages: e.g., 'Whoso sheddeth man's blood, by man shall his blood be shed.' (*Genesis* 9: 6) The early Christian church accepted the doctrine of reincarnation. It was first declared a heresy in A.D. 553. The 'Adam and Eve' story of the Hindus is recounted in the hoary *purana, Srimad Bhagavata*. (See also Note 2 on page 246).

17. *Sasi and the Three Sapphires*

"BECAUSE YOU and my son think so highly of Swami Sri Yukteswar, I will take a look at him." The tone of voice used by Dr. Narayan Chunder Roy implied that he was humouring the whim of half-wits. I concealed my indignation, in the best traditions of the proselyter.

My companion, a veterinary surgeon, was a confirmed agnostic. His young son Santosh had implored me to take an interest in his father. So far my invaluable aid had been a bit on the invisible side.

Dr. Roy accompanied me the following day to the Serampore hermitage. After Master had granted him a brief interview, marked for the most part by stoic silence on both sides, the visitor brusquely departed.

"Why bring a dead man to the ashram?" Sri Yukteswar looked at me inquiringly as soon as the door had closed on the Calcutta skeptic.

"Sir! The doctor is very much alive!"

"But in a short time he will be dead."

I was shocked. "Sir, this will be a terrible blow to his son. Santosh yet hopes for time to change his father's materialistic views. I beseech you, Master, to help the man."

"Very well; for your sake." My guru's face was impassive. "The proud horse doctor is far gone in diabetes, although he does not know it. In fifteen days he will take to his bed. The physicians will give him up for lost; his natural time to leave this earth is six weeks from today. Due to your intercession, however, on that date he will recover. But there is one condition. You must get him to wear an astrological bangle; he will doubtless object as violently as one of his horses before an operation!" Master chuckled.

After a silence, during which I wondered how Santosh and I could best employ the arts of cajolery on the recalcitrant doctor, Sri Yukteswar made further disclosures.

"As soon as the man gets well, advise him not to eat meat. He will not heed this counsel, however, and in six months, just as he is feeling at his best, he will drop dead. Even that six-month extension of life is granted him only because of your plea."

The following day I suggested to Santosh that he order an armlet at the jeweler's. It was ready in a week, but Dr. Roy refused to put it on.

"I am in the best of health. You will never impress me with these astrological superstitions." The doctor glanced at me belligerently.

I recalled with amusement that Master had justifiably compared the man to a balky horse. Another seven days passed; the doctor, suddenly ill, meekly consented to wear the bangle. Two weeks later the physician in attendance told me that his patient's case was hopeless. He supplied harrowing details of the ravages inflicted by diabetes.

I shook my head. "My guru has said that, after a sickness lasting one month, Dr. Roy will be well."

The physician stared at me incredulously. But he sought me out a fortnight later, with an apologetic air.

"Dr. Roy has made a complete recovery!" he exclaimed. "It is the most amazing case in my experience. Never before have I seen a dying man show such an inexplicable comeback. Your guru must indeed be a healing prophet!"

After one interview with Dr. Roy, during which I repeated Sri Yukteswar's advice about a meatless diet, I did not see the man again for six months. He stopped for a chat one evening as I sat on the piazza of my family home on Gurpar Road.

"Tell your teacher that by eating meat frequently, I have wholly regained my strength. His unscientific ideas on diet have not influenced me." It was true that Dr. Roy looked a picture of health.

But the next day Santosh came running to me from his home on the next block. "This morning Father dropped dead!"

This case was one of my strangest experiences with Master. He healed the rebellious veterinary surgeon in spite of his disbelief, and extended the man's natural term on earth by six months, just because of my earnest supplication. Sri Yukteswar was boundless in his kindness when confronted by the urgent prayer of a devotee.

It was my proudest privilege to bring college friends to meet my guru. Many of them would lay aside – at least in the ashram! – their fashionable academic cloak of religious skepticism.

One of my friends, Sasi, spent a number of happy week-ends in Serampore. Master became immensely fond of the boy, and lamented that his private life was wild and disorderly.

"Sasi, unless you reform, one year hence you will be dangerously ill." Sri Yukteswar gazed at my friend with affectionate exasperation. "Mukunda is the witness: don't say later that I didn't warn you."

Sasi laughed. "Master, I will leave it to you to interest a sweet charity of cosmos in my own sad case! My spirit is willing but my will is weak. You are my only savior on earth; I believe in nothing else."

"At least you should wear a two-carat blue sapphire. It will help you."

"I can't afford one. Anyhow, dear guruji, if trouble comes, I fully believe you will protect me."

"In a year you will bring three sapphires," Sri Yukteswar replied cryptically. "They will be of no use then."

Variations on this conversation took place regularly. "I can't reform!" Sasi would say in comical despair. "And my trust in you, Master, is more precious to me than any stone!"

A year later I was visiting my guru at the Calcutta home of his disciple, Naren Babu. About ten o'clock in the morning, as Sri Yukteswar and I were sitting quietly in the second-floor parlour, I heard the front door open. Master straightened stiffly.

"It is that Sasi," he remarked gravely. "The year is now up; both his lungs are gone. He has ignored my counsel; tell him I don't want to see him."

Half stunned by Sri Yukteswar's sternness, I raced down the stairway. Sasi was ascending.

"O Mukunda! I do hope Master is here; I had a hunch he might be."

"Yes, but he doesn't wish to be disturbed."

Sasi burst into tears and brushed past me. He threw himself at Sri Yukteswar's feet, placing there three beautiful sapphires.

"Omniscient guru, the doctors say I have galloping tuberculosis! They give me no longer than three more months! I humbly implore your aid; I know you can heal me!"

"Isn't it a bit late now to be worrying over your life? Depart with your jewels; their time of usefulness is past." Master then sat sphinx-like in an unrelenting silence, punctuated by the boy's sobs for mercy.

An intuitive conviction came to me that Sri Yukteswar was merely testing the depth of Sasi's faith in the divine healing power. I was not surprised a tense hour later when Master turned a sympathetic gaze on my prostrate friend.

"Get up, Sasi; what a commotion you make in other people's houses! Return your sapphires to the jeweler's; they are an unnecessary expense now. But get an astrological bangle and wear it. Fear not; in a few weeks you shall be well."

Sasi's smile illumined his tear-marred face like sudden sun over a sodden landscape. "Beloved guru, shall I take the medicines prescribed by the doctors?"

Sri Yukteswar's glance was longanimous. "Just as you wish – drink them or discard them; it does not matter. It is more possible for the sun and moon to interchange their positions than for you to die of tuberculosis." He added abruptly, "Go now, before I change my mind!"

With an agitated bow, my friend hastily departed. I visited him several times during the next few weeks, and was aghast to find his condition increasingly worse.

"Sasi cannot last through the night." These words from his physician, and the spectacle of my friend, now reduced almost to a skeleton, sent me post-haste to Serampore. My guru listened coldly to my tearful report.

"Why do you come here to bother me? You have already heard me assure Sasi of his recovery."

I bowed before him in great awe, and retreated to the door. Sri Yukteswar said no parting word, but sank into silence, his unwinking eyes half-open, their vision fled to another world.

I returned at once to Sasi's home in Calcutta. With astonishment I found my friend sitting up, drinking milk.

"O Mukunda! What a miracle! Four hours ago I felt Master's presence in the room; my terrible symptoms immediately disappeared. I feel that through his grace I am entirely well."

In a few weeks Sasi was stouter and in better health than ever before.[1] But his singular reaction to his healing had an ungrateful tinge: he seldom visited Sri Yukteswar again! My friend told me one day that he so deeply regretted his previous mode of life that he was ashamed to face Master.

I could only conclude that Sasi's illness had had the contrasting effect of stiffening his will and impairing his manners.

The first two years of my course at Scottish Church College were drawing to a close. My classroom attendance had been very spasmodic; what little studying I did was only to keep peace with my family. My two private tutors came regularly to my house; I was regularly absent: I can discern at least this one regularity in my scholastic career!

In India two successful years of college bring an Intermediate Arts diploma; the student may then look forward to another two years and his A.B. degree.

The Intermediate Arts final examinations loomed ominously ahead. I fled to Puri, where my guru was spending a few weeks. Vaguely hoping that he would sanction my non-appearance at the finals, I related my embarrassing unpreparedness.

But Master smiled consolingly. "You have whole-heartedly pursued your spiritual duties, and could not help neglecting your college work. Apply yourself diligently to your books for the next week: you shall get through your ordeal without failure."

I returned to Calcutta, firmly suppressing all reasonable doubts that occasionally arose with unnerving ridicule. Surveying the mountain of books on my table, I felt like a traveller lost in a wilderness. A long period of meditation brought me a labour-saving inspiration. Opening each book at random, I studied only those pages which lay thus exposed. Pursuing this

1 In 1936, I heard from a friend that Sasi was still in excellent health.

course during eighteen hours a day for a week, I considered myself entitled to advise all succeeding generations on the art of cramming.

The following days in the examination halls were a justification of my seemingly haphazard procedure. I passed all the tests, though by a hairbreadth. The congratulations of my friends and family were ludicrously mixed with ejaculations betraying their astonishment.

On his return from Puri, Sri Yukteswar gave me a pleasant surprise. "Your Calcutta studies are now over. I will see that you pursue your last two years of university work right here in Serampore."

I was puzzled. "Sir, there is no Bachelor of Arts course in this town." Serampore College, the sole institution of higher learning, offered only a two-year course in Intermediate Arts.

Master smiled mischievously. "I am too old to go about collecting donations to establish an A.B. college for you. I guess I shall have to arrange the matter through someone else."

Two months later Professor Howells, president of Serampore College, publicly announced that he had succeeded in raising sufficient funds to offer a four-year course. Serampore College became a branch affiliation of the University of Calcutta. I was one of the first students to enroll in Serampore as an A.B. candidate.

"Guruji, how kind you are to me! I have been longing to leave Calcutta and be near you every day in Serampore. Professor Howells does not dream how much he owes to your silent help!"

Sri Yukteswar gazed at me with mock severity. "Now you won't have to spend so many hours on trains; what a lot of free time for your studies! Perhaps you will become less of a last-minute crammer and more of a scholar." But somehow his tone lacked conviction.[2]

2 (Chap. 17) Sri Yukteswar grieved at the materialistic trend in the modern education that does not expound the spiritual laws for happiness, or teach the wisdom of inculcating the awe in one's maker.

Young people, who today hear in high schools and colleges that man is merely a 'higher animal,' often become atheists. They do not attempt any soul exploration or consider themselves in their essential nature. 'Images of God.' Emerson observed: 'that only which we have within, can we see without. If we meet no Gods, it is because we harbour none.' He who imagines his animal nature to be his only reality is cut off from divine aspirations.

An educational system that does not present Spirit as the central Fact of man's existence is offering *avidya*, false knowledge. "Thou sayest, I am rich, and increased with goods, and have need of nothing; knowest not that thou art wretched, and miserable, and poor, and blind and naked." – *Revelation* 3: 17.

The education of youth in ancient India was ideal. At the age of nine, the pupil was received 'as a son' in *gurukula* (Guru's family home as a seat of learning). 'The modern boy spends, annually, an eighth of his time at school, whereas the ancient Indian child spent his whole time there,' Professor S.V. Venkateswara writes in *Indian Culture Through the Ages* (vol. I; Longmans, Green & Co.). 'There was a healthy feeling of solidarity and responsibility, and ample opportunity for the exercise of self-reliance and individuality. There was a high standard of culture, self-imposed discipline, and stern regard for duty, selfless action, and sacrifice, combined with self-respect and reverence for others; a high standard of academic dignity, and a sense of…. the nobility and the great purpose of human life.'

18. *A Mohammedan Wonder-Worker*

"YEARS AGO, right in this very room you now occupy, a Mohammedan wonder-worker performed four miracles before me!"

Sri Yukteswar made this surprising statement during his first visit to my new quarters. Immediately after entering Serampore College, I had taken a room in a nearby boarding-house, called *Panthi*.[1] It was an old-fashioned brick mansion, fronting the Ganges.

"Master, what a coincidence! Are these newly decorated walls really ancient with memories?" I looked around my simply furnished room with awakened interest.

"It is a long story." My guru smiled reminiscently. "The name of the *fakir*[2] was Afzal Khan. He had acquired his extraordinary powers through a chance encounter with a Hindu yogi.

" 'Son, I am thirsty; fetch me some water.' A dust-covered *sannyasi* made this request of Afzal one day during his early boyhood in a small village of eastern Bengal.

" 'Master, I am a Mohammedan. How could you, a Hindu, accept a drink from my hands?'

" 'Your truthfulness pleases me, my child. I do not observe the ostracizing rules of ungodly sectarianism. Go; bring me water quickly.'

"Afzal's reverent obedience was rewarded by a loving glance from the yogi.

" 'You possess good karma from former lives,' he observed solemnly. 'I am going to teach you a certain yoga method which will give you command over one of the invisible realms. The great powers that will be yours should be exercised for worthy ends; never employ them selfishly! I perceive, alas! that you have brought over from the past some seeds of destructive tendencies. Do not allow them to sprout by watering them with fresh evil actions. The complexity of your previous karma is such that you must use this life to reconcile your yogic accomplishments with the highest humanitarian goals.'

"After instructing the amazed boy in a complicated technique, the master vanished.

"Afzal faithfully followed his yoga exercise for twenty years. His miraculous feats began to attract widespread attention. It seems that he was always accompanied by a disembodied spirit whom he called 'Hazrat.' This invisible entity was able to fulfill the *fakir's* slightest wish.

1 (Chap. 18) Residence for students; from Pantha: wanderer or seeker of knowledge.
2 A Moslem yogi; from the Arabic *faqir:* poor; originally applied to dervishes under a vow of poverty.

"Ignoring his master's warning, Afzal began to misuse his powers. Whatever object he touched and then replaced would soon disappear without a trace. This disconcerting eventuality usually made the Mohammedan an objectionable guest!

"He visited large jewelry stores in Calcutta from time to time, representing himself as a possible purchaser. Any jewel he handled would vanish shortly after he had left the shop.

"Afzal was often surrounded by several hundred students, attracted by the hope of learning his secrets. The *fakir* occasionally invited them to travel with him. At the railway station he would manage to touch a roll of tickets. These he would return to the clerk, remarking: 'I have changed my mind, and won't buy them now.' But when he boarded the train with his retinue, Afzal would be in possession of the required tickets.[3]

"These exploits created an indignant uproar; Bengali jewelers and ticket-sellers were succumbing to nervous breakdowns! The police who sought to arrest Afzal found themselves helpless; the *fakir* could remove incriminating evidence merely by saying: 'Hazrat, take this away.' "

Sri Yukteswar rose from his seat and walked to the balcony of my room which overlooked the Ganges. I followed him, eager to hear more of the baffling Mohammedan Raffles.

"This *Panthi* house formerly belonged to a friend of mine. He became acquainted with Afzal and asked him here. My friend also invited about twenty neighbors, including myself. I was only a youth then, and felt a lively curiosity about the notorious *fakir*." Master laughed. "I took the precaution of not wearing anything valuable! Afzal looked me over inquisitively, then remarked:

" 'You have powerful hands. Go downstairs to the garden; get a smooth stone and write your name on it with chalk; then throw the stone as far as possible into the Ganges.'

"I obeyed. As soon as the stone had vanished under distant waves, the Mohammedan addressed me again:

" 'Fill a pot with Ganges water near the front of this house.'

"After I had returned with a vessel of water, the *fakir* cried, 'Hazrat, put the stone in the pot!'

"The stone appeared at once. I pulled it from the vessel and found my signature as legible as when I had written it.

"Babu,[4] one of my friends in the room, was wearing a heavy antique gold watch and chain. The *fakir* examined them with ominous admiration. Soon they were missing!

3 My father later told me that his company, the Bengal-Nagpur Railway, had been one of the firms victimized by Afzal Khan.
4 I do not recall the name of Sri Yukteswar's friend, and must refer to him simply as 'Babu' (Mister).

" 'Afzal, please return my prized heirloom!' Babu was nearly in tears.

"The Mohammedan was stoically silent for awhile, then said, 'You have five hundred rupees in an iron safe. Bring them to me, and I will tell you where to locate your timepiece.'

"The distraught Babu left immediately for his home. He came back shortly and handed Afzal the required sum.

" 'Go to the little bridge near your house,' the *fakir* instructed Babu. 'Call on Hazrat to give you the watch and chain.'

"Babu rushed away. On his return, he was wearing a smile of relief and no jewelry whatever.

" 'When I commanded Hazrat as directed,' he announced, 'my watch came tumbling down from the air into my right hand! You may be sure I locked the heirloom in my safe before rejoining the group here!'

"Babu's friends, witnesses of the comicotragedy of the ransom for a watch, were staring with resentment at Afzal. He now spoke placatingly.

" 'Please name any drink you want; Hazrat will produce it.'

"A number asked for milk, others for fruit juices. I was not too much shocked when the unnerved Babu requested whisky! The Mohammedan gave an order; the obliging Hazrat sent sealed containers sailing down the air and thudding to the floor. Each man found his desired beverage.

"The promise of the fourth spectacular feat of the day was doubtless gratifying to our host: Afzal offered to supply an instantaneous lunch!

" 'Let us order the most expensive dishes,' Babu suggested gloomily. 'I want an elaborate meal for my five hundred rupees! Everything should be served on gold plates!'

"As soon as each man had expressed his preferences, the *fakir* addressed himself to the inexhaustible Hazrat. A great rattle ensued; gold platters filled with intricately-prepared curries, hot *luchis*, and many out-of-season fruits, landed from nowhere at our feet. All the food was delicious. After feasting for an hour, we started to leave the room. A tremendous noise, as though dishes were being piled up, caused us to turn around. Lo! there was no sign of the glittering plates or the remnants of the meal."

"Guruji," I interrupted, "if Afzal could easily secure such things as gold dishes, why did he covet the property of others?"

"The *fakir* was not highly developed spiritually," Sri Yukteswar explained. "His mastery of a certain yoga technique gave him access to an astral plane where any desire is immediately materialized. Through the agency of an astral being, Hazrat, the Mohammedan could summon the atoms of any object from etheric energy by an act of powerful will. But such astrally-produced objects are structurally evanescent; they cannot be long retained.[5] Afzal still yearned for worldly wealth which, though more hardly earned, has a more dependable durability."

I laughed. "It too sometimes vanishes most unaccountably!"

"Afzal was not a man of God-realization," Master went on. "Miracles of a permanent and beneficial nature are performed by true saints because they have attuned themselves to the omnipotent Creator. Afzal was merely an ordinary man with an extraordinary power of penetrating a subtle realm not usually entered by mortals until death."

"I understand now, Guruji. The after-world appears to have some charming features."

Master agreed. "I never saw Afzal after that day, but a few years later Babu came to my home to show me a newspaper account of the Mohammedan's public confession. From it I learned the facts I have just told you about Afzal's early initiation from a Hindu guru."

The gist of the latter part of the published document, as recalled by Sri Yukteswar, was as follows: "I, Afzal Khan, am writing these words as an act of penance and as a warning to those who seek the possession of miraculous powers. For years I have been misusing the wondrous abilities imparted to me through the grace of God and my master. I became drunk with egotism, feeling that I was beyond the ordinary laws of morality. My day of reckoning finally arrived.

"Recently I met an old man on a road outside Calcutta. He limped along painfully, carrying a shining object which looked like gold. I addressed him with greed in my heart.

" 'I am Afzal Khan, the great *fakir*. What have you there?'

" 'This ball of gold is my sole material wealth; it can be of no interest to a *fakir*. I implore you, sir, to heal my limp.'

"I touched the ball and walked away without reply. The old man hobbled after me. He soon raised an outcry: 'My gold is gone!'

"As I paid no attention, he suddenly spoke in a stentorian voice that issued oddly from his frail body:

" 'Do you not recognize me?'

"I stood speechless, aghast at the belated discovery that this unimpressive old cripple was none other than the great saint who, long, long ago, had initiated me into yoga. He straightened himself; his body instantly became strong and youthful.

" 'So!' My guru's glance was fiery. 'I see with my own eyes that you use your powers, not to help suffering humanity, but to prey on it like a

[5] I had a silver amulet, an astrally produced artifact that eventually vanished as it came. *See* the Astral world in Chap. 43.

common thief! I withdraw your occult gifts; Hazrat is now freed from you. No longer shall you be a terror in Bengal!'

"I called on Hazrat in anguished tones; for the first time, he did not appear to my inner sight. But some dark veil suddenly lifted within me; I saw clearly the blasphemy of my life.

" 'My guru, I thank you for coming to banish my long delusion.' I was sobbing at his feet. 'I promise to forsake my worldly ambitions. I will retire to the mountains for lonely meditation on God, hoping to atone for my evil past.'

"My master regarded me with silent compassion. 'I feel your sincerity,' he said finally. 'Because of your earlier years of strict obedience, and because of your present repentance, I will grant you one boon. Your other powers are now gone, but whenever food and clothing are needed, you may still call successfully on Hazrat to supply them. Devote yourself whole-heartedly to divine understanding in the mountain solitudes.'

"My guru then vanished; I was left to my tears and reflections. Farewell, world! I go to seek the forgiveness of the Cosmic Beloved."

19. *My Master, in Calcutta, appears in Serampore*

"I AM OFTEN BESET by atheistic doubts. Yet a torturing surmise sometimes haunts me: may not untapped soul possibilities exist? Is man not missing his real destiny if he fails to explore them?"

These remarks of Dijen Babu, my roommate at the *Panthi* boarding-house, were called forth by my invitation that he meet my guru.

"Sri Yukteswarji will initiate you into *Kriya Yoga*," I replied. "It calms the dualistic turmoil by a divine inner certainty."

That evening Dijen accompanied me to the hermitage. In Master's presence my friend received such spiritual peace that he was soon a constant visitor. The trivial preoccupations of daily life are not enough for man; wisdom too is a native hunger. In Sri Yukteswar's words Dijen found an incentive to those attempts – first painful, then effortlessly liberating – to locate a realer self within his bosom than the humiliating ego of a temporary birth, seldom ample enough for the Spirit.

As Dijen and I were both pursuing the A.B. course at Serampore College, we got into the habit of walking together to the ashram as soon as classes were over. We would often see Sri Yukteswar standing on his second-floor balcony, welcoming our approach with a smile.

One afternoon Kanai, a young hermitage resident, met Dijen and me at the door with disappointing news.

"Master is not here; he was summoned to Calcutta by an urgent note."

The following day I received a post card from my guru. "I shall leave Calcutta Wednesday morning," he had written. "You and Dijen meet the nine o'clock train at Serampore station."

About eight-thirty on Wednesday morning, a telepathic message from Sri Yukteswar flashed insistently to my mind: "I am delayed; don't meet the nine o'clock train."

I conveyed the latest instructions to Dijen, who was already dressed for departure.

"You and your intuition!" My friend's voice was edged in scorn. "I prefer to trust Master's written word."

I shrugged my shoulders and seated myself with quiet finality. Muttering angrily, Dijen made for the door and closed it noisily behind him.

As the room was rather dark, I moved nearer to the window overlooking the street. The scant sunlight suddenly increased to an intense brilliancy in which the iron-barred window completely vanished. Against this dazzling background appeared the clearly materialized figure of Sri Yukteswar!

Bewildered to the point of shock, I rose from my chair and knelt before him. With my customary gesture of respectful greeting at my guru's feet, I touched his shoes. These were a pair familiar to me, of orange-dyed canvas, soled with rope. His ochre swami cloth brushed against me; I distinctly felt not only the texture of his robe, but also the gritty surface of the shoes, and the pressure of his toes within them. Too much astounded to utter a word, I stood up and gazed at him questioningly.

"I was pleased that you got my telepathic message." Master's voice was calm, entirely normal. "I have now finished my business in Calcutta, and shall arrive in Serampore by the ten o'clock train."

As I still stared mutely, Sri Yukteswar went on, "This is not an apparition, but my flesh and blood form. I have been divinely commanded to give you this experience, rare to achieve on earth. Meet me at the station; you and Dijen will see me coming toward you, dressed as I am now. I shall be preceded by a fellow passenger – a little boy carrying a silver jug."

My guru placed both hands on my head, with a murmured blessing. As he concluded with the words, '*Tabe asi*,'[1] I heard a peculiar rumbling sound.[2] His body began to melt gradually within the piercing light. First his feet and legs vanished, then his torso and head, like a scroll being rolled up. To the very last, I could feel his fingers resting lightly on my hair. The

1 Bengali 'Good-bye'; literally, it is a hopeful paradox: 'Then I come.' (In the Japanese too, they say "I come back.").
2 The characteristic sound of dematerialization of bodily atoms.

effulgence faded; nothing remained before me but the barred window and a pale stream of sunlight.

I remained in a half-stupor of confusion, questioning whether I had not been the victim of a hallucination. A crestfallen Dijen soon entered the room.

"Master was not on the nine o'clock train, nor even the nine-thirty." My friend made his announcement with a slightly apologetic air.

"Come then; I know he will arrive at ten o'clock." I took Dijen's hand and rushed him forcibly along with me, heedless of his protests. In about ten minutes we entered the station, where the train was already puffing to a halt.

"The whole train is filled with the light of Master's aura! He is there!" I exclaimed joyfully.

"You dream so?" Dijen laughed mockingly.

"Let us wait here." I told my friend details of the way in which our guru would approach us. As I finished my description, Sri Yukteswar came into view, wearing the same clothes I had seen a short time earlier. He walked slowly in the wake of a small lad bearing a silver jug.

For a moment a wave of cold fear passed through me, at the unprecedented strangeness of my experience. I felt the materialistic, twentieth-century world slipping from me; was I back in the ancient days when Jesus appeared before Peter on the sea?

As Sri Yukteswar, a modern Yogi-Christ, reached the spot where Dijen and I were speechlessly rooted, Master smiled at my friend and remarked:

"I sent you a message too, but you were unable to grasp it."

Dijen was silent, but glared at me suspiciously. After we had escorted our guru to his hermitage, my friend and I proceeded toward Serampore College. Dijen halted in the street, indignation streaming from his every pore.

"So! Master sent me a message! Yet you concealed it! I demand an explanation!"

"Can I help it if your mental mirror oscillates with such restlessness that you cannot register our guru's instructions?" I retorted.

The anger vanished from Dijen's face. "I see what you mean," he said ruefully. "But please explain how you could know about the child with the jug."

By the time I had finished the story of Master's phenomenal appearance at the boarding-house that morning, my friend and I had reached Serampore College.

"The account I have just heard of our guru's powers," Dijen said, "makes me feel that any university in the world is only a kindergarten."[3]

3 St. Thomas Aquinas (1224-1274), the foremost theologian of the Roman Catholic Church, who had experienced a profound mystical insight once said: "Such things have been revealed to me that all I have written appears to me of no greater value than straw."
In Plato's Dialogues (*Phaedrus*), Socrates says "As for me, all I know is that I know nothing."

20. *We do not visit Kashmir*

"FATHER, I want to invite Master and four friends to accompany me to the Himalayan foothills during my summer vacation. May I have six train passes to Kashmir and enough money to cover our travel expenses?"

As I had expected, Father laughed heartily. "This is the third time you have given me the same cock-and-bull story. Didn't you make a similar request last summer, and the year before that? At the last moment, Sri Yukteswarji refuses to go."

"It is true, Father; I don't know why my guru will not give me his definite word about Kashmir.[1] But if I tell him that I have already secured the passes from you, somehow I think that this time he will consent to make the journey."

Father was unconvinced at the moment, but the following day, after some good-humoured gibes, he handed me six passes and a roll of ten-rupee bills.

"I hardly think your theoretical trip needs such practical props," he remarked, "but here they are."

That afternoon I exhibited my booty to Sri Yukteswar. Though he smiled at my enthusiasm, his words were noncommittal: "I would like to go; we shall see." He made no comment when I asked his little hermitage disciple, Kanai, to accompany us. I also invited three other friends – Rajendra Nath Mitra, Jotin Auddy, and one other boy. Our date of departure was set for the following Monday.

On Saturday and Sunday I stayed in Calcutta, where marriage rites for a cousin were being celebrated at my family home. I arrived in Serampore with my luggage early Monday morning. Rajendra met me at the hermitage door.

"Master is out, walking. He has refused to go."

I was equally grieved and obdurate. "I will not give Father a third chance to ridicule my chimerical plans for Kashmir. Come; the rest of us will go anyhow."

Rajendra agreed; I left the ashram to find a servant. Kanai, I knew, would not take the trip without Master, and someone was needed to look after the luggage. I bethought myself of Behari, previously a servant in my family home, who was now employed by a Serampore schoolmaster. As I walked along briskly, I met my guru in front of the Christian church near Serampore Courthouse.

"Where are you going?" Sri Yukteswar's face was unsmiling.

"Sir, I hear that you and Kanai will not take the trip we have been planning. I am seeking Behari. You will recall that last year he was so anxious to see Kashmir that he even offered to serve without pay."

"I remember. Nevertheless, I don't think Behari will be willing to go."

I was exasperated. "He is just eagerly waiting for this opportunity!"

---

1 Although Master failed to make any explanation, his reluctance to visit Kashmir during those two summers may have been a foreknowledge that the time was not ripe for his illness there. (see page 145).

My guru silently resumed his walk; I soon reached the schoolmaster's house. Behari, in the courtyard, greeted me with friendly warmth that abruptly vanished as soon as I mentioned Kashmir. With a murmured word of apology, the servant left me and entered his employer's house. I waited half an hour, nervously assuring myself that Behari's delay was being caused by preparations for his trip. Finally I knocked at the front door.

"Behari left by the back stairs about thirty minutes ago," a man informed me. A slight smile hovered about his lips.

I departed sadly, wondering whether my invitation had been too coercive or whether Master's unseen influence were at work. Passing the Christian church, again I saw my guru walking slowly toward me. Without waiting to hear my report, he exclaimed:

"So Behari would not go! Now, what are your plans?"

I felt like a recalcitrant child who is determined to defy his masterful father. "Sir, I am going to ask my uncle to lend me his servant, Lal Dhari."

"See your uncle if you want to," Sri Yukteswar replied with a chuckle. "But I hardly think you will enjoy the visit."

Apprehensive but rebellious, I left my guru and entered Serampore Courthouse. My paternal uncle, Sarada Ghosh, a government attorney, welcomed me affectionately.

"I am leaving today with some friends for Kashmir," I told him. "For years I have been looking forward to this Himalayan trip."

"I am happy for you, Mukunda. Is there anything I can do to make your journey more comfortable?"

These kind words gave me a lift of encouragement. "Dear uncle," I said, "could you possibly spare me your servant, Lal Dhari?"

My simple request had the effect of an earthquake. Uncle jumped so violently that his chair overturned, the papers on the desk flew in every direction, and his pipe, a long, coconut-stemmed hubble-bubble, fell to the floor with a great clatter.

"You selfish young man," he shouted, quivering with wrath, "what a preposterous idea! Who will look after me, if you take my servant on one of your pleasure jaunts?"

I concealed my surprise, reflecting that my amiable uncle's sudden change of front was only one more enigma in a day fully devoted to incomprehensibility. My retreat from the courthouse office was more alacritous than dignified.

I returned to the hermitage, where my friends were expectantly gathered. Conviction was growing on me that some sufficient if exceedingly recondite motive was behind Master's attitude. Remorse seized me that I had been trying to thwart my guru's will.

"Mukunda, wouldn't you like to stay awhile longer with me?" Sri Yukteswar inquired. "Rajendra and the others can go ahead now, and wait for you at Calcutta. There will be plenty of time to catch the last evening train leaving Calcutta for Kashmir."

"Sir, I don't care to go without you," I said mournfully.

My friends paid not the slightest attention to my remark. They summoned a hackney carriage and departed with all the luggage. Kanai and I sat quietly at our guru's feet. After a half hour of complete silence, Master rose and walked toward the second-floor dining patio.

"Kanai, please serve Mukunda's food. His train leaves soon."

Getting up from my blanket seat, I staggered suddenly with nausea and a ghastly churning sensation in my stomach. The stabbing pain was so intense that I felt I had been abruptly hurled into some violent hell. Groping blindly toward my guru, I collapsed before him, attacked by all symptoms of the dread Asiatic cholera. Sri Yukteswar and Kanai carried me to the sitting room.

Racked with agony, I cried, "Master, I surrender my life to you;" for I believed it was indeed fast ebbing from the shores of my body.

Sri Yukteswar put my head on his lap, stroking my forehead with angelic tenderness.

"You see now what would have happened if you were at the station with your friends," he said. "I had to look after you in this strange way, because you chose to doubt my judgment about taking the trip at this particular time."

I understood at last. Inasmuch as great masters seldom see fit to display their powers openly, a casual observer of the day's events would have imagined that their sequence was quite natural. My guru's intervention had been too subtle to be suspected. He had worked his will through Behari and my Uncle Sarada and Rajendra and the others in such an inconspicuous manner that probably everyone but myself thought the situations had been logically normal.

As Sri Yukteswar never failed to observe his social obligations, he instructed Kanai to go for a specialist, and to notify my uncle.

"Master," I protested, "only you can heal me. I am too far gone for any doctor."

"Child, you are protected by the Divine Mercy. Don't worry about the doctor; he will not find you in this state. You are already healed."

With my guru's words, the excruciating suffering left me. I sat up feebly. A doctor soon arrived and examined me carefully.

"You appear to have passed through the worst," he said. "I will take some specimens with me for laboratory tests."

The following morning the physician arrived hurriedly. I was sitting up, in good spirits.

"Well, well, here you are, smiling and chatting as though you had had no close call with death." He patted my hand gently. "I hardly expected to find you alive, after I had discovered from the specimens that your disease was Asiatic cholera. You are fortunate, young man, to have a guru with divine healing powers! I am convinced of it!"

I agreed wholeheartedly. As the doctor was preparing to leave, Rajendra and Auddy appeared at the door. The resentment in their faces changed into sympathy as they glanced at the physician and then at my somewhat wan countenance.

"We were angry when you didn't turn up as agreed at the Calcutta train. You have been sick?"

"Yes." I could not help laughing as my friends placed the luggage in the same corner it had occupied yesterday. I quoted:

"There was a ship that sailed for Spain;
before it arrived, it was back again!"

Master entered the room. I permitted myself a convalescent's liberty, and captured his hand lovingly.

"Guruji." I said, "from my twelfth year on, I have made many unsuccessful attempts to reach the Himalayas. I am finally convinced that without your blessings the Goddess Parvati[2] will not receive me!"

21. *We visit Kashmir*

"YOU ARE STRONG enough now to travel. I will accompany you to Kashmir," Sri Yukteswar informed me two days after my miraculous recovery from Asiatic cholera.

That evening our party of six entrained for the north. Our first leisurely stop was at Simla, a queenly city resting on the throne of Himalayan hills. We strolled over the steep streets, admiring the magnificent views.

"English strawberries for sale," cried an old woman, squatting in a picturesque open market place.

Master was curious about the strange little red fruits. He bought a basketful and offered it to Kanai and myself, who were near-by. I tasted one berry but spat it hastily on the ground.

"Sir, what a sour fruit! I could never like strawberries!"

My guru laughed. "Oh, you will like them – in America. At a dinner there, your hostess will serve them with sugar and cream. After she has mashed the berries with a fork, you will taste them and say: 'What delicious strawberries!' Then you will remember this day in Simla."

Literally, 'of the mountains.' Parvati, mythologically represented as a daughter of Himavat or the sacred mountains, is a name given to the *shakti* or 'cansort' of Shiva. (Parvati, Kali, Durga, Uma and other goddesses are aspects of *Jaganmatri* 'Divine Mother of the World.')

(Sri Yukteswar's forecast vanished from my mind, but reappeared there many years later, shortly after my arrival in America. I was a dinner guest at the home of Mrs. Alice T. Hasey [Sister Yogmata] in West Somerville, Massachusetts. When a dessert of strawberries was put on the table, my hostess picked up her fork and mashed my berries, adding cream and sugar. "The fruit is rather tart; I think you will like it fixed this way," she remarked.

I took a mouthful. "What delicious strawberries!" I exclaimed. At once my guru's prediction in Simla emerged from the fathomless cave of memory. It was staggering to realize that long ago Sri Yukteswar's God-tuned mind had sensitively detected the program of karmic events wandering in the ether of futurity.)

Our party soon left Simla and entrained for Rawalpindi. There we hired a large landau, drawn by two horses, in which we started a seven-day trip to Srinagar, capital city of Kashmir. The second day of our northbound journey brought into view the true Himalayan vastness. As the iron wheels of our carriage creaked along the hot, stony roads, we were enraptured with changing vistas of mountainous grandeur.

"Sir," Auddy said to Master, "I am greatly enjoying these glorious scenes in your holy company."

I felt a throb of pleasure at Auddy's appreciation, for I was acting as host on this trip. Sri Yukteswar caught my thought; he turned to me and whispered:

"Don't flatter yourself; Auddy is not nearly as entranced with the scenery as he is with the prospect of leaving us long enough to have a cigarette."

I was shocked. "Sir," I said in an undertone, "please do not break our harmony by these unpleasant words. I can hardly believe that Auddy is hankering for a smoke."[1] I looked apprehensively at my usually irrepressible guru.

"Very well; I won't say anything to Auddy." Master chuckled. "But you will soon see, when the landau halts, that Auddy is quick to seize his opportunity."

The carriage arrived at a small caravanserai. As our horses were led to be watered, Auddy inquired, "Sir, do you mind if I ride awhile with the driver? I would like to get a little outside air."

Sri Yukteswar gave permission, but remarked to me, "He wants fresh smoke and not fresh air."

The landau resumed its noisy progress over the dusty roads. Master's eyes were twinkling; he instructed me, "Crane up your neck through the carriage door and see what Auddy is doing with the air."

I obeyed, and was astounded to observe Auddy in the act of exhaling rings of cigarette smoke. My glance toward Sri Yukteswar was apologetic.

1 It is a mark of disrespect, in India, to smoke in the presence of one's elders and superiors.

"You are right, as always, sir. Auddy is enjoying a puff along with a panorama." I surmised that my friend had received a gift from the cab driver; I knew Auddy had not carried any cigarettes from Calcutta.

We continued on the labyrinthine way, adorned by views of rivers, valleys, precipitous crags, and multitudinous mountain tiers. Every night we stopped at rustic inns, and prepared our own food. Sri Yukteswar took special care of my diet, insisting that I have lime juice at all meals. I was still weak, but daily improving, though the rattling carriage was strictly designed for discomfort.

Joyous anticipations filled our hearts as we neared central Kashmir, paradise land of lotus lakes, floating gardens, gaily canopied houseboats, the many-bridged Jhelum River, and flower-strewn pastures, all ringed round by the Himalayan majesty. Our approach to Srinagar was through an avenue of tall, welcoming trees. We engaged rooms at a double-storied inn overlooking the noble hills. No running water was available; we drew our supply from a near-by well. The summer weather was ideal, with warm days and slightly cold nights.

We made a pilgrimage to the ancient Srinagar temple of Swami Shankara. As I gazed upon the mountain-peak hermitage, standing bold against the sky, I fell into an ecstatic trance. A vision appeared of a hilltop mansion in a distant land. The lofty Shankara ashram before me was transformed into the structure where, years later, I established the Self-Realization Fellowship headquarters in America. When I first visited Los Angeles, and saw the large building on the crest of Mount Washington, I recognized it at once from my long-past visions in Kashmir and elsewhere.

A few days at Srinagar; then on to Gulmarg ('mountain paths of flowers'), elevated by six thousand feet. There I had my first ride on a large horse. Rajendra mounted a small trotter, whose heart was fired with ambition for speed. We ventured onto the very steep Khilanmarg; the path led through a dense forest, abounding in tree-mushrooms, where the mist-shrouded trails were often precarious. But Rajendra's little animal never permitted my oversized steed a moment's rest, even at the most perilous turns. On, on, untiringly came Rajendra's horse, oblivious to all but the joy of competition.

Our strenuous race was rewarded by a breath-taking view. For the first time in this life, I gazed in all directions at sublime snow-capped Himalayas, lying tier upon tier like silhouettes of huge polar bears. My eyes feasted exultingly on endless reaches of icy mountains against sunny blue skies.

I rolled merrily with my young companions, all wearing overcoats, on the sparkling white slopes. On our downward trip we saw afar a vast carpet of yellow flowers, wholly transfiguring the bleak hills.

Our next excursions were to the famous royal 'pleasure gardens' of the Emperor Jehangir, at Shalimar and Nishat Bagh. The ancient palace at

Nishat Bagh is built directly over a natural waterfall. Rushing down from the mountains, the torrent has been regulated through ingenious contrivances to flow over colourful terraces and to gush into fountains amidst the dazzling flower-beds. The stream also enters several of the palace rooms, ultimately dropping fairy like into the lake below. The immense gardens are riotous with colour – roses of a dozen hues, snapdragons, lavender, pansies, poppies. An emerald enclosing outline is given by symmetrical rows of *chinars*,[2] cypresses, cherry trees; beyond them tower the white austerities of the Himalayas.

Kashmir grapes are considered a rare delicacy in Calcutta. Rajendra, who had been promising himself a veritable feast on reaching Kashmir, was disappointed to find there no large vineyards. Now and then I chaffed him jocosely over his baseless anticipation.

"Oh, I have become so much gorged with grapes I can't walk!" I would say. "The invisible grapes are brewing within me!" Later I heard that sweet grapes grow abundantly in Kabul, west of Kashmir. We consoled ourselves with ice cream made of *rabri,* a heavily condensed milk, and flavored with whole pistachio nuts.

We took several trips in the *shikaras* or houseboats, shaded by red-embroidered canopies, coursing along the intricate channels of Dal Lake, a network of canals like a watery spider web. Here the numerous floating gardens, crudely improvised with logs and earth, strike one with amazement, so incongruous is the first sight of vegetables and melons growing in the midst of vast waters. Occasionally one sees a peasant, disdaining to be 'rooted to the soil,' towing his square plot of 'land' to a new location in the many-fingered lake.

In this storied vale one finds an epitome of all the earth's beauties. The Lady of Kashmir is mountain-crowned, lake-garlanded, and flower-shod. In later years, after I had toured many distant lands, I understood why Kashmir is often called the world's most scenic spot. It possesses some of the charms of the Swiss Alps, and of Loch Lomond in Scotland, and of the exquisite English lakes. An American traveller in Kashmir finds much to remind him of the rugged grandeur of Alaska and of Pikes Peak near Denver.

As entries in a scenic beauty contest, I offer for first prize either the gorgeous view of Xochimilco in Mexico, where mountains, skies, and poplars reflect themselves in myriad lanes of water amidst the playful fish, or the jewel-like lakes of Kashmir, guarded like beautiful maidens by the stern surveillance of the Himalayas. These two places stand out in my memory as the loveliest spots on earth.

Yet I was awed also when I first beheld the wonders of Yellowstone National Park and of the Grand Canyon of the Colorado, and of Alaska. Yellowstone Park

2 The Oriental plane tree.

is perhaps the only region where one can see innumerable geysers shooting high into the air, performing year after year with clockwork regularity. Its opal and sapphire pools and hot sulphurous springs, its bears and wild creatures, remind one that here Nature left a specimen of her earliest creation. Motoring along the roads of Wyoming to the 'Devil's Paint Pot' of hot bubbling mud, with gurgling springs, vaporous fountains, and spouting geysers in all directions, I was disposed to say that Yellowstone deserves a special prize for uniqueness.

The ancient majestic redwoods of Yosemite, stretching their huge columns far into the unfathomable sky, are green natural cathedrals designed with skill divine. Though there are wonderful falls in the Orient, none match the torrential beauty of Niagara near the Canadian border. The Mammoth Caves of Kentucky and the Carlsbad Caverns in New Mexico, with colourful icicle-like formations, are stunning fairylands. Their long needles of stalactite spires, hanging from cave ceilings and mirrored in underground waters, present a glimpse of other worlds as fancied by man.

Most of the Hindus of Kashmir, world-famed for their beauty, are as white as Europeans and have similar features and bone structure; many have blue eyes and blonde hair. Dressed in Western clothes, they look like Americans. The cold Himalayas protect the Kashmiris from the sultry sun and preserve their light complexions. As one travels to the southern and tropical latitudes of India, he finds progressively that the people become darker and darker.

After spending happy weeks in Kashmir, I was forced to return to Bengal for the fall term of Serampore College. Sri Yukteswar remained in Srinagar, with Kanai and Auddy. Before I departed, Master hinted that his body would be subject to suffering in Kashmir.

"Sir, you look a picture of health," I protested.

"There is a chance that I may even leave this earth."

"Guruji!" I fell at his feet with an imploring gesture. "Please promise that you won't leave your body now. I am utterly unprepared to carry on without you."

Sri Yukteswar was silent, but smiled at me so compassionately that I felt reassured. Reluctantly I left him.

"MASTER DANGEROUSLY ILL." This telegram from Auddy reached me shortly after my return to Serampore.

"Sir," I wired my guru frantically, "I asked for your promise not to leave me. Please keep your body; otherwise, I also shall die."

"Be it as you wish." This was Sri Yukteswar's reply from Kashmir.

A letter from Auddy arrived in a few days, informing me that Master had recovered. On his return to Serampore during the next fortnight, I was grieved to find my guru's body reduced to half its usual weight.

Fortunately for his disciples, Sri Yukteswar burned many of their sins in the fire of his severe fever in Kashmir. The metaphysical method of physical transfer of disease is known to highly advanced yogis. A strong man can assist a weaker one by helping to carry his heavy load; a spiritual superman is able to minimize his disciples' physical or mental burdens by sharing the karma of their past actions. Just as a rich man loses some money when he pays off a large debt for his prodigal son, who is thus saved from dire consequences of his own folly, so a master willingly sacrifices a portion of his bodily wealth to lighten the misery of disciples.[3]

By a secret yogic method, the saint unites his mind and astral vehicle with those of a suffering individual; the disease is conveyed, wholly or in part, to the saint's body. Having harvested God on the physical field, a master no longer cares what happens to that material form. Though he may allow it to register a certain disease in order to relieve others, his mind is never affected; he considers himself fortunate in being able to render such aid.

The devotee who has achieved final salvation in the Lord finds that his body has completely fulfilled its purpose; he can then use it in any way he deems fit. His work in the world is to alleviate the sorrows of mankind, whether through spiritual means or by intellectual counsel or through will-power or by the physical transfer of disease. Escaping to the superconsciousness whenever he so desires, a master can remain oblivious of physical suffering; sometimes he chooses to bear bodily pain stoically, as an example to disciples. By putting on the ailments of others, a yogi can satisfy, for them, the karmic law of cause and effect. This law is mechanically or mathematically operative; its workings can be scientifically manipulated by men of divine wisdom.

The spiritual law does not require a master to become ill whenever he heals another person. Healings ordinarily take place through the saint's knowledge of various methods of instantaneous cure in which no hurt to the spiritual healer is involved. On rare occasions, however, a master who wishes to greatly quicken his disciples' evolution may then voluntarily work out on his own body a large measure of their undesirable karma.

Jesus signified himself as a ransom for the sins of many. With his divine powers,[4] his body could never have been subjected to death by crucifixion if he had not willingly cooperated with the subtle cosmic law of cause and effect. He thus took on himself the consequences of others' karma, especially that of his disciples. In this manner they were highly purified and made fit to receive the omnipresent consciousness which later descended on them.

3 Many Christian saints, including Therese Neumann (see chapter 39), are familiar with the metaphysical transfer of disease.

4 Christ said, just before he was led away to be crucified: "Thinkest thou that I cannot now pray to my Father, and he shall presently give me more than twelve legions of angels? But how then shall the scriptures be fulfilled, that thus it must be?" – Matthew, 26: 53-54.

Only a self-realized master can transfer his life force, or convey into his own body the diseases of others. An ordinary man cannot employ this yogic method of cure, nor is it desirable that he should do so; for an unsound physical instrument is a hindrance to God-meditation. The Hindu scriptures teach that the first duty of man is to keep his body in good condition; otherwise his mind is unable to remain fixed in devotional concentration.

A very strong mind, however, can transcend all physical difficulties and attain to God-realization. Many saints have ignored illness and succeeded in their divine quest. St. Francis of Assisi, severely afflicted with ailments, healed others and even raised the dead.

I once knew an Indian saint, half of whose body was festering with sores. His diabetic condition was so acute that under ordinary conditions he could not sit still at one time for more than fifteen minutes. But his spiritual aspiration was undeterrable. "Lord," he prayed, "wilt Thou come into my broken temple?" With ceaseless command of will, the saint gradually became able to sit daily in the lotus posture for eighteen continuous hours, engrossed in the ecstatic trance.

"And," he told me, "at the end of three years, I found the Infinite Light blazing within my shattered form. Rejoicing in the joyful splendour, I forgot the body. Later I saw that it had become whole through the Divine Mercy."

A historical healing incident concerns King Baber (1483-1530), founder of the Mogul empire in India. His son, Prince Humayun,[5] was mortally ill. The father prayed with anguished determination that he receive the sickness, and that his son be spared. After all physicians had given up hope, Humayun recovered. Baber immediately fell sick and died of the same disease which had stricken his son. Humayun succeeded Baber as Emperor of Hindustan.

Many people imagine that every spiritual master has, or should have, the health and strength of a Sandow. The assumption is unfounded. A sickly body does not indicate that a guru is not in touch with divine powers, any more than lifelong health necessarily indicates an inner illumination. The condition of the physical body, in other words, cannot rightfully be made a test of a master. His distinguishing qualifications must be sought in his own domain, the spiritual.

Numerous bewildered seekers in the West erroneously think that an eloquent speaker or writer on metaphysics must be a master. The rishis, however, have pointed out that the acid test of a master is a man's ability to enter at will the breathless state, and to maintain the unbroken *samadhi* of *nirbikalpa*.[6] Only by these achievements can a human being prove that

---

5 Humayun's son Akbar at first persecuted the Hindus. "As I grew in knowledge, I was overwhelmed with shame," he said later. "Miracles occur in the temples of every creed." He arranged for a Persian translation of the *Bhagavad Gita*, and invited to his court several Jesuit Fathers from Rome. Akbar inaccurately but lovingly attributed to Christ the following saying (inscribed on the Victory Arch in Akbar's new city of Fatehpur Sikri): 'Jesus son of Mary (on whom be peace), said: *The World is a bridge; pass over it, but build no house upon it.*'

6 See page 188 & Note 1 on page 309.

he has 'mastered' *maya* or the dualistic Cosmic Delusion. He alone can say from the depths of realization: '*Ekam sat*,' – 'Only One exists.'

"The *Vedas* declare that the ignorant man who rests content with making the slightest distinction between the individual soul and the Supreme Self is exposed to danger," Shankara the great monist has written. "Where there is duality by virtue of ignorance, one sees all things as distinct from the Self. When everything is seen as the Self, then there is not even an atom other than the Self . . .

"As soon as the knowledge of the Reality has sprung up, there can be no fruits of past actions to be experienced, owing to the unreality of the body, in the same way as there can be no dream after waking."

Only great gurus are able to assume the karma of disciples. Sri Yukteswar would not have suffered in Srinagar[7] unless he had received permission from the Spirit within him to help his disciples in that strange way. Few saints were ever more sensitively equipped with wisdom to carry out divine commands than my God-tuned Master.

When I ventured a few words of sympathy over his emaciated figure, my guru said gaily:

"It has its good points; I am able now to get into some small *ganjis* (undershirts) that I haven't worn in years!"

Listening to Master's jovial laugh, I remembered the words of St. Francis de Sales: "A saint that is sad is a sad saint!"

22. *The Heart of a Stone Image*

"As a loyal Hindu wife, I do not wish to complain of my husband. But I yearn to see him turn from his materialistic views. He delights in ridiculing the pictures of saints in my meditation room. Dear brother, I have deep faith that you can help him. Will you?"

My eldest sister Roma gazed beseechingly at me. I was paying a short visit at her Calcutta home on Girish Vidyaratna Lane. Her plea touched me, for she had exercised a profound spiritual influence over my early life, and had lovingly tried to fill the void left in the family circle by Mother's death.

"Beloved sister, of course I will do anything I can." I smiled, eager to lift the gloom plainly visible on her face, in contrast to her usual calm and cheerful expression.

7 Srinagar, capital city of Kashmir, was founded in the third century B.C. by Emperor Asoka. He built there 500 monasteries, of which 100 were still standing when the Chinese pilgrim Hiuen Tsiang visited Kashmir 1000 years later. Another Chinese writer, Fa-Hsien (fifth century), viewing the ruins of Asoka's last palace at Pa-taliputra (modern Patna), tells us the structure was of such incredible beauty in its architecture and decorative sculpture that it 'could have been the work of no mortal hands.'

Roma and I sat a while in silent prayer for guidance. A year earlier, my sister had asked me to initiate her into *Kriya Yoga,* in which she was making notable progress.

An inspiration seized me. "Tomorrow," I said, "I am going to the Dakshineswar temple. Please come with me, and persuade your husband to accompany us. I feel that in the vibrations of that holy place, Divine Mother will touch his heart. But don't disclose our object in wanting him to go."

Sister agreed hopefully. Very early the next morning I was pleased to find that Roma and her husband were in readiness for the trip. As our hackney carriage rattled along Upper Circular Road toward Dakshineswar, my brother-in-law, Satish Chandra Bose, amused himself by deriding spiritual gurus of the past, present, and future. I noticed that Roma was quietly weeping.

"Sister, cheer up!" I whispered. "Don't give your husband the satisfaction of believing that we take his mockery seriously."

"Mukunda, how can you admire worthless humbugs?" Satish was saying. "A *sadhu's* very appearance is repulsive. He is either as thin as a skeleton, or as unholily fat as an elephant!"

I shook with laughter. My good-natured reaction was annoying to Satish; he retired into sullen silence. As our cab entered the Dakshineswar grounds, he grinned sarcastically.

"This excursion, I suppose, is a scheme to reform me?"

As I turned away without reply, he caught my arm. "Young Mr. Monk," he said, "don't forget to make proper arrangements with the temple authorities to provide for our noon meal."

"I am going to meditate now. Do not worry about your lunch," I replied sharply. "Divine Mother will look after it."

"I don't trust Divine Mother to do a single thing for me. But I do hold you responsible for my food." Satish's tones were threatening.

I proceeded alone to the colonnaded hall which fronts the large temple of Kali, or Mother Nature. Selecting a shady spot near one of the pillars, I arranged my body in the lotus posture. Although it was only about seven o'clock, the morning sun would soon be oppressive.

The world receded as I became devotionally entranced. My mind was concentrated on Goddess Kali, whose image at Dakshineswar had been the special object of adoration by the great master, Sri Ramakrishna Paramahansa. In answer to his anguished demands, the stone image of this very temple had often taken a living form and conversed with him.

"Silent Mother with stony heart," I prayed, "Thou didst become filled with life at the request of Thy beloved devotee Ramakrishna; why dost Thou not also heed the wails of this yearning son of Thine?"

My aspiring zeal increased boundlessly, accompanied by a divine peace. Yet, when five hours had passed, and the Goddess whom I was inwardly visualizing had made no response, I felt slightly disheartened. Sometimes it is a test by God to delay the fulfillment of prayers. But He eventually appears to the persistent devotee in whatever form he holds dear. A devout Christian sees Jesus; a Hindu beholds Krishna, or the Goddess Kali, or an expanding Light if his worship takes an impersonal turn.

Reluctantly I opened my eyes, and saw that the temple doors were being locked by a priest, in conformance with a noon-hour custom. I rose from my secluded seat under the open, roofed hall, and stepped into the courtyard. Its stone floor was scorching under the midday sun; my bare feet were painfully burned.

"Divine Mother," I silently remonstrated, "Thou didst not come to me in vision, and now Thou art hidden in the temple behind closed doors. I wanted to offer a special prayer to Thee today on behalf of my brother-in-law."

My inward petition was instantly acknowledged. First, a delightful cold wave descended over my back and under my feet, banishing all discomfort. Then, to my amazement, the temple became greatly magnified. Its large door slowly opened, revealing the stone figure of Goddess Kali. Gradually it changed into a living form, smilingly nodding in greeting, thrilling me with joy indescribable. As if by a mystic syringe, the breath was withdrawn from my lungs; my body became very still, though not inert.

An ecstatic enlargement of consciousness followed. I could see clearly for several miles over the Ganges River to my left, and beyond the temple into the entire Dakshineswar precincts. The walls of all buildings glimmered transparently; through them I observed people walking to and fro over distant acres.

Though I was breathless and my body in a strangely quiet state, yet I was able to move my hands and feet freely. For several minutes I experimented in closing and opening my eyes; in either state I saw distinctly the whole Dakshineswar panorama.

Spiritual sight, x-raylike, penetrates into all matter; the divine eye is centre everywhere, circumference nowhere. I realized anew, standing there in the sunny courtyard, that when man ceases to be a prodigal child of God, engrossed in a physical world indeed dream, baseless as a bubble, he reinherits his eternal realms. If 'escapism' be a need of man, cramped in his narrow personality, can any escape compare with the majesty of omnipresence?

In my sacred experience at Dakshineswar, the only extraordinarily-enlarged objects were the temple and the form of the Goddess. Everything else appeared in its normal dimensions, although each was enclosed in a halo of mellow light – white, blue, and pastel rainbow hues. My body seemed to be of ethereal substance, ready to levitate. Fully conscious of my material surroundings, I was looking about me and taking a few steps without disturbing the continuity of the blissful vision.

Behind the temple walls I suddenly glimpsed my brother-in-law as he sat under the thorny branches of a sacred *bel* tree. I could effortlessly discern the course of his thoughts. Somewhat uplifted under the holy influence of Dakshineswar, his mind yet held unkind reflections about me. I turned directly to the gracious form of the Goddess.

"Divine Mother," I prayed, "wilt Thou not spiritually change my sister's husband?"

The beautiful figure, hitherto silent, spoke at last: "Thy wish is granted!"

I looked happily at Satish. As though instinctively aware that some spiritual power was at work, he rose resentfully from his seat on the ground. I saw him running behind the temple; he approached me, shaking his fist.

The all-embracing vision disappeared. No longer could I see the glorious Goddess; the towering temple was reduced to its ordinary size, minus its transparency. Again my body sweltered under the fierce rays of the sun. I jumped to the shelter of the pillared hall, where Satish pursued me angrily. I looked at my watch. It was one o'clock; the divine vision had lasted an hour.

"You little fool," my brother-in-law blurted out, "you have been sitting there cross-legged and cross-eyed for six hours. I have gone back and forth watching you. Where is my food? Now the temple is closed; you failed to notify the authorities; we are left without lunch!"

The exaltation I had felt at the Goddess' presence was still vibrant within my heart. I was emboldened to exclaim, "Divine Mother will feed us!"

Satish was beside himself with rage. "Once and for all," he shouted, "I would like to see your Divine Mother giving us food here without prior arrangements!"

His words were hardly uttered when a temple priest crossed the courtyard and joined us.

"Son," he addressed me, "I have been observing your face serenely glowing during hours of meditation. I saw the arrival of your party this morning, and felt a desire to put aside ample food for your lunch. It is against the temple rules to feed those who do not make a request beforehand, but I have made an exception for you."

I thanked him, and gazed straight into Satish's eyes. He flushed with emotion, lowering his gaze in silent repentance. When we were served a lavish meal, including out-of-season mangoes, I noticed that my brother-in-law's appetite was meagre. He was bewildered, diving deep into the ocean of thought. On the return journey to Calcutta, Satish, with softened expression, occasionally glanced at me pleadingly. But he did not speak a single word after the moment the priest had appeared to invite us to lunch, as though in direct answer to Satish's challenge.

The following afternoon I visited my sister at her home. She greeted me affectionately.

"Dear brother," she cried, "what a miracle! Last evening my husband wept openly before me.

" 'Beloved *devi*,'[1] he said, 'I am happy beyond expression that this reforming scheme of your brother's has wrought a transformation. I am going to undo every wrong I have done you. From tonight we will use our large bedroom only as a place of worship; your small meditation room shall be changed into our sleeping quarters. I am sincerely sorry that I have ridiculed your brother. For the shameful way I have been acting, I will punish myself by not talking to Mukunda until I have progressed in the spiritual path. Deeply I will seek the Divine Mother from now on; someday I must surely find Her!' "

Years later, I visited my brother-in-law in Delhi. I was overjoyed to perceive that he had developed highly in self-realization, and had been blessed by the vision of Divine Mother. During my stay with him, I noticed that Satish secretly spent the greater part of every night in divine meditation, though he was suffering from a serious ailment, and was engaged during the day at his office.

The thought came to me that my brother-in-law's life span would not be a long one. Roma must have read my mind.

"Dear brother," she said, "I am well, and my husband is sick. Nevertheless, I want you to know that, as a devoted Hindu wife, I am going to be the first one to die.[2] It won't be long now before I pass on."

Taken aback at her ominous words, I yet realized their sting of truth. I was in America when my sister died, about a year after her prediction. My youngest brother Bishnu later gave me the details.

"Roma and Satish were in Calcutta at the time of her death," Bishnu told me. "That morning she dressed herself in her bridal finery.

" 'Why this special costume?' Satish inquired.

" 'This is my last day of service to you on earth,' Roma replied. A short time later she had a heart attack. As her son was rushing out for aid, she said:

" 'Son, do not leave me. It is no use; I shall be gone before a doctor could arrive.' Ten minutes later, holding the feet of her husband in reverence, Roma consciously left her body, happily and without suffering.

1 Goddess.

2 A Hindu wife believes it is a sign of spiritual advancement if she dies before her husband, as a proof of her loyal service to him, or 'dying in harness.'

"Satish became very reclusive after his wife's death," Bishnu continued. "One day he and I were looking at a large smiling photograph of Roma.

" 'Why do you smile?' Satish suddenly exclaimed, as though his wife were present. 'You think you were clever in arranging to go before me. I shall prove that you cannot long remain away from me; soon I shall join you.'

"Although at this time Satish had fully recovered from his sickness, and was enjoying excellent health, he died without apparent cause shortly after his strange remark before the photograph."

Thus prophetically passed my dearly beloved eldest sister Roma, and her husband Satish – he who changed at Dakshineswar from an ordinary worldly man to a silent saint.

23. *I receive my University Degree*

"YOU IGNORE your textbook assignments in philosophy. No doubt you are depending on an unlaborious 'intuition' to get you through the examinations. But unless you apply yourself in a more scholarly manner, I shall see to it that you don't pass this course."

Professor D.C. Ghoshal of Serampore College was addressing me sternly. If I failed to pass his final written classroom test, I would be ineligible to take the conclusive examinations. These are formulated by the faculty of Calcutta University, which numbers Serampore College among its affiliated branches. A student in Indian universities who is unsuccessful in one subject in the A.B. finals must be examined anew in *all* his subjects the following year.

My instructors at Serampore College usually treated me with kindness, not untinged by an amused tolerance. "Mukunda is a bit over-drunk with religion." Thus summing me up, they tactfully spared me the embarrassment of answering classroom questions; they trusted the final written tests to eliminate me from the list of A.B. candidates. The judgment passed by my fellow students was expressed in their nickname for me – 'Mad Monk.'

I took an ingenious step to nullify Professor Ghoshal's threat to me of failure in philosophy. When the results of the final tests were about to be publicly announced, I asked a classmate to accompany me to the professor's study.

"Come along; I want a witness," I told my companion. "I shall be very much disappointed if I have not succeeded in outwitting the instructor."

Professor Ghoshal shook his head after I had inquired what rating he had given my paper.

"You are not among those who have passed," he said in triumph. He hunted through a large pile on his desk. "Your paper isn't here at all; you have failed, in any case, through non-appearance at the examination."

I chuckled. "Sir, I was there. May I look through the stack myself?"

The professor, nonplused, gave his permission; I quickly found my paper, where I had carefully omitted any identification mark except my roll call number. Unwarned by the 'red flag' of my name, the instructor had given a high rating to my answers even though they were unembellished by textbook quotations.[1]

Seeing through my trick, he now thundered, "Sheer brazen luck!" He added hopefully, "You are sure to fail in the A.B. finals."

For the tests in my other subjects, I received some coaching, particularly from my dear friend and cousin, Prabhas Chandra Ghose,[2] son of my Uncle Sarada. I staggered painfully but successfully – with the lowest possible passing marks – through all my final tests.

Now, after four years of college, I was eligible to sit for the A.B. examinations. Nevertheless, I hardly expected to avail myself of the privilege. The Serampore College finals were child's play compared to the stiff ones which would be set by Calcutta University for the A.B. degree. My almost daily visits to Sri Yukteswar had left me little time to enter the college halls. There it was my presence rather than my absence that brought forth ejaculations of amazement from my classmates!

My customary routine was to set out on my bicycle about nine-thirty in the morning. In one hand I would carry an offering for my guru – a few flowers from the garden of my *Panthi* boarding-house. Greeting me affably, Master would invite me to lunch. I invariably accepted with alacrity, glad to banish the thought of college for the day. After hours with Sri Yukteswar, listening to his incomparable flow of wisdom, or helping with ashram duties, I would reluctantly depart around midnight for the *Panthi*. Occasionally I stayed all night with my guru, so happily engrossed in his conversation that I scarcely noticed when darkness changed into dawn.

One night about eleven o'clock, as I was putting on my shoes[3] in preparation for the ride to the boarding-house, Master questioned me gravely.

"When do your A.B. examinations start?"

"Five days hence, sir."

---

1 I must do Professor Ghoshal the justice of admitting that the strained relationship between us was not due to any fault of his, but due solely to my absences from classes and inattention in them. Professor Ghoshal was, and is, a remarkable orator with vast philosophical knowledge. In later years we came to a cordial understanding.

2 Although my cousin and I have the same family name of Ghosh, Prabhas has accustomed himself to transliterating his name in English as Ghose; therefore I follow his own spelling here.

3 A disciple always removes his shoes in an Indian hermitage.

"I hope you are in readiness for them."

Transfixed with alarm, I held one shoe in the air. "Sir," I protested, "you know how my days have been passed with you rather than with the professors. How can I enact a farce by appearing for those difficult finals?"

Sri Yukteswar's eyes were turned piercingly on mine. "You must appear." His tone was coldly peremptory. "We should not give cause for your father and other relatives to criticize your preference for ashram life. Just promise me that you will be present for the examinations; answer them the best way you can."

Uncontrollable tears were coursing down my face. I felt that Master's command was unreasonable, and that his interest was, to say the least, belated.

"I will appear if you wish it," I said amidst sobs. "But no time remains for proper preparation." Under my breath I muttered, "I will fill up the sheets with your teachings in answer to the questions!"

When I entered the hermitage the following day at my usual hour, I presented my bouquet with a certain mournful solemnity. Sri Yukteswar laughed at my woebegone air.

"Mukunda, has the Lord ever failed you, at an examination or elsewhere?"

"No, sir," I responded warmly. Grateful memories came in a revivifying flood.

"Not laziness but burning zeal for God has prevented you from seeking college honours," my guru said kindly. After a silence, he quoted, " 'Seek ye first the kingdom of God, and His righteousness; and all these things shall be added unto you.' "[4]

For the thousandth time, I felt my burdens lifted in Master's presence. When we had finished our early lunch, he suggested that I return to the *Panthi*.

"Does your friend, Romesh Chandra Dutt, still live in your boarding-house?"

"Yes, sir."

"Get in touch with him; the Lord will inspire him to help you with the examinations."

"Very well, sir; but Romesh is unusually busy. He is the honours man in our class, and carries a heavier course than the others."

Master waved aside my objections. "Romesh will find time for you. Now go."

I bicycled back to the *Panthi*. The first person I met in the boarding-house compound was the scholarly Romesh. As though his days were quite free, he obligingly agreed to my diffident request.

"Of course; I am at your service." He spent several hours of that

4 *Matthew* 6: 33.

afternoon and of succeeding days in coaching me in my various subjects.

"I believe many questions in English literature will be centred in the route of Childe Harold," he told me. "We must get an atlas at once."

I hastened to the home of my Uncle Sarada and borrowed an atlas. Romesh marked the European map at the places visited by Byron's romantic traveller.

A few classmates had gathered around to listen to the tutoring. "Romesh is advising you wrongly," one of them commented to me at the end of a session. "Usually only fifty per cent of the questions are about the books; the other half will involve the authors' lives."

When I sat for the examination in English literature the following day, my first glance at the questions caused tears of gratitude to pour forth, wetting my paper. The classroom monitor came to my desk and made a sympathetic inquiry.

"My guru foretold that Romesh would help me," I explained. "Look; the very questions dictated to me by Romesh are here on the examination sheet! Fortunately for me, there are very few questions this year on English authors, whose lives are wrapped in deep mystery so far as I am concerned!"

My boarding-house was in an uproar when I returned. The boys who had been ridiculing Romesh's method of coaching looked at me in awe, almost deafening me with congratulations. During the week of the examinations, I spent many hours with Romesh, who formulated questions that he thought were likely to be set by the professors. Day by day, Romesh's questions appeared in almost the same form on the examination sheets.

The news was widely circulated in the college that something resembling a miracle was occurring, and that success seemed probable for the absent-minded 'Mad Monk.' I made no attempt to hide the facts of the case. The local professors were powerless to alter the questions, which had been arranged by Calcutta University.

Thinking over the examination in English literature, I realized one morning that I had made a serious error. One section of the questions had been divided into two parts of A or B, and C or D. Instead of answering one question from each part, I had carelessly answered both questions in Group I, and had failed to consider anything in Group II. The best mark I could score in that paper would be 33, three less than the passing mark of 36. I rushed to Master and poured out my troubles.

"Sir, I have made an unpardonable blunder. I don't deserve the divine blessings through Romesh; I am quite unworthy."

"Cheer up, Mukunda." Sri Yukteswar's tones were light and unconcerned. He pointed to the blue vault of the heavens. "It is more possible for the sun and moon to interchange their positions in space than it is for you to fail in getting your degree!"

I left the hermitage in a more tranquil mood, though it seemed mathematically inconceivable that I could pass. I looked once or twice apprehensively into the sky; the Lord of Day appeared to be securely anchored in his customary orbit!

As I reached the *Panthi*, I overheard a classmate's remark: "I have just learned that this year, for the first time, the required passing mark in English literature has been lowered."

I entered the boy's room with such speed that he looked up in alarm. I questioned him eagerly.

"Long-haired monk," he said laughingly, "why this sudden interest in scholastic matters? Why cry in the eleventh hour? But it is true that the passing mark has just been lowered to 33 points."

A few joyous leaps took me into my own room, where I sank to my knees and praised the mathematical perfections of my Divine Father.

Every day I thrilled with the consciousness of a spiritual presence that I clearly felt to be guiding me through Romesh. A significant incident occurred in connection with the examination in Bengali. Romesh, who had touched little on that subject, called me back one morning as I was leaving the boarding-house on my way to the examination hall.

"There is Romesh shouting for you," a classmate said to me impatiently. "Don't return; we shall be late at the hall."

Ignoring the advice, I ran back to the house.

"The Bengali examination is usually easily passed by our Bengali boys," Romesh told me. "But I have just had a hunch that this year the professors have planned to massacre the students by asking questions from our ancient literature." My friend then briefly outlined two stories from the life of Vidyasagar, a renowned philanthropist of the nineteenth century.

I thanked Romesh and quickly bicycled to the college hall. The examination sheet in Bengali proved to contain two parts. The first instruction was: "Write two instances of the charities of Vidyasagar."[5] As I transferred to the paper the lore that I had so recently acquired, I whispered a few words of thanks-giving that I had heeded Romesh's last-minute summons. Had I been ignorant of Vidyasagar's benefactions to mankind (including ultimately myself), I could not have passed the Bengali examination. Failing in one subject, I would have been forced to stand examination anew in all subjects

5 Because of his erudition Pundit Ishwar Chandra Vidyasagar became widely known in Bengal simply by the title *Vidyasagar* ('Ocean of Learning').

the following year. Such a prospect was understandably abhorrent.

The second instruction on the sheet read: "Write an essay in Bengali on the life of the man who has most inspired you." Gentle reader, I need not inform you what man I chose for my theme. As I covered page after page with praise of my guru, I smiled to realize that my muttered prediction was coming true: "I will fill up the sheets with your teachings!"

I had not felt inclined to question Romesh about my course in philosophy. Trusting my long training under Sri Yukteswar, I safely disregarded the textbook explanations. The highest mark given to any of my papers was the one in philosophy. My score in all other subjects was just barely within the passing mark.

It is a pleasure to record that my unselfish friend Romesh received his own degree *cum laude* (with distinction).

Father was wreathed in smiles at my graduation. "I hardly thought you would pass, Mukunda," he confessed. "You spend so much time with your guru." Master had indeed correctly detected the unspoken criticism of my father.

For years I had been uncertain that I would ever see the day when an A.B. would follow my name. I seldom use the title without reflecting that it was a divine gift, conferred on me for reasons somewhat obscure. Occasionally I hear college men remark that very little of their crammed knowledge remained with them after graduation. That admission consoles me a bit for my undoubted academic deficiencies.

On the day in June 1915 that I received my degree from Calcutta University, I knelt at my guru's feet and thanked him for all the blessings flowing from his life[6] into mine.

"Get up, Mukunda," he said indulgently. "The Lord simply found it more convenient to make you a graduate than to re-arrange the sun and moon!"

---

6 The power of influencing others' minds and the course of events is a *vibhuti* (yogic power) mentioned in Patanjali's *Yoga Sutras* III: 24, which explains it to be a result of 'universal sympathy.' [Two scholarly books on the *Sutras* are *Yoga-System of Patanjali* (Vol. 17, Oriental Series, Harvard Univ.) and Dasgupta's *Yoga Philosophy* (Trubner's, London.)].

All scriptures proclaim that the Lord created man in His omnipotent image. Control over the universe appears to be supernatural, but in truth such power is inherent and natural in everyone who attains 'right remembrance' of his divine origin. Men of God-realization like Sri Yukteswar are devoid of the ego-principle (*ahamkara*) and its uprisings of personal desires; the actions of true masters are in effortless conformity with *rita*, natural righteousness. In Emerson's words, all great ones become 'not virtuous but Virtue; then is the end of the creation answered, and God is well pleased.'

Any man of divine realization could perform miracles, because, like Christ, he understands the subtle laws of creations; but not all masters choose to exercise phenomenal powers. (See Note 11 on page 164). Each saint reflects God in his own way; the expression of individuality is basic in a world where not two grains of sand are exactly alike.

Invariable rules may not be formulated about God-illumined saints: some perform miracles, others do not; some are inactive, while others (like King Janaka of ancient India, and St. Teresa of Avila) are concerned with large affairs; some teach, travel, and accept disciples, while others pass their lives as silently and unobtrusively as a shadow. No worldly critics can read the secret scroll of *karma* (past actions) that unrolls for each saint a different script.

24. *I become a Monk of the Swami Order*

"MASTER, my father has been anxious for me to accept an executive position with the Bengal-Nagpur Railway. But I have definitely refused it." I added hopefully, "Sir, will you not make me a monk of the Swami Order?" I looked pleadingly at my guru. During preceding years, in order to test the depth of my determination, he had refused this same request. Today, however, he smiled graciously.

"Very well; tomorrow I will initiate you into swamiship." He went on quietly, "I am happy that you have persisted in your desire to be a monk. Lahiri Mahasaya often said: 'If you don't invite God to be your summer Guest, He won't come in the winter of your life.' "

"Dear master, I could never falter in my goal to belong to the Swami Order like your revered self." I smiled at him with measureless affection.

"He that is unmarried careth for the things that belong to the Lord, how he may please the Lord: but he that is married careth for the things of the world, how he may please his wife."[1] I had analyzed the lives of many of my friends who, after undergoing certain spiritual discipline, had then married. Launched on the sea of worldly responsibilities, they had forgotten their resolutions to meditate deeply.

To allot God a secondary place[2] in life was, to me, inconceivable. Though He is the sole Owner of the cosmos, silently showering us with gifts from life to life, one thing yet remains which He does not own, and which each human heart is empowered to withhold or bestow – man's love. The Creator, in taking infinite pains to shroud with mystery His presence in every atom of creation, could have had but one motive – a sensitive desire that men seek Him only through free will. With what velvet glove of every humility has He not covered the iron hand of omnipotence!

The following day was one of the most memorable in my life. It was a sunny Thursday, I remember, in July, 1914, a few weeks after my graduation from college. On the inner balcony of his Serampore hermitage, Master dipped a new piece of white silk into a dye of ochre, the traditional colour of the Swami Order. After the cloth had dried, my guru draped it around me as a renunciate's robe.

"Someday you will go to the West, where silk is preferred," he said. "As a symbol, I have chosen for you this silk material instead of the customary cotton."

In India, where monks embrace the ideal of poverty, a silk-clad swami is an unusual sight. Many yogis, however, wear garments of silk, which preserves certain subtle bodily currents better than cotton.

1 I *Corinthians* 7: 32-33.
2 'He who offers God a second place offers Him no place' – *Ruskin*.

"I am averse to ceremonies," Sri Yukteswar remarked. "I will make you a swami in the *bidwat* (non-ceremonious) manner."

The *bibidisa* or elaborate initiation into swamiship includes a fire ceremony, during which symbolical funeral rites are performed. The physical body of the disciple is represented as dead, cremated in the flame of wisdom. The newly-made swami is then given a chant, such as: "This *atma* is Brahma" [3] or "Thou art That" or "I am He." Sri Yukteswar, however, with his love of simplicity, dispensed with all formal rites and merely asked me to select a new name.

"I will give you the privilege of choosing it yourself," he said, smiling.

"Yogananda," I replied, after a moment's thought. The name literally means "Bliss (*ananda*) through divine union (*yoga*)."

"Be it so. Forsaking your family name of Mukunda Lal Ghosh, henceforth you shall be called Yogananda of the Giri branch of the Swami Order."

As I knelt before Sri Yukteswar, and for the first time heard him pronounce my new name, my heart overflowed with gratitude. How lovingly and tirelessly had he laboured, that the boy Mukunda be someday transformed into the monk Yogananda! I joyfully sang a few verses from the long Sanskrit chant of Lord Shankara:

> "Mind, nor intellect, nor ego, feeling;
> Sky nor earth nor metals am I.
> I am He, I am He, Blessed Spirit, I am He!
> No birth, no death, no caste have I;
> Father, mother, have I none.
> I am He, I am He, Blessed Spirit, I am He!
> Beyond the flights of fancy, formless am I,
> Permeating the limbs of all life;
> Bondage I do not fear; I am free, ever free,
> I am He, I am He, Blessed Spirit, I am He!"

Every swami belongs to the ancient monastic order which was organized in its present form by Shankara.[4] Because it is a formal order, with an unbroken line of saintly representatives serving as active leaders, no man can give himself the title of swami. He rightfully receives it only from another swami; all monks thus trace their spiritual lineage to one common guru, Lord

---

3 Literally, 'This soul is Spirit.' The Supreme Spirit, the Uncreated, is wholly unconditioned (*neti, neti*: not this, not that) but is often referred to in *Vedanta* as *Sat-Chit-Ananda,* that is, Being-Intelligence-Bliss.

4 Sometimes called Shankaracharya. *Acharya* means 'religious teacher.' Shankara's date is a centre of the usual scholastic dispute. A few records indicate that the peerless monist lived from 510 to 478 B.C.; Western historians assign him to the late eighth century A.D. Readers who are interested in Shankara's famous exposition of the *Brahma Sutras* will find a careful English translation in Dr. Paul Deussen's *System of the Vedanta* (Chicago: Open Court Publishing Company, 1912). Short extracts from his writings will be found in *Selected Works of Sri Shankaracharya* (Natesan & Co., Madras).

Shankara. By vows of poverty, chastity, and obedience to the spiritual teacher, many Catholic Christian monastic orders resemble the Order of Swamis.

In addition to his new name, usually ending in *ananda,* the swami takes a tide which indicates his formal connection with one of the ten subdivisions of the Swami Order. These *dasanamis* or ten agnomens include the *Giri* (mountain), to which Sri Yukteswar, and hence myself, belong. Among the other branches are the *Sagar* (sea), *Bharati* (land), *Aranya* (forest), *Puri* (tract), *Tirtha* (place of pilgrimage), and *Saraswati* (wisdom of nature).

The new name received by a swami thus has a twofold significance, and represents the attainment of supreme bliss (*ananda*) through some divine quality or state – love, wisdom, devotion, service, yoga – and through a harmony with nature, as expressed in her infinite vastness of oceans, mountains, skies.

The ideal of selfless service to all mankind, and of renunciation of personal ties and ambitions, leads the majority of swamis to engage actively in humanitarian and educational work in India, or occasionally in foreign lands. Ignoring all prejudices of caste, creed, class, colour, sex, or race, a swami follows the precepts of human brotherhood. His goal is absolute unity with Spirit. Imbuing his waking and sleeping consciousness with the thought, "I am He," he roams contentedly, in the world but not of it. Thus only may he justify his title of swami – one who seeks to achieve union with the *Swa* or Self. It is needless to add that not all formally titled swamis are equally successful in reaching their high goal.

Sri Yukteswar was both a swami and a yogi. A swami, formally a monk by virtue of his connection with the ancient order, is not always a yogi. Anyone who practices a scientific technique of God-contact is a yogi; he may be either married or unmarried, either a worldly man or one of formal religious ties. A swami may conceivably follow only the path of dry reasoning, of cold renunciation; but a yogi engages himself in a definite, step-by-step procedure by which the body and mind are disciplined, and the soul liberated. Taking nothing for granted on emotional grounds, or by faith, a yogi practices a thoroughly tested series of exercises which were first mapped out by the early rishis. Yoga has produced, in every age of India, men who became truly free, truly Yogi-Christs.

Like any other science, yoga is applicable to people of every clime and rime. The theory advanced by certain ignorant writers that yoga is 'unsuitable for Westerners' is wholly false, and has lamentably prevented many sincere students from seeking its manifold blessings. Yoga is a method for restraining the natural turbulence of thoughts, which otherwise impartially prevent all men, of all lands, from glimpsing their true nature of Spirit. Yoga cannot know a barrier of East and West any more than does the healing and equitable light of the sun. So long as man possesses a mind with its restless thoughts, so long will there be a universal need for yoga or control.

The ancient rishi Patanjali defines 'yoga' as 'neutralization of the alternating waves in consciousness.'[5] His very short and masterly expositions, the *Yoga Sutras*, form one of the six systems of Hindu philosophy.[6] In contradistinction to Western philosophies, all six Hindu systems embody not only theoretical but practical teachings. In addition to every conceivable ontological inquiry, the six systems formulate six definite disciplines aimed at the permanent removal of suffering and the attainment of timeless bliss.

The common thread linking all six systems is the declaration that no true freedom for man is possible without knowledge of the ultimate Reality. The later *Upanishads* uphold the *Yoga Sutras,* among the six systems, as containing the most efficacious methods for achieving direct perception of truth. Through the practical techniques of yoga, man leaves behind forever the barren realms of speculation and cognizes in experience the veritable Essence.

The *Yoga* system as outlined by Patanjali is known as the Eightfold Path. The first steps, (1) *yama* and (2) *niyama,* require observance of ten negative and positive moralities – avoidance of injury to others, of untruthfulness, of stealing, of incontinence, of gift-receiving (which brings obligations); and purity of body and mind, contentment, self-discipline, study, and devotion to God.

The next steps are (3) *asana* (right posture); the spinal column must be held straight, and the body firm in a comfortable position for meditation; (4) *pranayama* (control of *prana,* subtle life currents); and (5) *pratyahara* (withdrawal of the senses from external objects).

The last steps are forms of yoga proper: (6) *dharana* (concentration); holding the mind to one thought; (7) *dhyana* (meditation), and (8) *samadhi* (superconscious perception). This is the Eightfold Path of Yoga[7] which leads one to the final goal of *Kaivalya* (Absoluteness), a term which might be more comprehensibly put as "realization of the Truth beyond all intellectual apprehension."

"Which is greater," one may ask, "a swami or a yogi?" If and when final oneness with God is achieved, the distinctions of the various paths

---

5 '*Chitta* (thinking principle) *vritti* (whirlpool) *nirodha* (neutralization)' – *Yoga Sutra* I: 2. Patanjali's date is unknown, though a number of scholars place him in the second century B.C. The rishis gave forth treatises on all subjects with such insight that ages have been powerless to outmode them; yet, to the subsequent consternation of historians, the sages made no effort to attach their own dates and personalities to their literary works. They knew their lives were only temporarily important as flashes of the great infinite Life; and that truth is timeless, impossible to trademark, and no private possession of their own.

6 The six orthodox systems (*saddarsana*) are *Sankhya, Yoga, Vedanta, Mimamsa, Nyaya,* and *Vaisesika.* Readers of a scholarly bent will delight in the subtleties and broad scope of these ancient formulations as summarized, in English, in *History of Indian Philosophy,* Vol. I, by Prof. Surendranath DasGupta (Cambridge University Press, 1922).

7 Not to be confused with the 'Noble Eightfold Path' of Buddhism, a guide to man's conduct of life, as follows (1) Right Ideals, (2) Right Motive, (3) Right Speech, (4) Right Action, (5) Right Means of Livelihood, (6) Right Effort, (7) Right Remembrance (of the Self), (8) Right Realization (*samadhi*).

disappear. The *Bhagavad Gita*, however, points out that the methods of yoga are all-embracive. Its techniques are not meant only for certain types and temperaments, such as those few who incline toward the monastic life; yoga requires no formal allegiance. Because the yogic science satisfies a universal need, it has a natural universal applicability.

A true yogi may remain dutifully in the world; there he is like butter on water, and not like the easily-diluted milk of unchurned and undisciplined humanity. To fulfill one's earthly responsibilities is indeed the higher path, provided the yogi, maintaining a mental uninvolvement with egotistical desires, plays his part as a willing instrument of God.

There are a number of great souls, living in American or European or other non-Hindu bodies today who, though they may never have heard the words *yogi* and *swami,* are yet true exemplars of those terms. Through their disinterested service to mankind, or through their mastery over passions and thoughts, or through their single hearted love of God, or through their great powers of concentration, they are, in a sense, yogis; they have set themselves the goal of yoga – self-control. These men could rise to even greater heights if they were taught the definite science of yoga, which makes possible a more conscious direction of one's mind and life.

Yoga has been superficially misunderstood by certain Western writers, but its critics have never been its practitioners. Among many thoughtful tributes to yoga may be mentioned one by Dr. C. G. Jung, the famous Swiss psychologist.

"When a religious method recommends itself as 'scientific,' it can be certain of its public (interest) in the West. Yoga fulfills this expectation," Dr. Jung writes.[8] "Quite apart from the charm of the new, and the fascination of the half-understood, there is good cause for Yoga to have many adherents. It offers the possibility of controllable experience, and thus satisfies the scientific need of 'facts,' and besides this, by reason of its breadth and depth, its venerable age, its doctrine and method, which include every phase of life, it promises undreamed-of possibilities.

"Every religious or philosophical practice means a psychological discipline, that is, a method of mental hygiene. The manifold, purely bodily procedures of Yoga[9] also mean a physiological hygiene which is superior to ordinary gymnastics and breathing exercises, inasmuch

8 Dr. Jung attended the Indian Science Congress in 1937 and received an honorary degree from the University of Calcutta.

9 Dr. Jung here is referring to *Hatha Yoga*, a specialized branch of bodily postures and techniques for health and longevity. *Hatha* is useful, and produces spectacular physical results, but this branch of yoga is little used by yogis bent on spiritual liberation.

as it is not merely mechanistic and scientific, but also philosophical; in its training of the parts of the body, it unites them with the whole of the spirit, as is quite clear, for instance, in the *Pranayama* exercises where *Prana* is both the breath and the universal dynamics of the cosmos.

"When the thing which the individual is doing is also a cosmic event, the effect experienced in the body (the innervation), unites with the emotion of the spirit (the universal idea), and out of this there develops a lively unity which no technique, however scientific, can produce. Yoga practice is unthinkable, and would also be ineffectual, without the concepts on which Yoga is based. It combines the bodily and the spiritual with each other in an extraordinarily complete way.

"In the East, where these ideas and practices have developed, and where for several thousand years an unbroken tradition has created the necessary spiritual foundations, Yoga is, as I can readily believe, the perfect and appropriate method of fusing body and mind together so that they form a unity which is scarcely to be questioned. This unity creates a psychological disposition which makes possible intuitions that transcend consciousness."

The Western day is indeed nearing when the inner science of self-control will be found as necessary as the outer conquest of nature. This new Atomic Age will see men's minds sobered and broadened by the now scientifically indisputable truth that matter is in reality a concentrate of energy. Finer forces of the human mind can and must liberate energies greater than those within stones and metals, lest the material atomic giant, newly unleashed, turn on the world in mindless destruction.[10] An indirect benefit of mankind's concern over atomic bombs may be an increased interest in the science of yoga,[11] a 'bombproof shelter' truly.

10 In Plato's *Timaeus* story of Atlantis, he tells of the inhabitants' advanced state of scientific knowledge. The lost continent is believed to have vanished about 9500 B.C. through a cataclysm of nature; certain metaphysical writers state that the Atlanteans were destroyed as a result of their misuse of atomic power. Two French writers have compiled a *Bibliography of Atlantis*, with 1700 historical and other references.

11 The uninformed consider yoga as *Hatha Yoga,* magic, or dark mysterious rites for attaining spectacular powers. The scholars mean the system expounded in Patanjali's *Yoga Sutras,* the treatise that embodies philosophic concepts with grandeur. They are based on the concept of 'moral purity' (*yama* and *niyama*). The cosmic order (*rita*) that upholds the universe is not different from the moral order that rules man's destiny. He who does not observe universal moral precepts is not serious to pursue truth.

Yogic powers (*vibhutis* and *siddhis*) are mentioned in section III of *Yoga Sutras*. True knowledge is always power. Emergence of characteristic powers is evidence of the scientific structure of the yoga system. Patanjali warns the devotee against delusions about one's 'spiritual progress' and exhorts unity with Spirit as the sole goal, not the incidental possession of *vibhutis*, along the sacred path. May the Eternal Giver be sought, not His phenomenal gifts! God does not reveal Himself to a seeker who is satisfied with any lesser attainment. The striving yogi is careful not to exercise his phenomenal powers lest they arouse false pride and distract him from entering the ultimate state of *Kaivalya*.

When the Yogi has reached his Infinite Goal, he optionally exercises the *Vibhutis* without Karmic involvement. The iron filings of karma are attracted only where a magnet of the personal ego still exists.

25. *Brother Ananta and Sister Nalini*

"ANANTA CANNOT LIVE; the sands of his karma for this life have run out."

These inexorable words reached my inner consciousness as I sat one morning in deep meditation. Shortly after I had entered the Swami Order, I paid a visit to my birthplace, Gorakhpur, as a guest of my elder brother Ananta. A sudden illness confined him to his bed; I nursed him lovingly.

The solemn inward pronouncement filled me with grief. I felt that I could not bear to remain longer in Gorakhpur, only to see my brother removed before my helpless gaze. Amidst uncomprehending criticism from my relatives, I left India on the first available boat. It cruised along Burma and the China Sea to Japan. I disembarked at Kobe, where I spent only a few days. My heart was too heavy for sightseeing.

On the return trip to India, the boat touched at Shanghai. There Dr. Misra, the ship's physician, guided me to several curio shops, where I selected various presents for Sri Yukteswar and my family and friends. For Ananta I purchased a large carved bamboo piece. No sooner had the Chinese salesman handed me the bamboo souvenir than I dropped it on the floor, crying out, "I have bought this for my dear dead brother!"

A clear realization had swept over me that his soul was just being freed in the Infinite. The souvenir was sharply and symbolically cracked by its fall; amidst sobs, I wrote on the bamboo surface: "For my beloved Ananta, now gone."

My companion, the doctor, was observing these proceedings with a sardonic smile.

"Save your tears," he remarked. "Why shed them until you are sure he is dead?"

When our boat reached Calcutta, Dr. Misra again accompanied me. My youngest brother Bishnu was waiting to greet me at the dock.

"I know Ananta has departed this life," I said to Bishnu, before he had had time to speak. "Please tell me, and the doctor here, when Ananta died."

Bishnu named the date, which was the very day that I had bought the souvenirs in Shanghai.

"Look here!" Dr. Misra ejaculated. "Don't let any word of this get around! The professors will be adding a year's study of mental telepathy to the medical course, which is already long enough!"

Father embraced me warmly as I entered our Gurpar Road home. "You have come," he said tenderly. Two large tears dropped from his eyes.

Ordinarily undemonstrative, he had never before shown me these signs of affection. Outwardly the grave father, inwardly he possessed the melting heart of a mother. In all his dealings with the family, his dual parental role was distinctly manifest.

Soon after Ananta's passing, my younger sister Nalini was brought back from death's door by a divine healing. Before relating the story, I will refer to a few phases of her earlier life.

The childhood relationship between Nalini and myself had not been of the happiest nature. I was very thin; she was thinner still. Through an unconscious motive or 'complex' which psychiatrists will have no difficulty in identifying, I often used to tease my sister about her cadaverous appearance. Her retorts were equally permeated with the callous frankness of extreme youth. Sometimes Mother intervened, ending the childish quarrels, temporarily, by a gentle box on my ear, (as the elder ear).

Time passed; Nalini was betrothed to a young Calcutta physician, Panchanon Bose. He received a generous dowry from Father, presumably (as I remarked to Sister) to compensate the bridegroom-to-be for his fate in allying himself with a human bean-pole.

Elaborate marriage rites were celebrated in due time. On the wedding night, I joined the large and jovial group of relatives in the living room of our Calcutta home. The bridegroom was leaning on an immense gold-brocaded pillow, with Nalini at his side. A gorgeous purple silk *sari*[1] could not, alas, wholly hide her angularity. I sheltered myself behind the pillow of my new brother-in-law and grinned at him in friendly fashion. He had never seen Nalini until the day of the nuptial ceremony, when he finally learned what he was getting in the matrimonial lottery.

Feeling my sympathy, Dr. Bose pointed unobtrusively to Nalini, and whispered in my ear, "Say, what's this?"

"Why, Doctor," I replied, "it is a skeleton for your observation!"

Convulsed with mirth, my brother-in-law and I were hard put to it to maintain the proper decorum before our assembled relatives.

As the years went on, Dr. Bose endeared himself to our family, who called on him whenever illness arose. He and I became fast friends, often joking together, usually with Nalini as our target.

"It is a medical curiosity," my brother-in-law remarked to me one day. "I have tried everything on your lean sister – cod-liver oil, butter, malt,

1 Gracefully draped dress of Indian women.

honey, fish, meat, eggs, tonics. Still she fails to bulge even one-hundredth of an inch." We both chuckled.

A few days later I visited the Bose home. My errand there took only a few minutes; I was leaving, unnoticed, I thought, by Nalini. As I reached the front door, I heard her voice, cordial but commanding.

"Brother, come here. You are not going to give me the slip this time. I want to talk to you."

I mounted the stairs to her room. To my surprise, she was in tears.

"Dear brother," she said, "let us bury the old hatchet. I see that your feet are now firmly set on the spiritual path. I want to become like you in every way." She added hopefully, "You are now robust in appearance; can you help me? My husband does not come near me, and I love him so dearly! But still more I want to progress in God-realization, even if I must remain thin[2] and unattractive."

My heart was deeply touched at her plea. Our new friendship steadily progressed: one day she asked to become my disciple.

"Train me in any way you like. I put my trust in God instead of tonics." She gathered together an armful of medicines and poured them down the roof drain.

As a test of her faith, I asked her to omit from her diet all fish, meat, and eggs.

After several months, during which Nalini had strictly followed the various rules I had outlined, and had adhered to her vegetarian diet in spite of numerous difficulties, I paid her a visit.

"Sis, you have been conscientiously observing the spiritual injunctions; your reward is near." I smiled mischievously. "How plump do you want to be – as fat as our aunt who hasn't seen her feet in years?"

"No! But I long to be as stout as you are."

I replied solemnly. "By the grace of God, as I have spoken truth always, I speak truly now.[3] Through the divine blessings, your body shall verily change from today; in one month it shall have the same weight as mine."

These words from my heart found fulfillment. In thirty days, Nalini's weight equalled mine. The new roundness gave her beauty; her husband fell deeply in love. Their marriage, begun so inauspiciously, turned out to be ideally happy.

2 Because most persons in India are thin, reasonable plumpness is considered very desirable.

3 The Hindu scriptures declare that those who habitually speak the truth will develop the power of materializing their words. What commands they utter from the heart will come true in life. Because the worlds are built on truth, all scriptures extol it as a virtue by which man may tune his life with the Infinite. Mahatma Gandhi often said: "Truth is God"; his lifelong striving was for perfect truth in thought, speech, and act.

On my return from Japan, I learned that during my absence Nalini had been stricken with typhoid fever. I rushed to her home, and was aghast to find her reduced to a mere skeleton. She was in a coma.

"Before her mind became confused by illness," my brother-in-law told me, "she often said: 'If brother Mukunda were here, I would not be faring thus.'" He added despairingly, "The other doctors and myself see no hope. Blood dysentery has set in, after her long bout with typhoid."

I began to move heaven and earth with my prayers. Engaging an Anglo-Indian nurse, who gave me full cooperation, I applied to my sister various yoga techniques of healing. The blood dysentery disappeared.

But Dr. Bose shook his head mournfully. "She simply has no more blood left to shed."

"She will recover," I replied stoutly. "In seven days her fever will be gone."

A week later I was thrilled to see Nalini open her eyes and gaze at me with loving recognition. From that day her recovery was swift. Although she regained her usual weight, she bore one sad scar of her nearly fatal illness: her legs were paralyzed. Indian and English specialists pronounced her a hopeless cripple.

The incessant war for her life which I had waged by prayer had exhausted me. I went to Serampore to ask Sri Yukteswar's help. His eyes expressed deep sympathy as I told him of Nalini's plight.

"Your sister's legs will be normal at the end of one month." He added, "Let her wear, next to her skin, a band with an un-perforated two-carat pearl, held on by a clasp."

I prostrated myself at his feet with joyful relief.

"Sir, you are a master; your word of her recovery is enough But if you insist I shall immediately get her a pearl."

My guru nodded. "Yes, do that." He went on to correctly describe the physical and mental characteristics of Nalini, whom he had never seen.

"Sir," I inquired, "is this an astrological analysis? You do not know her birth day or hour."

Sri Yukteswar smiled. "There is a deeper astrology, not dependent on the testimony of calendars and clocks. Each man is a part of the Creator, or Cosmic Man; he has a heavenly body as well as one of earth. The human eye sees the physical form, but the inward eye penetrates more profoundly, even to the universal pattern of which each man is an integral and individual part."

I returned to Calcutta and purchased a pearl[4] for Nalini. A month later, her paralyzed legs were completely healed.

Sister asked me to convey her heartfelt gratitude to my guru. He listened to her message in silence. But as I was taking my leave, he made a pregnant comment.

"Your sister has been told by many doctors that she can never bear children. Assure her that in a few years she will give birth to two daughters."

Some years later, to Nalini's joy, she bore a girl, followed in a few years by another daughter.

"Your master blessed our home, our entire family," my sister said. "The presence of such a man is a sanctification on the whole of India. Dear brother, please tell Sri Yukteswarji that, through you, I humbly count myself as one of his *Kriya Yoga* disciples."

---

4 Pearls and other Jewels as well as metals and plants, applied to the human skin exercise an electromagnetic influence over the physical cells. Man's body also contains carbon and metallic elements. The discoveries of rishis in these fields will, someday, receive confirmation from physiologists, for, as yet, man's sensitive body with its electrical life currents remains unexplored.

Though jewels and metal bangles have remedial values for the body, Swami Sri Yukteswar had another reason for recommending them. Masters never wish to appear as great healers: God alone is the Healer. Saints therefore cloak their powers humbly received from the Lord. When my guru was approached for healing, he advised them to wear these tangibles to arouse their faith and to divert attention from himself. Apart from their intrinsic electromagnetic healing potencies, the bangles and jewels possessed the Master's hidden spiritual blessings.

170

GYANA PRABHA GHOSH (1868-1904)
Mother of Sri Paramahansa Yogananda
Disciple of Sri Sri Lahiri Mahasaya

BHAGABATI CHARAN GHOSH (1853-1942)
Father of Sri Paramahansa Yogananda
Disciple of Sri Sri Lahiri Mahasaya

Sri Yogananda at the age of 6

Sri Yogananda's elder sister
Uma as a young girl

Sri Sri Mahavtar Babaji
Guru of Sri Lahiri Mahasaya

Sri Sri Lahiri Mahasaya (1828-1895)
Disciple of Mahavatar Babaji
Guru of Sri Yukteswar Giri

Sri Sri Swami Yukteswar Giri (1855-1936)
Disciple of Sri Sri Lahiri Mahasaya
Guru of Sri Yoganandji, and
all YSS-SRF Kriya Yogis

172

Sri Yogananda with sisters
Eldest, Roma (left); and younger, Nalini (right)

Sri Yogananda as high-school student
with elder brother Ananta

(top) Kashi at Ranchi School (ref. Ch. 28)

(left) Sri Yogananda's companion
Jitendra Mazumdar (ref. Ch. 11)

173

Sri Nagendra Nath Bhaduri
The Levitating Saint

Swami Kebalanana
Sri Yogananda's Sanskrit tutor

Swami Pranabananda
The Banaras Saint with Two Bodies

Master Mahasaya
'The Blissful Devotee'

174

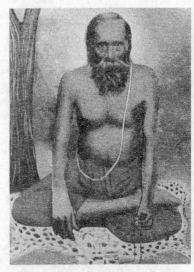

Ram Gopal Mazumdar
'The Sleepless Saint'

Sri Sri Babaji's cave near Ranikhet
Lahiri Mahasaya's grandson
Ananda Mohan is seen

Sri Yogananda's Family Home
Garpar road Kolkata

Swami Sri Yukteswar's Ashram
Sea-side Puri

175

Rabindranath Tagore (1817-1905)

Jagadis Chandra Bose (1858-1937)

Sri Yogananda among the Delegates to International Congress of Religious Liberals
Boston USA (October 1920)

Addressing the gathering
Denver, Colorado USA (1924)

Lecturing at the Philharmonic Auditorium,
Los Angeles, California USA (1925)

177

With Mr John Balfour at the White House
prior to meeting President Coolidge of USA

With Luther Burbank, Santa Rosa
California USA (1924)

178

SRF International HQ established by Sri Yogananda,
Los Angeles USA, (1925)

Swami Sri Yukteswar celebrates Last Solstice Festival,
Serampore (1935)

With Swami Keshabananda and C Richard Wright, Brindaban (1936)

In religious procession with the Guru, Kolkata (1935)

With Swami Sri Yukteswar
Serampore Ashram (1935)

112 years old Shankari Mai Jiew
At Haridwar Kumbh Mela (1938)

With Sri Ramana Maharshi
Sri Ramana's Arunachal Ashram

With Swami Dayananda
Mahamandal Hermitage Banaras (1936)

182

Swami Sri Yukteswar's
Samadhi Mandir, Puri

Panchanon Bhattacharya
Disciple of Sri Sri Lahiri Mahasaya

Swami Krishnananda and his
Vegetarian lioness (Ref. Ch. 42)

Reading a Note to Mahatma Gandhi at his Wardha Ashram (1935)

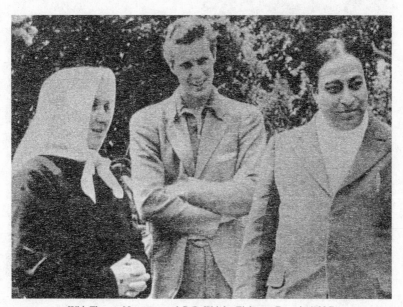

With Therese Neumann and C. R. Wright, Eichstätt, Bavaria (1935)

184

Giri Bala
Non-eating Saint

Sri Daya Mata
The third President of YSS/SRF

With Sri Ananda Moyi Ma and
Her husband Bholanath, Kolkata (1935)

Swami Sri Janakananda (James J. Lynn)
(b. 1892 – Samadhi: 1955)

185

Yogoda Math on the Ganges (YSS Regd. Off.)
founded by Sri Yogananda at Dakshineshwar (1939)

Self-Realization Fellowship (SRF) Ashram
Encinitas California USA

The Last Smile of a Yogi
Taken barely one hour before his Mahasamadhi
March 07, 1952

Guru Sri Shankaracharya of Puri at SRF Int'l HQ
Los Angeles (1958)

26. *The Science of Kriya Yoga*

THE SCIENCE of *Kriya Yoga,* mentioned so often in these pages, became widely known in modern India through the instrumentality of Lahiri Mahasaya, my guru's guru. The Sanskrit root of *Kriya* is *kri,* to do, to act and react; the same root is found in the word *karma,* the natural principle of cause and effect. *Kriya Yoga* is thus 'union (yoga) with the Infinite through a certain action or rite.' A yogi who faithfully follows its technique is gradually freed from karma or the universal chain of causation.

Because of certain ancient yogic injunctions, I cannot give a full explanation of *Kriya Yoga* in the pages of a book intended for the general public. The actual technique must be learned from a *Kriyaban* or *Kriya Yogi;* here a broad reference must suffice.

Kriya Yoga is a simple, psycho-physiological method by which the human blood is decarbonized and recharged with oxygen. The atoms of this extra oxygen are transmuted into life current to rejuvenate the brain and spinal centres.[1] By stopping the accumulation of venous blood, the yogi is able to lessen or prevent the decay of tissues; the advanced yogi transmutes his cells into pure energy. Elijah, Jesus, Kabir and other prophets were past masters in the use of *Kriya* or a similar technique, by which they caused their bodies to dematerialize at will.

Kriya is an ancient science. Lahiri Mahasaya received it from his guru, Babaji, who rediscovered and clarified the technique after it had been lost in the Dark Ages.

"The *Kriya Yoga* which I am giving to the world through you in this nineteenth century," Babaji told Lahiri Mahasaya, "is a revival of the same science which Krishna gave, millenniums ago, to Arjuna, and which was later known to Patanjali, and to Christ, St. John, St. Paul, and other disciples."

Kriya Yoga is twice referred to by Krishna, India's greatest prophet, in a stanza of the *Bhagavad Gita*: "Offering inhaling breath into the outgoing breath, and offering the outgoing breath into the inhaling breath, the yogi neutralizes both these breaths; he thus releases the life force from the heart and brings it under his control."[2] The interpretation is: "The yogi arrests decay in the body by an addition of life force, and arrests the mutations of growth in the body by *apan* (eliminating current). Thus neutralizing decay and growth, by quieting the heart, the yogi learns life-force control."

---

1 The noted scientist, Dr. George W. Crile of Cleveland explained before a 1940 meeting of the American Association for the Advancement of Science the experiments by which he had proved that all bodily tissues are electrically negative, except the brain and nervous system tissues which remain electrically positive because they take up revivifying oxygen at a more rapid rate.

2 *Bhagavad Gita*, IV: 29.

Krishna also relates[3] that it was he, in a former incarnation, who communicated the indestructible yoga to an ancient illuminato, Vivasvat, who gave it to Manu, the great legislator.[4] He, in turn, instructed Ikshwaku, the father of India's solar warrior dynasty. Passing thus from one to another, the royal yoga was guarded by the rishis until the coming of the materialistic ages.[5] Then, due to priestly secrecy and man's indifference, the sacred knowledge gradually became inaccessible.

Kriya Yoga is mentioned twice by the ancient sage Patanjali, foremost exponent of yoga, who wrote: "*Kriya Yoga* consists of body discipline, mental control, and meditating on *Aum*."[6] Patanjali speaks of God as the actual Cosmic Sound of *Aum* heard in meditation.[7] *Aum* is the Creative Word,[8] the sound of the Vibratory Motor. Even the yoga-beginner soon inwardly hears the wondrous sound of *Aum*. Receiving this blissful spiritual encouragement, the devotee becomes assured that he is in actual touch with divine realms.

Patanjali refers a second time to the life-control or *Kriya* technique thus: "Liberation can be accomplished by that *pranayama* which is attained by disjoining the course of inspiration and expiration."[9]

St. Paul knew *Kriya Yoga,* or a technique very similar to it, by which he could switch life currents to and from the senses. He was therefore able to say: "Verily, I protest by our rejoicing which I have in Christ, *I die daily*."[10] By daily withdrawing his bodily life force, he united it by yoga union with the rejoicing (eternal bliss) of the Christ consciousness. In that felicitous state, he was consciously aware of being dead to the delusive sensory world of *maya*.

In the initial states of God-contact (*sabikalpa samadhi*) the devotee's consciousness merges with the Cosmic Spirit; his life force is withdrawn from the body, which appears 'dead,' or motionless and rigid. The yogi is fully aware of his bodily condition of suspended animation. As he progresses

3 *Ibid*. IV: 1-2.
4 The author of *Manava Dharma Shastras*. These institutes of canonized common law are effective in India to this day. The French scholar, Louis Jacolliot, writes that the date of Manu 'is lost in the night of the ante-historical period of India; and no scholar has dared to refuse him the title of the most ancient law giver in the world.' In *La Bible dans l'Inde*, pages 33-37, Jacolliot reproduces parallel textual references to prove that the Roman *Code of Justinian* follows closely the *Laws of Manu*.
5 The start of the materialistic ages, according to Hindu scriptural reckonings, was 3102B.C. This was the beginning of the Descending Dwapara Age (see page 122 & Note 6 on page 123). Modern scholars, blithely believing that 10,000 years ago all men were sunk in a barbarous Stone Age, summarily dismiss as 'myths' all records and traditions of very ancient civilizations in India, China, Egypt, and other lands.
6 Patanjali's *Yoga Sutras*, II: 1. In using the words *Kriya Yoga,* Patanjali was referring to either the exact technique taught by Babaji, or one very similar to it. That it was a definite technique of life control is proved by Patanjali's *Yoga Sutras* II: 49.
7 *Yoga Sutras* I: 27.
8 All things were made by Him; and without Him was not any thing made that was made. – *John* 1: 1-3. *Aum* (*Om*) of the *Vedas* became the sacred word *Amin* of the Moslems, *Hum* of the Tibetans, and *Amen* of the Christians (its meaning in Hebrew being *sure, faithful*). 'These things saith the Amen, the faithful and true witness, the beginning of the creation of *God*' – *Revelations* 3: 14.
9 *Yoga Sutras* II: 49.
10 I *Corinthians* 15: 31. 'Our rejoicing' is the correct translation; not, as usually given, 'your rejoicing.' St. Paul was referring to the *omnipresence* of the Christ consciousness.

to higher spiritual states (*nirbikalpa samadhi*), however, he communes with God without bodily fixation, and in his ordinary waking consciousness, even in the midst of exacting worldly duties.[11]

"*Kriya Yoga* is an instrument through which human evolution can be quickened," Sri Yukteswar explained to his students. "The ancient yogis discovered that the secret of cosmic consciousness is intimately linked with breath mastery. This is India's unique and deathless contribution to the world's treasury of knowledge. The life force, which is ordinarily absorbed in maintaining the heart-pump, must be freed for higher activities by a method of calming and stilling the ceaseless demands of the breath."

The *Kriya Yogi* mentally directs his life energy to revolve, upward and downward, around the six spinal centres (medullary, cervical, dorsal, lumbar, sacral, and coccygeal plexuses) which correspond to the twelve astral signs of the zodiac, the symbolic Cosmic Man. One-half minute of revolution of energy around the sensitive spinal cord of man effects subtle progress in his evolution; that half-minute of *Kriya* equals one year of natural spiritual un-foldment.

The astral system of a human being, with six (twelve by polarity) inner constellations revolving around the sun of the omniscient spiritual eye, is interrelated with the physical sun and the twelve zodiacal signs. All men are thus affected by an inner and an outer universe. The ancient rishis discovered that man's earthly and heavenly environment, in twelve-year cycles, push him forward on his natural path. The scriptures aver that man requires a million years of normal, disease-less evolution to perfect his human brain sufficiently to express cosmic consciousness.

One thousand *Kriya*s practiced in eight hours gives the yogi, in one day, the equivalent of one thousand years of natural evolution: 365,000 years of evolution in one year. In three years, a *Kriya Yogi* can thus accomplish by intelligent self-effort the same result which nature brings to pass in a million years. The *Kriya* short cut, of course, can be taken only by deeply developed yogis. With the guidance of a guru, such yogis have carefully prepared their bodies and brains to receive the power created by intensive practice.

The *Kriya* beginner employs his yogic exercise only fourteen to twenty-eight times, twice daily. A number of yogis achieve emancipation in six or twelve or twenty-four or forty-eight years. A yogi who dies before achieving full realization carries with him the good karma of his past *Kriya* effort; in his new life he is harmoniously propelled toward his Infinite Goal.

The body of the average man is like a fifty-watt lamp, which cannot accommodate the billion watts of power roused by an excessive practice of

11 *Bikalpa* means time, or aeon. *Sabikalpa* means subject to time, or change; some link with *prakriti* or matter remains. *Nirbikalpa* means timeless, changeless; this is the highest state of *samadhi*.

Kriya. Through gradual and regular increase of the simple and 'foolproof' methods of *Kriya,* man's body becomes astrally transformed day by day, and is finally fitted to express the infinite potentials of cosmic energy – the first materially active expression of Spirit.

Kriya Yoga has nothing in common with the unscientific breathing exercises taught by a number of misguided zealots. Their attempts to forcibly hold breath in the lungs is not only unnatural but decidedly unpleasant. *Kriya,* on the other hand, is accompanied from the very beginning by an accession of peace, and by soothing sensations of regenerative effect in the spine.

The ancient yogic technique converts the breath into mind. By spiritual advancement, one is able to cognize the breath as an act of mind – a dream-breath.

Many illustrations could be given of the mathematical relationship between man's respiratory rate and the variations in his states of consciousness. A person whose attention is wholly engrossed, as in following some closely knit intellectual argument, or in attempting some delicate or difficult physical feat, automatically breathes very slowly. Fixity of attention depends on slow breathing; quick or uneven breaths are an inevitable accompaniment of harmful emotional states: fear, lust, anger. The restless monkey breaths at the rate of 32 times a minute, in contrast to man's average of 18 times. The elephant, tortoise, snake and other animals noted for their longevity have a respiratory rate which is less than man's. The tortoise, for instance, who may attain the age of 300 years,[12] breathes only 4 times per minute.

The rejuvenating effects of sleep are due to man's temporary unawareness of body and breathing. The sleeping man becomes a yogi; each night he unconsciously performs the yogic rite of releasing himself from bodily identification, and of merging the life force with healing currents in the main brain region and the six sub-dynamos of his spinal centres. The sleeper thus dips unknowingly into the reservoir of cosmic energy which sustains all life.

The voluntary yogi performs a simple, natural process consciously, not unconsciously like the slow-paced sleeper. The *Kriya Yogi* uses his technique to saturate and feed all his physical cells with undecaying light and keep them in a magnetized state. He scientifically makes breath unnecessary, without producing the states of subconscious sleep or unconsciousness, or death.

By *Kriya,* the outgoing life force is not wasted and abused in the senses, but constrained to reunite with subtler spinal energies. By such

12 According to the *Lincoln Library of Essential Information,* p. 1030, the giant tortoise lives between 200 and 300 years.

reinforcement of life, the yogi's body and brain cells are electrified with the spiritual elixir. Thus he removes himself from studied observance of natural laws, which can only take him – by circuitous means as given by proper food, sunlight, and harmonious thoughts – to a million-year Goal. It needs twelve years of normal healthful living to effect even slight perceptible change in brain structure, and a million solar returns are exacted to sufficiently refine the cerebral tenement for manifestation of cosmic consciousness.

Untying the cord of breath which binds the soul to the body, *Kriya* serves to prolong life and enlarge the consciousness to infinity. The yoga method overcomes the tug of war between the mind and the matter-bound senses, and frees the devotee to reinherit his eternal kingdom. He knows his real nature is bound neither by physical encasement nor by breath, symbol of the mortal enslavement to air, to nature's elemental compulsions.

Introspection, or 'sitting in the silence,' is an unscientific way of trying to force apart the mind and senses, tied together by the life force. The contemplative mind, attempting its return to divinity, is constantly dragged back toward the senses by the life currents. *Kriya,* controlling the mind *directly* through the life force, is the easiest, most effective, and most scientific avenue of approach to the Infinite. In contrast to the slow, uncertain 'bullock cart' theological path to God, *Kriya* may justly be called the 'airplane' route.

The yogic science is based on an empirical consideration of all forms of concentration and meditation exercises. Yoga enables the devotee to switch off or on, at will, life current from the five sense telephones of sight, sound, smell, taste, and touch. Attaining this power of sense-disconnection, the yogi finds it simple to unite his mind at will with divine realms or with the world of matter. No longer is he unwillingly brought back by the life force to the mundane sphere of rowdy sensations and restless thoughts. Master of his body and mind, the Kriya Yogi ultimately achieves victory over the 'last enemy,'[13] death.

So shalt thou feed on Death, that feeds on men: And Death once dead, there's no more dying then.[14]

The life of an advanced *Kriya Yogi* is influenced, not by effects of past actions, but solely by directions from the soul. The devotee thus avoids the slow, evolutionary monitors of egoistic actions, good and bad, of common life, cumbrous and snail-like to the eagle hearts.

The superior method of soul living frees the yogi who, shorn of his ego-prison, tastes the deep air of omnipresence. The thralldom of natural living is, in contrast, set in a pace humiliating. Conforming his life to the evolutionary order,

13 'The last enemy that shall be destroyed is death' – I *Corinthians* 15: 26. The incorruptibility of Paramahansa Yogananda's body after death (see Epilogue) proved him a perfect *Kriya Yogi*. – Ed.
14 Shakespeare: *Sonnet* # 146.

a man can command no concessionary haste from nature but, living without error against the laws of his physical and mental endowment, still requires about a million years of masquerading incarnations to attain final emancipation.

The telescopic methods of yogis, disengaging themselves from physical and mental identifications in favour of soul-individuality, thus commend themselves to those who eye with revolt a thousand thousand years. This numerical periphery is enlarged for the ordinary man, who lives in harmony not even with nature, let alone his soul, but pursues instead unnatural complexities, thus offending in his body and thoughts the sweet sanities of nature. For him, two times a million years can scarce suffice for liberation.

Gross man seldom or never realizes that his body is a kingdom, governed by Emperor Soul on the throne of the cranium, with subsidiary regents in the six spinal centres or spheres of consciousness. This theocracy extends over a throng of obedient subjects: twenty-seven thousand billion cells – endowed with a sure if automatic intelligence by which they perform all duties of bodily growths, transformations, and dissolutions – and fifty million substratal thoughts, emotions, and variations of alternating phases in man's consciousness in an average life of sixty years. Any apparent insurrection of bodily or cerebral cells toward Emperor Soul, manifesting as disease or depression, is due to no disloyalty among the humble citizens, but to past or present misuse by man of his individuality or free will, given to him simultaneous with a soul, and revocable never.

Identifying himself with a shallow ego, man takes for granted that it is he who thinks, wills, feels, digests meals, and keeps himself alive, never admitting through reflection (only a little would suffice!) that in his ordinary life he is naught but a puppet of past actions (karma) and of nature or environment. Each man's intellectual reactions, feelings, moods, and habits are circumscribed by effects of past causes, whether of this or a prior life. Lofty above such influences, however, is his regal soul. Spurning the transitory truths and freedoms, the *Kriya Yogi* passes beyond all disillusionment into his unfettered Being. All scriptures declare man to be not a corruptible body, but a living soul; by *Kriya* he is given a method to prove the scriptural truth.

'Outward ritual cannot destroy ignorance, because they are not mutually contradictory,' wrote Shankara in his famous *Century of Verses*. 'Realized knowledge alone destroys ignorance. . . . Knowledge cannot spring up by any other means than inquiry. *Who am I? How was this universe born? Who is its maker? What is its material cause?* This is the kind of inquiry referred to.' The intellect has no answer for these questions; hence the rishis evolved yoga as the technique of spiritual inquiry.

Kriya Yoga is the real 'fire rite' often extolled in *Bhagavad Gita*. The purifying fires of yoga bring eternal illumination, and thus differ much from outward and little-effective religious fire ceremonies, where perception of truth is oft burnt, to solemn chanted accompaniment, along with the incense!

The advanced yogi, withholding all his mind, will, and feeling from false identification with bodily desires, uniting his mind with superconscious forces in the spinal shrines, thus lives in this world as God hath planned, not impelled by impulses from the past nor by new witlessnesses of fresh human motivations. Such a yogi receives fulfillment of his Supreme Desire, safe in the final haven of inexhaustibly blissful Spirit.

The yogi offers his labyrinthine human longings to a monotheistic bonfire dedicated to the unparalleled God. This is indeed the true yogic fire ceremony, in which all past and present desires are fuel consumed by love divine. The Ultimate Flame receives the sacrifice of all human madness, and man is pure of dross. His bones stripped of all desirous flesh, his karmic skeleton bleached in the antiseptic suns of wisdom, he is clean at last, inoffensive before man and Maker.

On yoga's sure and methodical efficacy, Lord Krishna praises the technological yogi in the following words: "The yogi is greater than body-disciplining ascetics, greater even than the followers of the path of wisdom (*Jnana Yoga*), or of the path of action (*Karma Yoga*); be thou, O disciple Arjuna, a yogi!"[15]

27. *Founding a Yoga School in Ranchi*

"WHY ARE YOU averse to organizational work?"

Master's question startled me a bit. It is true that my private conviction at the time was that organizations were 'hornets' nests.'

"It is a thankless task, sir," I answered. "No matter what the leader does or does not, he is criticized."

"Do you want the whole divine *channa* (milk curd) for yourself alone?" My guru's retort was accompanied by a stern glance. "Could you or anyone else achieve God-contact through yoga if a line of generous-hearted masters had not been willing to convey their knowledge to others?" He added, "God is the Honey, organizations are the hives; both are necessary. Any *form* is useless, of course, without the spirit, but why should you not start busy hives full of the spiritual nectar?"

His counsel moved me deeply. Although I made no outward reply, an adamant resolution arose in my breast: I would share with my fellows, so far as lay in my power, the unshackling truths I had learned at my guru's feet. "Lord," I prayed, "may Thy Love shine forever on the sanctuary of my devotion, and may I be able to awaken that Love in other hearts."

15 *Bhagavad Gita*, VI: 46. Benefiting from *Kriya Yoga* and non-breathing the Yogi recevies rewards in body and mind, and in soul-awareness.

On a previous occasion, before I had joined the monastic order, Sri Yukteswar had made a most unexpected remark.

"How you will miss the companionship of a wife in your old age!" he had said. "Do you not agree that the family man, engaged in useful work to maintain his wife and children, thus plays a rewarding role in God's eyes?"

"Sir," I had protested in alarm, "you know that my desire in this life is to espouse only the Cosmic Beloved."

Master had laughed so merrily that I understood his observation was made merely as a test of my faith.

"Remember," he had said slowly, "that he who discards his worldly duties can justify himself only by assuming some kind of responsibility toward a much larger family."

The ideal of an all-sided education for youth had always been close to my heart. I saw clearly the arid results of ordinary instruction, aimed only at the development of body and intellect. Moral and spiritual values, without whose appreciation no man can approach happiness, were yet lacking in the formal curriculum. I determined to found a school where young boys could develop to the full stature of manhood. My first step in that direction was made with seven children at Dihika, a small country site in Bengal.

A year later, in 1918, through the generosity of Sir Manindra Chandra Nundy, the Maharaja of Kasimbazar, I was able to transfer my fast-growing group to Ranchi. This town in Bihar, about two hundred miles from Calcutta, is blessed with one of the most healthful climates in India. The Kasimbazar Palace at Ranchi was transformed into the headquarters for the new school, which I called *Brahmacharya Vidyalaya*[1] in accordance with the educational

---

1 *Vidyalaya*: school. *Brahmacharya* here refers to one of the four stages in the Vedic plan for man's life, as comprising that of (1) the celibate student (*brahmachari*); (2) the householder with worldly responsibilities (*grihastha*); (3) the hermit (*vanaprastha*); (4) the forest dweller or wanderer, free from all earthly concerns (*sannyasi*). This ideal scheme of life, while not widely observed in modern India, still has many devout followers. The four stages are carried out religiously under the lifelong direction of a guru.

Solitude is necessary to become established in the Self, but masters then return to the world to serve it. Even saints who engage in no outward work bestow, through their thoughts and holy vibrations, more precious benefits on the world than can be given by the most strenuous humanitarian activities of unenlightened men. The great ones, each in his own way and often against bitter opposition, strive selflessly to inspire and uplift their fellow beings. No Hindu religious or social ideal is merely negative. *Ahimsa*, 'non-injury' called 'virtue entire' (*sakalo dharma*) in the *Mahabharata*, is a positive injunction by reason of its conception that one who is not helping others in some way is injuring them.

The *Bhagwad Gita* (III: 4-8) points out that activity is inherent in man's very nature. Sloth is simply 'wrong activity.'

"No man shall 'scape from act
By shunning action; nay, and none shall come
By mere renouncements unto perfectness.
Nay, and not jot of time, at any time,
Rests any action-less; his nature's law
Compels him, even unwilling, into act.
(For thought is act in fancy.)
....He who with strong body serving mind,
Gives up his mortal powers to worthy work,
Not seeking gain, Arjuna! such a one
Is honourable. Do thine allotted tasks!"

(*Arnold's Translation*)

ideals of the rishis. Their forest ashrams had been the ancient seats of learning, secular and divine, for the youth of India.

At Ranchi I organized an educational program for both grammar and high school grades. It included agricultural, industrial, commercial, and academic subjects. The students were also taught yoga concentration and meditation, and a unique system of physical development, 'Yogoda,' whose principles I had discovered in 1916.

Realizing that man's body is like an electric battery, I reasoned that it could be recharged with energy through the direct agency of the human will. As no action, slight or large, is possible without *willing,* man can avail himself of his prime mover, will, to renew his bodily tissues without burdensome apparatus or mechanical exercises. I therefore taught the Ranchi students my simple 'Yogoda' techniques by which the life force, centred in man's medulla oblongata, can be consciously and instantly recharged from the unlimited supply of cosmic energy.

The boys responded wonderfully to this training, developing extraordinary ability to shift the life energy from one part of the body to another part, and to sit in perfect poise in difficult body postures.[2] They performed feats of strength and endurance which many powerful adults could not equal. My youngest brother, Bishnu Charan Ghosh, joined the Ranchi school; he later became a leading physical culturist in Bengal. He and one of his students travelled to Europe and America, giving exhibitions of strength and skill which amazed the university savants, including those at Columbia University in New York.

At the end of the first year at Ranchi, applications for admission reached two thousand. But the school, which at that time was solely residential, could accommodate only about one hundred. Instruction for day students was soon added.

In the *Vidyalaya* I had to play father-mother to the little children, and to cope with many organizational difficulties. I often remembered Christ's words: "Verily I say unto you, There is no man that hath left house, or brethren or sisters, or father, or mother, or wife, or children, or lands, for my sake, and the gospel's, but he shall receive an hundredfold now in this time, houses and brethren, and sisters, and mothers, and children, and lands, with persecutions; and in the world to come eternal life."[3]

Sri Yukteswar had interpreted these words: "The devotee who forgoes the life-experiences of marriage and family, and exchanges the problems of a small household and limited activities for the larger responsibilities of service to society in general, is undertaking a task which is often

2 A number of American students also have mastered various *asanas* or postures, including Bernard Cole, an instructor in Los Angeles of the Self-Realization Fellowship teachings.
3 *Mark* 10: 29-30.

accompanied by persecution from a misunderstanding world, but also by a divine inner contentment."

One day my father arrived in Ranchi to bestow a paternal blessing, long withheld because I had hurt him by refusing his offer of a position with the Bengal-Nagpur Railway.

"Son," he said, "I am now reconciled to your choice in life. It gives me joy to see you amidst these happy, eager youngsters; you belong here rather than with the lifeless figures of railroad timetables." He waved toward a group of a dozen little ones who were tagging at my heels. "I had only eight children," he observed with twinkling eyes, "but I can feel for you!"

With a large fruit orchard and twenty-five fertile acres at our disposal, the students, teachers, and myself enjoyed many happy hours of outdoor labour in these ideal surroundings. We had many pets, including a young deer who was fairly idolized by the children. I too loved the fawn so much that I allowed it to sleep in my room. At the light of dawn, the little creature would toddle over to my bed for a morning caress.

One day I fed the pet earlier than usual, as I had to attend to some business in the town of Ranchi. Although I cautioned the boys not to feed the fawn until my return, one of them was disobedient, and gave the baby deer a large quantity of milk. When I came back in the evening, sad news greeted me: "The little fawn is nearly dead, through overfeeding."

In tears, I placed the apparently lifeless pet on my lap. I prayed piteously to God to spare its life. Hours later, the small creature opened its eyes, stood up, and walked feebly. The whole school shouted for joy.

But a deep lesson came to me that night, one I can never forget. I stayed up with the fawn until two o'clock, when I fell asleep. The deer appeared in a dream, and spoke to me:

"You are holding me back. Please let me go; let me go!"

"All right," I answered in the dream.

I awoke immediately, and cried out, "Boys, the deer is dying!" The children rushed to my side.

I ran to the corner of the room where I had placed the pet. It made a last effort to rise, stumbled toward me, then dropped at my feet, dead.

According to the mass karma which guides and regulates the destinies of animals, the deer's life was over, and it was ready to progress to a higher form. But by my deep attachment, which I later realized was selfish, and by my fervent prayers, I had been able to hold it in the limitations of the animal form from which the soul was struggling for release. The soul of the deer made its plea in a dream because, without my loving permission, it either would not or could not go. As soon as I agreed, it departed.

All sorrow left me; I realized anew that God wants His children to love everything as a part of Him, and not to feel delusively that death ends all. The ignorant man sees only the unsurmountable wall of death, hiding, seemingly forever, his cherished friends. But the man of unattachment, he who loves others as expressions of the Lord, understands that at death the dear ones have only returned for a breathing-space of joy in Him.

The Ranchi school grew from small and simple beginnings to an institution now well-known in India. Many departments of the school are supported by voluntary contributions from those who rejoice in perpetuating the educational ideals of the rishis. Under the general name of *Yogoda Sat-Sanga,*[4] flourishing branch schools have been established at Midnapore, Lakshmanpur, and Puri.

The Ranchi headquarters maintains a Medical Department where medicines and the services of doctors are supplied free to the poor of the locality. The number treated has averaged more than 18,000 persons a year. The *Vidyalaya* has made its mark, too, in Indian competitive sports, and in the scholastic field, where many Ranchi alumni have distinguished themselves in later university life.

The school, now in its twenty-eighth year and the centre of many activities,[5] has been honoured by visits of eminent men from the East and the West. One of the earliest great figures to inspect the *Vidyalaya* in its first year was Swami Pranabananda, the Benares 'saint with two bodies.' As the great master viewed the picturesque outdoor classes, held under the trees, and saw in the evening that young boys were sitting motionless for hours in yoga meditation, he was profoundly moved.

"Joy comes to my heart," he said, "to see that Lahiri Mahasaya's ideals for the proper training of youth are being carried on in this institution. My guru's blessings be on it."

A young lad sitting by my side ventured to ask the great yogi a question.

"Sir," he said, "shall I be a monk? Is my life only for God?"

Though Swami Pranabananda smiled gently, his eyes were piercing the future.

"Child," he replied, "when you grow up, there is a beautiful bride waiting for you." The boy did eventually marry, after having planned for years to enter the Swami Order.

Sometime after Swami Pranabananda had visited Ranchi, I accompanied my father to the Calcutta house where the yogi was temporarily staying. Pranabananda's prediction, made to me so many years before, came rushing to my mind: "I shall see you, with your father, later on."

4 Yogoda: *yoga,* union, harmony, equilibrium; *da,* that which imparts. Sat-Sanga: *sat,* truth; *sanga,* fellowship. In the West, to avoid the use of a Sanskrit name, the *Yogoda Sat-Sanga* movement has been called the *Self-Realization Fellowship.*
5 The activities at Ranchi are described more fully in chapter 40. The Lakshmanpur school is in the capable charge of Mr. G. C. Dey, B.A. The medical department is ably supervised by Dr. S. N. Pal and Sasi Bhusan Mullick.

As Father entered the swami's room, the great yogi rose from his seat and embraced my parent with loving respect.

"Bhagabati," he said, "what are you doing about yourself? Don't you see your son racing to the Infinite?" I blushed to hear his praise before my father. The swami went on, "You recall how often our blessed guru used to say: '*Banat, banat, ban jai.*'[6] So keep up *Kriya Yoga* ceaselessly, and reach the divine portals quickly."

The body of Pranabananda, which had appeared so well and strong during my amazing first visit to him in Benares, now showed definite aging, though his posture was still admirably erect.

"Swamiji," I inquired, looking straight into his eyes, "please tell me the truth: Aren't you feeling the advance of age? As the body is weakening, are your perceptions of God suffering any diminution?"

He smiled angelically. "The Beloved is more than ever with me now." His complete conviction overwhelmed my mind and soul. He went on, "I am still enjoying the two pensions – one from Bhagabati here, and one from above." Pointing his finger heavenward, the saint fell into an ecstasy, his face lit with a divine glow – an ample answer to my question.

Noticing that Pranabananda's room contained many plants and packages of seed, I asked their purpose.

"I have left Benares permanently," he said, "and am now on my way to the Himalayas. There I shall open an ashram for my disciples. These seeds will produce spinach and a few other vegetables. My dear ones will live simply, spending their time in blissful God-union. Nothing else is necessary."

Father asked his brother disciple when he would return to Calcutta.

"Never again," the saint replied. "This year is the one in which Lahiri Mahasaya told me I would leave my beloved Benares forever and go to the Himalayas, there to throw off my mortal frame."

My eyes filled with tears at his words, but the swami smiled tranquilly. He reminded me of a little heavenly child, sitting securely on the lap of the Divine Mother. The burden of the years has no ill effect on a great yogi's full possession of supreme spiritual powers. He is able to renew his body at will; yet sometimes he does not care to retard the aging process, but allows his karma to work itself out on the physical plane, using his old body as a time-saving device to exclude the necessity of working out karma in a new incarnation.

Months later I met an old friend, Sanandan, who was one of Pranabananda's close disciples.

"My adorable guru is gone," he told me, amidst sobs. "He established a

6 One of Lahiri Mahasaya's favourite remarks, given as encouragement for his students' perseverance. A free translation is: 'Striving, striving, one day behold! the Divine Goal is attained!'

hermitage near Rishikesh, and gave us loving training. When we were pretty well settled, and making rapid spiritual progress in his company, he proposed one day to feed a huge crowd from Rishikesh. I inquired why he wanted such a large number.

" 'This is my last festival ceremony,' he said. I did not understand the full implications of his words.

"Pranabanandaji helped with the cooking of great amounts of food. We fed about 2000 guests. After the feast, he sat on a high platform and gave an inspired sermon on the Infinite. At the end, before the gaze of thousands, he turned to me, as I sat beside him on the dais, and spoke with unusual force.

" 'Sanandan, be prepared; I am going to kick the frame.'[7]

"After a stunned silence, I cried loudly, 'Master, don't do it! Please, please, don't do it!' The crowd was tongue-tied, watching us curiously. My guru smiled at me, but his solemn gaze was already fixed on Eternity.

" 'Be not selfish,' he said, 'nor grieve for me. I have been long cheerfully serving you all; now rejoice and wish me Godspeed. I go to meet my Cosmic Beloved.' In a whisper, Pranabanandaji added, 'I shall be reborn shortly. After enjoying a short period of the Infinite Bliss, I shall return to earth and join Babaji.[8] You shall soon know when and where my soul has been encased in a new body.'

"He cried again, 'Sanandan, here I kick the frame by the second *Kriya Yoga*.'[9]

"He looked at the sea of faces before us, and gave a blessing. Directing his gaze inwardly to the spiritual eye, he became immobile. While the bewildered crowd thought he was meditating in an ecstatic state, he had already left the tabernacle of flesh and plunged his soul into the cosmic vastness. The disciples touched his body, seated in the lotus posture, but it was no longer the warm flesh. Only a stiffened frame remained; the tenant had fled to the immortal shore."

I inquired where Pranabananda was to be reborn.

"That's a sacred trust I cannot divulge to anyone," Sanandan replied. "Perhaps you may find out some other way."

Years later I discovered from Swami Keshabananda[10] that Pranabananda, a few years after his birth in a new body, had gone to Badrinarayan in the Himalayas, and there joined the group of saints around the great Babaji.

---

7 *i.e.*, give up the body.

8 Lahiri Mahasaya's guru, who is still living. (See chapter 33.)

9 The second Kriya, as taught by Lahiri Mahasaya, enables the devotee that has mastered it to leave and return to the body consciously at any time. Advanced yogis use the second *Kriya* technique during the last exit of death, a moment they invariably know beforehand.

Great yogis go 'in and out' of the spiritual eye, the pranic star 'door' of salvation. Christ said: "I am the door: by me if any man enter in, he shall be saved, and shall go in and out, and find pleasure. The thief (*maya* of delusion) cometh not but for to steal, and to kill, and to destroy: I (the Christ-Consciousness) am come that they might have life, and that they might have it more abundantly." – *John* 10: 9-10.

10 My meeting with Keshabananda is described in chapter 42.

28. *Kashi, Reborn and Rediscovered*

"PLEASE DO NOT go into the water. Let us bathe by dipping our buckets."

I was addressing the young Ranchi students who were accompanying me on an eight-mile hike to a neighboring hill. The pond before us was inviting, but a distaste for it had arisen in my mind. The group around me followed my example of dipping buckets, but a few lads yielded to the temptation of the cool waters. No sooner had they dived than large water snakes wiggled around them. The boys came out of the pond with comical alacrity.

We enjoyed a picnic lunch after we reached our destination. I sat under a tree, surrounded by a group of students. Finding me in an inspirational mood, they plied me with questions.

"Please tell me, sir," one youth inquired, "if I shall always stay with you in the path of renunciation."

"Ah, no." I replied, "you will be forcibly taken away to your home, and later you will marry."

Incredulous, he made a vehement protest. "Only if I am dead can I be carried home." But in a few months, his parents arrived to take him away, in spite of his tearful resistance; some years later, he did marry.

After answering many questions, I was addressed by a lad named Kashi. He was about twelve years old, a brilliant student, and beloved by all.

"Sir," he said, "what will be my fate?"

"You shall soon be dead." The reply came from my lips with an irresistible force.

This unexpected disclosure shocked and grieved me as well as everyone present. Silently rebuking myself as an *enfant terrible*, I refused to answer further questions.

On our return to the school, Kashi came to my room.

"If I die, will you find me when I am reborn, and bring me again to the spiritual path?" He sobbed.

I felt constrained to refuse this difficult occult responsibility. But for weeks afterward, Kashi pressed me doggedly. Seeing him unnerved to the breaking point, I finally consoled him.

"Yes," I promised. "If the Heavenly Father lends His aid, I will try to find you."

During the summer vacation, I started on a short trip. Regretting that I could not take Kashi with me, I called him to my room before leaving, and carefully instructed him to remain, against all persuasion, in the spiritual vibrations of the school. Somehow I felt that if he did not go home, he might avoid the impending calamity.

No sooner had I left than Kashi's father arrived in Ranchi. For fifteen days he tried to break the will of his son, explaining that if Kashi would go to Calcutta for only four days to see his mother, he could then return. Kashi persistently refused. The father finally said he would take the boy away with the help of the police. The threat disturbed Kashi, who was unwilling to be the cause of any unfavourable publicity to the school. He saw no choice but to go.

I returned to Ranchi a few days later. When I heard how Kashi had been removed, I entrained at once for Calcutta. There I engaged a horse cab. Very strangely, as the vehicle passed beyond the Howrah bridge over the Ganges, I beheld Kashi's father and other relatives in mourning clothes. Shouting to my driver to stop, I rushed out and glared at the unfortunate father.

"Mr. Murderer," I cried somewhat unreasonably, "you have killed my boy!"

The father had already realized the wrong he had done in forcibly bringing Kashi to Calcutta. During the few days the boy had been there, he had eaten contaminated food, contracted cholera, and passed on.

My love for Kashi, and the pledge to find him after death, night and day haunted me. No matter where I went, his face loomed up before me. I began a memorable search for him, even as long ago I had searched for my lost mother.

I felt that inasmuch as God had given me the faculty of reason, I must utilize it and tax my powers to the utmost in order to discover the subtle laws by which I could know the boy's astral whereabouts. He was a soul vibrating with unfulfilled desires, I realized – a mass of light floating somewhere amidst millions of luminous souls in the astral regions. How was I to tune in with him, among so many vibrating lights of other souls?

Using a secret yoga technique, I broadcasted my love to Kashi's soul through the microphone of the spiritual eye, the inner point between the eyebrows. With the antenna of upraised hands and fingers, I often turned myself round and round, trying to locate the direction in which he had been reborn as an embryo. I hoped to receive response from him in the concentration-tuned radio of my heart.[1]

I intuitively felt that Kashi would soon return to the earth, and that if I kept unceasingly broadcasting my call to him, his soul would reply. I knew that the slightest impulse sent by Kashi would be felt in my fingers, hands, arms, spine, and nerves.

With undiminished zeal, I practiced the yoga method steadily for about six months after Kashi's death. Walking with a few friends one morning in

1 The will, projected from the point between the eyebrows, is known by yogis as the broadcasting apparatus of thought. When the feeling is calmly concentrated on the heart, it acts as a mental radio, and can receive the messages of others from far or near. In telepathy the fine vibrations of thoughts in one person's mind are transmitted through the subtle vibrations of astral ether and then through the grosser earthly ether, creating electrical waves which, in turn, translate themselves into thought waves in the mind of the other person.

the crowded Bowbazar section of Calcutta, I lifted my hands in the usual manner. For the first time, there was response. I was thrilled to detect electrical impulses trickling down my fingers and palms. These currents translated themselves into one overpowering thought from a deep recess of my consciousness: "I am Kashi; I am Kashi; come to me!"

The thought became almost audible as I concentrated on my heart radio. In the characteristic, slightly hoarse whisper of Kashi,[2] I heard his summons again and again. I seized the arm of one of my companions, Prokash Das,[3] and smiled at him joyfully.

"It looks as though I have located Kashi!"

I began to turn round and round, to the undisguised amusement of my friends and the passing throng. The electrical impulses tingled through my fingers only when I faced toward a near-by path, aptly named 'Serpentine Lane.' The astral currents disappeared when I turned in other directions.

"Ah," I exclaimed, "Kashi's soul must be living in the womb of some mother whose home is in this lane."

My companions and I approached closer to Serpentine Lane; the vibrations in my upraised hands grew stronger, more pronounced. As if by a magnet, I was pulled toward the right side of the road. Reaching the entrance of a certain house, I was astounded to find myself transfixed. I knocked at the door in a state of intense excitement, holding my very breath. I felt that the successful end had come for my long, arduous, and certainly unusual quest!

The door was opened by a servant, who told me her master was at home. He descended the stairway from the second floor and smiled at me inquiringly. I hardly knew how to frame my question, at once pertinent and impertinent.

"Please tell me, sir, if you and your wife have been expecting a child for about six months?"[4]

---

2 Every soul in its pure state is omniscient. Kashi's soul remembered all the characteristics of Kashi, the boy, and therefore mimicked his hoarse voice in order to stir my recognition.

3 Prokash Das is the present director of Yogoda Math (hermitage) at Dakshineswar in Bengal.

4 Though many men, after physical death, remain in an astral world for 500 or 1000 years, there is no invariable rule about the length of time between incarnations. (See chap. 43). A man's allotted span in a physical or an astral embodiment is karmically predetermined.

Death, and indeed sleep, 'the little death' are a mortal necessity, freeing the unenlightened human being temporarily from sense trammels. As man's essential nature is Spirit, he receives in sleep and in death certain revivifying reminders of his incorporeity.

The equilibrating law of karma, as expounded in Hindu scriptures, is that of action and reaction, cause and effect, sowing and reaping. In the course of natural righteousness (*rita*), each man, by his thoughts and actions, becomes the moulder of his destiny. Whatever universal energies he himself, wisely or unwisely, has set in motion must return to him as their starting point, like a circle inexorably completing itself. 'The world looks like a mathematical equation, which, turn it how you will, balances itself. Every secret is told, every crime is punished, every virtue rewarded, every wrong redressed, in silence and certainty.' – Emerson in *Compensation*.

An understanding of karma as the law of justice underlying life's inequalities serves to free the human mind from resentment against God and man. (See Note 20 on page 125).

"Yes, it is so." Seeing that I was a swami, a renunciate attired in the traditional orange cloth, he added politely, "Pray inform me how you know my affairs."

When he heard about Kashi and the promise I had given, the astonished man believed my story.

"A male child of fair complexion will be born to you," I told him. "He will have a broad face, with a cowlick[5] atop his forehead. His disposition will be notably spiritual." I felt certain that the coming child would bear these resemblances to Kashi.

Later I visited the child, whose parents had given him his old name of Kashi. Even in infancy he was strikingly similar in appearance to my dear Ranchi student. The child showed me an instantaneous affection; the attraction of the past awoke with redoubled intensity.

Years later the teen-age boy wrote me, during my stay in America. He explained his deep longing to follow the path of a renunciate. I directed him to a Himalayan master who, to this day, guides the reborn Kashi.

29. *Rabindranath Tagore and I Compare Schools*

"RABINDRANATH TAGORE taught us to sing, as a natural form of self-expression, like the birds."

Bhola Nath, a bright fourteen-year-old lad at my Ranchi school, gave me this explanation after I had complimented him one morning on his melodious outbursts. With or without provocation, the boy poured forth a tuneful stream. He had previously attended the famous Tagore school of 'Santiniketan' (Haven of Peace) at Bolpur.

"The songs of Rabindranath have been on my lips since early youth." I told my companion. "All Bengal, even the unlettered peasants, delights in his lofty verse."

Bhola and I sang together a few refrains from Tagore, who has set to music thousands of Indian poems, some original and others of hoary antiquity.

"I met Rabindranath soon after he had received the Nobel Prize for literature." I remarked after our vocalizing. "I was drawn to visit him because I admired his undiplomatic courage in disposing of his literary critics." I chuckled.

Bhola curiously inquired the story.

"The scholars severely flayed Tagore for introducing a new style into Bengali poetry," I began. "He mixed colloquial and classical expressions, ignoring all the prescribed limitations dear to the pundits' hearts. His songs

5 A tuft or a bunch of hair.

embody deep philosophic truth in emotionally appealing terms, with little regard for the accepted literary forms.

"One influential critic slightingly referred to Rabindranath as a 'pigeon-poet who sold his cooings in print for a rupee.' But Tagore's revenge was at hand; the whole Western world paid homage at his feet soon after he had translated into English his *Gitanjali* ('Song Offerings'). A train-load of pundits, including his one-time critics, went to Santiniketan to offer their congratulations.

"Rabindranath received his guests only after an intentionally long delay, and then heard their praise in stoic silence. Finally he turned against them their own habitual weapons of criticism.

" 'Gentlemen,' he said, 'the fragrant honours you here bestow are incongruously mingled with the putrid odours of your past contempt. Is there possibly any connection between my award of the Nobel Prize, and suddenly acute powers of your appreciation? I am still the same poet who displeased you when I first offered my humble flowers at the shrine of Bengal.'

"The newspapers published an account of the bold chastisement given by Tagore. I admired the outspoken words of a man unhypnotized by flattery," I went on. "I was introduced to Rabindranath in Calcutta by his secretary, Mr. C.F. Andrews,"[1] who was simply attired in a Bengali *dhoti*. He referred lovingly to Tagore as his *gurudeva*.

"Rabindranath received me graciously. He emanated a soothing aura of charm, culture, and courtliness. Replying to my question about his literary background, Tagore told me that one ancient source of his inspiration, besides our religious epics, had been the classical poet, Bidyapati."

Inspired by these memories, I began to sing Tagore's version of an old Bengali song, "Light the Lamp of Thy Love." Bhola and I chanted joyously as we strolled over the *Vidyalaya* grounds.

About two years after founding the Ranchi school, I received an invitation from Rabindranath to visit him at Santiniketan in order to discuss our educational ideals. I went gladly. The poet was seated in his study when I entered; I thought then, as at our first meeting, that he was as striking a model of superb manhood as any painter could desire. His beautifully chiselled face, nobly patrician, was framed in long hair and flowing beard. Large, melting eyes; an angelic smile; and a voice of flutelike quality which was literally enchanting. Stalwart, tall, and grave, he combined an almost womanly tenderness with the delightful spontaneity of a child. No idealized conception of a poet could find more suitable embodiment than in this gentle singer.

Tagore and I were soon deep in a comparative study of our schools, both

---

1 The English writer and publicist, close friend of Mahatma Gandhi. Mr. Andrews is honoured in India for his many services to his adopted land.

founded along unorthodox lines. We discovered many identical features – outdoor instruction, simplicity, ample scope for the child's creative spirit. Rabindranath, however, laid considerable stress on the study of literature and poetry, and the self-expression through music and song which I had already noted in the case of Bhola. The Santiniketan children observed periods of silence, but were given no special yoga training.

The poet listened with flattering attention to my description of the energizing 'Yogoda' exercises and the yoga concentration techniques which are taught to all students at Ranchi.

Tagore told me of his own early educational struggles. "I fled from school after the fifth grade," he said, laughing. I could readily understand how his innate poetic delicacy had been affronted by the dreary, disciplinary atmosphere of a schoolroom.

"That is why I opened Santiniketan under the shady trees and the glories of the sky." He motioned eloquently to a little group studying in the beautiful garden. "A child is in his natural setting amidst the flowers and songbirds. Only thus may he fully express the hidden wealth of his individual endowment. True education can never be crammed and pumped from without; rather it must aid in bringing spontaneously to the surface the infinite hoards of wisdom within."[2]

I agreed. "The idealistic and hero-worshiping instincts of the young are starved on an exclusive diet of statistics and chronological eras."

The poet spoke lovingly of his father, Devendranath, who had inspired the Santiniketan beginnings.

"Father presented me with this fertile land, where he had already built a guest house and temple," Rabindranath told me. "I started my educational experiment here in 1901, with only ten boys. The eight thousand pounds which came with the Nobel Prize all went for the upkeep of the school."

The elder Tagore, Devendranath, known far and wide as *Maharishi*, was a very remarkable man, as one may discover from his *Autobiography*. Two years of his manhood were spent in meditation in the Himalayas. In turn, his father, Dwarkanath Tagore, had been celebrated throughout Bengal for his munificent public benefactions. From this illustrious tree has sprung a family of geniuses. Not Rabindranath alone; all his relatives have distinguished themselves in creative expression. His brothers, Gogonendra and Abanindra, are among the foremost artists[3] of India; another brother,

---

[2] The soul having been often born, or, as the Hindus say, 'travelling the path of existence through thousands of births'... there is nothing of which she has not gained the knowledge; no wonder that she is able to recollect... what formerly she knew.... For inquiry and learning is reminiscence all. – Emerson in *Representative Men*.

[3] Rabindranath, too, in his sixties, engaged in a serious study of painting. Exhibitions of his 'futuristic' work were given some years ago in European capitals and New York.

Dwijendra, is a deep-seeing philosopher, at whose gentle call the birds and woodland creatures respond.

Rabindranath invited me to stay overnight in the guest house. It was indeed a charming spectacle, in the evening, to see the poet seated with a group in the patio. Time unfolded backward: the scene before me was like that of an ancient hermitage – the joyous singer encircled by his devotees, all aureoled in divine love. Tagore knitted each tie with the cords of harmony. Never assertive, he drew and captured the heart by an irresistible magnetism. Rare blossom of poesy blooming in the garden of the Lord, attracting others by a natural fragrance!

In his melodious voice, Rabindranath read to us a few of his exquisite poems, newly created. Most of his songs and plays, written for the delectation of his students, have been composed at Santiniketan. The beauty of his lines, to me, lies in his art of referring to God in nearly every stanza, yet seldom mentioning the sacred Name. "Drunk with the bliss of singing," he wrote, "I forget myself and call thee friend who art my lord."

The following day, after lunch, I bade the poet a reluctant farewell. I rejoice that his little school has now grown to an international university, 'Viswa-Bharati,'[4] where scholars of all lands have found an ideal setting.

Where the mind is without fear and the head is held high;

Where knowledge is free;

Where the world has not been broken up into fragments by narrow domestic walls;

Where words come out from the depth of truth;

Where tireless striving stretches its arms toward perfection;

Where the clear stream of reason has not lost its way into the dreary desert sand of dead habit;

Where the mind is led forward by Thee into ever-widening thought and action;

Into that heaven of freedom, my Father, let my country awake![5]

                                                    – RABINDRANATH TAGORE

---

4 Although the beloved poet died in 1941, his Visva-Bharati institution is still flourishing. In January 1950, sixty-five teachers and students from Santiniketan paid a ten-day visit to the Yogoda Satsanga school in Ranchi.

5 *Gitanjali* (New York: Macmillan Co.). A thoughtful study of the poet will be found in *The Philosophy of Rabindranath Tagore,* by the celebrated scholar, Sir S. Radhakrishnan (Macmillan, 1918). Another expository volume is B. K. Roy's *Rabindranath Tagore: The Man and His Poetry* (New York: Dodd, Mead, 1915). *Buddha and the Gospel of Buddhism* (New York: Putnam's, 1916), by the eminent Oriental art authority, Ananda K. Coomaraswamy, contains a number of illustrations in colour by the poet's brother, Abanindra Nath Tagore.

30. *The Law of Miracles*

THE GREAT NOVELIST Leo Tolstoy wrote a delightful story, *The Three Hermits*. His friend Nicholas Roerich[1] has summarized the tale, as follows:

"On an island there lived three old hermits. They were so simple that the only prayer they used was: 'We are three; Thou art Three – have mercy on us!' Great miracles were manifested during this naive prayer.

"The local bishop[2] came to hear about the three hermits and their inadmissible prayer, and decided to visit them in order to teach them the canonical invocations. He arrived on the island, told the hermits that their heavenly petition was undignified, and taught them many of the customary prayers. The bishop then left on a boat. He saw, following the ship, a radiant light. As it approached, he discerned the three hermits, who were holding hands and running upon the waves in an effort to overtake the vessel.

" 'We have forgotten the prayers you taught us,' they cried as they reached the bishop, 'and have hastened to ask you to repeat them.' The awed bishop shook his head.

" 'Dear ones,' he replied humbly, 'continue to live with your old prayer!' "

How did the three saints walk on the water?

How did Christ resurrect his crucified body?

How did Lahiri Mahasaya and Sri Yukteswar perform their miracles?

Modern science has, as yet, no answer; though with the advent of the atomic bomb and the wonders of radar, the scope of the world-mind has been abruptly enlarged. The word 'impossible' is becoming less prominent in the scientific vocabulary.

The ancient Vedic scriptures declare that the physical world operates under one fundamental law of *maya,* the principle of relativity and duality. God, the Sole Life, is an Absolute Unity; He cannot appear as the separate and diverse manifestations of a creation except under a false or unreal veil. That cosmic illusion is *maya.* Every great scientific discovery of modern times has served as a confirmation of this simple pronouncement of the rishis.

Newton's Law of Motion is a law of *maya*: 'To every action there is always an equal and contrary reaction; the mutual actions of any two bodies are always equal and oppositely directed.' Action and reaction are thus exactly equal. 'To have a single force is impossible. There must be, and always is, a pair of forces equal and opposite.'

1 This famous Russian artist and philosopher has been living for many years in India near the Himalayas. 'From the peaks comes revelation,' he has written. 'In caves and upon the summits lived the rishis. Over the snowy peaks of the Himalayas burns a bright glow, brighter than stars and the fantastic flashes of lightning.'
2 The story may have a historical basis; an editorial note informs us that the bishop met the three monks while he was sailing from Archangel to the Slovetsky Monastery, at the mouth of the Dvina River.

Fundamental natural activities all betray their mayic origin. Electricity, for example, is a phenomenon of repulsion and attraction; its electrons and protons are electrical opposites. Another example: the atom or final particle of matter is, like the earth itself, a magnet with positive and negative poles. The entire phenomenal world is under the inexorable sway of polarity; no law of physics, chemistry, or any other science is ever found free from inherent opposite or contrasted principles.

Physical science, then, cannot formulate laws outside of *maya,* the very texture and structure of creation. Nature herself is *maya;* natural science must perforce deal with her ineluctable quiddity. In her own domain, she is eternal and inexhaustible; future scientists can do no more than probe one aspect after another of her varied infinitude. Science thus remains in a perpetual flux, unable to reach finality; fit indeed to formulate the laws of an already existing and functioning cosmos, but powerless to detect the Law Framer and Sole Operator. The majestic manifestations of gravitation and electricity have become known, but what gravitation and electricity are, no mortal knoweth.[3]

To surmount *maya* was the task assigned to the human race by the millennial prophets. To rise above the duality of creation and perceive the unity of the Creator was conceived of as man's highest goal. Those who cling to the cosmic illusion must accept its essential law of polarity: flow and ebb, rise and fall, day and night, pleasure and pain, good and evil, birth and death. This cyclic pattern assumes a certain anguishing monotony, after man has gone through a few thousand human births; he begins to cast a hopeful eye beyond the compulsions of *maya.*

To tear the veil of *maya* is to pierce the secret of creation. The yogi who thus denudes the universe is the only true monotheist. All others are worshiping heathen images. So long as man remains subject to the dualistic delusions of nature, the Janus-faced *Maya* is his goddess; he cannot know the one true God.

The world illusion, *maya,* is individually called *avidya,* literally, 'not-knowledge,' ignorance, delusion. *Maya* or *avidya* can never be destroyed through intellectual conviction or analysis, but solely through attaining the interior state of *nirbikalpa samadhi.* The Old Testament prophets, and seers of all lands and ages, spoke from that state of consciousness. Ezekiel says (43: 1-2): "Afterwards he brought me to the gate, even the gate that looketh toward the east: and, behold, the glory of the God of Israel came from the way of the east: and his voice was like a noise of many waters: and the earth

3 Marconi, the great inventor, made the following admission of scientific inadequacy before the finalities: "The inability of science to solve life is absolute. This fact would be truly frightening were it not for faith. The mystery of life is certainly the most persistent problem ever placed before the thought of man."

shined with his glory." Through the divine eye in the forehead (east), the yogi sails his consciousness into omnipresence, hearing the Word or *Aum,* divine sound of many waters or vibrations which is the sole reality of creation.

Among the trillion mysteries of the cosmos, the most phenomenal is light. Unlike sound-waves, whose transmission requires air or other material media, light-waves pass freely through the vacuum of interstellar space. Even the hypothetical ether, held as the interplanetary medium of light in the undulatory theory, can be discarded on the Einsteinian grounds that the geometrical properties of space render the theory of ether unnecessary. Under either hypothesis, light remains the most subtle, the freest from material dependence, of any natural manifestation.

In the gigantic conceptions of Einstein, the velocity of light – 186,000 miles per second – dominates the whole Theory of Relativity. He proves mathematically that the velocity of light is, so far as man's finite mind is concerned, the only *constant* in a universe of unstayable flux. On the sole absolute of light-velocity depend all human standards of time and space. Not abstractly eternal as hitherto considered, time and space are relative and finite factors, deriving their measurement validity only in reference to the yardstick of light-velocity. In joining space as a dimensional relativity, time has surrendered age-old claims to a changeless value. Time is now stripped to its rightful nature – a simple essence of ambiguity! With a few equational strokes of his pen, Einstein has banished from the cosmos every fixed reality except that of light.

In a later development, his Unified Field Theory, the great physicist embodies in one mathematical formula the laws of gravitation and of electromagnetism. Reducing the cosmical structure to variations on a single law, Einstein[4] reaches across the ages to the rishis who proclaimed a sole texture of creation – that of a protean *maya.*

On the epochal Theory of Relativity have arisen the mathematical possibilities of exploring the ultimate atom. Great scientists are now boldly asserting not only that the atom is energy rather than matter, but that atomic energy is essentially mind-stuff.

"The frank realization that physical science is concerned with a world of shadows is one of the most significant advances," Sir Arthur Stanley Eddington writes in *The Nature of the Physical World.* "In the world of physics we watch a shadowgraph performance of the drama of familiar life. The shadow of my elbow rests on the shadow table as the shadow ink

---

4 A clue to the direction taken by Einstein's genius is given by the fact that he is a lifelong disciple of the great Dutch philosopher Benedict de Spinoza (1632-1677), whose best-known work is *Ethics Demonstrated in Geometrical Order.*

flows over the shadow paper. It is all symbolic, and as a symbol the physicist leaves it. Then comes the alchemist Mind who transmutes the symbols. . . . To put the conclusion crudely, the stuff of the world is mind-stuff. . . . The realistic matter and fields of force of former physical theory are altogether irrelevant except in so far as the mind-stuff has itself spun these imaginings. . . . The external world has thus become a world of shadows. In removing our illusions we have removed the substance, for indeed we have seen that substance is one of the greatest of our illusions."

With the recent discovery of the electron microscope came definite proof of the light-essence of atoms and of the inescapable duality of nature. *The New York Times* gave the following report of a 1937 demonstration of the electron microscope before a meeting of the American Association for the Advancement of Science:

> "The crystalline structure of tungsten, hitherto known only indirectly by means of X-rays, stood outlined boldly on a fluorescent screen, showing nine atoms in their correct positions in the space lattice, a cube, with one atom in each corner and one in the center. The atoms in the crystal lattice of the tungsten appeared on the fluorescent screen as points of light, arranged in geometric pattern. Against this crystal cube of light the bombarding molecules of air could be observed as dancing points of light, similar to points of sunlight shimmering on moving waters. . . .
>
> "The principle of the electron microscope was first discovered in 1927 by Drs. Clinton J. Davisson and Lester H. Germer of the Bell Telephone Laboratories, New York City, who found that the electron had a dual personality partaking of the characteristic of both a particle and a wave. The wave quality gave the electron the characteristic of light, and a search was begun to devise means for 'focusing' electrons in a manner similar to the focusing of light by means of a lens.
>
> "For his discovery of the *Jekyll-Hyde* quality of the electron, which corroborated the prediction made in 1924 by De Broglie, French Nobel Prize winning physicist, and showed that the entire realm of physical nature had a dual personality, Dr. Davisson also received the Nobel Prize in physics."

'The stream of knowledge,' Sir James Jeans writes in *The Mysterious Universe*, 'is heading towards a non-mechanical reality; the universe begins to look more like a great thought than like a great machine.' Twentieth-century science is thus sounding like a page from the hoary *Vedas*.

From science, then, if it must be so, let man learn the philosophic truth that there is no material universe; its warp and woof is *maya,* illusion. Its mirages of reality all break down under analysis. As one by one the reassuring props of a physical cosmos crash beneath him, man dimly perceives his idolatrous reliance, his past transgression of the divine command: 'Thou shalt have no other gods before Me.'

In his famous equation outlining the equivalence of mass and energy, Einstein proved that the energy in any particle of matter is equal to its mass or weight multiplied by the square of the velocity of light. The release of the atomic energies is brought about through the annihilation of the material particles. The 'death' of matter has been the 'birth' of an Atomic Age.

Light-velocity is a mathematical standard or constant not because there is an absolute value in 186,000 miles a second, but because no material body, whose mass increases with its velocity, can ever attain the velocity of light. Stated another way: only a material body whose mass is infinite could equal the velocity of light.

This conception brings us to the law of miracles.

The masters who are able to materialize and dematerialize their bodies or any other object, and to move with the velocity of light, and to utilize the creative light-rays in bringing into instant visibility any physical manifestation, have fulfilled the necessary Einsteinian condition: their mass is infinite.

The consciousness of a perfected yogi is effortlessly identified, not with a narrow body, but with the universal structure. Gravitation, whether the 'force' of Newton or the Einsteinian 'manifestation of inertia,' is powerless to *compel* a master to exhibit the property of 'weight' which is the distinguishing gravitational condition of all material objects. He who knows himself as the omnipresent Spirit is subject no longer to the rigidities of a body in time and space. Their imprisoning 'rings-pass-not' have yielded to the solvent: *I am He.*

"*Fiat lux*! And there was light." God's first command to His ordered creation (*Genesis* 1: 3) brought into being the only atomic reality: light. On the beams of this immaterial medium occur all divine manifestations. Devotees of every age testify to the appearance of God as flame and light. 'The King of kings, and Lord of lords; who only hath immortality, dwelling in the light which no man can approach unto.'[5]

A yogi who through perfect meditation has merged his consciousness with the Creator perceives the cosmical essence as light; to him there is no difference

I *Timothy* 6: 15-16.

between the light rays composing water and the light rays composing land. Free from matter-consciousness, free from the three dimensions of space and the fourth dimension of time, a master transfers his body of light with equal ease over the light rays of earth, water, fire, or air. Long concentration on the liberating spiritual eye has enabled the yogi to destroy all delusions concerning matter and its gravitational weight; thenceforth he sees the universe as an essentially undifferentiated mass of light.

"Optical images," Dr. L. T. Troland of Harvard tells us, "are built up on the same principle as the ordinary 'half-tone' engravings; that is, they are made up of minute dottings or stripplings far too small to be detected by the eye. . . . The sensitiveness of the retina is so great that a visual sensation can be produced by relatively few Quanta of the right kind of light." Through a master's divine knowledge of light phenomena, he can instantly project into perceptible manifestation the ubiquitous light atoms. The actual form of the projection, whether it be a tree, a medicine, a human body, is in conformance with a yogi's powers of will and of visualization.

In man's dream-consciousness, where he has loosened in sleep his clutch on the egoistic limitations that daily hem him round, the omnipotence of his mind has a nightly demonstration. Lo! there in the dream stand the long-dead friends, the remotest continents, the resurrected scenes of his childhood. With that free and unconditioned consciousness, known to all men in the phenomena of dreams, the God-tuned master has forged a never-severed link. Innocent of all personal motives, and employing the creative will bestowed on him by the Creator, a yogi rearranges the light atoms of the universe to satisfy any sincere prayer of a devotee. For this purpose were man and creation made: that he should rise up as master of *maya,* knowing his dominion over the cosmos.

"And God said, Let us make man in our image, after our likeness: and let them have dominion over the fish of the sea, and over the fowl of the air, and over the cattle, and over all the earth, and over every creeping thing that creepeth upon the earth."[6]

In 1915, shortly after I had entered the Swami Order, I witnessed a vision of violent contrasts. In it the relativity of human consciousness was vividly established; I clearly perceived the unity of the Eternal Light behind the painful dualities of *maya.* The vision descended on me as I sat one morning in my little attic room in Father's Gurpar Road home. For months World War-I had been raging in Europe; I reflected sadly on the vast toll of death.

As I closed my eyes in meditation, my consciousness was suddenly transferred to the body of a captain in command of a battleship. The thunder

6 *Genesis* 1: 26.

of guns split the air as shots were exchanged between shore batteries and the ship's cannons. A huge shell hit the powder magazine and tore my ship asunder. I jumped into the water, together with the few sailors who had survived the explosion.

Heart pounding, I reached the shore safely. But alas! a stray bullet ended its furious flight in my chest. I fell groaning to the ground. My whole body was paralyzed, yet I was aware of possessing it as one is conscious of a leg gone to sleep.

"At last the mysterious footstep of Death has caught up with me," I thought. With a final sigh, I was about to sink into unconsciousness when lo! I found myself seated in the lotus posture in my Gurpar Road room.

Hysterical tears poured forth as I joyfully stroked and pinched my regained possession – a body free from any bullet hole in the breast. I rocked to and fro, inhaling and exhaling to assure myself that I was alive. Amidst these self-congratulations, again I found my consciousness transferred to the captain's dead body by the gory shore. Utter confusion of mind came upon me.

"Lord," I prayed, "am I dead or alive?"

A dazzling play of light filled the whole horizon. A soft rumbling vibration formed itself into words:

"What has life or death to do with Light? In the image of My Light I have made you. The relativities of life and death belong to the cosmic dream. Behold your dreamless being! Awake, my child, awake!"

As steps in man's awakening, the Lord inspires scientists to discover, at the right time and place, the secrets of His creation. Many modern discoveries help men to apprehend the cosmos as a varied expression of one power – light, guided by divine intelligence. The wonders of the motion picture, of radio, of television, of radar, of the photo-electric cell – the all-seeing 'electric eye,' of atomic energies, are all based on the electromagnetic phenomenon of light.

The motion picture art can portray any miracle. From the impressive visual standpoint, no marvel is barred to trick photography. A man's transparent astral body can be seen rising from his gross physical form, he can walk on the water, resurrect the dead, reverse the natural sequence of developments, and play havoc with time and space. Assembling the light images as he pleases, the photographer achieves optical wonders which a true master produces with actual light rays.

The lifelike images of the motion picture illustrate many truths concerning creation. The Cosmic Director has written His own plays, and assembled the tremendous casts for the pageant of the centuries. From the dark booth of eternity, He pours His creative beam through the films of successive ages, and the pictures are thrown on the screen of space. Just as the motion-picture images appear to be real, but are only combinations of light and shade, so is the universal variety a delusive seeming. The planetary spheres, with their countless forms of life, are naught but figures in a cosmic motion picture, temporarily true to five sense perceptions as the scenes are cast on the screen of man's consciousness by the infinite creative beam.

A cinema audience can look up and see that all screen images are appearing through the instrumentality of one imageless beam of light. The colourful universal drama is similarly issuing from the single white light of a Cosmic Source. With inconceivable ingenuity God is staging an entertainment for His human children, making them actors as well as audience in His planetary theater.

One day I entered a motion picture house to view a newsreel of the European battlefields. World War-I was still being waged in the West; the newsreel recorded the carnage with such realism that I left the theater with a troubled heart.

"Lord," I prayed, "why dost Thou permit such suffering?"

To my intense surprise, an instant answer came in the form of a vision of the actual European battlefields. The horror of the struggle, filled with the dead and dying, far surpassed in ferocity any representation of the newsreel.

"Look intently!" A gentle voice spoke to my inner conscious-ness. "You will see that these scenes now being enacted in France are nothing but a play of chiaroscuro[7]. They are the cosmic motion picture, as real and as unreal as the theater newsreel you have just seen – a play within a play."

My heart was still not comforted. The divine voice went on: "Creation is light and shadow both, else no picture is possible. The good and evil of *maya* must ever alternate in supremacy. If joy were ceaseless in this world, would man ever seek another? Without suffering he scarcely cares to recall that he has forsaken his eternal home. Pain is a prod to remembrance. The escape is through wisdom! The tragedy of death is unreal; those who shudder at it are like an ignorant actor who dies of fright on the stage when nothing more is fired at him than a blank cartridge. My sons are the children of light; they will not sleep forever in delusion."

Although I had read scriptural accounts of *maya*, they had not given me the deep insight that came with the personal visions and their accompanying words of consolation. One's values are profoundly changed when he is

7 Interplay of light and shadow.

finally convinced that creation is only a vast motion picture, and that not in it, but beyond it, lies his own reality.

As I finished writing this chapter, I sat on my bed in the lotus posture. My room[8] was dimly lit by two shaded lamps. Lifting my gaze, I noticed that the ceiling was dotted with small mustard-coloured lights, scintillating and quivering with a radiumlike lustre. Myriads of pencilled rays, like sheets of rain, gathered into a transparent shaft and poured silently upon me.

At once my physical body lost its grossness and became metamorphosed into astral texture. I felt a floating sensation as, barely touching the bed, the weightless body shifted slightly and alternately to left and right. I looked around the room; the furniture and walls were as usual, but the little mass of light had so multiplied that the ceiling was invisible. I was wonder-struck.

"This is the cosmic motion picture mechanism." A voice spoke as though from within the light. "Shedding its beam on the white screen of your bed sheets, it is producing the picture of your body. Behold, your form is nothing but light!"

I gazed at my arms and moved them back and forth, yet could not feel their weight. An ecstatic joy overwhelmed me. This cosmic stem of light, blossoming as my body, seemed a divine replica of the light beams streaming out of the projection booth in a cinema house and manifesting as pictures on the screen.

For a long time I experienced this motion picture of my body in the dimly lighted theater of my own bedroom. Despite the many visions I have had, none was ever more singular. As my illusion of a solid body was completely dissipated, and my realization deepened that the essence of all objects is light, I looked up to the throbbing stream of lifetrons and spoke entreatingly.

"Divine Light, please withdraw this, my humble bodily picture, into Thyself, even as Elijah was drawn up to heaven by a flame."

This prayer was evidently startling; the beam disappeared. My body resumed its normal weight and sank on the bed; the swarm of dazzling ceiling lights flickered and vanished.[9] My time to leave this earth had apparently not arrived.

"Besides," I thought philosophically, "the prophet Elijah might well be displeased at my presumption!"

8 In Encinitas hermitage, in California.
9 A 'miracle' is considered an event without law or beyond law but not so in our precisely adjusted universe. The so-called powers of a great master are a natural accompaniment to his exact understanding of subtle laws that operate in the inner cosmos of consciousness. In this chapter I have given the Vedic explanation of *maya*. *Maya* is 'from the beginning' because of its structural inheritance in the phenomenal worlds. These are ever in transitional flux as antithesis to the Divine Immutability.

31. *An Interview with the Sacred Mother*

"REVERED MOTHER, I was baptized in infancy by your prophet-husband. He was the guru of my parents and of my own guru Sri Yukteswarji. Will you therefore give me the privilege of listening to a few incidents in your sacred life?"

I was addressing Srimati Kashi Moni, the life-companion of Lahiri Mahasaya. Finding myself in Benares for a short period, I was fulfilling a long-felt desire to visit the venerable lady. She received me graciously at the old Lahiri homestead in the Garudeswar Mohulla (precinct) of Benares. Although aged, she was blooming like a lotus, silently emanating a spiritual fragrance. She was of medium build, with a slender neck and fair skin. Large, lustrous eyes softened her motherly face.

"Son, you are welcome here. Come upstairs."

Kashi Moni led the way to a very small room where, for a time, she had lived with her husband. I felt honoured to witness the shrine in which the peerless master had condescended to play the human drama of matrimony. The gentle lady motioned me to a pillow seat by her side.

"It was years before I came to realize the divine stature of my husband," she began. "One night, in this very room, I had a vivid dream. Glorious angels floated in unimaginable grace above me. So realistic was the sight that I awoke at once; the room was strangely enveloped in dazzling light.

"My husband, in lotus posture, was levitated in the centre of the room, surrounded by angels who were worshiping him with the supplicating dignity of palm folded hands. Astonished beyond measure, I was convinced that I was still dreaming.

" 'Woman,' Lahiri Mahasaya said, 'you are not dreaming. Forsake your sleep forever and forever.' As he slowly descended to the floor, I prostrated myself at his feet.

" 'Master,' I cried, 'again and again I bow before you! Will you pardon me for having considered you as my husband? I die with shame to realize that I have remained asleep in ignorance by the side of one who is divinely awakened. From this night, you are no longer my husband, but my guru. Will you accept my insignificant self as your disciple?'[1]

"The master touched me gently. 'Sacred soul, arise. You are accepted.' He motioned toward the angels. 'Please bow in turn to each of these holy saints.'

"When I had finished my humble genuflections, the angelic voices sounded together, like a chorus from an ancient scripture.

---

1 One is reminded here of Milton's line: *He for God only, she for God in him.*

" 'Consort of the Divine One, thou art blessed. We salute thee.' They bowed at my feet and lo! their refulgent forms vanished. The room darkened.

"My guru asked me to receive initiation into *Kriya Yoga*.

" 'Of course,' I responded. 'I am sorry not to have had its blessing earlier in my life.'

" 'The time was not ripe.' Lahiri Mahasaya smiled consolingly. 'Much of your *karma* I have silently helped you to work out. Now you are willing and ready.'

"He touched my forehead. Masses of whirling light appeared; the radiance gradually formed itself into the opal-blue spiritual eye, ringed in gold and centred with a white pentagonal star.

" 'Penetrate your consciousness through the star into the kingdom of the Infinite.' My guru's voice had a new note, soft like distant music.

"Vision after vision broke as oceanic surf on the shores of my soul. The panoramic spheres finally melted in a sea of bliss. I lost myself in ever-surging blessedness. When I returned hours later to awareness of this world, the master gave me the technique of *Kriya Yoga*.

"From that night on, Lahiri Mahasaya never slept in my room again. Nor, thereafter, did he ever sleep. He remained in the front room downstairs, in the company of his disciples both by day and by night."

The illustrious lady fell into silence. Realizing the uniqueness of her relationship with the sublime yogi, I finally ventured to ask for further reminiscences.

"Son, you are greedy. Nevertheless you shall have one more story." She smiled shyly. "I will confess a sin which I committed against my guru-husband. Some months after my initiation, I began to feel forlorn and neglected. One morning Lahiri Mahasaya entered this little room to fetch an article; I quickly followed him. Overcome by violent delusion, I addressed him scathingly.

" 'You spend all your time with the disciples. What about your responsibilities for your wife and children? I regret that you do not interest yourself in providing more money for the family.'

"The master glanced at me for a moment, then lo! he was gone. Awed and frightened, I heard a voice resounding from every part of the room:

" 'It is all nothing, don't you see? How could a nothing like me produce riches for you?'

" 'Guruji,' I cried, 'I implore pardon a million times! My sinful eyes can see you no more; please appear in your sacred form.'

" 'I am here.' This reply came from above me. I looked up and saw the master materialize in the air, his head touching the ceiling. His eyes were like blinding flames. Beside myself with fear, I lay sobbing at his feet after he had quietly descended to the floor.

" 'Woman,' he said, 'seek divine wealth, not the paltry tinsel of earth. After acquiring inward treasure, you will find that outward supply is always forthcoming.' He added, 'One of my spiritual sons will make provision for you.'

"My guru's words naturally came true; a disciple did leave a considerable sum for our family."

I thanked Kashi Moni for sharing with me her wondrous experiences.[2] On the following day I returned to her home and enjoyed several hours of philosophical discussion with Tincouri and Ducouri Lahiri. These two saintly sons of India's great yogi followed closely in his ideal footsteps. Both men were fair, tall, stalwart, and heavily bearded, with soft voices and an old-fashioned charm of manner.

His wife was not the only woman disciple of Lahiri Mahasaya; there were hundreds of others, including my mother. A woman chela once asked the guru for his photograph. He handed her a print, remarking, "If you deem it a protection, then it is so; otherwise it is only a picture."

A few days later this woman and Lahiri Mahasaya's daugher-in-law happened to be studying the *Bhagavad Gita* at a table behind which hung the guru's photograph. An electrical storm broke out with great fury.

"Lahiri Mahasaya, protect us!" The women bowed before the picture. Lightning struck the book which they had been reading, but the two devotees were unhurt.

"I felt as though a sheet of ice had been placed around me to ward off the scorching heat," the chela explained.

Lahiri Mahasaya performed two miracles in connection with a woman disciple, Abhoya. She and her husband, a Calcutta lawyer, started one day for Benares to visit the guru. Their carriage was delayed by heavy traffic; they reached the Howrah main station only to hear the Benares train whistling for departure.

Abhoya, near the ticket office, stood quietly.

"Lahiri Mahasaya, I beseech thee to stop the train!" she silently prayed. "I cannot suffer the pangs of delay in waiting another day to see thee."

The wheels of the snorting train continued to move round and round, but there was no onward progress. The engineer and passengers descended to the platform to view the phenomenon. An English railroad guard approached Abhoya and her husband. Contrary to all precedent, he volunteered his services.

2 The venerable mother passed on at Benares in 1930.

"Babu," he said, "give me the money. I will buy your tickets while you get aboard."

As soon as the couple was seated and had received the tickets, the train slowly moved forward. In panic, the engineer and passengers clambered again to their places, knowing neither how the train started, nor why it had stopped in the first place.

Arriving at the home of Lahiri Mahasaya in Benares, Abhoya silently prostrated herself before the master, and tried to touch his feet.

"Compose yourself, Abhoya," he remarked. "How you love to bother me! As if you could not have come here by the next train!"

Abhoya visited Lahiri Mahasaya on another memorable occasion. This time she wanted his intercession, not with a train, but with the stork.

"I pray you to bless me that my ninth child may live," she said. "Eight babies have been born to me; all died soon after birth."

The master smiled sympathetically. "Your coming child will live. Please follow my instructions carefully. The baby, a girl, will be born at night. See that the oil lamp is kept burning until dawn. Do not fall asleep and thus allow the light to become extinguished."

Abhoya's child was a daughter, born at night, exactly as foreseen by the omniscient guru. The mother instructed her nurse to keep the lamp filled with oil. Both women kept the urgent vigil far into the early morning hours, but finally fell asleep. The lamp oil was almost gone; the light flickered feebly.

The bedroom door unlatched and flew open with a violent sound. The startled women awoke. Their astonished eyes beheld the form of Lahiri Mahasaya.

"Abhoya, behold, the light is almost gone!" He pointed to the lamp, which the nurse hastened to refill. As soon as it burned again brightly, the master vanished. The door closed; the latch was affixed without visible agency.

Abhoya's ninth child survived; in 1935, when I made inquiry, she was still living.

One of Lahiri Mahasaya's disciples, the venerable Kali Kumar Roy, related to me many fascinating details of his life with the master.

"I was often a guest at his Benares home for weeks at a time," Roy told me. "I observed that many saintly figures, *danda*[3] swamis, arrived in the quiet of night to sit at the guru's feet. Sometimes they would engage in discussion of meditational and philosophical points. At dawn the exalted guests would depart. I found during my visits that Lahiri Mahasaya did not once lie down to sleep.

3 Staff, symbolizing the spinal cord, carried ritually by certain orders of monks.

"During an early period of my association with the master, I had to contend with the opposition of my employer," Roy went on. "He was steeped in materialism.

" 'I don't want religious fanatics on my staff,' he would sneer. 'If I ever meet your charlatan guru, I shall give him some words to remember.'

"This alarming threat failed to interrupt my regular program; I spent nearly every evening in my guru's presence. One night my employer followed me and rushed rudely into the parlour. He was doubtless fully bent on uttering the pulverizing remarks he had promised. No sooner had the man seated himself than Lahiri Mahasaya addressed the little group of about twelve disciples.

" 'Would you all like to see a picture?'

"When we nodded, he asked us to darken the room. 'Sit behind one another in a circle,' he said, 'and place your hands over the eyes of the man in front of you.'

"I was not surprised to see that my employer also was following, albeit unwillingly, the master's directions. In a few minutes Lahiri Mahasaya asked us what we were seeing.

" 'Sir,' I replied, 'a beautiful woman appears. She wears a red-bordered *sari,* and stands near an elephant-ear plant.' All the other disciples gave the same description. The master turned to my employer. 'Do you recognize that woman?'

" 'Yes.' The man was evidently struggling with emotions new to his nature. 'I have been foolishly spending my money on her, though I have a good wife. I am ashamed of the motives which brought me here. Will you forgive me, and receive me as a disciple?'

" 'If you lead a good moral life for six months, I shall accept you.' The master enigmatically added, 'Otherwise I won't have to initiate you.'

"For three months my employer refrained from temptation; then he resumed his former relationship with the woman. Two months later he died. Thus I came to understand my guru's veiled prophecy about the improbability of the man's initiation."

Lahiri Mahasaya had a very famous friend, Swami Trailanga, who was reputed to be over three hundred years old. The two yogis often sat together in meditation. Trailanga's fame is so widespread that few Hindus would deny the possibility of truth in any story of his astounding miracles. If Christ returned to earth and walked the streets of New York, displaying his divine powers, it would cause the same excitement that was created by Trailanga decades ago as he passed through the crowded lanes of Benares.

On many occasions the swami was seen to drink, with no ill effect, the most deadly poisons. Thousands of people, including a few who are still living, have seen Trailanga floating on the Ganges. For days together he would sit on top of the water, or remain hidden for very long periods under the waves. A common sight at the Benares bathing *ghats* was the swami's motionless body on the blistering stone slabs, wholly exposed to the merciless Indian sun. By these feats Trailanga sought to teach men that a yogi's life does not depend upon oxygen or ordinary conditions and precautions. Whether he were above water or under it, and whether or not his body lay exposed to the fierce solar rays, the master proved that he lived by divine consciousness: death could not touch him.

The yogi was great not only spiritually, but physically. His weight exceeded three hundred pounds: a pound for each year of his life! As he ate very seldom, the mystery is increased. A master, however, easily ignores all usual rules of health, when he desires to do so for some special reason, often a subtle one known only to himself. Great saints who have awakened from the cosmic mayic dream and realized this world as an idea in the Divine Mind, can do as they wish with the body, knowing it to be only a manipulatable form of condensed or frozen energy. Though physical scientists now understand that matter is nothing but congealed energy, fully-illumined masters have long passed from theory to practice in the field of matter-control.

Trailanga always remained completely nude. The harassed police of Benares came to regard him as a baffling problem child. The natural swami, like the early Adam in the garden of Eden, was utterly unconscious of his nakedness. The police were quite conscious of it, however, and unceremoniously committed him to jail. General embarrassment ensued; the enormous body of Trailanga was soon seen, in its usual entirety, on the prison roof. His cell, still securely locked, offered no clue to his mode of escape.

The discouraged officers of the law once more performed their duty. This time a guard was posted before the swami's cell. Might again retired before Right. Trailanga was soon observed in his nonchalant stroll over the roof. Justice is blind; the outwitted police decided to follow her example.

The great yogi preserved a habitual silence.[4] In spite of his round face and huge, barrel-like stomach, Trailanga ate only occasionally. After weeks without food, he would break his fast with potfuls of clabbered milk offered to him by devotees. A skeptic once determined to expose Trailanga as a

4 He was a *muni,* a monk who observes *mauna,* spiritual silence. The Sanskrit root muni is akin to Greek *monos,* 'alone, single,' from which are derived the English words *monk, monism,* etc.

charlatan. A large bucket of calcium-lime mixture, used in whitewashing walls, was placed before the swami.

"Master," the materialist said, in mock reverence, "I have brought you some clabbered milk. Please drink it."

Trailanga unhesitatingly drained, to the last drop, the containerful of burning lime. In a few minutes the evildoer fell to the ground in agony.

"Help, swami, help!" he cried. "I am on fire! Forgive my wicked test!"

The great yogi broke his habitual silence. "Scoffer," he said, "you did not realize when you offered me poison that my life is one with your own. Except for my knowledge that God is present in my stomach, as in every atom of creation, the lime would have killed me. Now that you know the divine meaning of boomerang, never again play tricks on anyone."

The well-purged sinner, healed by Trailanga's words, slunk feebly away.

The reversal of pain was not due to any volition of the master, but came about through unerring application of the law of justice which upholds creation's farthest swinging orb. Men of God-realization like Trailanga allow the divine law to operate instantaneously; they have banished forever all thwarting crosscurrents of ego.

The automatic adjustments of righteousness, often paid in an unexpected coin as in the case of Trailanga and his would be murderer, assuage our hasty indignance at human injustice. 'Vengeance is mine; I will repay, saith the Lord.'[5] What need for man's brief resources? the universe duly conspires for retribution. Dull minds discredit the possibility of divine justice, love, omniscience, immortality. 'Airy scriptural conjectures!' This insensitive viewpoint, aweless before the cosmic spectacle, arouses a train of events which brings its own awakening.

The omnipotence of spiritual law was referred to by Christ on the occasion of his triumphant entry into Jerusalem. As the disciples and the multitude shouted for joy, and cried, "Peace in heaven, and glory in the highest," certain Pharisees complained of the undignified spectacle. "Master," they protested, "rebuke thy disciples."

"I tell you," Jesus replied, "that, if these should hold their peace, the stones would immediately cry out."[6]

In this reprimand to the Pharisees, Christ was pointing out that divine justice is no figurative abstraction, and that a man of peace, though his tongue be torn from its roots, will yet find his speech and his defense in the bedrock of creation, the universal order itself.

5 *Romans* 12: 19.   6 *Luke* 19: 37-40.

"Think you," Jesus was saying, "to silence men of peace? As well may you hope to throttle the voice of God, whose very stones sing His glory and His omnipresence. Will you demand that men not celebrate in honour of the peace in heaven, but should only gather together in multitudes to shout for war on earth? Then make your preparations, O Pharisees, to overtopple the foundations of the world; for it is not gentle men alone, but stones or earth, and water and fire and air that will rise up against you, to bear witness of His ordered harmony."

The grace of the Christ-like yogi, Trailanga, was once bestowed on my *sejo mama* (maternal uncle). One morning Uncle saw the master surrounded by a crowd of devotees at a Benares ghat. He managed to edge his way close to Trailanga, whose feet he touched humbly. Uncle was astonished to find himself instantly freed from a painful chronic disease.[7]

The only known living disciple of the great yogi is a woman, Shankari Mai Jiew. Daughter of one of Trailanga's disciples, she received the swami's training from her early childhood. She lived for forty years in a series of lonely Himalayan caves near Badrinath, Kedarnath, Amarnath, and Pasupatinath. The *brahmacharini* (woman ascetic), born in 1826, is now well over the century mark. Not aged in appearance, however, she has retained her black hair, sparkling teeth, and amazing energy. She comes out of her seclusion every few years to attend the periodical *melas* or religious fairs.

This woman saint often visited Lahiri Mahasaya. She has related that one day, in the Barrackpore section near Calcutta, while she was sitting by Lahiri Mahasaya's side, his great guru Babaji quietly entered the room and held converse with them both.

On one occasion her master Trailanga, forsaking his usual silence, honoured Lahiri Mahasaya very pointedly in public. A Benares disciple objected.

"Sir," he said, "why do you, a swami and a renunciate, show such respect to a householder?"

"My son," Trailanga replied, "Lahiri Mahasaya is like a divine kitten, remaining wherever the Cosmic Mother has placed him. While dutifully playing the part of a worldly man, he has received that perfect self-realization for which I have renounced everything – even my loincloth!"

---

7 The lives of Trailanga and other great masters remind us of Jesus' words: "And these signs shall follow them that believe: In my name (the Christ-consciousness) they shall cast out devils; they shall speak with new tongues; they shall take up serpents; and if they drink any deadly thing, it shall not hurt them; they shall lay hands on the sick, and they shall recover." – *Mark* 16: 17-18.

224

32. *Rama is raised from the Dead*

"Now a CERTAIN MAN was sick, named Lazarus. . . . When Jesus heard that, he said, This sickness is not unto death, but for the glory of God, that the Son of God might be glorified thereby.' "[1]

Sri Yukteswar was expounding the Christian scriptures one sunny morning on the balcony of his Serampore hermitage. Besides a few of Master's other disciples, I was present with a small group of my Ranchi students.

"In this passage Jesus calls himself the Son of God. Though he was truly united with God, his reference here has a deep impersonal significance," my guru explained. "The Son of God is the Christ or Divine Consciousness in man. No *mortal* can glorify God. The only honour that man can pay his Creator is to seek Him; man cannot glorify an Abstraction that he does not know. The 'glory' or nimbus around the head of the saints is a symbolic witness of their *capacity* to render divine homage."

Sri Yukteswar went on to read the marvellous story of Lazarus' resurrection. At its conclusion Master fell into a long silence, the sacred book open on his knee.

"I too was privileged to behold a similar miracle." My guru finally spoke with solemn unction. "Lahiri Mahasaya resurrected one of my friends from the dead."

The young lads at my side smiled with keen interest. There was enough of the boy in me, too, to enjoy not only the philosophy but, in particular, any story I could get Sri Yukteswar to relate about his wondrous experiences with his guru.

"My friend Rama and I were inseparable," Master began. "Because he was shy and reclusive, he chose to visit our guru Lahiri Mahasaya only during the hours of midnight and dawn, when the crowd of daytime disciples was absent. As Rama's closest friend, I served as a spiritual vent through which he let out the wealth of his spiritual perceptions. I found inspiration in his ideal companionship." My guru's face softened with memories.

"Rama was suddenly put to a severe test," Sri Yukteswar continued. "He contracted the disease of Asiatic cholera. As our master never objected to the services of physicians at times of serious illness, two specialists were summoned. Amidst the frantic rush of ministering to the stricken man, I was deeply praying to Lahiri Mahasaya for help. I hurried to his home and sobbed out the story.

" 'The doctors are seeing Rama. He will be well.' My guru smiled jovially.

"I returned with a light heart to my friend's bedside, only to find him in a dying state.

1 *John* 11: 1-4.

" 'He cannot last more than one or two hours,' one of the physicians told me with a gesture of despair. Once more I hastened to Lahiri Mahasaya.

" 'The doctors are conscientious men. I am sure Rama will be well.' The master dismissed me blithely.

"At Rama's place I found both doctors gone. One had left me a note: 'We have done our best, but his case is hopeless.'

"My friend was indeed the picture of a dying man. I did not understand how Lahiri Mahasaya's words could fail to come true, yet the sight of Rama's rapidly ebbing life kept suggesting to my mind: 'All is over now.' Tossing thus on the seas of faith and apprehensive doubt, I ministered to my friend as best I could. He roused himself to cry out:

" 'Yukteswar, run to Master and tell him I am gone. Ask him to bless my body before its last rites.' With these words Rama sighed heavily and gave up the ghost.[2]

"I wept for an hour by his beloved form. Always a lover of quiet, now he had attained the utter stillness of death. Another disciple came in; I asked him to remain in the house until I returned. Half-dazed, I trudged back to my guru.

" 'How is Rama now?' Lahiri Mahasaya's face was wreathed in smiles.

" 'Sir, you will soon see how he is,' I blurted out emotionally. 'In a few hours you will see his body, before it is carried to the crematory grounds.' I broke down and moaned openly.

" 'Yukteswar, control yourself. Sit calmly and meditate.' My guru retired into *samadhi*. The afternoon and night passed in unbroken silence; I struggled unsuccessfully to regain an inner composure.

"At dawn Lahiri Mahasaya glanced at me consolingly. 'I see you are still disturbed. Why didn't you explain yesterday that you expected me to give Rama tangible aid in the form of some medicine?' The master pointed to a cup-shaped lamp containing crude castor oil. 'Fill a little bottle from the lamp; put seven drops into Rama's mouth.'

" 'Sir,' I remonstrated, 'he has been dead since yesterday noon. Of what use is the oil now?'

" 'Never mind; just do as I ask.' Lahiri Mahasaya's cheerful mood was incomprehensible; I was still in the unassuaged agony of bereavement. Pouring out a small amount of oil, I departed for Rama's house.

"I found my friend's body rigid in the death-clasp. Paying no attention to his ghastly condition, I opened his lips with my right finger and managed,

2 A cholera victim is often rational and fully conscious right up to the moment of death.

with my left hand and the help of the cork, to put the oil drop by drop over his clenched teeth.

"As the seventh drop touched his cold lips, Rama shivered violently. His muscles vibrated from head to foot as he sat up wonderingly.

" 'I saw Lahiri Mahasaya in a blaze of light,' he cried. 'He shone like the sun. "Arise; forsake your sleep," he commanded me. "Come with Yukteswar to see me." ' "

"I could scarcely believe my eyes when Rama dressed himself and was strong enough after that fatal sickness to walk to the home of our guru. There he prostrated himself before Lahiri Mahasaya with tears of gratitude.

"The master was beside himself with mirth. His eyes twinkled at me mischievously.

" 'Yukteswar,' he said, 'surely henceforth you will not fail to carry with you a bottle of castor oil! Whenever you see a corpse, just administer the oil! Why, seven drops of lamp oil must surely foil the power of Yama!'[3]

" 'Guruji, you are ridiculing me. I don't understand; please point out the nature of my error.'

" 'I told you twice that Rama would be well; yet you could not fully believe me,' Lahiri Mahasaya explained. 'I did not mean the doctors would be able to cure him; I remarked only that they were in attendance. There was no causal connection between my two statements. I didn't want to interfere with the physicians; they have to live, too.' In a voice resounding with joy, my guru added, 'Always know that the inexhaustible Paramatman[4] can heal anyone, doctor or no doctor.'

" 'I see my mistake,' I acknowledged remorsefully. 'I know now that your simple word is binding on the whole cosmos.' "

As Sri Yukteswar finished the awesome story, one of the spellbound listeners ventured a question that, from a child, was doubly understandable.

"Sir," he said, "why did your guru use castor oil?"

"Child, giving the oil had no meaning except that I expected something material and Lahiri Mahasaya chose the near-by oil as an objective symbol for awakening my greater faith. The master allowed Rama to die, because I had partially doubted. But the divine guru knew that inasmuch as he had said the disciple would be well, the healing must take place, even though he had to cure Rama of death, a disease usually final!"

Sri Yukteswar dismissed the little group, and motioned me to a blanket seat at his feet.

3 The god of death.   4 Literally, 'Supreme Soul.'

"Yogananda," he said with unusual gravity, "you have been surrounded from birth by direct disciples of Lahiri Mahasaya. The great master lived his sublime life in partial seclusion, and steadfastly refused to permit his followers to build any organization around his teachings. He made, nevertheless, a significant prediction.

" 'About fifty years after my passing,' he said, 'my life will be written because of a deep interest in yoga which the West will manifest. The yogic message will encircle the globe, and aid in establishing that brotherhood of man which results from direct perception of the One Father.'

"My son Yogananda," Sri Yukteswar went on, "you must do your part in spreading that message, and in writing that sacred life."

Fifty years after Lahiri Mahasaya's passing in 1895 culminated in 1945, the year of completion of this present book. I cannot but be struck by the coincidence that the year 1945 has also ushered in a new age – the era of revolutionary atomic energies. All thoughtful minds turn as never before to the urgent problems of peace and brotherhood, lest the continued use of physical force banish all men along with the problems.

Though the human race and its works disappear tracelessly by time or bomb, the sun does not falter in its course; the stars keep their invariable vigil. Cosmic law cannot be stayed or changed, and man would do well to put himself in harmony with it. If the cosmos is against might, if the sun wars not with the planets but retires at dueful time to give the stars their little sway, what avails our mailed fist? Shall any peace indeed come out of it? Not cruelty but good-will arms the universal sinews; a humanity at peace will know the endless fruits of victory, sweeter to the taste than any nurtured on the soil of blood.

The effective League of Nations will be a natural, nameless league of human hearts. The broad sympathies and discerning insight needed for the healing of earthly woes cannot flow from a mere intellectual consideration of man's diversities, but from knowledge of man's sole unity – his kinship with God. Toward realization of the world's highest ideal – peace through brotherhood – may yoga, the science of personal contact with the Divine, spread in time to all men in all lands.

Though India's civilization is ancient above any other, few historians have noted that her feat of national survival is by no means an accident, but a logical incident in the devotion to eternal verities which India has offered through her best men in every generation. By sheer continuity of being, by intransitivity before the ages – can dusty scholars truly tell us how many? – India has given the worthiest answer of any people to the challenge of time.

The Biblical story[5] of Abraham's plea to the Lord that the city of Sodom be spared if ten righteous men could be found therein, and the divine reply: "I will not destroy it for ten's sake," gains new meaning in the light of India's escape from the oblivion of Babylon, Egypt and other mighty nations who were once her contemporaries. The Lord's answer clearly shows that a land lives, not by its material achievements, but in its masterpieces of man.

Let the divine words be heard again, in this twentieth century, twice dyed in blood ere half over: No nation that can produce ten men, great in the eyes of the Unbribable Judge, shall know extinction. Heeding such persuasions, India has proved herself not witless against the thousand cunnings of time. Self-realized masters in every century have hallowed her soil; modern Christ-like sages, like Lahiri Mahasaya and his disciple Sri Yukteswar, rise up to proclaim that the science of yoga is more vital than any material advances to man's happiness and to a nation's longevity.

Very scanty information about the life of Lahiri Mahasaya and his universal doctrine has ever appeared in print. For three decades in India, America, and Europe, I have found a deep and sincere interest in his message of liberating yoga; a written account of the master's life, even as he foretold, is now needed in the West, where lives of the great modern yogis are little known.

Nothing but one or two small pamphlets in English has been written on the guru's life. One biography in Bengali, *Sri Sri[6] Shyama Charan Lahiri Mahasaya,* appeared in 1941. It was written by my disciple, Swami Satyananda, who for many years has been the *acharya* (spiritual preceptor) at our *Vidyalaya* in Ranchi. I have translated a few passages from his book and have incorporated them into this section devoted to Lahiri Mahasaya.

It was into a pious Brahmin family of ancient lineage that Lahiri Mahasaya was born September 30, 1828. His birthplace was the village of Ghurni in the Nadia district near Krishnagar, Bengal. He was the youngest son of Muktakashi, the second wife of the esteemed Gaur Mohan Lahiri. (His first wife, after the birth of three sons, had died during a pilgrimage.) The boy's mother passed away during his childhood; little about her is known except the revealing fact that she was an ardent devotee of Lord Shiva,[7] scripturally designated as the 'King of Yogis.'

The boy Lahiri, whose given name was Shyama Charan, spent his early years in the ancestral home at Nadia. At the age of three or four he was often

5 *Genesis* 18: 23-32.

6 *Sri,* a prefix meaning 'holy,' is attached (generally twice or thrice) to names of great Indian teachers.

7 One of the trinity of Godhead – Brahma, Vishnu. Shiva – whose universal work is, respectively, that of creation, preservation, and dissolution-restoration. Shiva (sometimes spelled Siva), represented in mythology as the Lord of Renunciates, appears in visions to His devotees under various aspects, such as Mahadeva, the matted-haired Ascetic, and Nataraja, the Cosmic Dancer.

observed sitting under the sands in the posture of a yogi, his body completely hidden except for the head.

The Lahiri estate was destroyed in the winter of 1833, when the nearby Jalangi River changed its course and disappeared into the depths of the Ganges. One of the Shiva temples founded by the Lahiris went into the river along with the family home. A devotee rescued the stone image of Lord Shiva from the swirling waters and placed it in a new temple, now well-known as the Ghurni Shiva Site.

Gaur Mohan Lahiri and his family left Nadia and became residents of Benares, where the father immediately erected a Shiva temple. He conducted his household along the lines of Vedic discipline, with regular observance of ceremonial worship, acts of charity, and scriptural study. Just and open-minded, however, he did not ignore the beneficial current of modern ideas.

The boy Lahiri took lessons in Hindi and Urdu in Benares study-groups. He attended a school conducted by Joy Narayan Ghosal, receiving instruction in Sanskrit, Bengali, French, and English. Applying himself to a close study of the *Vedas,* the young yogi listened eagerly to scriptural discussions by learned Brahmins, including a Marhatta pundit named Nag-Bhatta.

Shyama Charan was a kind, gentle, and courageous youth, beloved by all his companions. With a well-proportioned, bright, and powerful body, he excelled in swimming and in many skillful activities.

In 1846 Shyama Charan Lahiri was married to Srimati Kashi Moni, daughter of Sri Debnarayan Sanyal. A model Indian housewife, Kashi Moni cheerfully carried on her home duties and the traditional householder's obligation to serve guests and the poor. Two saintly sons, Tincouri and Ducouri, blessed the union.

At the age of 23, in 1851, Lahiri Mahasaya took the post of accountant in the Military Engineering Department of the English government. He received many promotions during the time of his service. Thus not only was he a master before God's eyes, but also a success in the little human drama where he played his given role as an office worker in the world.

As the offices of the Army were shifted, Lahiri Mahasaya was transferred to Gazipur, Mirjapur, Danapur, Nainital, Benares, and other localities. After the death of his father, Lahiri had to assume the entire responsibility of his family, for whom he bought a quiet residence in the Garudeswar Mohulla neighborhood of Benares.

It was in his thirty-third year that Lahiri Mahasaya saw fulfillment of the purpose for which he had been reincarnated on earth. The ash-hidden flame, long smouldering, received its opportunity to burst into flame. A divine decree, resting beyond the gaze of human beings, works mysteriously to bring all things into outer manifestation at the proper time. He met his great guru, Babaji, near Ranikhet, and was initiated by him into *Kriya Yoga*.

This auspicious event did not happen to him alone; it was a fortunate moment for all the human race, many of whom were later privileged to receive the soul-awakening gift of *Kriya*. The lost, or long-vanished, highest art of yoga was again being brought to light. Many spiritually thirsty seekers eventually found their way to the cool waters of *Kriya Yoga*. Just as in the Hindu legend, where Mother Ganges[8] offers her divine draught to the parched devotee Bhagirath, so the celestial flood of *Kriya* rolled from the secret fastnesses of the Himalayas into the dusty haunts of men.

33. *Babaji, the Yogi-Christ of Modern India*

THE NORTHERN HIMALAYAN crags near Badrinarayan are still blessed by the living presence of Babaji, guru of Lahiri Mahasaya. The secluded master has retained his physical form for centuries, perhaps for millenniums. The deathless Babaji is an *avatara*. This Sanskrit word means 'descent'; its roots are *ava,* 'down,' and *tri,* 'to pass.' In the Hindu scriptures, *avatara* signifies the descent of Divinity into flesh.

"Babaji's spiritual state is beyond human comprehension." Sri Yukteswar explained to me. "The dwarfed vision of men cannot pierce to his transcendental star. One attempts in vain even to picture the avatar's attainment. It is inconceivable."

The *Upanishads* have minutely classified every stage of spiritual advancement. A *siddha* ('perfected being') has progressed from the state of a *jivanmukta* ('freed while living') to that of a *paramukta* ('supremely free' – full power over death); the latter has completely escaped from the mayic thralldom and its reincarnational round. The *paramukta* therefore seldom returns to a physical body; if he does, he is an avatar, a divinely appointed medium of supernal blessings on the world.

An avatar is unsubject to the universal economy; his pure body, visible as a light image, is free from any debt to nature. The casual gaze may see nothing

8 The Ganga, holy river of the Hindus, originates in the icy Himalayas of the eternal snows and silence. Down the centuries thousands of saints have delighted in remaining near the Ganges, leaving its banks an aura of blessing. An extraordinary and unique feature of the Ganges is its unpollutability. No bacteria live in its changeless sterility. Millions of Hindus, without harm, use its waters for bathing and drinking. This fact is baffling to modern scientists. One of them, Nobel laureate (for chemistry) Dr. John Howard Northrop, opined: "We know that the Ganges is highly contaminated. Yet Indians drink out of it but, apparently, are not effected," adding, "Perhaps bacteriophage (the virus that destroys bacteria) renders the river sterile." The Vedas inculcate reverence for all natural phenomena. The devout Hindu understands St. Francis's words: "Blessed be my Lord for our Sister Water, so useful, humble, chaste, and precious."

extraordinary in an avatar's form, but it may cast no shadow nor make any footprint on the ground. These are outward symbolic proofs of an inward lack of darkness and material bondage. Such a God-man alone knows the Truth behind the relativities of life and death. Omar Khayyám, so grossly misunderstood, sang of this liberated man in his immortal scripture, the *Rubáiyát:*

> Ah, Moon of my Delight who know'st no wane,
> The Moon of Heav'n is rising once again;
> How oft hereafter rising shall she look
> Through this same Garden after me – in vain!
>
> – Edward FitzGerald's translation

The 'Moon of Delight' is God, eternal Polaris, anachronous never. The 'Moon of Heav'n' is the outward cosmos, fettered to the law of periodic recurrence. Its chains had been dissolved forever by the Persian seer through his self-realization. 'How oft hereafter rising shall she look . . . after me – in vain!' What frustration of search by a frantic universe for an absolute omission!

Christ expressed his freedom in another way: "And a certain scribe came, and said unto him, Master, I will follow thee whithersoever thou goest. And Jesus saith unto him, The foxes have holes, and the birds of the air have nests; but the Son of man hath not where to lay his head."[1]

Spacious with omnipresence, could Christ indeed be followed except in the overarching Spirit?

Krishna, Rama, Buddha, and Patanjali were among the ancient Indian avatars. A considerable poetic literature in Tamil has grown up around Agastya, a South Indian avatar. He worked many miracles during the centuries preceding and following the Christian era, and is credited with retaining his physical form even to this day.

Babaji's mission in India has been to assist prophets in carrying out their special dispensations. He thus qualifies for the scriptural classification of *Mahavatar* (Great Avatar). He has stated that he gave yoga initiation to Shankara, ancient founder of the Swami Order, and to Kabir, famous medieval saint. His chief nineteenth-century disciple was, as we know, Lahiri Mahasaya, revivalist of the lost *Kriya* art.

The *Mahavatar* is in constant communion with Christ; together they send out vibrations of redemption, and have planned the spiritual technique of salvation for this age. The work of these two fully-illumined masters – one with the body, and one without it – is to inspire the nations to forsake suicidal wars, race hatreds, religious sectarianism, and the boomerang-evils of

---

1 *Matthew* 8: 19-20.

materialism. Babaji is well aware of the trend of modern times, especially of the influence and complexities of Western civilization, and realizes the necessity of spreading the self-liberations of yoga equally in the West and in the East.

That there is no historical reference to Babaji need not surprise us. The great guru has never openly appeared in any century; the misinterpreting glare of publicity has no place in his millennial plans. Like the Creator, the sole but silent Power, Babaji works in a humble obscurity.

Great prophets like Krishna and Christ come to earth for a specific and spectacular purpose; they depart as soon as it is accomplished. Other avatars, like Babaji, undertake work which is concerned more with the slow evolutionary progress of man during the centuries than with any one outstanding event of history. Such masters always veil themselves from the gross public gaze, and have the power to become invisible at will. For these reasons, and because they generally instruct their disciples to maintain silence about them, a number of towering spiritual figures remain world-unknown. I give in these pages on Babaji merely a hint of his life – only a few facts which he deems it fit and helpful to be publicly imparted.

No limiting facts about Babaji's family or birthplace, dear to the annalist's heart, have ever been discovered. His speech is generally in Hindi, but he converses easily in any language. He has adopted the simple name of Babaji (revered father); other titles of respect given him by Lahiri Mahasaya's disciples are Mahamuni Babaji Maharaj (supreme ecstatic saint), Maha Yogi (greatest of yogis), Trambak Baba and Shiva Baba (titles of avatars of Shiva). Does it matter that we know not the patronymic of an earth-released master?

"Whenever anyone utters with reverence the name of Babaji," Lahiri Mahasaya said, "that devotee attracts an instant spiritual blessing."

The deathless guru bears no marks of age on his body; he appears to be no more than a youth of twenty-five. Fair-skinned, of medium build and height, Babaji's beautiful, strong body radiates a perceptible glow. His eyes are dark, calm, and tender; his long, lustrous hair is copper-coloured. A very strange fact is that Babaji bears an extraordinarily exact resemblance to his disciple Lahiri Mahasaya. The similarity is so striking that, in his later years. Lahiri Mahasaya might have passed as the father of the youthful-looking Babaji.

Swami Kebalananda, my saintly Sanskrit tutor, spent some time with Babaji in the Himalayas.

"The peerless master moves with his group from place to place in the mountains," Kebalananda told me. "His small band contains two highly advanced American disciples. After Babaji has been in one locality for some time, he says: '*Dera danda uthao.*' ('Let us lift our camp and staff.') He carries a symbolic *danda* (bamboo staff). His words are the signal for moving with his group instantaneously to another place. He does not always employ this method of astral travel; sometimes he goes on foot from peak to peak.

"Babaji can be seen or recognized by others only when he so desires. He is known to have appeared in many slightly different forms to various devotees – sometimes without beard and moustache, and sometimes with them. As his undecaying body requires no food, the master seldom eats. As a social courtesy to visiting disciples, he occasionally accepts fruits, or rice cooked in milk and clarified butter.

"Two amazing incidents of Babaji's life are known to me," Kebalananda went on. "His disciples were sitting one night around a huge fire which was blazing for a sacred Vedic ceremony. The master suddenly seized a burning log and lightly struck the bare shoulder of a chela who was close to the fire.

" 'Sir, how cruel!' Lahiri Mahasaya, who was present, made this remonstrance.

" 'Would you rather have seen him burned to ashes before your eyes, according to the decree of his past karma?'

"With these words Babaji placed his healing hand on the chela's disfigured shoulder. 'I have freed you tonight from painful death. The karmic law has been satisfied through your slight suffering by fire.'

"On another occasion Babaji's sacred circle was disturbed by the arrival of a stranger. He had climbed with astonishing skill to the nearly inaccessible ledge near the camp of the master.

" 'Sir, you must be the great Babaji.' The man's face was lit with inexpressible reverence. 'For months I have pursued a ceaseless search for you among these forbidding crags. I implore you to accept me as a disciple.'

"When the great guru made no response, the man pointed to the rocky chasm at his feet.

" 'If you refuse me, I will jump from this mountain. Life has no further value if I cannot win your guidance to the Divine.'

" 'Jump then,' Babaji said unemotionally. 'I cannot accept you in your present state of development.'

"The man immediately hurled himself over the cliff. Babaji instructed the shocked disciples to fetch the stranger's body. When they returned with the mangled form, the master placed his divine hand on the dead man. Lo! he opened his eyes and prostrated himself humbly before the omnipotent one.

" 'You are now ready for discipleship.' Babaji beamed lovingly on his resurrected chela. 'You have courageously passed a difficult test. Death shall not touch you again; now you are one of our immortal flock.' Then he spoke his usual words of departure, '*Dera danda uthao*'; the whole group vanished from the mountain."

An avatar lives in the omnipresent Spirit; for him there is no distance inverse to the square. Only one reason, therefore, can motivate Babaji in maintaining his physical form from century to century: the desire to furnish humanity with a concrete example of its own possibilities. Were man never vouchsafed a glimpse of Divinity in the flesh, he would remain oppressed by the heavy *mayic* delusion that he cannot transcend his mortality.

Jesus knew from the beginning the sequence of his life; he passed through each event not for himself, not from any karmic compulsion, but solely for the upliftment of reflective human beings. His four reporter-disciples – Matthew, Mark, Luke, and John – recorded the ineffable drama for the benefit of later generations.

For Babaji, also, there is no relativity of past, present, future; from the beginning he has known all phases of his life. Yet, accommodating himself to the limited understanding of men, he has played many acts of his divine life in the presence of one or more witnesses. Thus it came about that a disciple of Lahiri Mahasaya was present when Babaji deemed the time to be ripe for him to proclaim the possibility of bodily immortality. He uttered this promise before Ram Gopal Muzumdar, that it might finally become known for the inspiration of other seeking hearts. The great ones speak their words and participate in the seemingly natural course of events, solely for the good of man, even as Christ said: "Father . . . I knew that thou hearest me always: but *because of the people which stand by I said it*, that they may believe that thou hast sent me."[2]

During my visit at Ranbajpur with Ram Gopal, 'the sleepless saint,'[3] he related the wondrous story of his first meeting with Babaji.

"I sometimes left my isolated cave to sit at Lahiri Mahasaya's feet in Benares," Ram Gopal told me. "One midnight as I was silently meditating in a group of his disciples, the master made a surprising request.

" 'Ram Gopal,' he said, 'go at once to the Dasasamedh bathing *ghat*.'

"I soon reached the secluded spot. The night was bright with moonlight and the glittering stars. After I had sat in patient silence for awhile, my attention was drawn to a huge stone slab near my feet. It rose gradually, revealing an underground cave. As the stone remained balanced in some unknown manner, the draped form of a young and surpassingly lovely woman was levitated from the cave high into the air. Surrounded by a soft

2 *John* 11: 41-42.
3 The omnipresent yogi who observed that I failed to bow before the Tarakeswar shrine. (See chapter 13).

halo, she slowly descended in front of me and stood motionless, steeped in an inner state of ecstasy. She finally stirred, and spoke gently.

" 'I am Mataji,[4] the sister of Babaji. I have asked him and also Lahiri Mahasaya to come to my cave tonight to discuss a matter of great importance.'

"A nebulous light was rapidly floating over the Ganges; the strange luminescence was reflected in the opaque waters. It approached nearer and nearer until, with a blinding flash, it appeared by the side of Mataji and condensed itself instantly into the human form of Lahiri Mahasaya. He bowed humbly at the feet of the woman saint.

"Before I had recovered from my bewilderment, I was further wonder-struck to behold a circling mass of mystical light travelling in the sky. Descending swiftly, the flaming whirlpool neared our group and materialized itself into the body of a beautiful youth who, I understood at once, was Babaji. He looked like Lahiri Mahasaya, the only difference being that Babaji appeared much younger, and had long, bright hair.

"Lahiri Mahasaya, Mataji, and myself knelt at the guru's feet. An ethereal sensation of beatific glory thrilled every fiber of my being as I touched his divine flesh.

" 'Blessed sister,' Babaji said, 'I am intending to shed my form and plunge into the Infinite Current.'

" 'I have already glimpsed your plan, beloved master. I wanted to discuss it with you tonight. Why should you leave your body?' The glorious woman looked at him beseechingly.

" 'What is the difference if I wear a visible or invisible wave on the ocean of my Spirit?'

"Mataji replied with a quaint flash of wit. 'Deathless guru, if it makes no difference, then please do not ever relinquish your form.'[5]

" 'Be it so,' Babaji said solemnly. 'I will never leave my physical body. It will always remain visible to at least a small number of people on this earth. The Lord has spoken His own wish through your lips.'

"As I listened in awe to the conversation between these exalted beings, the great guru turned to me with a benign gesture.

" 'Fear not, Ram Gopal,' he said, 'you are blessed to be a witness at the scene of this immortal promise.'

"As the sweet melody of Babaji's voice faded away, his form and that of Lahiri Mahasaya slowly levitated and moved backward over the Ganges. An aureole of dazzling light templed their bodies as they vanished into the

'Holy Mother.' Mataji also has lived through the centuries; she is almost as far advanced spiritually as her brother. She remains in ecstasy in a hidden underground cave near the *Dasaswamedh* ghat.
This incident reminds one of Thales. The great Greek philosopher taught that there was no difference between life and death. "Why, then," inquired a critic, "do you not die?" "Because," answered Thales, "it makes no difference."

night sky. Mataji's form floated to the cave and descended; the stone slab closed of itself, as if working on an invisible leverage.

"Infinitely inspired, I wended my way back to Lahiri Mahasaya's place. As I bowed before him in the early dawn, my guru smiled at me understandingly.

" 'I am happy for you, Ram Gopal,' he said. 'The desire of meeting Babaji and Mataji, which you have often expressed to me, has found at last a sacred fulfillment.'

"My fellow disciples informed me that Lahiri Mahasaya had not moved from his dais since early the preceding evening.

" 'He gave a wonderful discourse on immortality after you had left for the Dasasamedh *ghat,*' one of the chelas told me. For the first time I fully realized the truth in the scriptural verses which state that a man of self-realization can appear at different places in two or more bodies at the same time.

"Lahiri Mahasaya later explained to me many metaphysical points concerning the hidden divine plan for this earth," Ram Gopal concluded. "Babaji has been chosen by God to remain in his body for the duration of this particular world cycle. Ages shall come and go – still the deathless master,[6] beholding the drama of the centuries, shall be present on this stage terrestrial."

34. *Materializing a Palace in the Himalayas*

"BABAJI'S FIRST MEETING with Lahiri Mahasaya is an enthralling story, and one of the few which gives us a detailed glimpse of the deathless guru."

These words were Swami Kebalananda's preamble to a wondrous tale. The first time he recounted it I was literally spellbound. On many other occasions I coaxed my gentle Sanskrit tutor to repeat the story, which was later told me in substantially the same words by Sri Yukteswar. Both these Lahiri Mahasaya disciples had heard the awesome tale direct from the lips of their guru.

"My first meeting with Babaji took place in my thirty-third year," Lahiri Mahasaya had said. "In the autumn of 1861 I was stationed in Danapur as a government accountant in the Military Engineering Department. One morning the office manager summoned me.

" 'Lahiri,' he said, 'a telegram has just come from our main office. You are

---

6 'Verily, verily, I say unto you, if a man keep my saying, he shall never see death.' – *John* 8: 51.

In these words Jesus was not referring to immortal life in the physical body – a monotonous confinement one would hardly mete out to a sinner, much less a saint! The illumined man of whom Christ spoke is one who has awakened from the deathly trance of ignorance to Eternal Life.

Man's essential nature is formless omnipresent Spirit. Karmic embodiment is the result of *avidya*, ignorance. The Hindu scriptures teach that birth and death are manifestations of *maya*, cosmic delusion. Babaji is not limited to a physical body or to this planet, but, at God's wish, is fulfilling a special mission for the earth.

to be transferred to Ranikhet, where an army post[1] is now being established.'

"With one servant, I set out on the 500-mile trip. Travelling by horse and buggy, we arrived in thirty days at the Himalayan site of Ranikhet.[2]

"My office duties were not onerous; I was able to spend many hours roaming in the magnificent hills. A rumour reached me that great saints blessed the region with their presence; I felt a strong desire to see them. During a ramble one early afternoon, I was astounded to hear a distant voice calling my name. I continued my vigorous upward climb on Drongiri Mountain. A slight uneasiness beset me at the thought that I might not be able to retrace my steps before darkness had descended over the jungle.

"I finally reached a small clearing whose sides were dotted with caves. On one of the rocky ledges stood a smiling young man, extending his hand in welcome. I noticed with astonishment that, except for his copper-coloured hair, he bore a remarkable resemblance to myself.

" 'Lahiri, you have come!' The saint addressed me affectionately in Hindi. 'Rest here in this cave. It was I who called you.'

"I entered a neat little grotto which contained several woollen blankets and a few *kamandulus* (begging bowls).

" 'Lahiri, do you remember that seat?' The yogi pointed to a folded blanket in one corner.

" 'No, sir.' Somewhat dazed at the strangeness of my adventure, I added, 'I must leave now, before nightfall. I have business in the morning at my office.'

"The mysterious saint replied in English, 'The office was brought for you, and not you for the office.'

"I was dumbfounded that this forest ascetic should not only speak English but also paraphrase the words of Christ.[3]

" 'I see my telegram took effect.' The yogi's remark was incomprehensible to me; I inquired his meaning.

" 'I refer to the telegram that summoned you to these isolated parts. It was I who silently suggested to the mind of your superior officer that you be transferred to Ranikhet. When one feels his unity with mankind, all minds become transmitting stations through which he can work at will.' He added gently, 'Lahiri, surely this cave seems familiar to you?'

"As I maintained a bewildered silence, the saint approached and struck me gently on the forehead. At his magnetic touch, a wondrous current swept through my brain, releasing the sweet seed-memories of my previous life.

1. Now a military sanatorium. By 1861 the British Govt. had already established a tele-communication centre here.
2. Ranikhet, in the Almora dist. of U.P., is at the foot of Himalayan peak Nanda Devi. (The peak is at 25,661 feet, above mean sea level).
3. 'The Sabbath was made for man, and not man for the Sabbath.' – *Mark* 2: 27.

" 'I remember!' My voice was half-choked with joyous sobs. 'You are my guru Babaji, who has belonged to me always! Scenes of the past arise vividly in my mind; here in this cave I spent many years of my last incarnation!' As ineffable recollections overwhelmed me, I tearfully embraced my master's feet.

" 'For more than three decades I have waited for you here – waited for you to return to me!' Babaji's voice rang with celestial love. 'You slipped away and vanished into the tumultuous waves of the life beyond death. The magic wand of your karma touched you, and you were gone! Though you lost sight of me, never did I lose sight of you! I pursued you over the luminescent astral sea where the glorious angels sail. Through gloom, storm, upheaval, and light I followed you, like a mother bird guarding her young. As you lived out your human term of womb-life, and emerged a babe, my eye was ever on you. When you covered your tiny form in the lotus posture under the Nadia sands in your childhood, I was invisibly present! Patiently, month after month, year after year, I have watched over you, waiting for this perfect day. Now you are with me! Lo, here is your cave, loved of yore! I have kept it ever clean and ready for you. Here is your hallowed *asana*-blanket, where you daily sat to fill your expanding heart with God! Behold there your bowl, from which you often drank the nectar prepared by me! See how I have kept the brass cup brightly polished, that you might drink again therefrom! My own, do you now understand?'

" 'My guru, what can I say?' I murmured brokenly. 'Where has one ever heard of such deathless love?' I gazed long and ecstatically on my eternal treasure, my guru in life and death.

" 'Lahiri, you need purification. Drink the oil in this bowl and lie down by the river.' Babaji's practical wisdom, I reflected with a quick, reminiscent smile, was ever to the fore.

"I obeyed his directions. Though the icy Himalayan night was descending, a comforting warmth, an inner radiation, began to pulsate in every cell of my body. I marvelled. Was the unknown oil endued with a cosmical heat?

"Bitter winds whipped around me in the darkness, shrieking a fierce challenge. The chill wavelets of the Gogash River lapped now and then over my body, outstretched on the rocky bank. Tigers howled near-by, but my heart was free of fear: the radiant force newly generated within me conveyed an assurance of unassailable protection. Several hours passed swiftly; faded memories of another life wove themselves into the present brilliant pattern of reunion with my divine guru.

"My solitary musings were interrupted by the sound of approaching footsteps. In the darkness, a man's hand gently helped me to my feet, and gave me some dry clothing.

" 'Come, brother,' my companion said. 'The master awaits you.'

"He led the way through the forest. The sombre night was suddenly lit by a steady luminosity in the distance.

" 'Can that be the sunrise?' I inquired. 'Surely the whole night has not passed?'

" 'The hour is midnight.' My guide laughed softly. 'Yonder light is the glow of a golden palace, materialized here tonight by the peerless Babaji. In the dim past, you once expressed a desire to enjoy the beauties of a palace. Our master is now satisfying your wish, thus freeing you from the bonds of karma.'[4] He added, 'The magnificent palace will be the scene of your initiation tonight into *Kriya Yoga*. All your brothers here join in a paean of welcome, rejoicing at the end of your long exile. Behold!'

"A vast palace of dazzling gold stood before us. Studded with countless jewels, and set amidst landscaped gardens, it presented a spectacle of unparalleled grandeur. Saints of angelic countenance were stationed by resplendent gates, half-reddened by the glitter of rubies. Diamonds, pearls, sapphires, and emeralds of great size and lustre were imbedded in the decorative arches.

"I followed my companion into a spacious reception hall. The odour of incense and of roses wafted through the air; dim lamps shed a multicoloured glow. Small groups of devotees, some fair, some dark-skinned, chanted musically, or sat in the meditative posture, immersed in an inner peace. A vibrant joy pervaded the atmosphere.

" 'Feast your eyes; enjoy the artistic splendours of this palace, for it has been brought into being solely in your honour.' My guide smiled sympathetically as I uttered a few ejaculations of wonderment.

" 'Brother,' I said, 'the beauty of this structure surpasses the bounds of human imagination. Please tell me the mystery of its origin.'

" 'I will gladly enlighten you.' My companion's dark eyes sparkled with wisdom. 'In reality there is nothing inexplicable about this materialization. The whole cosmos is a materialized thought of the Creator. This heavy, earthly clod, floating in space, is a dream of God. He made all things out of His consciousness, even as man in his dream consciousness reproduces and vivifies a creation with its creatures.

" 'God first created the earth as an idea. Then He quickened it; energy atoms came into being. He coordinated the atoms into this solid sphere. All its molecules are held together by the will of God. When He withdraws His will, the earth again will disintegrate into energy. Energy will dissolve into consciousness; the earth-idea will disappear from objectivity.

___

[4] The karmic law requires that every human wish find ultimate fulfillment. Desire is thus the chain which binds man to the reincarnational wheel.

" 'The substance of a dream is held in materialization by the subconscious thought of the dreamer. When that cohesive thought is withdrawn in wakefulness, the dream and its elements dissolve. A man closes his eyes and erects a dream-creation which, on awakening, he effortlessly dematerializes. He follows the divine archetypal pattern. Similarly, when he awakens in cosmic consciousness, he will effortlessly dematerialize the illusions of the cosmic dream universe.

" 'Being one with the infinite all-accomplishing Will, Babaji can summon the elemental atoms to combine and manifest themselves in any form. This golden palace, instantaneously created, is real, even as this earth is real. Babaji created this palatial mansion out of his mind and is holding its atoms together by the power of his will, even as God created this earth and is maintaining it intact.' He added, 'When this structure has served its purpose, Babaji will dematerialize it.'

"As I remained silent in awe, my guide made a sweeping gesture. 'This shimmering palace, superbly embellished with jewels, has not been built by human effort or with laboriously mined gold and gems. It stands solidly, a monumental challenge to man.[5] Whoever realizes himself as a son of God, even as Babaji has done, can reach any goal by the infinite powers hidden within him. A common stone locks within itself the secret of stupendous atomic energy;[6] even so, a mortal is yet a powerhouse of divinity.'

"The sage picked up from a near-by table a graceful vase whose handle was blazing with diamonds. 'Our great guru created this palace by solidifying myriads of free cosmic rays,' he went on. 'Touch this vase and its diamonds; they will satisfy all the tests of sensory experience.'

"I examined the vase, and passed my hand over the smooth room-walls, thick with glistening gold. Each of the jewels scattered lavishly about was worthy of a king's collection. Deep satisfaction spread over my mind. A submerged desire, hidden in my subconsciousness from lives now gone, seemed simultaneously gratified and extinguished.

"My stately companion led me through ornate arches and corridors into a series of chambers richly furnished in the style of an emperor's palace. We entered an immense hall. In the centre stood a golden throne, encrusted with jewels shedding a dazzling medley of colours. There, in lotus posture, sat the supreme Babaji. I knelt on the shining floor at his feet.

5 'What is a miracle? – 'Tis a reproach,
 'Tis an implicit satire on mankind.' – Edward Young, in *Night Thoughts*.
6 The theory of the atomic structure of matter was expounded in the ancient Indian *Vaisesika* and *Nyaya* treatises. 'There are vast worlds all placed away within the hollows of each atom, multifarious as the motes in a sunbeam.' – *Yoga Vasishtha*.

" 'Lahiri, are you still feasting on your dream desires for a golden palace?' My guru's eyes were twinkling like his own sapphires. 'Wake! All your earthly thirsts are about to be quenched forever.' He murmured some mystic words of blessing. 'My son, arise. Receive your initiation into the kingdom of God through *Kriya Yoga*.'

"Babaji stretched out his hand; a *homa* (sacrificial) fire appeared, surrounded by fruits and flowers. I received the liberating yogic technique before this flaming altar.

"The rites were completed in the early dawn. I felt no need for sleep in my ecstatic state, and wandered around the palace, filled on all sides with treasures and priceless *objects d'art*. Descending to the gorgeous gardens, I noticed, near-by, the same caves and barren mountain ledges which yesterday had boasted no adjacency to palace or flowered terraces.

"Re-entering the palace, fabulously glistening in the cold Himalayan sunlight, I sought the presence of my master. He was still enthroned, surrounded by many quiet disciples.

" 'Lahiri, you are hungry.' Babaji added, 'Close your eyes.'

"When I reopened them, the enchanting palace and its picturesque gardens had disappeared. My own body and the forms of Babaji and the cluster of chelas were all now seated on the bare ground at the exact site of the vanished palace, not far from the sunlit entrances of the rocky grottos. I recalled that my guide had remarked that the palace would be dematerialized, its captive atoms released into the thought-essences from which it had sprung. Although stunned, I looked trustingly at my guru. I knew not what to expect next on this day of miracles.

" 'The purpose for which the palace was created has now been served,' Babaji explained. He lifted an earthen vessel from the ground. 'Put your hand there and receive whatever food you desire.'

"As soon as I touched the broad, empty bowl, it became heaped with hot butter-fried *luchis,* curry, and rare sweet-meats. I helped myself, observing that the vessel was ever-filled. At the end of my meal I looked around for water. My guru pointed to the bowl before me. Lo! the food had vanished; in its place was water, clear as from a mountain stream.

" 'Few mortals know that the kingdom of God includes the kingdom of mundane fulfillments,' Babaji observed. 'The divine realm extends to the earthly, but the latter, being illusory, cannot include the essence of reality.'

" 'Beloved guru, last night you demonstrated for me the link of beauty in heaven and earth!' I smiled at memories of the vanished palace; surely no simple yogi had ever received initiation into the august mysteries of Spirit amidst surroundings of more impressive luxury! I gazed tranquilly at the stark contrast of the present scene. The gaunt ground, the skyey roof, the caves offering primitive shelter – all seemed a gracious natural setting for the seraphic saints around me.

"I sat that afternoon on my blanket, hallowed by associations of past-life realizations. My divine guru approached and passed his hand over my head. I entered the *nirbikalpa samadhi* state, remaining unbrokenly in its bliss for seven days. Crossing the successive strata of self-knowledge, I penetrated the deathless realms of reality. All delusive limitations dropped away; my soul was fully established on the eternal altar of the Cosmic Spirit. On the eighth day I fell at my guru's feet and implored him to keep me always near him in this sacred wilderness.

" 'My son,' Babaji said, embracing me, 'your role in this incarnation must be played on an outward stage. Prenatally blessed by many lives of lonely meditation, you must now mingle in the world of men.

" 'A deep purpose underlay the fact that you did not meet me this time until you were already a married man, with modest business responsibilities. You must put aside your thoughts of joining our secret band in the Himalayas; your life lies in the crowded marts, serving as an example of the ideal yogi-householder.

" 'The cries of many bewildered worldly men and women have not fallen unheard on the ears of the Great Ones,' he went on. 'You have been chosen to bring spiritual solace through *Kriya Yoga* to numerous earnest seekers. The millions who are encumbered by family ties and heavy worldly duties will take new heart from you, a householder like themselves. You must guide them to see that the highest yogic attainments are not barred to the family man. Even in the world, the yogi who faithfully discharges his responsibilities, without personal motive or attachment, treads the sure path of enlightenment.

" 'No necessity compels you to leave the world, for inwardly you have already sundered its every karmic tie. Not of this world, you must yet be in it. Many years still remain during which you must conscientiously fulfill your family, business, civic, and spiritual duties. A sweet new breath of divine hope will penetrate the arid hearts of worldly men. From your balanced life, they will understand that liberation is dependent on inner, rather than outer, renunciations.'

"How remote seemed my family, the office, the world, as I listened to my guru in the high Himalayan solitudes. Yet adamantine truth rang in his words; I submissively agreed to leave this blessed haven of peace. Babaji instructed me in the ancient rigid rules which govern the transmission of the yogic art from guru to disciple.

" 'Bestow the *Kriya* key only on qualified chelas,' Babaji said. 'He who vows to sacrifice all in the quest of the Divine is fit to unravel the final mysteries of life through the science of meditation.'

" 'Angelic guru, as you have already favoured mankind by resurrecting the lost *Kriya* art, will you not increase that benefit by relaxing the strict requirements for discipleship?' I gazed beseechingly at Babaji. 'I pray that you permit me to communicate *Kriya* to all seekers, even though at first they cannot vow themselves to complete inner renunciation. The tortured men and women of the world, pursued by the threefold suffering,[7] need special encouragement. They may never attempt the road to freedom if *Kriya* initiation be withheld from them.'

" 'Be it so. The divine wish has been expressed through you.' With these simple words, the merciful guru banished the rigorous safeguards that for ages had hidden *Kriya* from the world. 'Give *Kriya* freely to all who humbly ask for help.'

"After a silence, Babaji added, 'Repeat to each of your disciples this majestic promise from the *Bhagavad Gita*: "*Swalpamapyasya dharmasya, trayate mahato bhayat*" – "Even a little practice of this religion will save you from dire fears and colossal sufferings inherent cycles of birth and death." ' "[8]

"As I knelt the next morning at my guru's feet for his farewell blessing, he sensed my deep reluctance to leave him.

" 'There is no separation for us, my beloved child.' He touched my shoulder affectionately. 'Wherever you are, whenever you call me, I shall be with you instantly.'

"Consoled by his wondrous promise, and rich with the newly found gold of God-wisdom, I wended my way down the mountain. At the office I was welcomed by my fellow employees, who for ten days had thought me lost in the Himalayan jungles. A letter soon arrived from the head office.

" 'Lahiri should return to the Danapur office,' it read. 'His transfer to Ranikhet occurred by error. Another man should have been sent to assume the Ranikhet duties.'

"I smiled, reflecting on the hidden crosscurrents in the events which had led me to this furthermost spot of India.

"Before returning to Danapur,[9] I spent a few days with a Bengali family at Moradabad. A party of six friends gathered to greet me. As I turned the conversation to spiritual subjects, my host observed gloomily:

7 Physical, mental, and spiritual suffering; manifested respectively in disease, in psychological inadequacies or 'complexes,' and in soul-ignorance.

8 *Gita* Chapter II: 40.   9 A town near Benares.

" 'Oh, in these days India is destitute of saints!'

" 'Babu,' I protested warmly, 'of course there are still great masters in this land!'

"In a mood of exalted fervor, I felt impelled to relate my miraculous experiences in the Himalayas. The little company was politely incredulous.

" 'Lahiri,' one man said soothingly, 'your mind has been under a strain in those rarefied mountain airs. This is some daydream you have recounted.'

"Burning with the enthusiasm of truth, I spoke without due thought. 'If I call him, my guru will appear right in this house.'

"Interest gleamed in every eye; it was no wonder that the group was eager to behold a saint materialized in such a strange way. Half-reluctantly, I asked for a quiet room and two new woollen blankets.

" 'The master will materialize from the ether,' I said. 'Remain silently outside the door; I shall soon call you.'

"I sank into the meditative state, humbly summoning my guru. The darkened room soon filled with a dim aural moonlight; the luminous figure of Babaji emerged.

" 'Lahiri, do you call me for a trifle?' The master's gaze was stern. 'Truth is for earnest seekers, not for those of idle curiosity. It is easy to believe when one sees; there is nothing then to deny. Supersensual truth is deserved and discovered by those who overcome their natural materialistic skepticism.' He added gravely, 'Let me go!'

"I fell entreatingly at his feet. 'Holy guru, I realize my serious error; I humbly ask pardon. It was to create faith in these spiritually blinded minds that I ventured to call you. Because you have graciously appeared at my prayer, please do not depart without bestowing a blessing on my friends. Unbelievers though they be, at least they were willing to investigate the truth of my strange assertions.'

" 'Very well; I will stay awhile. I do not wish your word discredited before your friends.' Babaji's face had softened, but he added gently, 'Henceforth, my son, I shall come when you need me, and not always when you call me.'[10]

"Tense silence reigned in the little group when I opened the door. As if mistrusting their senses, my friends stared at the lustrous figure on the blanket seat.

" 'This is mass-hypnotism!' One man laughed blatantly. 'No one could possibly have entered this room without our knowledge!'

"Babaji advanced smilingly and motioned to each one to touch the warm, solid flesh of his body. Doubts dispelled, my friends prostrated themselves on the floor in awed repentance.

10 In the path to the Infinite, even illumined masters like Lahiri Mahasaya may suffer from excess zeal, and subjected to discipline. In the *Bhagavad Gita*, the divine guru Krishna often chastises the prince of devotees, Arjuna.

" 'Let *halua*[11] be prepared.' Babaji made this request, I knew, to further assure the group of his physical reality. While the porridge was boiling, the divine guru chatted affably. Great was the metamorphosis of these doubting Thomases into devout St. Pauls. After we had eaten, Babaji blessed each of us in turn. There was a sudden flash; we witnessed the instantaneous dechemicalization of the electronic elements of Babaji's body into a spreading vaporous light. The God-tuned will-power of the master had loosened its grasp of the ether atoms held together as his body; forthwith the trillions of tiny lifetronic sparks faded into the infinite reservoir.

" 'With my own eyes I have seen the conqueror of death.' Maitra,[12] one of the group, spoke reverently. His face was transfigured with the joy of his recent awakening. 'The supreme guru played with time and space, as a child plays with bubbles. I have beheld one with the keys of heaven and earth.'

"I soon returned to Danapur. Firmly anchored in the Spirit, again I assumed the manifold business and family obligations of a householder."

Lahiri Mahasaya also related to Swami Kebalananda and Sri Yukteswar the story of another meeting with Babaji, under circumstances which recalled the guru's promise: "I shall come whenever you need me."

"The scene was a *Kumbha Mela* at Allahabad," Lahiri Mahasaya told his disciples. "I had gone there during a short vacation from my office duties. As I wandered amidst the throng of monks and sadhus who had come from great distances to attend the holy festival, I noticed an ash-smeared ascetic who was holding a begging bowl. The thought arose in my mind that the man was hypocritical, wearing the outward symbols of renunciation without a corresponding inward grace.

"No sooner had I passed the ascetic than my astounded eye fell on Babaji. He was kneeling in front of a matted-haired anchorite.

" 'Guruji!' I hastened to his side. 'Sir, what are you doing here?'

" 'I am washing the feet of this renunciate, and then I shall clean his cooking utensils.' Babaji smiled at me like a little child; I knew he was intimating that he wanted me to criticize no one, but to see the Lord as residing equally in all body-temples, whether of superior or inferior men. The great guru added, 'By serving wise and ignorant sadhus, I am learning the greatest of virtues, pleasing to God above all others – humility.' "[13]

---

11 A porridge made of cream of wheat fried in butter, and boiled with milk.

12 Maitra later attained self-realization. When I met him at the Mahamandal hermitage in Benares, he told me of Babaji's materialization before the group in Moradabad. "As a result of the miracle," Maitra said, "I became a lifelong disciple of Lahiri Mahasaya."

13 (Chap. 34) "(He) humbleth himself to behold the things that are in heaven and in the earth." – *Psalms* 113: 6.
"Whosoever shall exalt himself shall be abased; and he that shall humble himself shall be exalted." – *Matthew* 23: 12.

To humble the ego or false self is to discover one's eternal identity.

246

35. *The Christlike Life of Lahiri Mahasaya*

THUS IT BECOMETH us to fulfil all righteousness."[1] In these words to John the Baptist, and in asking John to baptize him, Jesus was acknowledging the divine rights of his guru.

From a reverent study of the Bible from an Oriental viewpoint,[2] and from intuitional perception, I am convinced that John the Baptist was, in past lives, the guru of Christ. There are numerous passages in the Bible which infer that John and Jesus in their last incarnations were, respectively, Elijah and his disciple Elisha. (These are the spellings in the Old Testament. The Greek translators spelled the names as Elias and Eliseus; they reappear in the New Testament in these changed forms.)

The very end of the Old Testament is a prediction of the reincarnation of Elijah and Elisha: "Behold, I will send you Elijah the prophet before the coming of the great and dreadful day of the Lord."[3] Thus John (Elijah), sent "before the coming . . . of the Lord," was born slightly earlier to serve as a herald for Christ. An angel appeared to Zacharias the father to testify that his coming son John would be no other than Elijah (Elias).

"But the angel said unto him, Fear not, Zacharias: for thy prayer is heard; and thy wife Elisabeth shall bear thee a son, and thou shalt call his name John. . . . And many of the children of Israel shall he turn to the Lord their God. And he shall go before Him *in the spirit and power of Elias,* to turn the hearts of the fathers to the children, and the disobedient to the wisdom of the just; to make ready a people prepared for the Lord."[4]

Jesus twice unequivocally identified Elijah (Elias) as John: "Elias is come already, and they knew him not. . . . Then the disciples understood that he spake unto them of John the Baptist."[5] Again, Christ says: "For all the prophets and the law prophesied until John. And if ye will receive it, this is Elias, which was for to come."[6]

When John denied that he was Elias (Elijah),[7] he meant that in the humble garb of John he came no longer in the outward elevation of Elijah the great guru. In his former incarnation he had given the 'mantle' of his glory and his spiritual wealth to his disciple Elisha. "And Elisha said, I pray thee, let a double portion of thy spirit be upon me. And he said, Thou hast asked a

1 (Chap. 35) *Matthew* 3: 15.
2 The Bible reveals that the law of reincarnation was understood and accepted. Reincarnational cycles are a more reasonable explanation for the different states of evolution of the mankind, than the Western assumtion that something (consciousness of egoity) came out of nothing, existed with varying degrees of lustihood for thirty or ninety years, and then returned to the original void. The enigma of such a void only delights the heart of a medieval Schoolman. (See also Note 20 on page 162).
3 *Malachi* 4: 5.   4 *Luke* 1: 13-17.   5 *Matthew* 17: 12-13.   6 *Matthew* 11: 13-14.   7 *John* 1: 21.

hard thing: nevertheless, if thou see me when I am taken from thee, it shall be so unto thee. . . . And he took the *mantle* of Elijah that fell from him."[8]

The roles became reversed, because Elijah-John was no longer needed to be the ostensible guru of Elisha-Jesus, now perfected in divine realization.

When Christ was transfigured on the mountain[9] it was his guru Elias, with Moses, whom he saw. Again, in his hour of extremity on the cross, Jesus cried out the divine name: "*Eli, Eli, lama sabachthani?* that is to say, My God, my God, why hast thou forsaken me? Some of them that stood there, when they heard that, said, This man calleth for Elias. . . . Let us see whether Elias will come to save him."[10]

The eternal bond of guru and disciple that existed between John and Jesus was present also for Babaji and Lahiri Mahasaya. With tender solicitude the deathless guru swam the abysmal waters that swirled between the last two lives of his chela, and guided the successive steps taken by the child and then by the man Lahiri Mahasaya. It was not until the disciple had reached his thirty-third year that Babaji deemed the time to be ripe to openly re-establish the never-severed link. Then, after their brief meeting near Ranikhet, the selfless master banished his dearly beloved disciple from the little mountain group, releasing him for an outward world mission. "My son, I shall come whenever you need me." What mortal lover can bestow that infinite promise?

Unknown to society in general, a great spiritual renaissance began to flow from a remote corner of Benares. Just as the fragrance of flowers cannot be suppressed, so Lahiri Mahasaya, quietly living as an ideal householder, could not hide his innate glory. Slowly, from every part of India, the devotee-bees sought the divine nectar of the liberated master.

The English office superintendent was one of the first to notice a strange transcendental change in his employee, whom he endearingly called 'Ecstatic Babu.'

"Sir, you seem sad. What is the trouble?" Lahiri Mahasaya made this sympathetic inquiry one morning to his employer.

"My wife in England is critically ill. I am torn by anxiety."

"I shall get you some word about her." Lahiri Mahasaya left the room and sat for a short time in a secluded spot. On his return he smiled consolingly.

"Your wife is improving; she is now writing you a letter." The omniscient yogi quoted some parts of the missive.

"Ecstatic Babu, I already know that you are no ordinary man. Yet I am unable to believe that, at will, you can banish time and space!"

8 II *Kings* 2: 9-14.   9 *Matthew* 17: 3.   10 *Matthew* 27: 46-49.

The promised letter finally arrived. The astounded superintendent found that it contained not only the good news of his wife's recovery, but also the same phrases which, weeks earlier, Lahiri Mahasaya had repeated.

The wife came to India some months later. She visited the office, where Lahiri Mahasaya was quietly sitting at his desk. The woman approached him reverently.

"Sir," she said, "it was your form, haloed in glorious light, that I beheld months ago by my sickbed in London. At that moment I was completely healed! Soon after, I was able to undertake the long ocean voyage to India."

Day after day, one or two devotees besought the sublime guru for *Kriya* initiation. In addition to these spiritual duties, and to those of his business and family life, the great master took an enthusiastic interest in education. He organized many study groups, and played an active part in the growth of a large high school in the Bengalitola section of Benares. His regular discourses on the scriptures came to be called his '*Gita* Assembly,' eagerly attended by many truth-seekers.

By these manifold activities, Lahiri Mahasaya sought to answer the common challenge: "After performing one's business and social duties, where is the time for devotional meditation?" The harmoniously balanced life of the great householder-guru became the silent inspiration of thousands of questioning hearts. Earning only a modest salary, thrifty, unostentatious, accessible to all, the master carried on naturally and happily in the path of worldly life.

Though ensconced in the seat of the Supreme One, Lahiri Mahasaya showed reverence to all men, irrespective of their differing merits. When his devotees saluted him, he bowed in turn to them. With a childlike humility, the master often touched the feet of others, but seldom allowed them to pay him similar honour, even though such obeisance toward the guru is an ancient Oriental custom.

A significant feature of Lahiri Mahasaya's life was his gift of *Kriya* initiation to those of every faith. Not Hindus only, but Moslems and Christians were among his foremost disciples. Monists and dualists, those of all faiths or of no established faith, were impartially received and instructed by the universal guru. One of his highly advanced chelas was Abdul Gufoor Khan, a Mohammedan. It shows great courage on the part of Lahiri Mahasaya that, although a high-caste Brahmin, he tried his utmost to dissolve the rigid caste bigotry of his time. Those from every walk of life found shelter under the master's omnipresent wings. Like all God-inspired prophets, Lahiri Mahasaya gave new hope to the outcastes and downtrodden of society.

"Always remember that you belong to no one, and no one belongs to you. Reflect that some day you will suddenly have to leave everything in this world – so make the acquaintanceship of God now," the great guru told his disciples. "Prepare yourself for the coming astral journey of death by daily riding in the balloon of God-perception. Through delusion you are perceiving yourself as a bundle of flesh and bones, which at best is a nest of troubles.[11] Meditate unceasingly, that you may quickly behold yourself as the Infinite Essence, free from every form of misery. Cease being a prisoner of the body; using the secret key of *Kriya,* learn to escape into Spirit."

The great guru encouraged his various students to adhere to the good traditional discipline of their own faith. Stressing the all-inclusive nature of *Kriya* as a practical technique of liberation, Lahiri Mahasaya then gave his chelas liberty to express their lives in conformance with environment and upbringing.

"A Moslem should perform his *namaj*[12] worship four times daily," the master pointed out. "Four times daily a Hindu should sit in meditation. A Christian should go down on his knees four times daily, praying to God and then reading the Bible."

With wise discernment the guru guided his followers into the paths of *Bhakti* (devotion), *Karma* (action), *Jnana* (wisdom), or *Raja* (royal or complete) *Yogas,* according to each man's natural tendencies. The master, who was slow to give his permission to devotees wishing to enter the formal path of monkhood, always cautioned them to first reflect well on the austerities of the monastic life.

The great guru taught his disciples to avoid theoretical discussion of the scriptures. "He only is wise who devotes himself to realizing, not reading only, the ancient revelations," he said. "Solve all your problems through meditation.[13] Exchange unprofitable religious speculations for actual God-contact. Clear your mind of dogmatic theological debris; let in the fresh, healing waters of direct perception. Attune yourself to the active inner Guidance; the Divine Voice has the answer to every dilemma of life. Though man's ingenuity for getting himself into trouble appears to be endless, the Infinite Succour is no less resourceful."

The master's omnipresence was demonstrated one day before a group of disciples who were listening to his exposition of the *Bhagavad Gita.* As he was explaining the meaning of *Kutastha Chaitanya* or the Christ Consciousness in all vibratory creation, Lahiri Mahasaya suddenly gasped and cried out:

"I am drowning in the bodies of many souls off the coast of Japan!"

11 "How many sorts of death are in our bodies! Nothing is therein but death." – Martin Luther, in *'Table-Talk.'*
12 The chief prayer of the Mohammedans, usually repeated four or five times daily.
13 'Seek truth in meditation, not in mouldy books. Look in the sky to find the moon, not in the pond.' – *A Persian proverb.*

The next morning the chelas read a newspaper account of the death of many people whose ship had foundered the preceding day near Japan.

Many distant disciples of Lahiri Mahasaya were often made aware of his enfolding presence. "I am ever with those who practice *Kriya*," he said consolingly to chelas who could not remain near him. "I will guide you to the Cosmic Home through your enlarging perceptions."

Sri Bhupendra Nath Sanyal, an eminent disciple of the great guru stated that, unable to go to Benares, he had nevertheless received precise *Kriya* initiation in a dream. Lahiri Mahasaya had appeared to instruct the *chela* in answer to his prayers.

If a disciple neglected any of his worldly obligations, the master would gently correct and discipline him.

"Lahiri Mahasaya's words were mild and healing, even when he was forced to speak openly of a chela's faults," Sri Yukteswar once told me. He added ruefully. "No disciple ever fled from our master's barbs." I could not help laughing, but I truthfully assured Sri Yukteswar that, sharp or not, his every word was music to my ears.

Lahiri Mahasaya carefully graded *Kriya* into four progressive initiations.[14] He bestowed the three higher techniques only after the devotee had manifested definite spiritual progress. One day a certain chela, convinced that his worth was not being duly evaluated, gave voice to his discontent.

"Master," he said, "surely I am ready now for the second initiation."

At this moment the door opened to admit a humble disciple, Brinda Bhagat. He was a Benares postman.

"Brinda, sit by me here." The great guru smiled at him affectionately. "Tell me, are you ready for the second technique of *Kriya*?"

The little postman folded his hands in supplication. "Gurudeva," he said in alarm, "no more initiations, please! How can I assimilate any higher teachings? I have come today to ask your blessings, because the first divine *Kriya* has filled me with such intoxication that I cannot deliver my letters!"

"Already Brinda swims in the sea of Spirit." At these words from Lahiri Mahasaya, his other disciple hung his head.

"Master," he said, "I see I have been a poor workman, finding fault with my tools."

The postman, who was an uneducated man, later developed his insight through *Kriya* to such an extent that scholars occasionally sought his interpretation on involved scriptural points. Innocent alike of sin and syntax, little Brinda won renown in the domain of learned pundits.

14 As *Kriya Yoga* is capable of many subdivisions, Lahiri Mahasaya wisely sifted out four steps which he discerned to be those which contained the essential marrow, and which were of the highest value in actual practice.

Besides the numerous Benares disciples of Lahiri Mahasaya, hundreds came to him from distant parts of India. He himself travelled to Bengal on several occasions, visiting at the homes of the fathers-in-law of his two sons. Thus blessed by his presence, Bengal became honeycombed with small *Kriya* groups. Particularly in the districts of Krishnagar and Bishnupur, many silent devotees to this day have kept the invisible current of spiritual meditation flowing.

Among many saints who received *Kriya* from Lahiri Mahasaya may be mentioned the illustrious Swami Bhaskarananda Saraswati of Benares, and the Deogarh ascetic of high stature, Balananda Brahmachari. For a time Lahiri Mahasaya served as private tutor to the son of Maharaja Iswari Narayan Sinha Bahadur of Benares. Recognizing the master's spiritual attainment, the maharaja, as well as his son, sought *Kriya* initiation, as did the Maharaja Jotindra Mohan Thakur.

A number of Lahiri Mahasaya's disciples with influential worldly position were desirous of expanding the *Kriya* circle by publicity. The guru refused his permission. One chela, the royal physician to the Lord of Benares, started an organized effort to spread the master's name as 'Kashi Baba' (Exalted One of Benares).[15] Again the guru forbade it.

"Let the fragrance of the *Kriya* flower be wafted naturally, without any display," he said. "Its seeds will take root in the soil of spiritually fertile hearts."

Although the great master did not adopt the system of preaching through the modern medium of an organization, or through the printing press, he knew that the power of his message would rise like a resistless flood, inundating by its own force the banks of human minds. The changed and purified lives of devotees were the simple guarantees of the deathless vitality of *Kriya*.

In 1886, twenty-five years after his Ranikhet initiation, Lahiri Mahasaya was retired on a pension.[16] With his availability in the daytime, disciples sought him out in ever-increasing numbers. The great guru now sat in silence most of the time, locked in the tranquil lotus posture. He seldom left his little parlour, even for a walk or to visit other parts of the house. A quiet stream of chelas arrived, almost ceaselessly, for a *darshan* (holy sight) of the guru.

To the awe of all beholders, Lahiri Mahasaya's habitual physiological state exhibited the superhuman features of breathlessness, sleeplessness, cessation of pulse and heartbeat, calm eyes unblinking for hours, and a profound aura of peace. No visitors departed without upliftment of spirit; all knew they had received the silent blessing of a true man of God.

15 Other titles bestowed on Lahiri Mahasaya by his disciples were *Yogivar* (greatest of yogis). *Yogiraj* (king of yogis), and *Munivar* (greatest of saints), to which I have added *Yogavatar* (incarnation of yoga).
16 He had given, altogether, thirty-five years of service in one department of the government.

The master now permitted his disciple, Panchanon Bhattacharya, to open an 'Arya Mission Institution' in Calcutta. Here the saintly disciple spread the message of *Kriya Yoga,* and prepared for public benefit certain yogic herbal[17] medicines.

In accordance with ancient custom, the master gave to people in general a *neem*[18] oil for the cure of various diseases. When the guru requested a disciple to distil the oil, he could easily accomplish the task. If anyone else tried, he would encounter strange difficulties, finding that the medicinal oil had almost evaporated after going through the required distilling processes. Evidently the master's blessing was a necessary ingredient.

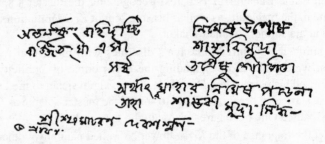

Lahiri Mahasaya's handwriting and signature, in Bengali script, are shown above. The lines occur in a letter to a chela; the great master interprets a Sanskrit verse as follows:

> 'He who has attained a state of calmness wherein his eyelids do
> not blink, has achieved *Sambhabi Mudra.*'

(*signed*) '*Sri Shyama Charan Deva Sharman*'

The Arya Mission undertook the publication of many of the guru's scriptural commentaries. Like Jesus and other great prophets, Lahiri Mahasaya himself wrote no books, but his penetrating interpretations were

17 Vast herbal knowledge is found in ancient Sanskrit treatises. Himalayan herbs were employed in a rejuvenation treatment which aroused the attention of the world in 1938 when the method was used on Pundit Madan Mohan Malaviya, the 77-year-old Vice-Chancellor of Benares Hindu University. Within 45 days he regained his health, strength, memory, normal eyesight; indications of a third set of teeth appeared, while all wrinkles vanished. The herbal treatment, known as *Kaya Kalpa,* is one of 80 rejuvenation methods outlined in Hindu *Ayurveda* or medical science. Pundit Malaviya was treated by Sri Kalpacharya Swami Beshundasji, who claims 1766 as his birth year. He possesses documents proving him to be more than 100 years old: *Associated Press* reporters remarked that he looked about 40. Ancient Hindu treatises divided medical science into 8 branches: *salya* (surgery); *salakya* (diseases above the neck); *kayachikitsa* (medicine proper); *bhutavidya* (mental diseases); *kaumara* (care of infancy); *agada* (toxicology); *rasayana* (longevity); *vagikarana* (tonics). Vedic physicians used delicate surgical instruments, employed plastic surgery, understood medical methods to counteract the effects of poison gas, performed Caesarean sections and brain operations, were skilled in dynamization of drugs. Hippocrates, famous physician of the 5th century B.C., borrowed much of his *Materia Medica* from Hindu sources.

18 The East Indian margosa tree. Its medicinal values have now become recognized in the West, where the bitter *neem* bark is used as a tonic, and the oil from seeds and fruit has been found of utmost worth in the treatment of leprosy and other diseases.

recorded by various disciples. Some of these voluntary amanuenses were more discerning than others in correctly conveying the profound insight of the guru; yet, on the whole, their efforts were successful. Through their zeal, the world possesses unparalleled commentaries by Lahiri Mahasaya on twenty-six ancient scriptures.

Sri Ananda Mohan Lahiri, a grandson of the master, has written an interesting booklet on *Kriya*. "The text of the *Bhagavad Gita* is a part of the great epic, the *Mahabharata,* which possesses several knot-points (*vyas-kutas*)," Sri Ananda wrote. "Keep those knot-points unquestioned, and we find nothing but mythical stones of a peculiar and easily-misunderstood type. Keep those knot-points unexplained, and we have lost a science which the East has preserved with superhuman patience after a quest of thousands of years of experiment.[19] It was the commentaries of Lahiri Mahasaya which brought to light, clear of allegories, the very science of religion that had been so cleverly put out of sight in the riddle of scriptural letters and imagery. No longer a mere unintelligible jugglery of words, the otherwise unmeaning formulas of Vedic worship have been proved by the master to be full of scientific significance. . . .

"We know that man is usually helpless against the insurgent sway of evil passions, but these are rendered powerless and man finds no motive in their indulgence when there dawns on him a consciousness of superior and lasting bliss through *Kriya.* Here the give-up, the negation of the lower passions, synchronizes with a take-up, the assertion of a beatitude. Without such a course, hundreds of moral maxims which run in mere negatives are useless to us.

"Our eagerness for worldly activity kills in us the sense of spiritual awe. We cannot comprehend the Great Life behind all names and forms, just because science brings home to us how we can use the powers of nature; this familiarity has bred a contempt for her ultimate secrets. Our relation with nature is one of practical business. We tease her, so to speak, to know how she can be used to serve our purposes; we make use of her energies, whose Source yet remains unknown. In science our relation with nature is one that exists between a man and his servant, or in a philosophical sense she is like a captive in the witness box. We cross-examine her, challenge her, and minutely weigh her evidence in human scales which cannot measure her hidden values. On the other hand,

---

[19] 'A number of seals recently excavated from archaeological sites of the Indus valley, datable in the third millennium B.C. show figures seated in meditative postures now used in the system of Yoga, and warrant the inference that even at that time some of the rudiments of Yoga were already known. We may not unreasonably draw the conclusion that systematic introspection with the aid of studied methods has been practiced in India for five thousand years. . . . India has developed certain valuable religious attitudes of mind and ethical notions which are unique, at least in the wideness of their application to life. One of these has been a tolerance in questions of intellectual belief – doctrine – that is amazing to the West, where for many centuries heresy-hunting was common, and bloody wars between nations over sectarian rivalries were frequent.' – Extracts from an article by Professor W. Norman Brown in the May, 1939 issue of the *Bulletin* of the American Council of Learned Societies, Washington, D.C.

when the self is in communion with a higher power, nature automatically obeys, without stress or strain, the will of man. This effortless command over nature is called 'miraculous' by the uncomprehending materialist.

"The life of Lahiri Mahasaya set an example which changed the erroneous notion that yoga is a mysterious practice. Every man may find a way through *Kriya* to understand his proper relation with nature, and to feel spiritual reverence for all phenomena, whether mystical or of everyday occurrence, in spite of the matter-of-factness of physical science.[20] We must bear in mind that what was mystical a thousand years ago is no longer so, and what is mysterious now may become lawfully intelligible a hundred years hence. It is the Infinite, the Ocean of Power, that is at the back of all manifestations.

"The science of *Kriya Yoga* is eternal. It is true like mathematics; like the simple rules of addition and subtraction, the law of *Kriya* can never be destroyed. Burn to ashes all the books on mathematics, the logically-minded will always rediscover such truths; destroy all the sacred books on yoga, its fundamental laws will come out whenever there appears a true yogi who comprises within himself pure devotion and consequently pure knowledge."

Just as Babaji is among the greatest of avatars, a *Mahavatar*, and Sri Yukteswar a *Jnanavatar* or Incarnation of Wisdom, so Lahiri Mahasaya may justly be called *Yogavatar,* or Incarnation of Yoga.[21] By the standards of both qualitative and quantitative good, he elevated the spiritual level of society. In his power to raise his close disciples to Christ-like stature and in his wide dissemination of truth among the masses, Lahiri Mahasaya ranks among the saviors of mankind. His uniqueness as a prophet lies in his practical stress on a definite method, *Kriya*, opening for the first time the doors of yoga freedom to all men. Apart from the miracles of his own life, surely the *Yogavatar* reached the zenith of all wonders in reducing the ancient complexities of yoga to an effective simplicity not beyond the ordinary grasp.

In reference to miracles, Lahiri Mahasaya often said, "The operation of subtle laws which are unknown to people in general should not be publicly discussed or published without due discrimination." If in these pages I have appeared to flout his cautionary words, it is because he has given me an inward reassurance. Also, in recording the lives of Babaji, Lahiri Mahasaya, and Sri Yukteswar, I have thought it advisable to omit many true miraculous stories, which could hardly have been included without writing, also, an explanatory volume of abstruse philosophy.

20 One thinks here of Carlyle's observation in *Sartor Resartus*: 'The man who cannot wonder, who does not habitually wonder (and worship), were he president of innumerable Royal Societies and carried . . . the epitome of all laboratories and observatories, with their results, in his single head, – is but a pair of spectacles behind which there is no eye.'
21 Sri Yukteswar had refferred to his disciple Paramahansa Yogananda as an incarnation of divine love. After Paramahansaji's passing, his spiritual successor James J. Lynn (later Rajarsi Janakananda) bestowed on him the title of *Premavatar* or Incarnation of Love.

As a householder-yogi, Lahiri Mahasaya brought a practical message suited to the needs of today's world. The excellent economic and religious conditions of ancient India no longer obtain. The great master therefore did not encourage the old ideal of a yogi as a wandering ascetic with a begging bowl. He stressed, rather, the advantage of a yogi of earning his own living, of not being dependent on a hard-pressed society for support, and of practicing yoga in the privacy of his home. To this counsel Lahiri Mahasaya added the heartening force of his own example. He was a modern, 'streamlined' model of a yogi. His way of life, as planned by Babaji, was intended to be a guide for aspiring yogis in all parts of the world.

New hope for new men! "Divine union," the *Yogavatar* proclaimed, "is possible through self-effort, and is not dependent on theological beliefs or on the arbitrary will of a Cosmic Dictator."

Through use of the *Kriya* key, persons who cannot bring themselves to believe in the divinity of any man will behold at last the full divinity of their own selves.

36. *Babaji's Interest in the West*

"MASTER, did you ever meet Babaji?"

It was a calm summer night in Serampore; the large stars of the tropics gleamed over our heads as I sat by Sri Yukteswar's side on the second-story balcony of the hermitage.

"Yes." Master smiled at my direct question; his eyes lit with reverence. "Three times I have been blessed by the sight of the deathless guru. Our first meeting was in Allahabad at a *Kumbha Mela.*"

These religious fairs held in India since the time immemorial are known as *Kumbha Melas*; they have kept spiritual goals in constant sight of the multitude. Devout Hindus gather by the millions every six years to meet thousands of sadhus, yogis, swamis, and ascetics of all kinds. Many are hermits who never leave their secluded haunts except to attend the *melas* and bestow their blessings on worldly men and women.

"I was not a swami at the time I met Babaji," Sri Yukteswar went on. "But I had already received *Kriya* initiation from Lahiri Mahasaya. He encouraged me to attend the *mela* which was convening in January, 1894 at Allahabad. It was my first experience of a *kumbha*; I felt slightly dazed by the clamour and surge of the crowd. In my searching gazes around I saw no illumined face of a master. Passing a bridge on the bank of the Ganges, I noticed an acquaintance standing nearby, his begging bowl extended.

" 'Oh, this fair is nothing but a chaos of noise and beggars.' I thought in disillusionment. 'I wonder if Western scientists, patiently enlarging the realms of knowledge for the practical good of mankind, are not more pleasing to God than these idlers who profess religion but concentrate on alms.'

"My smouldering reflections on social reform were interrupted by the voice of a tall sannyasi who halted before me.

" 'Sir,' he said, 'a saint is calling you.'

" 'Who is he?'

" 'Come and see for yourself.'

"Hesitantly following this laconic advice, I soon found myself near a tree whose branches were sheltering a guru with an attractive group of disciples. The master, a bright unusual figure, with sparkling dark eyes, rose at my approach and embraced me.

" 'Welcome, Swamiji,' he said affectionately.

" 'Sir," I replied emphatically, 'I am *not* a swami.'

" 'Those on whom I am divinely directed to bestow the title of "swami" never cast it off.' The saint addressed me simply, but deep conviction of truth rang in his words; I was engulfed in an instant wave of spiritual blessing. Smiling at my sudden elevation into the ancient monastic order,[1] I bowed at the feet of the obviously great and angelic being in human form who had thus honoured me.

"Babaji – for it was indeed he – motioned me to a seat near him under the tree. He was strong and young, and looked like Lahiri Mahasaya; yet the resemblance did not strike me, even though I had often heard of the extraordinary similarities in the appearance of the two masters. Babaji possesses a power by which he can prevent any specific thought from arising in a person's mind. Evidently the great guru wished me to be perfectly natural in his presence, not overawed by knowledge of his identity.

" 'What do you think of the *Kumbha Mela*?'

" 'I was greatly disappointed, sir.' I added hastily, 'Up until the time I met you. Somehow saints and this commotion don't seem to belong together.'

" 'Child,' the master said, though apparently I was nearly twice his own age, 'for the faults of the many, judge not the whole. Everything on earth is of mixed character, like a mingling of sand and sugar. Be like the wise ant which seizes only the sugar, and leaves the sand untouched. Though many sadhus here still wander in delusion, yet the *mela* is blessed by a few men of God-realization.'

"In view of my own meeting with this exalted master, I quickly agreed with his observation.

" 'Sir,' I commented, 'I have been thinking of the scientific men of the West,

1 Sri Yukteswar was later formally initiated into the Swami Order by the *Mahant* (monastery head) of Buddh Gaya in Bihar.

greater by far in intelligence than most people congregated here, living in distant Europe and America, professing different creeds, and ignorant of the real values of such *melas* as the present one. They are the men who could benefit greatly by meetings with India's masters. But, although high in intellectual attainments, many Westerners are wedded to rank materialism. Others, famous in science and philosophy, do not recognize the essential unity in religion. Their creeds serve as insurmountable barriers that threaten to separate them from us forever.'

" 'I saw that you are interested in the West, as well as the East.' Babaji's face beamed with approval. 'I felt the pangs of your heart, broad enough for all men, whether Oriental or Occidental. That is why I summoned you here.

" 'East and West must establish a golden middle path of activity and spirituality combined,' he continued. 'India has much to learn from the West in material development; in return, India can teach the universal methods by which the West will be able to base its religious beliefs on the unshakable foundations of yogic science.

" 'You, Swamiji, have a part to play in the coming harmonious exchange between Orient and Occident. Some years hence I shall send you a disciple whom you can train for yoga dissemination in the West. The vibrations there of many spiritually seeking souls come flood-like to me. I perceive potential saints in America and Europe, waiting to be awakened.' "

At this point in his story, Sri Yukteswar turned his gaze fully on mine.

"My son," he said, smiling in the moonlight, "you are the disciple that, years ago, Babaji promised to send me."

I was happy to learn that Babaji had directed my steps to Sri Yukteswar, yet it was hard for me to visualize myself in the remote West, away from my beloved guru and the simple hermitage peace.

"Babaji then spoke of the *Bhagavad Gita*," Sri Yukteswar went on. "To my astonishment, he indicated by a few words of praise that he was aware of the fact that I had written interpretations on various *Gita* chapters.

" 'At my request, Swamiji, please undertake another task,' the great master said. 'Will you not write a short book on the underlying basic unity between the Christian and Hindu scriptures? Show by parallel references that the inspired sons of God have spoken the same truths, now obscured by men's sectarian differences.'

" 'Maharaj,'[2] I answered diffidently, 'what a command! Shall I be able to fulfill it?'

"Babaji laughed softly. 'My son, why do you doubt?' he said reassuringly. 'Indeed, Whose work is all this, and Who is the Doer of all actions? Whatever the Lord has made me say is bound to materialize as truth.'

"I deemed myself empowered by the blessings of the saint, and agreed to write the book. Feeling reluctantly that the parting-hour had arrived, I rose from my leafy seat.

" 'Do you know Lahiri?'[3] the master inquired. 'He is a great soul, isn't he? Tell him of our meeting.' He then gave me a message for Lahiri Mahasaya.

"After I had bowed humbly in farewell, the saint smiled benignly. 'When your book is finished, I shall pay you a visit,' he promised. 'Good-by for the present.'

"I left Allahabad the following day and entrained for Benares. Reaching my guru's home, I poured out the story of the wonderful saint at the *Kumbha Mela.*

" 'Oh, didn't you recognize him?' Lahiri Mahasaya's eyes were dancing with laughter. 'I see you couldn't, for he prevented you. He is my incomparable guru, the celestial Babaji!'

" 'Babaji!' I repeated, awestruck. 'The Yogi-Christ Babaji! The invisible-visible savior Babaji! Oh, if I could just recall the past and be once more in his presence, to show my devotion at his lotus feet!'

" 'Never mind,' Lahiri Mahasaya said consolingly. 'He has promised to see you again.'

" 'Gurudeva, the divine master asked me to give you a message. "Tell Lahiri," he said, "that the stored-up power for this life now runs low: it is nearly finished." ' "

"At my utterance of these enigmatic words, Lahiri Mahasaya's figure trembled as though touched by a lightning current. In an instant everything about him fell silent; his smiling countenance turned incredibly stern. Like a wooden statue, sombre and immovable in its seat, his body became colourless. I was alarmed and bewildered. Never in my life had I seen this joyous soul manifest such awful gravity. The other disciples present stared apprehensively.

"Three hours passed in utter silence. Then Lahiri Mahasaya resumed his natural, cheerful demeanor, and spoke affectionately to each of the chelas. Everyone sighed in relief.

"I realized by my master's reaction that Babaji's message had been an unmistakable signal by which Lahiri Mahasaya understood that his body would soon be untenanted. His awesome silence proved that my guru had instantly controlled his being, cut his last cord of attachment to the material world, and fled to his ever-living identity in Spirit. Babaji's remark had been his way of saying: 'I shall be ever with you.'

"Though Babaji and Lahiri Mahasaya were omniscient, and had no need of communicating with each other through me or any other intermediary, the great ones often condescend to play a part in the human drama. Occasionally

2 'Great King' – a title of respect.
3 A guru's address is simply by name, omitting any title. Thus, Babaji said "Lahiri," not "Lahiri Mahasaya."

they transmit their prophecies through messengers in an ordinary way, that the final fulfillment of their words may infuse greater divine faith in a wide circle of men who later learn the story.

"I soon left Benares, and set to work in Serampore on the scriptural writings requested by Babaji." Sri Yukteswar continued. "No sooner had I begun my task than I was able to compose a poem dedicated to the deathless guru. The melodious lines flowed effortlessly from my pen, though never before had I attempted Sanskrit poetry.

"In the quiet of night I busied myself over a comparison of the Bible and the scriptures of *Sanatan Dharma*.[4] Quoting the words of the blessed Lord Jesus, I showed that his teachings were in essence one with the revelations of the *Vedas*. To my relief, my book was finished in a short time; I realized that this speedy blessing was due to the grace of my *Param-Guru-Maharaj*.[5] The chapters first appeared in the *Sadhusambad* journal; later they were privately printed as a book by one of my Kidderpore disciples.

"The morning after I had concluded my literary efforts," Master continued, "I went to the Rai Ghat here to bathe in the Ganges. The ghat was deserted; I stood still for awhile, enjoying the sunny peace. After a dip in the sparkling waters, I started for home. The only sound in the silence was that of my Ganges-drenched cloth, swish-swashing with every step. As I passed beyond the site of the large banyan tree near the river bank, a strong impulse urged me to look back. There, under the shade of the banyan, and surrounded by a few disciples, sat the great Babaji!

" 'Greetings, Swamiji!' The beautiful voice of the master rang out to assure me I was not dreaming. 'I see you have successfully completed your book. As I promised, I am here to thank you.'

"With a fast-beating heart, I prostrated myself fully at his feet. 'Paramguruji,' I said imploringly, 'will you and your chelas not honour my near-by home with your presence?'

"The supreme guru smilingly declined. 'No, child,' he said, 'we are people who like the shelter of trees; this spot is quite comfortable.'

---

4 Literally, 'eternal religion,' the name given to the body of Vedic teachings. It came to be called *Hinduism* since the time of the Greeks, who designated the people on the banks of the river Indus as *Indoos,* or *Hindus.* The word *Hindu,* properly speaking, refers only to followers of *Sanatan Dharma* or Hinduism. The term *Indian* applies equally to Hindus and Mohammedans and other *inhabitants* of the soil of secular India (and also, through the confusing geographical error of Columbus, to the American Mongoloid aboriginals).

The ancient name for India is *Aryavarta,* literally, 'abode of the Aryans.' The Sanskrit root of *arya* is 'worthy, holy, noble.' The later ethnological misuse of *Aryan* to signify not spiritual, but physical, characteristics, led the great Orientalist Max Muller, to say quaintly: "To me an ethnologist who speaks of an Aryan race, Aryan blood, Aryan eyes and hair, is as great a sinner as a linguist who speaks of a dolichocephalic dictionary or a brachycephalic grammar."

5 *Param-Guru* is literally 'guru supreme' or 'guru beyond,' signifying a line or succession of teachers Babaji, the *guru* of Lahiri Mahasaya, was the *param-guru* of Sri Yukteswar.

" 'Please tarry awhile, Master.' I gazed entreatingly at him. 'I shall be back at once with some special sweetmeats.'

"When I returned in a few minutes with a dish of delicacies, lo! the lordly banyan no longer sheltered the celestial troupe. I searched all around the ghat, but in my heart I knew the little band had already fled on etheric wings.

"I was deeply hurt. 'Even if we meet again, I would not care to talk to him,' I assured myself. 'He was unkind to leave me so suddenly.' This was a wrath of love, of course, and nothing more.

"A few months later I visited Lahiri Mahasaya in Benares. As I entered his little parlour, my guru smiled in greeting.

" 'Welcome, Yukteswar,' he said. 'Did you just meet Babaji at the threshold of my room?'

" 'Why, no,' I answered in surprise.

" 'Come here.' Lahiri Mahasaya touched me gently on the forehead; at once I beheld, near the door, the form of Babaji, blooming like a perfect lotus.

"I remembered my old hurt, and did not bow. Lahiri Mahasaya looked at me in astonishment.

"The divine guru gazed at me with fathomless eyes. 'You are annoyed with me.'

" 'Sir, why shouldn't I be?' I answered. 'Out of the air you came with your magic group, and into the thin air you vanished.'

" 'I told you I would see you, but didn't say how long I would remain.' Babaji laughed softly. 'You were full of excitement. I assure you that I was fairly extinguished in the ether by the gust of your restlessness.'

"I was instantly satisfied by this unflattering explanation. I knelt at his feet; the supreme guru patted me kindly on the shoulder.

" 'Child, you must meditate more,' he said. 'Your gaze is not yet faultless – you could not see me hiding behind the sunlight.' With these words in the voice of a celestial flute, Babaji disappeared into the hidden radiance.

"That was one of my last visits to Benares to see my guru," Sri Yukteswar concluded. "Even as Babaji had foretold at the *Kumbha Mela,* the householder-incarnation of Lahiri Mahasaya was drawing to a close. During the summer of 1895 his stalwart body developed a small boil on the back. He protested against lancing; he was working out in his own flesh the evil karma of some of his disciples. Finally a few chelas became very insistent; the master replied cryptically:

" 'The body has to find a cause to go; I will be agreeable to whatever you want to do.'

"A short time later the incomparable guru gave up his body in Benares. No longer need I seek him out in his little parlour; I find every day of my life blessed by his omnipresent guidance."

Years later, from the lips of Swami Keshabananda, an advanced disciple, I heard many wonderful details about the passing of Lahiri Mahasaya.

"A few days before my guru relinquished his body," Keshabananda told me, "he materialized himself before me as I sat in my hermitage at Hardwar.

" 'Come at once to Benares.' With these words Lahiri Mahasaya vanished.

"I entrained immediately for Benares. At my guru's home I found many disciples assembled. For hours that day[6] the master expounded the *Gita;* then he addressed us simply.

" 'I am going home.'

"Sobs of anguish broke out like an irresistible torrent.

" 'Be comforted; I shall rise again.' After this utterance Lahiri Mahasaya thrice turned his body around in a circle, faced the north in his lotus posture, and gloriously entered the final *maha-samadhi*.[7]

"Lahiri Mahasaya's beautiful body, so dear to the devotees, was cremated with solemn householder rites at Manikarnika Ghat by the holy Ganges," Keshabananda continued. "The following day, at ten o'clock in the morning, while I was still in Benares, my room was suffused with a great light. Lo! before me stood the flesh and blood form of Lahiri Mahasaya! It looked exactly like his old body, except that it appeared younger and more radiant. My divine guru spoke to me.

" 'Keshabananda,' he said, 'it is I. From the disintegrated atoms of my cremated body, I have resurrected a remodeled form. My householder work in the world is done; but I do not leave the earth entirely. Henceforth I shall spend some time with Babaji in the Himalayas, and with Babaji in the cosmos.'

"With a few words of blessing to me, the transcendent master vanished. Wondrous inspiration filled my heart; I was uplifted in Spirit even as were the disciples of Christ and Kabir[8] when they had gazed on their living gurus after physical death.

"When I returned to my isolated Hardwar hermitage," Keshabananda

6 On September 26, 1895 Lahiri Mahasaya left his body. In a few more days he would have reached his 68th birthday.

7 Facing the north, and thrice revolving the body, are parts of a Vedic rite used by masters who know beforehand when the final hour is about to strike for the physical body. The last meditation, during which the master merges himself in the Cosmic AUM, is called the *maha* – or great, *samadhi*.

8 Kabir was a great sixteenth-century saint whose large following included both Hindus and Mohammedans. At the time of his death, the disciples quarreled over the manner of conducting the funeral ceremonies. The exasperated master rose from his final sleep, and gave his instructions. "Half of my remains shall be buried by the Moslem rites;" he said, "let the other half be cremated with a Hindu sacrament." He then vanished. When the disciples opened the coffin which had contained his body, nothing was found but a dazzling array of gold-coloured *champak* flowers. Half of these were obediently buried by the Moslems, who revere his shrine to this day.

In his youth Kabir was approached by two disciples seeking intellectual guidance along the mystic path. His reply was:
  'Path presupposes distance; If He be near, no path needest thou at all.
  Verily it maketh me smile, to hear of a fish in water athirst!'

went on, "I carried with me the sacred ashes of my guru. I know he has escaped the spatio-temporal cage; the bird of omnipresence is freed. Yet it comforted my heart to enshrine his sacred remains."

Another disciple who was blessed by the sight of his resurrected guru was the saintly Panchanon Bhattacharya, founder of the Calcutta Arya Mission Institution.[9]

I visited Panchanon at his Calcutta home, and listened with delight to the story of his many years with the master. In conclusion, he told me of the most marvellous event in his life.

"Here in Calcutta," Panchanon said, "at ten o'clock of the morning which followed his cremation, Lahiri Mahasaya appeared before me in living glory."

Swami Pranabananda, the 'saint with two bodies,' also confided to me the details of his own supernal experience.

"A few days before Lahiri Mahasaya left his body," Pranabananda told me at the time he visited my Ranchi school, "I received a letter from him, requesting me to come at once to Benares. I was delayed, however, and could not leave immediately. As I was in the midst of my travel preparations, about ten o'clock in the morning, I was suddenly overwhelmed with joy to see the shining figure of my guru.

" 'Why hurry to Benares?' Lahiri Mahasaya said, smiling. 'You shall find me there no longer.'

"As the import of his words dawned on me, I sobbed broken-heartedly, believing that I was seeing him only in a vision.

"The master approached me comfortingly. 'Here, touch my flesh,' he said. 'I am living, as always. Do not lament; am I not with you forever?' "

From the lips of these three great disciples, a story of wondrous truth has emerged: At the morning hour of ten, on the day after the body of Lahiri Mahasaya had been consigned to the flames, the resurrected master, in a real but transfigured body, appeared before three disciples, each one in a different city.

"So when this corruptible shall have put on incorruption, and this mortal shall have put on immortality, then shall be brought to pass the saying that is written, Death is swallowed up in victory. O death, where is thy sting? O grave, where is thy victory?"[10]

---

9 Panchanon established, in a seventeen-acre garden at Deogarh in Bihar, a temple containing a stone statue of Lahiri Mahasaya. Another statue of the great master has been set by disciples in the little parlour of his Benares home.

10 I *Corinthians* 15: 54-55.
  'Why should it be thought a thing incredible with you, that God should raise the dead?' – *Acts* 26: 8

37. *I go to America*

"AMERICA! Surely these people are Americans!" This was my thought as a panoramic vision of Western faces passed before my inward view.

Immersed in meditation, I was sitting behind some dusty boxes in the storeroom of the Ranchi school. A private spot was difficult to find during those busy years with the youngsters!

The vision continued; a vast multitude,[1] gazing at me intently, swept actor-like across the stage of consciousness.

The storeroom door opened; as usual, one of the young lads had discovered my hiding place.

"Come here, Bimal," I cried gaily. "I have news for you: the Lord is calling me to America!"

"To America?" The boy echoed my words in a tone that implied I had said "to the moon".

"Yes! I am going forth to discover America, like Columbus. He thought he had found India; surely there is a karmic link between those two lands!"

Bimal scampered away; soon the whole school was informed by the two-legged newspaper.[2] I summoned the bewildered faculty and gave the school into its charge.

"I know you will keep Lahiri Mahasaya's yoga ideals of education ever to the fore," I said. "I shall write you frequently; God willing, someday I shall be back."

Tears stood in my eyes as I cast a last look at the little boys and the sunny acres of Ranchi. A definite epoch in my life had now closed, I knew; henceforth I would dwell in far lands. I entrained for Calcutta a few hours after my vision. The following day I received an invitation to serve as the delegate from India to an International Congress of Religious Liberals in America. It was to convene that year in Boston, under the auspices of the American Unitarian Association.

My head in a whirl, I sought out Sri Yukteswar in Serampore.

"Guruji, I have just been invited to address a religious congress in America. Shall I go?"

"All doors are open for you." Master replied simply. "It is now or never."

"But, sir," I said in dismay, "what do I know about public speaking? Seldom have I given a lecture, and never in English."

"English or no English, your words on yoga shall be heard in the West."

1 Many of those faces I have since seen in the West, and instantly recognized.
2 Swami Premananda, now the leader of the Self-Realization Church of All Religions in Washington, D.C., was one of the students at the Ranchi school at the time I left for America. (He was then Brahmachari Jotin.)

I laughed. "Well, dear guruji, I hardly think the Americans will learn Bengali! Please bless me with a push over the hurdles of the English language."[3]

When I broke the news of my plans to Father, he was utterly taken aback. To him America seemed incredibly remote; he feared he might never see me again.

"How can you go?" he asked sternly. "Who will finance you?" As he had affectionately borne the expenses of my education and whole life, he doubtless hoped that his question would bring my project to an embarrassing halt.

"The Lord will surely finance me." As I made this reply, I thought of the similar one I had given long ago to my brother Ananta in Agra. Without very much guile, I added, "Father, perhaps God will put it into your mind to help me."

"No, never!" He glanced at me piteously.

I was astounded, therefore, when Father handed me, the following day, a check made out for a large amount.

"I give you this money," he said, "not in my capacity as a father, but as a faithful disciple of Lahiri Mahasaya. Go then to that far Western land; spread there the creedless teachings of *Kriya Yoga*."

I was immensely touched at the selfless spirit in which Father had been able to quickly put aside his personal desires. The just realization had come to him during the preceding night that no ordinary desire for foreign travel was motivating my voyage.

"Perhaps we shall not meet again in this life." Father, who was sixty-seven at this time, spoke sadly.

An intuitive conviction prompted me to reply, "Surely the Lord will bring us together once more."

As I went about my preparations to leave Master and my native land for the unknown shores of America, I experienced not a little trepidation. I had heard many stories about the materialistic Western atmosphere, one very different from the spiritual background of India, pervaded with the centuried aura of saints. "An Oriental teacher who will dare the Western airs," I thought, "must be hardy beyond the trials of any Himalayan cold!"

One early morning I began to pray, with an adamant determination to continue, to even the praying, until I heard the voice of God. I wanted His blessing and assurance that I would not lose myself in the fogs of modern utilitarianism. My heart was set to go to America, but even more strongly was it resolved to hear the solace of divine permission.

I prayed and prayed, muffling my sobs. No answer came. My silent petition increased in excruciating crescendo until, at noon, I had reached

3 Sri Yukteswar and I normally conversed in Bengali.

a zenith; my brain could no longer withstand the pressure of my agonies. If I cried once more with an increased depth of my inner passion, I felt as though my brain would split. At that moment there came a knock outside the vestibule adjoining the Gurpar Road room in which I was sitting. Opening the door, I saw a young man in the scanty garb of a renunciate. He came in, closed the door behind him and, refusing my request to sit down, indicated with a gesture that he wished to talk to me while standing.

"He must be Babaji!" I thought, dazed, because the man before me had the features of a younger Lahiri Mahasaya.

He answered my thought. "Yes, I am Babaji." He spoke melodiously in Hindi. "Our Heavenly Father has heard your prayer. He commands me to tell you: Follow the behests of your guru and go to America. Fear not; you will be protected."

After a vibrant pause, Babaji addressed me again. "You are the one I have chosen to spread the message of *Kriya Yoga* in the West. Long ago I met your guru Yukteswar at a *Kumbha Mela;* I told him then I would send you to him for training."

I was speechless, choked with devotional awe at his presence, and deeply touched to hear from his own lips that he had guided me to Sri Yukteswar. I lay prostrate before the deathless guru. He graciously lifted me from the floor. Telling me many things about my life, he then gave me some personal instruction, and uttered a few secret prophecies.

"*Kriya Yoga,* the scientific technique of God-realization," he finally said with solemnity, "will ultimately spread in all lands, and aid in harmonizing the nations through man's personal, transcendental perception of the Infinite Father."

With a gaze of majestic power, the master electrified me by a glimpse of his cosmic consciousness.

If there should rise, Suddenly within the skies
Sunburst of a thousand suns, Flooding earth with beams undeemed-of,
Then might be, that Holy One's Majesty and radiance dreamed of!

– *Bhagavad Gita* XI: 12 (*Arnold's Translation*)

In a short while he started toward the door. "Do not try to follow me," he said. "You will not be able to do so."

"Please, Babaji, don't go away!" I cried repeatedly. "Take me with you!"

Looking back, he replied, "Not now. Some other time."

Overcome by emotion, I disregarded his warning. As I tried to pursue him, I discovered that my feet were firmly rooted to the floor. From the door, Babaji gave me a last affectionate glance. He raised his hand by way of benediction and walked away, my eyes fixed on him longingly.

After a few minutes my feet were free. I sat down and went into a deep meditation, unceasingly thanking God not only for answering my prayer but for blessing me by a meeting with Babaji. My whole body seemed sanctified through the touch of the ancient, ever-youthful master. Long had it been my burning desire to behold him.

Until now, I have never recounted to anyone this story of my meeting with Babaji. Holding it as the most sacred of my human experiences, I have hidden it in my heart. But the thought occurred to me that readers of this autobiography may be more inclined to believe in the reality of the secluded Babaji and his world interests if I relate that I saw him with my own eyes. I have helped an artist to draw a true picture of the great Yogi-Christ of modern India; it appears in this book.

The eve of my departure for the United States found me in Sri Yukteswar's holy presence.

"Forget you were born a Hindu, and don't be an American. Take the best of them both," Master said in his calm way of wisdom. "Be your true self, a child of God. Seek and incorporate into your being the best qualities of all your brothers, scattered over the earth in various races."

Then he blessed me: "All those who come to you with faith, seeking God, will be helped. As you look at them, the spiritual current emanating from your eyes will enter into their brains and change their material habits, making them more God-conscious."

He went on, "Your lot to attract sincere souls is very good. Everywhere you go, even in a wilderness, you will find friends."

Both of his blessings have been amply demonstrated. I came alone to America, into a wilderness without a single friend, but there I found thousands ready to receive the time-tested soul-teachings.

I left India in August, 1920, on *The City of Sparta,* the first passenger boat sailing for America after the close of World War-I. I had been able to book passage only after the removal, in ways fairly miraculous, of many 'red-tape' difficulties concerned with the granting of my passport.

During the two-months' voyage a fellow passenger found out that I was the Indian delegate to the Boston congress.

"Swami Yogananda," he said, with the first of many quaint pronunciations by which I was later to hear my name spoken by the Americans, "please favour the passengers with a lecture next Thursday night. I think we would all benefit by a talk on 'The Battle of Life and How to Fight it.'"

Alas! I had to fight the battle of my own life, I discovered on Wednesday. Desperately trying to organize my ideas into a lecture in English, I finally abandoned all preparations; my thoughts, like a wild colt eyeing a saddle, refused any cooperation with the laws of English grammar. Fully trusting in Master's past assurances, however, I appeared before my Thursday audience in the saloon of the steamer. No eloquence rose to my lips; speechlessly I stood before the assemblage. After an endurance contest lasting ten minutes, the audience realized my predicament and began to laugh.

The situation was not funny to me at the moment; indignantly I sent a silent prayer to Master.

"You *can*! Speak!" His voice sounded instantly within my consciousness.

My thoughts fell at once into a friendly relation with the English language. Forty-five minutes later the audience was still attentive. The talk won me a number of invitations to lecture later before various groups in America.

I never could remember, afterward, a word that I had spoken. By discreet inquiry I learned from a number of passengers: "You gave an inspiring lecture in stirring and correct English." At this delightful news I humbly thanked my guru for his timely help, realizing anew that he was ever with me, setting at naught all barriers of time and space.

Once in awhile, during the remainder of the ocean trip, I experienced a few apprehensive twinges about the coming English-lecture ordeal at the Boston congress.

"Lord," I prayed, "please let my inspiration be Thyself, and not again the laughter-bombs of the audience!"

The City of Sparta docked near Boston in late September. On the sixth of October I addressed the congress with my maiden speech in America. It was well received; I sighed in relief. The magnanimous secretary of the American Unitarian Association wrote the following comment in a published account[4] of the congress proceedings:

"Swami Yogananda, delegate from the Brahmacharya Ashram of Ranchi, India, brought the greetings of his Association to the Congress. In fluent English and a forceful delivery he gave an address of a philosophical character on 'The Science of Religion,' which has been printed in pamphlet form for a wider distribution. Religion, he maintained, is universal and it is one. We cannot possibly universalize particular customs and convictions, but the common element in religion can be universalized, and we can ask all alike to follow and obey it."

Due to Father's generous check, I was able to remain in America after the congress was over. Four happy years were spent in humble circumstances in Boston. I gave public lectures, taught classes, and wrote a book of poems, *Songs of the Soul,* with a preface by Dr. Frederick B. Robinson, president of the College of the City of New York.[5]

New Pilgrimages of the Spirit (Boston: Beacon Press, 1921).
Dr. and Mrs. Robinson visited India in 1939, and were the honoured guests at the Ranchi school.

Starting a transcontinental tour in the summer of 1924, I spoke before thousands in the principal cities, ending my western trip with a vacation in the beautiful Alaskan north.

With the help of large-hearted students, by the end of 1925, I had established an American headquarters on the Mount Washington Estates in Los Angeles. The building is the one I had seen years before in my vision at Kashmir. I hastened to send Sri Yukteswar pictures of these distant American activities. He replied with a postcard in Bengali, which I here translate:

11th August, 1926

Child of my heart, O Yogananda!

Seeing the photos of your school and students, what joy comes in my life I cannot express in words. I am melting in joy to see your yoga students of different cities. Beholding your methods in chant affirmations, healing vibrations, and divine healing prayers, I cannot refrain from thanking you from my heart. Seeing the gate, the winding hilly way upward, and the beautiful scenery spread out beneath the Mount Washington Estates, I yearn to behold it all with my own eyes.

Everything here is going on well. Through the grace of God, may you ever be in bliss.

– YUKTESWAR GIRI

Years sped by. I lectured in every part of my new land, and addressed hundreds of clubs, colleges, churches, and groups of every denomination. Tens of thousands of Americans received yoga initiation. To them all I dedicated a new book of prayer thoughts in 1929 – *Whispers From Eternity,* with a preface by Amelita Galli-Curci.[6] I give here, from the book, a poem entitled "God! God! God!", composed one night as I stood on a lecture platform:

From the depths of slumber,
As I ascend the spiral stairway of wakefulness,
I whisper:
God! God! God!
Thou art the food, and when I break my fast
Of nightly separation from Thee,
I taste Thee, and mentally say:
God! God! God!

6 Mme. Galli-Curci and her husband, Homer Samuels, the pianist, have been *Kriya Yoga* students for twenty years. The inspiring story of the famous prima donna's years of music has been recently published (*Galli-Curci's Life of Song,* by C. E. LeMassena, Paebar Co., New York, 1945).

No matter where I go, the spotlight of my mind
Ever keeps turning on Thee;
And in the battle din of activity
My silent war cry is ever:
God! God! God!
When boisterous storms of trials shriek,
And when worries howl at me,
I drown their clamour, loudly chanting:
God! God! God!
When my mind weaves dreams
With threads of memories,
Then on that magic cloth I find embossed:
God! God! God!
Every night, in time of deepest sleep,
My peace dreams and calls, Joy! Joy! Joy!
And my joy comes singing evermore:
God! God! God!
In waking, eating, working, dreaming, sleeping,
Serving, meditating, chanting, divinely loving,
My soul constantly hums, unheard by any:
God! God! God!

Sometimes – usually on the first of the month when the bills rolled in for upkeep of the Mount Washington and other Self-Realization Fellowship centres! – I thought longingly of the simple peace of India. But daily I saw a widening understanding between West and East; my soul rejoiced.

I have found the great heart of America expressed in the wondrous lines by Emma Lazarus, carved at the base of the Statue of Liberty, the 'Mother of Exiles':

From her beacon-hand
Glows world-wide welcome; her mild eyes command
The air-bridged harbor that twin cities frame.
"Keep, ancient lands, your storied pomp!" cries she
With silent lips. "Give me your tired, your poor,
Your huddled masses yearning to breathe free,
The wretched refuse of your teeming shore.
Send these, the homeless, tempest-tos'd to me,
I lift my lamp beside the golden door."

George Washington, the 'father of his country,' who felt on many occasions that he was being divinely guided, uttered (in his 'Farewell Address') the following words of spiritual inspiration for America.

"It will be worthy of a free, an enlightened, and at no distant period a great nation to give to mankind the magnanimous and too novel example of a people always guided by an exalted justice and benevolence. Who can doubt that in the course of time and things, the fruits of such a plan would richly repay any temporary advantages which might be lost by a steady adherence to it? Can it be that Providence has not connected the permanent felicity of a nation with its virtue?"

* *

Walt Whitman's[7] 'Hymn to America'
From *Thou Mother with Thy Equal Brood*

Thee in thy future,
Thee in thy larger, saner brood of female, male, – thee in thy athletes,
moral, spiritual, South, North, West, East.
Thee in thy moral wealth and civilization (until which thy proudest material
     civilization must remain in vain),
Thee in thy all-supplying, all-enclosing worship – thee in no single bible,
saviour, merely,
Thy saviours countless, latent within thyself, equal to any, divine as any....
These!... these in thee (are certain to come) today I prophesy.

38. *Luther Burbank – A Saint amidst the Roses*

"THE SECRET of improved plant breeding, apart from scientific knowledge, is love." Luther Burbank uttered this wisdom as I walked beside him in his Santa Rosa garden. We halted near a bed of edible cacti.

"While I was conducting experiments to make 'spineless' cacti," he continued, "I often talked to the plants to create a vibration of love. 'You have nothing to fear,' I would tell them. 'You don't need your defensive thorns. I will protect you.' Gradually the useful plant of the desert emerged in a thorn-less variety."

I was charmed at this miracle. "Please, dear Luther, give me a few cacti leaves to plant in my garden at Mount Washington."

A workman standing near-by started to strip off some leaves; Burbank prevented him.

"I myself will pluck them for the swami." He handed me three leaves, which later I planted, rejoicing as they grew to huge estate.

7 American poet and author of *Leaves of Grass* Walter Whitman (1819-92) celebrated the collective experience of an idealised democratic American life in his works – *Ed.*

The great horticulturist told me that his first notable triumph was the large potato, now known by his name. With the indefatigability of genius, he went on to present the world with hundreds of crossed improvements on nature – his new Burbank varieties of tomato, corn, squash, cherries, plums, nectarines, berries, poppies, lilies, roses.

I focused my camera as Luther led me before the famous walnut tree by which he had proved that natural evolution can be telescopically hastened.

"In only sixteen years," he said, "this walnut tree reached a state of abundant nut production to which an unaided nature would have brought the tree in twice that time."

Burbank's little adopted daughter came romping with her dog into the garden.

"She is my human plant." Luther waved to her affectionately. "I see humanity now as one vast plant, needing for its highest fulfillments only love, the natural blessings of the great outdoors, and intelligent crossing and selection. In the span of my own lifetime I have observed such wondrous progress in plant evolution that I look forward optimistically to a healthy, happy world as soon as its children are taught the principles of simple and rational living. We must return to nature and nature's God."

"Luther, you would delight in my Ranchi school, with its outdoor classes, and atmosphere of joy and simplicity."

My words touched the chord closest to Burbank's heart – child education. He plied me with questions, interest gleaming from his deep, serene eyes.

"Swamiji," he said finally, "schools like yours are the only hope of a future millennium. I am in revolt against the educational systems of our time, severed from nature and stifling of all individuality. I am with you heart and soul in your practical ideals of education."

As I was taking leave of the gentle sage, he autographed a small volume and presented it to me.[1]

"Here is my book on *The Training of the Human Plant*,"[2] he said. "New types of training are needed – fearless experiments. At times the most daring trials have succeeded in bringing out the best in fruits and flowers. Educational innovations for children should likewise become more numerous, more courageous."

I read his little book that night with intense interest. His eye envisioning a glorious future for the race, he wrote: "The most stubborn living thing in this world, the most difficult to swerve, is a plant once fixed in certain habits. . . .

Burbank also gave me an autographed picture of himself. I treasure it just as a Hindu merchant once treasured a picture of Lincoln. This Hindu, who was in America during the Civil War years, conceived such an admiration for Lincoln that he was unwilling to return to India until he had obtained a portrait of the Great Emancipator. Planting himself adamantly on Lincoln's doorstep, the merchant refused to leave until the astonished President permitted him to engage the services of Daniel Huntington, the famous New York artist. The Hindu then triumphantly carried it home.

New York: Century Co., 1922.

Remember that this plant has preserved its individuality all through the ages; perhaps it is one which can be traced backward through eons of time in the very rocks themselves, never having varied to any great extent in all these vast periods. Do you suppose, after all these ages of repetition, the plant does not become possessed of a will, if you so choose to call it, of unparalleled tenacity? Indeed, there are plants, like certain of the palms, so persistent that no human power has yet been able to change them. The human will is a weak thing beside the will of a plant. But see how this whole plant's lifelong stubbornness is broken simply by blending a new life with it, making, by crossing, a complete and powerful change in its life. Then when the break comes, fix it by these generations of patient supervision and selection, and the new plant sets out upon its new way never again to return to the old, its tenacious will broken and changed at last.

"When it comes to so sensitive and pliable a thing as the nature of a child, the problem becomes vastly easier."

Magnetically drawn to this great American, I visited him again and again. One morning I arrived at the same time as the postman, who deposited in Burbank's study about a thousand letters. Horticulturists wrote him from all parts of the world.

"Swamiji, your presence is just the excuse I need to get out into the garden," Luther said gaily. He opened a large desk-drawer containing hundreds of travel folders.

"See," he said, "this is how I do my travelling. Tied down by my plants and correspondence, I satisfy my desire for foreign lands by a glance now and then at these pictures."

My car was standing before his gate; Luther and I drove along the streets of the little town, its gardens bright with his own varieties of Santa Rosa, Peachblow, and Burbank roses.

"My friend Henry Ford and I both believe in the ancient theory of reincarnation." Luther told me. "It sheds light on aspects of life otherwise inexplicable. Memory is not a test of truth; just because man fails to remember his past lives does not prove he never had them. Memory is blank concerning his womb-life and infancy, too; but he probably passed through them!" He chuckled.

The great scientist had received *Kriya* initiation during one of my earlier visits. "I practice the technique devoutly, Swamiji," he said. After many thoughtful questions to me about various aspects of yoga, Luther remarked slowly:

"The East indeed possesses immense hoards of knowledge which the West has scarcely begun to explore."[3]

---

3 Dr. Julian Huxley, famous English biologist and director of UNESCO, asked Western scientists to "learn the Oriental techniques" for entering the trance state and for control of breathing. "*What* happens? *How* is it possible?" he asked. An *Associated Press* dispatch from London, dated Aug. 21, 1948, reported: 'Dr. Huxley told the World Federation for Mental Health it might well look into the mystic lore of the East and investigate it scientifically, adding, "then I think an immense step forward could be made."

Intimate communion with nature, who unlocked to him many of her jealously guarded secrets, had given Burbank a boundless spiritual reverence.

"Sometimes I feel very close to the Infinite Power," he confided shyly. His sensitive, beautifully modeled face lit with his memories. "Then I have been able to heal sick persons around me, as well as many ailing plants."

He told me of his mother, a sincere Christian. "Many times after her death," Luther said, "I have been blessed by her appearance in visions; she has spoken to me."

We drove back reluctantly toward his home and those waiting thousand letters.

"Luther," I remarked, "next month I am starting a magazine to present the truth-offerings of East and West. Please help me decide on a good name for the journal."

We discussed titles for awhile, and finally agreed on *East-West*. After we had re-entered his study, Burbank gave me an article he had written on 'Science and Civilization.'

"This will go in the first issue of *East-West*," I said gratefully.

As our friendship grew deeper, I called Burbank my 'American saint.' "Behold a man," I quoted, "in whom there is no guile!" His heart was fathomlessly deep, long acquainted with humility, patience, sacrifice. His little home amidst the roses was austerely simple; he knew the worthlessness of luxury, the joy of few possessions. The modesty with which he wore his scientific fame repeatedly reminded me of the trees that bend low with the burden of ripening fruits; it is the barren tree that lifts its head high in an empty boast.

I was in New York when, in 1926, my dear friend passed away. In tears I thought, "Oh, I would gladly walk all the way from here to Santa Rosa for one more glimpse of him!" Locking myself away from secretaries and visitors, I spent the next twenty-four hours in seclusion.

The following day I conducted a Vedic memorial rite around a large picture of Luther. A group of my American students, garbed in Hindu ceremonial clothes, chanted the ancient hymns as an offering was made of flowers, water, and fire – symbols of the bodily elements and their release in the Infinite Source.

Though the form of Burbank lies in Santa Rosa under a Lebanon cedar that he planted years ago in his garden, his soul is enshrined for me in every wide-eyed flower that blooms by the wayside. Withdrawn for a time into the spacious spirit of nature, is that not Luther whispering in her winds, walking her dawns?

His name has now passed into the heritage of common speech. Listing 'burbank' as a transitive verb, Webster's New International Dictionary defines it: "To cross or graft (a plant). Hence, figuratively, to improve (anything, as a process or institution) by selecting good features and rejecting bad, or by adding good features."

"Beloved Burbank," I cried after reading the definition, "your very name is now a synonym for goodness!"

LUTHER BURBANK
SANTAROSA,CALIFORNIAU.S.A.

December 22, 1924

I have examined the Yogoda system of Swami Yogananda and in my opinion it is ideal for training and harmonizing man's physical, mental, and spiritual natures. Swami's aim is to establish 'How-to-Live' schools throughout the world, wherein education will not confine itself to intellectual development alone, but also training of the body, will, and feelings.

Through the Yogoda system of physical, mental, and spiritual unfoldment by simple and scientific methods of concentration and meditation, most of the complex problems of life may be solved, and peace and good-will come upon earth. The Swami's idea of right education is plain commonsense, free from all mysticism and non-practicality; otherwise it would not have my approval.

I am glad to have this opportunity of heartily joining with the Swami in his appeal for international schools on the art of living which, if established, will come as near to bringing the millennium as anything with which I am acquainted.

Luther Burbank

39. *Therese Neumann, the Catholic Stigmatist*

"RETURN TO INDIA. I have waited for you patiently for fifteen years. Soon I shall swim out of the body and on to the Shining Abode. Yogananda, come!"

Sri Yukteswar's voice sounded startlingly in my inner ear as I sat in meditation at my Mt. Washington headquarters. Traversing ten thousand miles in the twinkling of an eye, his message penetrated my being like a flash of lightning.

Fifteen years! Yes, I realized, now it is 1935: I have spent fifteen years in spreading my guru's teachings in America. Now he recalls me.

That afternoon I recounted my experience to a visiting disciple Mr James J. Lynn. His spiritual development under *Kriya Yoga* was so remarkable that I often called him 'saint Lynn,' remembering Babaji's prophecy that America too would produce men and women of divine realization through the ancient yogic path.

Mr. Lynn generously insisted on making a donation for my travels. The financial problem thus solved, I made arrangements to sail, via Europe, for India. Busy weeks of preparations at Mount Washington! In March, 1935 I had the Self-Realization Fellowship chartered under the laws of the State of California as a non-profit corporation. To this educational institution go all public donations as well as the revenue from the sale of my books, magazine, written courses, class tuition, and every other source of income.

"I shall be back," I told my students. "Never shall I forget America."

At a farewell banquet given to me in Los Angeles by loving friends, I looked long at their faces and thought gratefully, "Lord, he who remembers Thee as the Sole Giver will never lack the sweetness of friendship among mortals."

I sailed from New York on June 9, 1935[1] in the *Europa.* Two students accompanied me: my secretary, Mr. C. Richard Wright, and an elderly lady from Cincinnati, Miss Ettie Bletch. We enjoyed the days of ocean peace, a welcome contrast to the past hurried weeks. Our period of leisure was short-lived; the speed of modern boats has some regrettable features!

Like any other group of inquisitive tourists, we walked around the huge and ancient city of London. The following day I was invited to address a large meeting in Caxton Hall, at which I was introduced to the London audience by Sir Francis Younghusband. Our party spent a pleasant day as guests of Sir Harry Lauder at his estate in Scotland. We soon crossed the English Channel to the continent, for I wanted to make a special pilgrimage to Bavaria. This would be my only chance, I felt, to visit the great Catholic mystic, Therese Neumann of Konnersreuth.

---

[1] The remarkable inclusion here of a complete date is due to the fact that my secretary, Mr. Wright, kept a travel diary.

Years earlier I had read an amazing account of Therese. Information given in the article was as follows:

(1) Therese, born on a Good Friday in 1898, had been injured in an accident at the age of twenty; she became blind and paralyzed.

(2) She miraculously regained her sight in 1923 through prayers to St. Teresa, 'The Little Flower.' Later Therese Neumann's limbs were instantaneously healed.

(3) From 1923 onward, Therese has abstained completely from food and drink, except for the daily swallowing of one small consecrated wafer.

(4) The stigmata, or sacred wounds of Christ, appeared in 1926 on Therese's head, breast, hands, and feet. On Friday of every week thereafter, she has passed through the Passion of Christ, suffering in her own body all his historic agonies.

(5) Knowing ordinarily only the simple German of her village, during her Friday trances Therese utters phrases which scholars have identified as ancient Aramaic. At appropriate times in her vision, she speaks Hebrew or Greek.

(6) By ecclesiastical permission, Therese has several times been under close scientific observation. Dr. Fritz Gerlich, editor of a Protestant German newspaper, went to Konnersreuth to 'expose the Catholic fraud,' but ended up by reverently writing her biography.[2]

As always, whether in East or West, I was eager to meet a saint. I rejoiced as our little party entered, on July 16th, the quaint village of Konnersreuth. The Bavarian peasants exhibited lively interest in our Ford automobile (brought with us from America) and its assorted group – an American young man, an elderly lady, and an olive-hued Oriental with long hair tucked under his coat collar.

Therese's little cottage, clean and neat, with geraniums blooming by a primitive well, was alas! silently closed. The neighbors, and even the village postman who passed by, could give us no information. Rain began to fall; my companions suggested that we leave.

"No," I said stubbornly, "I will stay here until I find some clue leading to Therese."

Two hours later we were still sitting in our car amidst the dismal rain. "Lord," I sighed complainingly, "why didst Thou lead me here if she has disappeared?"

An English-speaking man halted beside us, politely offering his aid.

"I don't know for certain where Therese is," he said, "but she often visits at the home of Professor Wutz, a seminary master of Eichstätt, eighty miles from here."

The following morning our party motored to the quiet village of Eichstätt, narrowly lined with cobble-stoned streets. Dr. Wutz greeted us cordially

2 Other books on her life are *Therese Neumann: A Stigmatist of our Day,* and *Further Chronicles of Therese Neumann,* both by Friedrich Ritter von Lama (Milwaukee: Bruce Pub. Co.).

at his home; "Yes, Therese is here." He sent her word of the visitors. A messenger soon appeared with her reply.

"Though the bishop has asked me to see no one without his permission, I will receive the man of God from India."

Deeply touched at these words, I followed Dr. Wutz upstairs to the sitting room. Therese entered immediately, radiating an aura of peace and joy. She wore a black gown and spotless white head dress. Although her age was thirty-seven at this time, she seemed much younger, possessing indeed a childlike freshness and charm. Healthy, well-formed, rosy-cheeked, and cheerful, this is the saint that does not eat!

Therese greeted me with a very gentle handshaking. We both beamed in silent communion, each knowing the other to be a lover of God.

Dr. Wutz kindly offered to serve as interpreter. As we seated ourselves, I noticed that Therese was glancing at me with naive curiosity; evidently Hindus had been rare in Bavaria.

"Don't you eat anything?" I wanted to hear the answer from her own lips.

"No, except a consecrated rice-flour wafer, once every morning at six o'clock."

"How large is the wafer?"

"It is paper-thin, the size of a small coin." She added, "I take it for sacramental reasons; if it is unconsecrated, I am unable to swallow it."

"Certainly you could not have lived on that, for twelve whole years?"

"I live by God's light." How simple her reply, how Einsteinian!

"I see you realize that energy flows to your body from the ether, sun, and air."

A swift smile broke over her face. "I am so happy to know you understand how I live."

"Your sacred life is a daily demonstration of the truth uttered by Christ: 'Man shall not live by bread alone, but by every word that proceedeth out of the mouth of God.' "[3]

Again she showed joy at my explanation. "It is indeed so. One of the reasons I am here on earth today is to prove that man can live by God's invisible light, and not by food only."

"Can you teach others how to live without food?"

She appeared a trifle shocked. "I cannot do that; God does not wish it."

---

3 *Matthew* 4: 4. Man's body battery is not sustained by gross food (bread) alone, but by the vibratory cosmic energy (word, or AUM). The invisible power flows into the human body through the gate of the medulla oblongata. This sixth bodily centre is located at the back of the neck at the top of the five spinal *chakras* (Sanskrit for 'wheels' or centres of radiating force). The medulla is the principal entrance for the body's supply of universal life force (AUM), and is directly connected with man's power of will, concentrated in the seventh or Christ-Consciousness centre (*Kutastha*) in the third eye between the eyebrows. Cosmic energy is then stored up in the brain as a reservoir of infinite potentialities, poetically mentioned in the *Vedas* as the 'thousand-petaled lotus of light.' The Bible invariably refers to AUM as the 'Holy Ghost' or invisible life force which divinely upholds all creation. *'What? know ye not that your body is the temple of the Holy Ghost which is in you, which ye have of God, and ye are not your own?'* – I *Corinthians* 6: 19.

As my gaze fell on her strong, graceful hands, Therese showed me a little, square, freshly healed wound on each of her palms. On the back of each hand, she pointed out a smaller, crescent-shaped wound, freshly healed. Each wound went straight through the hand. The sight brought to my mind distinct recollection of the large square iron nails with crescent-tipped ends, still used in the Orient, but which I do not recall having seen in the West.

The saint told me something of her weekly trances. "As a helpless onlooker, I observe the whole Passion of Christ." Each week, from Thursday midnight until Friday afternoon at one o'clock, her wounds open and bleed; she loses ten pounds of her ordinary 121-pound weight. Suffering intensely in her sympathetic love, Therese yet looks forward joyously to these weekly visions of her Lord.

I realized at once that her strange life is intended by God to reassure all Christians of the historical authenticity of Jesus' life and crucifixion as recorded in the New Testament, and to dramatically display the ever-living bond between the Galilean Master and his devotees.

Professor Wutz related some of his experiences with the saint.

"Several of us, including Therese, often travel for days on sight-seeing trips throughout Germany," he told me. "It is a striking contrast – while we have three meals a day, Therese eats nothing. She remains as fresh as a rose, untouched by the fatigue which the trips cause us. As we grow hungry and hunt for wayside inns, she laughs merrily."

The professor added some interesting physiological details: "Because Therese takes no food, her stomach has shrunk. She has no excretions, but her perspiration glands function; her skin is always soft and firm."

At the time of parting, I expressed to Therese my desire to be present at her trance.

"Yes, please come to Konnersreuth next Friday," she said graciously. "The bishop will give you a permit. I am very happy you sought me out in Eichstätt."

Therese shook hands gently, many times, and walked with our party to the gate. Mr. Wright turned on the automobile radio; the saint examined it with little enthusiastic chuckles. Such a large crowd of youngsters gathered that Therese retreated into the house. We saw her at a window, where she peered at us, childlike, waving her hand.

From a conversation the next day with two of Therese's brothers, very kind and amiable, we learned that the saint sleeps only one or two hours at night. In spite of the many wounds in her body, she is active and full of energy. She loves birds, looks after an aquarium of fish, and works often in her garden. Her correspondence is large; Catholic devotees write her for prayers and healing blessings. Many seekers have been cured through her of serious diseases.

Her brother Ferdinand, about twenty-three, explained that Therese has the power, through prayer, of working out on her own body the ailments of others. The saint's abstinence from food dates from a time when she prayed that the throat disease of a young man of her parish, then preparing to enter holy orders, be transferred to her own throat.

On Thursday afternoon our party drove to the home of the bishop, who looked at my flowing locks with some surprise. He readily wrote out the necessary permit. There was no fee; the rule made by the Church is simply to protect Therese from the onrush of casual tourists, who in previous years had flocked on Fridays by the thousands.

We arrived Friday morning about nine-thirty in Konnersreuth. I noticed that Therese's little cottage possesses a special glass-roofed section to afford her plenty of light. We were glad to see the doors no longer closed, but wide-open in hospitable cheer. There was a line of about twenty visitors, armed with their permits. Many had come from great distances to view the mystic trance.

Therese had passed my first test at the professor's house by her intuitive knowledge that I wanted to see her for spiritual reasons, and not just to satisfy a passing curiosity.

My second test was connected with the fact that, just before I went upstairs to her room, I put myself into a yogic trance state in order to be one with her in telepathic and televisic rapport. I entered her chamber, filled with visitors; she was lying in a white robe on the bed. With Mr. Wright following closely behind me, I halted just inside the threshold, awestruck at a strange and most frightful spectacle.

Blood flowed thinly and continuously in an inch-wide stream from Therese's lower eyelids. Her gaze was focused upward on the spiritual eye within the central forehead. The cloth wrapped around her head was drenched in blood from the stigmata wounds of the crown of thorns. The white garment was redly splotched over her heart from the wound in her side at the spot where Christ's body, long ages ago, had suffered the final indignity of the soldier's spear-thrust.

Therese's hands were extended in a gesture maternal, pleading; her face wore an expression both tortured and divine. She appeared thinner, changed in many subtle as well as outward ways. Murmuring words in a foreign tongue, she spoke with slightly quivering lips to persons visible before her inner sight.

As I was in attunement with her, I began to see the scenes of her vision. She was watching Jesus as He carried the cross amidst the jeering multitude.[4] Suddenly she lifted her head in consternation: the Lord had fallen under the cruel weight. The vision disappeared. In the exhaustion of

---

4 During the hours preceding my arrival, Therese had already passed through many visions of the closing days in Christ's life. Her entrancement usually starts with scenes of the events which followed the Last Supper. Her visions end with Jesus' death on the cross or, occasionally, with his entombment.

fervid pity, Therese sank heavily against her pillow.

At this moment I heard a loud thud behind me. Turning my head for a second, I saw two men carrying out a prostrate body. But because I was coming out of the deep superconscious state, I did not immediately recognize the fallen person. Again I fixed my eyes on Therese's face, deathly pale under the rivulets of blood, but now calm, radiating purity and holiness. I glanced behind me later and saw Mr. Wright standing with his hand against his cheek, from which blood was trickling.

"Dick," I inquired anxiously, "were you the one who fell?"

"Yes, I fainted at the terrifying spectacle."

"Well," I said consolingly, "you are brave to return and look upon the sight again."

Remembering the patiently waiting line of pilgrims, Mr. Wright and I silently bade farewell to Therese and left her sacred presence.[5]

The following day our little group motored south, thankful that we were not dependent on trains, but could stop the Ford wherever we chose throughout the countryside. We enjoyed every minute of a tour through Germany, Holland, France, and the Swiss Alps. In Italy we made a special trip to Assisi to honour the apostle of humility, St. Francis. The European tour ended in Greece, where we viewed the Athenian temples, and saw the prison in which the gentle Socrates[6] had drunk his death potion. One is filled with admiration for the artistry with which the Greeks have everywhere wrought their very fancies in alabaster.

We took ship over the sunny Mediterranean, disembarking at Palestine. Wandering day after day over the Holy Land, I was more than ever convinced of the value of pilgrimage. The spirit of Christ is all-pervasive in Palestine; I walked reverently by his side at Bethlehem, Gethsemane, Calvary, the holy Mount of Olives, and by the River Jordan and the Sea of Galilee.

Our little party visited the Birth Manger, Joseph's carpenter shop, the tomb of Lazarus, the house of Martha and Mary, the hall of the Last Supper. Antiquity unfolded; scene by scene, I saw the divine drama that Christ once played for the ages.

On to Egypt, with its modern Cairo and ancient pyramids. Then a boat down the narrow Red Sea, over the vasty Arabian Sea; lo, India!

5 Therese has survived the Nazi persecution, and is still present in Konnersreuth, according to 1945 American news dispatches from Germany.

6 A passage in Eusebius relates an interesting encounter between Socrates and a Hindu sage. The passage runs: 'Aristoxenus the musician, tells the following story about the Indians. One of these men met Socrates at Athens, and asked him what was the scope of his philosophy. "An inquiry into human phenomena," replied Socrates. At this the Indian burst out laughing. "How can a man inquire into human phenomena," he said, "when he is ignorant of divine ones?"' The Aristoxenus mentioned was a pupil of Aristotle, and a noted writer on harmonics. His date is 330 B.C.

40. *I return to India*

GRATEFULLY I was inhaling the blessed air of India. Our boat *Rajputana* docked on August 22, 1935 in the huge harbour of Bombay. Even this, my first day off the ship, was a foretaste of the year ahead – twelve months of ceaseless activity. Friends had gathered at the dock with garlands and greetings; soon, at our suite in the Taj Mahal Hotel, there was a stream of reporters and photographers.

Bombay was a city new to me; I found it energetically modern, with many innovations from the West. Palms line the spacious boulevards; magnificent state structures vie for interest with ancient temples. Very little time was given to sightseeing, however; I was impatient, eager to see my beloved guru and other dear ones. Consigning the Ford to a baggage car, our party was soon speeding eastward by train toward Calcutta.[1]

Our arrival at Howrah Station found such an immense crowd assembled to greet us that for awhile we were unable to dismount from the train. The young Maharaja of Kasimbazar and my brother Bishnu headed the reception committee; I was unprepared for the warmth and magnitude of our welcome.

Preceded by a line of automobiles and motorcycles, and amidst the joyous sound of drums and conch shells, Miss Bletch, Mr. Wright, and myself, flower-garlanded from head to foot, drove slowly to my father's home.

My aged parent embraced me as one returning from the dead; long we gazed on each other, speechless with joy. Brothers and sisters, uncles, aunts, and cousins, students and friends of years long past were grouped around me, not a dry eye among us. Passed now into the archives of memory, the scene of loving reunion vividly endures, unforgettable in my heart.

As for my meeting with Sri Yukteswar, words fail me; let the following description from my secretary suffice:

"Today, filled with the highest anticipations, I drove Yoganandaji from Calcutta to Serampore," Mr. Wright recorded in his travel diary. "We passed by quaint shops, one of them the favourite eating haunt of Yoganandaji during his college days, and finally entered a narrow, walled lane. A sudden left turn, and there before us towered the simple but inspiring two-story ashram, its Spanish-style balcony jutting from the upper floor. The pervasive impression was that of peaceful solitude.

"In grave humility I walked behind Yoganandaji into the courtyard within the hermitage walls. Hearts beating fast, we proceeded up some old cement steps, trod, no doubt, by myriads of truth-seekers. The tension

[1] We broke our journey in Central Provinces, halfway across the continent, to see Mahatma Gandhi at Wardha. Those days are described in chapter 44.

grew keener and keener as on we strode. Before us, near the head of the stairs, quietly appeared the Great One, Swami Sri Yukteswarji, standing in the noble pose of a sage.

"My heart heaved and swelled as I felt myself blessed by the privilege of being in his sublime presence. Tears blurred my eager sight when Yoganandaji dropped to his knees, and with bowed head offered his soul's gratitude and greeting, touching with his hand his guru's feet and then, in humble obeisance, his own head. He rose then and was embraced on both sides of the bosom by Sri Yukteswarji.

"No words passed at the beginning, but the most intense feeling was expressed in the mute phrases of the soul. How their eyes sparkled and were fired with the warmth of renewed soul-union! A tender vibration surged through the quiet patio, and even the sun eluded the clouds to add a sudden blaze of glory.

"On bended knee before the master I gave my own unexpressed love and thanks, touching his feet, calloused by time and service, and receiving his blessing. I stood then and faced two beautiful deep eyes smouldering with introspection, yet radiant with joy. We entered his sitting room, whose whole side opened to the outer balcony first seen from the street. The master braced himself against a worn davenport, sitting on a covered mattress on the cement floor. Yoganandaji and I sat near the guru's feet, with orange-coloured pillows to lean against and ease our positions on the straw mat.

"I tried and tried to penetrate the Bengali conversation between the two Swamijis – for English, I discovered, is null and void when they are together, although Swamiji Maharaj, as the great guru is called by others, can and often does speak it. But I perceived the saintliness of the Great One through his heart-warming smile and twinkling eyes. One quality easily discernible in his merry, serious conversation is a decided positiveness in statement – the mark of a wise man, who knows he knows, because he knows God. His great wisdom, strength of purpose, and determination are apparent in every way.

"Studying him reverently from time to time, I noted that he is of large, athletic stature, hardened by the trials and sacrifices of renunciation. His poise is majestic. A decidedly sloping forehead, as if seeking the heavens, dominates his divine countenance. He has a rather large and homely nose, with which he amuses himself in idle moments, flipping and wiggling it with his fingers, like a child. His powerful dark eyes are haloed by an ethereal blue ring. His hair, parted in the middle, begins as silver and changes to streaks of silvery-gold and silvery-black, ending in ringlets at his shoulders. His beard and moustache are scant or thinned out, yet seem to enhance his features and, like his character, are deep and light at the same time.

"He has a jovial and rollicking laugh which comes from deep in his chest, causing him to shake and quiver throughout his body – very cheerful and sincere. His face and stature are striking in their power, as are his muscular fingers. He moves with a dignified tread and erect posture.

"He was clad simply in the common *dhoti* and shirt, both once dyed a strong ochre colour, but now a faded orange.

"Glancing about, I observed that this rather dilapidated room suggested the owner's non-attachment to material comforts. The weather-stained white walls of the long chamber were streaked with fading blue plaster. At one end of the room hung a picture of Lahiri Mahasaya, garlanded in simple devotion. There was also an old picture showing Yoganandaji as he had first arrived in Boston, standing with the other delegates to the Congress of Religions.

"I noted a quaint concurrence of modernity and antiquation. A huge, cut-glass, candle-light chandelier was covered with cobwebs through disuse, and on the wall was a bright, up-to-date calendar. The whole room emanated a fragrance of peace and calmness. Beyond the balcony I could see coconut trees towering over the hermitage in silent protection.

"It is interesting to observe that the master has merely to clap his hands together and, before finishing, he is served or attended by some small disciple. Incidentally, I am much attracted to one of them – a thin lad, named Prafulla,[2] with long black hair to his shoulders, a most penetrating pair of sparkling black eyes, and a heavenly smile; his eyes twinkle, as the corners of his mouth rise, like the stars and the crescent moon appearing at twilight.

"Swami Sri Yukteswarji's joy is obviously intense at the return of his 'product' (and he seems to be somewhat inquisitive about the 'product's product'). However, predominance of the wisdom-aspect in the Great One's nature hinders his outward expression of feeling.

"Yoganandaji presented him with some gifts, as is the custom when the disciple returns to his guru. We sat down later to a simple but well-cooked meal. All the dishes were vegetable and rice combinations. Sri Yukteswarji was pleased at my use of a number of Indian customs, 'finger-eating' for example.

2 Prafulla was the lad who had been present with Master when a cobra had approached (See page 80).

"After several hours of flying Bengali phrases and the exchange of warm smiles and joyful glances, we paid obeisance at his feet, bade adieu with a *pronam,*[3] and departed for Calcutta with an everlasting memory of a sacred meeting and greeting. Although I write chiefly of my external impressions of him, yet I was always conscious of the true basis of the saint – his spiritual glory. I felt his power, and shall carry that feeling as my divine blessing."

From America, Europe, and Palestine I had brought many presents for Sri Yukteswar. He received them smilingly, but without remark. For my own use, I had bought in Germany a combination umbrella-cane. In India I decided to give the cane to Master.

"This gift I appreciate indeed!" My guru's eyes were turned on me with affectionate understanding as he made the unwonted comment. From all the presents, it was the cane that he singled out to display to visitors.

"Master, please permit me to get a new carpet for the sitting room." I had noticed that Sri Yukteswar's tiger skin was placed over a torn rug.

"Do so if it pleases you." My guru's voice was not enthusiastic. "Behold, my tiger mat is nice and clean; I am monarch in my own little kingdom. Beyond it is the vast world, interested only in externals."

As he uttered these words I felt the years roll back; once again I am a young disciple, purified in the daily fires of chastisement!

As soon as I could tear myself away from Serampore and Calcutta, I set out, with Mr. Wright, for Ranchi. What a welcome there, a veritable ovation! Tears stood in my eyes as I embraced the selfless teachers who had kept the banner of the school flying during my fifteen years' absence. The bright faces and happy smiles of the residential and day students were ample testimony to the worth of their many-sided school and yoga training.

Yet, alas! the Ranchi institution was in dire financial difficulties. Sir Manindra Chandra Nundy, the old Maharaja whose Kasimbazar Palace had been converted into the central school building, and who had made many princely donations, was now dead. Many free, benevolent features of the school were now seriously endangered for lack of sufficient public support. I had not spent years in America without learning some of its practical wisdom, its undaunted spirit before obstacles. For one week I remained in Ranchi, wrestling with critical problems. Then came interviews in Calcutta with prominent leaders and educators, a long talk with the young Maharaja of Kasimbazar, a financial appeal to my father, and lo! the shaky foundations of Ranchi began to be righted. Many donations including one huge check arrived in the nick of time from my American students.

Within a few months after my arrival in India, I had the joy of seeing the Ranchi school legally incorporated. My lifelong dream of a permanently endowed yoga educational centre stood fulfilled. That vision had guided me in the humble beginnings in 1917 with a group of seven boys.

In the decade since 1935, Ranchi has enlarged its scope far beyond the boys' school. Widespread humanitarian activities are now carried on there in the Shyama Charan Lahiri Mahasaya Mission.

The school, or Yogoda Sat-Sanga Brahmacharya Vidyalaya, conducts outdoor classes in grammar and high school subjects. The residential students and day scholars also receive vocational training of some kind. The boys themselves regulate most of their activities through autonomous committees. Very early in my career as an educator I discovered that boys who impishly delight in outwitting a teacher will cheerfully accept disciplinary rules that are set by their fellow students. Never a model pupil myself, I had a ready sympathy for all boyish pranks and problems.

Sports and games are encouraged; the fields resound with hockey and football practice. Ranchi students often win the cup at competitive events. The outdoor gymnasium is known far and wide. Muscle recharging through will-power is the *Yogoda* feature: mental direction of life energy to any part of the body. The boys are also taught *asanas* (postures), sword and *lathi* (stick) play, and jujitsu. The Yogoda Health Exhibitions at the Ranchi Vidyalaya have been attended by thousands.

Instruction in primary subjects is given in Hindi to the *Kols, Santals,* and *Mundas,* aboriginal tribes of the province. Classes for girls only have been organized in near-by villages.

The unique feature at Ranchi is the initiation into *Kriya Yoga.* The boys daily practice their spiritual exercises, engage in *Gita* chanting, and are taught by precept and example the virtues of simplicity, self-sacrifice, honour, and truth. Evil is pointed out to them as being that which produces misery; good as those actions which result in true happiness. Evil may be compared to poisoned honey, tempting but laden with death.

Overcoming restlessness of body and mind by concentration techniques has achieved astonishing results: it is no novelty at Ranchi to see an appealing little figure, aged nine or ten years, sitting for an hour or more in unbroken poise, the unwinking gaze directed to the spiritual eye. Often the picture of these Ranchi students has returned to my mind, as I observed collegians over the world who are hardly able to sit still through one class period.[4]

Ranchi lies 2000 feet above sea level; the climate is mild and equable. The twenty-five acre site, by a large bathing pond, includes one of the finest orchards in India – five hundred fruit trees – mango, guava, litchi, jackfruit, date. The boys grow their own vegetables, and spin at their *charkas*.

A guest house is hospitably open for Western visitors. The Ranchi library contains numerous magazines, and about a thousand volumes in English and Bengali, donations from the West and the East. There is a collection of the scriptures of the world. A well-classified museum displays archeological, geological, and anthropological exhibits; trophies, to a great extent, of my wanderings over the Lord's varied earth.

The charitable hospital and dispensary of the Lahiri Mahasaya Mission, with many outdoor branches in distant villages, have already ministered to 150,000 of India's poor. The Ranchi students are trained in first aid, and have given praiseworthy service to their province at tragic times of flood or famine.

In the orchard stands a Shiva temple, with a statue of the blessed master, Lahiri Mahasaya. Daily prayers and scripture classes are held in the garden under the mango bowers.

Branch high schools, with the residential and yoga features of Ranchi, have been opened and are now flourishing. These are the Yogoda Sat-Sanga Vidyapith (School) for Boys, at Lakshmanpur in Bihar; and the Yogoda Sat-Sanga High School and hermitage at Ejmalichak in Midnapore.

A stately Yogoda Math was dedicated in 1939 at Dakshineswar, directly on the Ganges. Only a few miles north of Calcutta, the new hermitage affords a haven of peace for city dwellers. Suitable accommodations are available for Western guests, and particularly for those seekers who are intensely dedicating their lives to spiritual realization. The activities of the Yogoda Math include a fortnightly mailing of Self-Realization Fellowship teachings to students in various parts of India.

4 Mental training through concentration techniques has produced in each Indian generation men of prodigious memory. Sir T. Vijayaraghavachari, in the *Hindustan Times,* has described the tests put to the modern professional *memory men* of Madras. 'These men,' he wrote, 'were unusually learned in Sanskrit literature. Seated in the midst of a large audience, they were equal to the several tests put them. One person would start ringing a bell, the number of rings having to be counted by the *memory man*. A second person would dictate a long exercise in arithmetic. A third would go on reciting from the *Ramayana* or the *Mahabharata* a long series of poems, which had to be reproduced; a fourth would set problems in versification on a given subject, each line to end in a specified word; a fifth man would carry on with a sixth a theological disputation, the exact language of which had to be quoted in the precise order, and a seventh man was all the while turning a wheel, the number of revolutions of which had to be counted. The memory expert had simultaneously to do all these feats purely by mental processes, as he was allowed no paper and pencil. The strain on the faculties must have been terrific. Ordinarily men in unconscious envy are apt to depreciate such efforts by affecting to believe that they involve only the exercise of the lower functionings of the brain. It is not, however, a pure question of memory. The greater factor is the immense concentration of mind.'

It is needless to say that all these educational and humanitarian activities have required the self-sacrificing service and devotion of many teachers and workers. I do not list their names here, because they are so numerous; but in my heart each one has a lustrous niche. Inspired by the ideals of Lahiri Mahasaya, these teachers have abandoned promising worldly goals to serve humbly, to give greatly.

Mr. Wright formed many fast friendships with Ranchi boys; clad in a simple *dhoti,* he lived for awhile among them. At Ranchi, Calcutta, Serampore, everywhere he went, my secretary, who has a vivid gift of description, hauled out his travel diary to record his adventures. One evening I asked him a question.

"Dick, what is your impression of India?"

"Peace," he said thoughtfully. "The racial aura is peace."

41. *An Idyll*[1] *in South India*

"YOU ARE THE FIRST Westerner, Dick, ever to enter that shrine. Many others have tried in vain."

At my words Mr. Wright looked startled, then pleased. We had just left the beautiful Chamundi Temple in the hills overlooking Mysore in southern India. There we had bowed before the gold and silver altars of the Goddess Chamundi, patron deity of the family of the reigning maharaja.

"As a souvenir of the unique honour," Mr. Wright said, carefully stowing away a few blessed rose petals, "I will always preserve this flower, sprinkled by the priest with rose water."

My companion and I[2] were spending the month of November, 1935, as guests of the State of Mysore. The Maharaja, H.H. Sri Krishnaraja Wadiyar IV, is a model prince with intelligent devotion to his people. A pious Hindu, the Maharaja has empowered a Mohammedan, the able Mirza Ismail, as his Dewan or Premier. Popular representation is given to the seven million inhabitants of Mysore in both an Assembly and a Legislative Council.

The heir to the Maharaja, H.H. the Yuvaraja, Sir Sri Krishna Narasingharaj Wadiyar, had invited my secretary and me to visit his enlightened and progressive realm. During the past fortnight I had addressed thousands of Mysore citizens and students, at the Town Hall, the Maharajah's College, the University Medical School; and three mass meetings in Bangalore, at the National High School, the Intermediate College, and the Chetty Town Hall where over three thousand persons had assembled.

1 A narrative poem.
2 Miss Bletch, unable to maintain the pace set by Mr. Wright and myself, stayed with my relatives in Calcutta.

Whether the eager listeners had been able to credit the glowing picture I drew of America, I know not; but the applause had always been loudest when I spoke of the mutual benefits that could flow from exchange of the best features in East and West.

Mr. Wright and I were now relaxing in the tropical peace. His travel diary gives the following account of his impressions of Mysore:

"Brilliantly green rice fields, varied by tasseled sugar cane patches, nestle at the protective foot of rocky hills – hills dotting the emerald panorama like excrescences of black stone – and the play of colours is enhanced by the sudden and dramatic disappearance of the sun as it seeks rest behind the solemn hills.

"Many rapturous moments have been spent in gazing, almost absent-mindedly, at the ever-changing canvas of God stretched across the firmament, for His touch alone is able to produce colours that vibrate with the freshness of life. That youth of colours is lost when man tries to imitate with mere pigments, for the Lord resorts to a more simple and effective medium-oils that are neither oils nor pigments, but mere rays of light. He tosses a splash of light here, and it reflects red; He waves the brush again and it blends gradually into orange and gold; then with a piercing thrust He stabs the clouds with a streak of purple that leaves a ringlet or fringe of red oozing out of the wound in the clouds; and so, on and on, He plays, night and morning alike, ever-changing, ever-new, ever-fresh; no patterns, no duplicates, no colours just the same. The beauty of the Indian change in day to night is beyond compare elsewhere; often the sky looks as if God had taken all the colours in His kit and given them one mighty kaleidoscopic toss into the heavens.

"I must relate the splendour of a twilight visit to the huge Krishnaraja Sagar Dam,[3] constructed twelve miles outside of Mysore. Yoganandaji and I boarded a small bus and, with a small boy as official cranker or battery substitute, started off over a smooth dirt road, just as the sun was setting on the horizon and squashing like an overripe tomato.

"Our journey led past the omnipresent square rice fields, through a line of comforting banyan trees, in between a grove of towering coconut palms, with vegetation nearly as thick as in a jungle, and finally, approaching the crest of a hill, we came face-to-face with an immense

3 This dam, a huge hydro-electric installation, lights Mysore City and gives power to factories for silks, soaps, and sandalwood oil. The sandalwood souvenirs from Mysore possess a delightful permanent fragrance. The state boasts large pioneer industrial undertakings including the Kolar Gold Mines and Mysore Sugar Factory, the huge iron and steel works at Bhadravati, and the cheap and efficient Mysore State Railway which covers many of the state's 30,000 square miles. The Maharaja and Yuvaraja who were my hosts in Mysore in 1935 have both recently died. The son of the Yuvaraja, the present Maharaja, is an enterprising ruler, and has added a large airplane factory to Mysore's industries.

artificial lake, reflecting the stars and fringe of palms and other trees, surrounded by lovely terraced gardens and a row of electric lights on the brink of the dam – and below it our eyes met a dazzling spectacle of coloured beams playing on geyserlike fountains, like so many streams of brilliant ink pouring forth – gorgeously blue waterfalls, arresting red cataracts, green and yellow sprays, elephants spouting water, a miniature of the Chicago World's Fair, and yet modernly outstanding in this ancient land of paddy fields and simple people, who have given us such a loving welcome that I fear it will take more than my strength to bring Yoganandaji back to America.

"Another rare privilege – my first elephant ride. Yesterday the Yuvaraja invited us to his summer palace to enjoy a ride on one of his elephants, an enormous beast. I mounted a ladder provided to climb aloft to the *howdah* or saddle, which is silk-cushioned and boxlike; and then for a rolling, tossing, swaying, and heaving down into a gully, too much thrilled to worry or exclaim, but hanging on for dear life!"

Southern India, rich with historical and archaeological remains, is a land of definite and yet indefinable charm. To the north of Mysore is the largest native state in India, Hyderabad, a picturesque plateau cut by the mighty Godavari River. Broad fertile plains, the lovely Nilgiris or 'Blue Mountains,' other regions with barren hills of limestone or granite. Hyderabad history is a long, colourful story, starting three thousand years ago under the Andhra kings, and continuing under Hindu dynasties until A.D. 1294, when it passed to a line of Moslem rulers who reign to this day.

The most breath-taking display of architecture, sculpture, and painting in all India is found at Hyderabad in the ancient rock-sculptured caves of Ellora and Ajanta. The Kailasa at Ellora, a huge monolithic temple, possesses carved figures of gods, men, and beasts in the stupendous proportions of a Michelangelo. Ajanta is the site of five cathedrals and twenty-five monasteries, all rock excavations maintained by tremendous frescoed pillars on which artists and sculptors have immortalized their genius.

Hyderabad City is graced by the Osmania University and by the imposing Mecca Masjid Mosque, where ten thousand Mohammedans may assemble for prayer.

Mysore State too is a scenic wonderland, three thousand feet above sea level, abounding in dense tropical forests, the home of wild elephants, bison, bears, panthers, and tigers. Its two chief cities, Bangalore and Mysore, are clean, attractive, with many parks and public gardens.

Hindu architecture and sculpture achieved their highest perfection in Mysore under the patronage of Hindu kings from the eleventh to the fifteenth centuries. The temple at Belur, an eleventh-century masterpiece completed during the reign of King Vishnuvardhana, is unsurpassed in the world for its delicacy of detail and exuberant imagery.

The rock pillars found in northern Mysore date from the third century B.C., illuminating the memory of King Asoka. He succeeded to the throne of the Maurya dynasty then prevailing; his empire included nearly all of modern India, Afghanistan, and Baluchistan. This illustrious emperor, considered even by Western historians to have been an incomparable ruler, has left the following wisdom on a rock memorial:

> This religious inscription has been engraved in order that our sons and grandsons may not think a new conquest is necessary; that they may not think conquest by the sword deserves the name of conquest; that they may see in it nothing but destruction and violence; that they may consider nothing as true conquest save the conquest of religion. Such conquests have value in this world and in the next.

Asoka was a grandson of the formidable Chandragupta Maurya (known to the Greeks as Sandrocottus), who in his youth had met Alexander the Great. Later Chandragupta destroyed the Macedonian garrisons left in India, defeated the invading Greek army of Seleucus in the Punjab, and then received at his Patna court the Hellenic ambassador Megasthenes.

Intensely interesting stories have been minutely recorded by Greek historians and others who accompanied or followed after Alexander in his expedition to India. The narratives of Arrian, Diodoros, Plutarch, and Strabo the geographer have been translated by Dr. J. W. M'Crindle[4] to throw a shaft of light on ancient India. The most admirable feature of Alexander's unsuccessful invasion was the deep interest he displayed in Hindu philosophy and in the yogis and holy men whom he encountered from time to time and whose society he eagerly sought. Shortly after the Greek warrior had arrived in Taxila in northern India, he sent a messenger, Onesikritos, a disciple of the Hellenic school of Diogenes, to fetch an Indian teacher, Dandamis, a great sannyasi of Taxila.

"Hail to thee, O teacher of Brahmins!" Onesikritos said after seeking out Dandamis in his forest retreat. "The son of the mighty God Zeus, being Alexander who is the Sovereign Lord of all men, asks you to go to him, and if you comply, he will reward you with great gifts, but if you refuse, he will cut off your head!"

The yogi received this fairly compulsive invitation calmly, and "did not so much as lift up his head from his couch of leaves."

"I also am a son of Zeus, if Alexander be such," he commented. "I want

4 Six volumes on *Ancient India* (Calcutta: Chuckervertty, Chatterjee & Co., 15, College Square; 1879, re-issued 1927).

nothing that is Alexander's, for I am content with what I have, while I see that he wanders with his men over sea and land for no advantage, and is never coming to an end of his wanderings.

"Go and tell Alexander that God the Supreme King is never the Author of insolent wrong, but is the Creator of light, of peace, of life, of water, of the body of man and of souls; He receives all men when death sets them free, being in no way subject to evil disease. He alone is the God of my homage, who abhors slaughter and instigates no wars.

"Alexander is no god, since he must taste of death," continued the sage in quiet scorn. "How can such as he be the world's master, when he has not yet seated himself on a throne of inner universal dominion? Neither as yet has he entered living into Hades, nor does he know the course of the sun through the central regions of the earth, while the nations on its boundaries have not so much as heard his name!"

After this chastisement, surely the most caustic ever sent to assault the ears of the 'Lord of the World,' the sage added ironically, "If Alexander's present dominions be not capacious enough for his desires, let him cross the Ganges River; there he will find a region able to sustain all his men, if the country on this side be too narrow to hold him.[5]

"Know this, however, that what Alexander offers and the gifts he promises are things to me utterly useless; the things I prize and find of real use and worth are these leaves which are my house, these blooming plants which supply me with daily food, and the water which is my drink; while all other possessions which are amassed with anxious care are wont to prove ruinous to those who gather them, and cause only sorrow and vexation, with which every poor mortal is fully fraught. As for me, I lie upon the forest leaves, and having nothing which requires guarding, close my eyes in tranquil slumber; whereas had I anything to guard, that would banish sleep. The earth supplies me with everything, even as a mother her child with milk. I go wherever I please, and there are no cares with which I am forced to cumber myself.

"Should Alexander cut off my head, he cannot also destroy my soul. My head alone, then silent, will remain, leaving the body like a torn garment upon the earth, whence also it was taken. I then, becoming Spirit, shall ascend to my God, who enclosed us all in flesh and left us upon earth to prove whether, when here below, we shall live obedient to His ordinances and who also will require of us all, when we depart hence to His presence, an account of our life, since He is Judge of all proud wrongdoing; for the groans of the oppressed become the punishment of the oppressor.

5 Neither Alexander nor any of his generals ever crossed the Ganges. Finding determined resistance in the northwest, the Macedonian army refused to penetrate farther; Alexander was forced to leave India and seek his conquests in Persia.

"Let Alexander then terrify with these threats those who wish for wealth and who dread death, for against us these weapons are both alike powerless; the Brahmins neither love gold nor fear death. Go then and tell Alexander this: Dandamis has no need of aught that is yours, and therefore will not go to you, and if you want anything from Dandamis, come you to him."

With close attention Alexander received through Onesikritos the message from the yogi, and "felt a stronger desire than ever to see Dandamis who, though old and naked, was the only antagonist in whom he, the conqueror of many nations, had met more than his match."

Alexander invited to Taxila a number of Brahmin ascetics noted for their skill in answering philosophical questions with pithy wisdom. An account of the verbal skirmish is given by Plutarch; Alexander himself framed all the questions.

"Which be the more numerous, the living or the dead?"
"The living, for the dead are not."
"Which breeds the larger animals, the sea or the land?"
"The land, for the sea is only a part of land."
"Which is the cleverest of beasts?"
"That one with which man is not yet acquainted."
(Man fears the unknown.)
"Which existed first, the day or the night?"
"The day was first by one day." This reply caused
Alexander to betray surprise; the Brahmin added: "Impossible questions require impossible answers."
"How best may a man make himself beloved?"
"A man will be beloved if, possessed with great power, he still does not make himself feared."
"How may a man become a god?"[6]
"By doing that which it is impossible for a man to do."
"Which is stronger, life or death?"
"Life, because it bears so many evils."

Alexander succeeded in taking out of India, as his teacher, a true yogi. This man was Kalyana (Swami Sphines), called 'Kalanos' by the Greeks because the saint, a devotee of God in the form of Kali, greeted everyone by pronouncing Her auspicious name.

Kalanos accompanied Alexander to Persia. On a stated day, at Susa in Persia, Kalanos gave up his aged body by entering a funeral pyre in view of the whole Macedonian army. The historians record the astonishment

6 From this question we may surmise that the 'Son of Zeus' had some doubt that he had already attained perfection.

of the soldiers who observed that the yogi had no fear of pain or death, and who never once moved from his position as he was consumed in the flames. Before leaving for his cremation, Kalanos had embraced all his close companions, but refrained from bidding farewell to Alexander, to whom the Hindu sage had merely remarked:

"I shall see you shortly in Babylon."

Alexander left Persia, and died a year later in Babylon. His Indian guru's words had been his way of saying he would be present with Alexander in life and death.

The Greek historians have left us many vivid and inspiring pictures of Indian society. Hindu law, Arrian tells us, protects the people and "ordains that no one among them shall, under any circumstances, be a slave but that, enjoying freedom themselves, they shall respect the equal right to it which all possess. For those, they thought, who have learned neither to domineer over nor cringe to others will attain the life best adapted for all vicissitudes of lot."[7]

"The Indians," runs another text, "neither put out money at usury, nor know how to borrow. It is contrary to established usage for an Indian either to do or suffer a wrong, and therefore they neither make contracts nor require securities." Healing, we are told, was by simple and natural means. "Cures are effected rather by regulating diet than by the use of medicines. The remedies most esteemed are ointments and plasters. All others are considered to be in great measure pernicious." Engagement in war was restricted to the *Kshatriyas* or warrior caste. "Nor would an enemy coming upon a husbandman at his work on his land, do him any harm, for men of this class being regarded as public benefactors, are protected from all injury. The land thus remaining unravaged and producing heavy crops, supplies the inhabitants with the requisites to make life enjoyable."[8]

The Emperor Chandragupta who in 305 B.C. had defeated Alexander's general, Seleucus, decided seven years later to hand over the reins of India's government to his son. Travelling to South India. Chandragupta spent the last twelve years of his life as a penniless ascetic, seeking self-realization in a rocky cave at Sravanabelagola, now honoured as a Mysore shrine. Near-by stands the world's largest statue, carved out of an immense boulder by the Jains in A.D. 983 to honour the saint Comateswara.

The ubiquitous religious shrines of Mysore are a constant reminder of the many great saints of South India. One of these masters, Thayumanavar,

---

7 The Greek observers comment on the lack of slavery in India, a feature at complete variance with the structure of Hellenic society.

8 *Creative India* by Benoy Kumar Sarkar gives a comprehensive picture of India's ancient and modern achievements and distinctive values in economics, political science, literature, art, and social philosophy. (Lahore: Motilal Banarsi Dass, Publishers, 1937, 714 pp.) Another recommended volume is *Indian Culture Through the Ages,* by S. V. Venatesvara (New York: Longmans, Green & Co.).

has left us the following challenging poem:

> You may control a mad elephant;
> You may shut the mouth of the bear and the tiger;
> You may ride a lion;
> You may play with the cobra;
> By alchemy may can eke out your livelihood;
> You may wander through the universe incognito;
> You may make vassals of the gods;
> You may be ever youthful;
> You may walk on water and live in fire;
> But control of the mind is better and more difficult.

In the beautiful and fertile State of Travancore in the extreme south of India, where traffic is conveyed over rivers and canals, the Maharaja assumes every year a hereditary obligation to expiate the sin incurred by wars and the annexation in the distant past of several petty states to Travancore. For fifty-six days annually the Maharaja visits the temple thrice daily to hear Vedic hymns and recitations; the expiation ceremony ends with the *lakshadipam* or illumination of the temple by a hundred thousand lights.

Madras Presidency on the southeast coast of India contains the flat, spacious, sea-girt city of Madras, and Conjeeveram, the Golden City, capital site of the Pallava dynasty whose kings ruled during the early centuries of the Christian era. In modern Madras Presidency the nonviolent ideals of Mahatma Gandhi have made great headway; the white distinguishing 'Gandhi caps' are seen everywhere. In the south generally the Mahatma has effected many important temple reforms for 'untouchables' as well as caste-system reforms.

The great Hindu lawgiver Manu[9] has outlined the duties of a king. "He should shower amenities like Indra (lord of the gods); collect taxes gently and imperceptibly as the sun obtains vapor from water; enter into the life of his subjects as the wind goes everywhere; mete out even justice to all like Yama (god of death); bind transgressors in a noose like Varuna (Vedic deity of sky and wind); please all like the moon, burn up vicious enemies like the god of fire; and support all like the earth goddess.

"In war a king should not fight with poisonous or fiery weapons nor kill weak or unready or weaponless foes or men who are in fear or who pray for protection or who run away. War should be resorted to only as a last resort. Results are always doubtful in war."

---

9 Manu is the universal lawgiver; not just for the Hindu society. All systems of wise social regulations and even justice are patterned after Manu. Nietzsche has paid the following tribute: "I know of no book in which so many delicate and kindly things are said to woman as in the *Lawbook of Manu;* those old graybeards and saints have a manner of being gallant to women which perhaps cannot be surpassed . . . an incomparably intellectual and superior work . . . replete with noble values, it is filled with a feeling of perfection, with a saying of yea to life, and a triumphant sense of well-being in regard to itself and to life; the sun shines upon the whole book."

The origin of the caste system, formulated by the great legislator Manu, was admirable. He saw clearly that men are distinguished by natural evolution into four great classes: those capable of offering service to society through their bodily labour (*Sudras*); those who serve through mentality, skill, agriculture, trade, commerce, business life in general (*Vaisyas*); those whose talents are administrative, executive, and protective – rulers and warriors (*Kshatriyas*); those of contemplative nature, spiritually inspired and inspiring (*Brahmins*). "Neither birth nor sacraments nor study nor ancestry can decide whether a person is twice-born (i.e., a *Brahmin*);" the *Mahabharata* declares, "character and conduct only can decide."[10] Manu instructed society to show respect to its members insofar as they possessed wisdom, virtue, age, kinship or, lastly, wealth. Riches in Vedic India were always despised if they were hoarded or unavailable for charitable purposes. Ungenerous men of great wealth were assigned a low rank in society.

Serious evils arose when the caste system became hardened through the centuries into a hereditary halter. Social reformers like Gandhi and the members of very numerous societies in India today are making slow but sure progress in restoring the ancient values of caste, based solely on natural qualification and not on birth. Every nation on earth has its own distinctive misery-producing karma to deal with and remove; India, too, with her versatile and invulnerable spirit, shall prove herself equal to the task of caste-reformation.

So entrancing is southern India that Mr. Wright and I yearned to prolong our idyll. But time, in its immemorial rudeness, dealt us no courteous extensions. I was scheduled soon to address the concluding session of the Indian Philosophical Congress at Calcutta University. At the end of the visit to Mysore, I enjoyed a talk with Sir C. V. Raman, president of the Indian Academy of Sciences. This brilliant Hindu physicist was awarded the Nobel Prize in 1930 for his important discovery in the diffusion of light – the 'Raman Effect' now known to every schoolboy.

10 An article in *East-West* for January, 1935, tells us that inclusion in one of these four castes originally depended not on man's birth but on the goal in life he elected to achieve. This goal could be (1) *kama*, desire, activity of the life of the senses (*Sudra* stage), (2) *artha*, gain, fulfilling but controlling the desires (*Vaisya* stage), (3) *dharma*, self-discipline, the life of responsibility and right action (*Kshatriya* stage), (4) *moksha*, liberation, the life of spirituality and religious teaching (*Brahmin* stage). These four castes render service to humanity by (1) body, (2) mind, (3) will-power and (4) Spirit. These four stages relate to the eternal *gunas* or qualities of nature, *tamas, rajas,* and *sattva:* obstruction, activity, and expansion; or, mass, energy, and intelligence. The four natural castes are marked by the *gunas* as (1) *tamas* (ignorance), (2) *tamas-rajas* (mixture of ignorance and activity), (3) *rajas-sattva* (mixture of right activity and enlightenment), (4) *sattva* (enlightenment). Thus has nature marked every man with his caste, by the predominance in himself of one, or the mixture of two, of the *gunas*? Of course every human being has all three *gunas* in varying proportions. The guru will be able to determine rightly a man's caste or evolutionary status.

To a certain extent, all races and nations observe in practice, if not in theory, the features of caste. Where there is great license or so-called liberty, particularly in intermarriage between extremes in the natural castes, the race dwindles away and becomes extinct. The *Purana Samhita* compares the offspring of such unions to barren hybrids, like the mule which is incapable of propagation of its own species. Artificial species are eventually exterminated. History offers abundant proof of numerous great races which no longer have any living representatives. Manu's system is credited by India's most profound thinkers as a check or preventive against license which has preserved the purity of the race and brought it safely through millenniums of vicissitudes, while other races have vanished in oblivion."

Waving a reluctant farewell to a crowd of Madras students and friends, Mr. Wright and I set out for the north. On the way we stopped before a little shrine sacred to the memory of Sadasiva Brahman,[11] in whose eighteenth-century life story miracles cluster thickly. A larger Sadasiva shrine at Nerur, erected by the Raja of Pudukkottai, is a pilgrimage spot which has witnessed numerous divine healings.

Many quaint stories of Sadasiva, a lovable and fully-illumined master, are still current among the South Indian villagers. Immersed one day in *samadhi* on the bank of the Kaveri River, Sadasiva was seen to be carried away by a sudden flood. Weeks later he was found buried deep beneath a mound of earth. As the villagers' shovels struck his body, the saint rose and walked briskly away.

Sadasiva never spoke a word or wore a cloth. One morning the nude yogi unceremoniously entered the tent of a Mohammedan chieftain. His ladies screamed in alarm; the warrior dealt a savage sword thrust at Sadasiva, whose arm was severed. The master departed unconcernedly. Overcome by remorse, the Mohammedan picked up the arm from the floor and followed Sadasiva. The yogi quietly inserted his arm into the bleeding stump. When the warrior humbly asked for some spiritual instruction, Sadasiva wrote with his finger on the sands:

"Do not do what you want, and then you may do what you like."

The Mohammedan was uplifted to an exalted state of mind, and understood the saint's paradoxical advice to be a guide to soul freedom through mastery of the ego.

The village children once expressed a desire in Sadasiva's presence to see the Madura religious festival, 150 miles away. The yogi indicated to the little ones that they should touch his body. Lo! instantly the whole group was transported to Madura. The children wandered happily among the thousands of pilgrims. In a few hours the yogi brought his small charges home by his simple mode of transportation. The astonished parents heard the vivid tales of the procession of images, and noted that several children were carrying bags of Madura sweets.

An incredulous youth derided the saint and the story. The following morning he approached Sadasiva.

"Master," he said scornfully, "why don't you take me to the festival, even as you did yesterday for the other children?"

Sadasiva complied; the boy immediately found himself among the distant city throng. But alas! where was the saint when the youth wanted to leave? The weary boy reached his home by the ancient and prosaic method of foot locomotion.

11 His full title was Sri Sadasivendra Saraswati Swami. The illustrious successor in the formal Shankara line, Jagadguru Sri Shankaracharya of Sringeri Math, wrote an inspiring *Ode* dedicated to Sadasiva. *East-West* for July, 1942, carried an article on Sadasiva's life.

Before leaving South India, Mr. Wright and I made a pilgrimage to the holy hill of Arunachala near Tiruvannamalai to meet Sri Ramana Maharshi. At his ashram the sage welcomed us affectionately and pointed to a nearby stack of *East-West* magazines. During the hours that we spent with him and his disciples, he was mostly silent, his gentle face radiating divine love and wisdom.

To help suffering humanity regain its forgotten state of Perfection, Sri Ramana teaches that one should constantly ask himself: "Who am I?" – the Great Inquiry indeed. By stern rejection of all other thoughts the devotee soon finds himself going deeper and deeper into the true Self, and the sidetracking bewilderments of other thoughts cease to arise. This illumined rishi of South India has written:

> Dualities and trinities on something do hang,
> Supportless they never appear;
> That support searched for, they loosen and fall.
> There is the Truth. Who sees that never wavers.

42. *Last Days with my Guru*

"GURUJI, I am glad to find you alone this morning." I had just arrived at the Serampore hermitage, carrying a fragrant burden of fruit and roses. Sri Yukteswar glanced at me meekly.

"What is your question?" Master looked about the room as though he were seeking escape.

"Guruji, I came to you as a high-school youth; now I am a grown man, even with a gray hair or two. Though you have showered me with silent affection from the first hour to this, do you realize that once only, on the day of meeting, have you ever said, 'I love you'?" I looked at him pleadingly.

Master lowered his gaze. "Yogananda, must I bring out into the cold realms of speech the warm sentiments best guarded by the wordless heart?"

"Guruji, I know you love me, but my mortal ears ache to hear you say so."

"Be it as you wish. During my married life I often yearned for a son, to train in the yogic path. But when you came into my life, I was content; in you I have found my son." Two clear teardrops stood in Sri Yukteswar's eyes. "Yogananda, I love you always."

"Your answer is my passport to heaven." I felt a weight lift from my heart, dissolved forever at his words. Often had I wondered at his silence. Realizing that he was unemotional and self-contained, yet sometimes I feared I had been unsuccessful in fully satisfying him. His was a strange nature, never utterly to be known; a nature deep and still, unfathomable to the outer world, whose values he had long transcended.

A few days later, when I spoke before a huge audience at Albert Hall in Calcutta, Sri Yukteswar consented to sit beside me on the platform, with the Maharaja of Santosh and the Mayor of Calcutta. Though Master made no remark to me, I glanced at him from time to time during my address, and thought I detected a pleased twinkle in his eyes.

Then came a talk before the alumni of Serampore College. As I gazed upon my old classmates, and as they gazed on their own 'Mad Monk,' tears of joy showed unashamedly. My silver-tongued professor of philosophy, Dr. Ghoshal, came forward to greet me, all our past misunderstandings dissolved by the alchemist Time.

A Winter Solstice Festival was celebrated at the end of December in the Serampore hermitage. As always, Sri Yukteswar's disciples gathered from far and near. Devotional *sankirtans*, solos in the nectar-sweet voice of Kristo-da, a feast served by young disciples, Master's profoundly moving discourse under the stars in the thronged courtyard of the ashram – memories, memories! Joyous festivals of years long past! Tonight, however, there was to be a new feature.

"Yogananda, please address the assemblage – in English." Master's eyes were twinkling as he made this doubly unusual request; was he thinking of the shipboard predicament that had preceded my first lecture in English? I told the story to my audience of brother disciples, ending with a fervent tribute to our guru.

"His omnipresent guidance was with me not alone on the ocean steamer," I concluded, "but daily throughout my fifteen years in the vast and hospitable land of America."

After the guests had departed, Sri Yukteswar called me to the same bedroom where – once only, after a festival of my early years – I had been permitted to sleep on his wooden bed. Tonight my guru was sitting there quietly, a semicircle of disciples at his feet. He smiled as I quickly entered the room.

"Yogananda, are you leaving now for Calcutta? Please return here tomorrow. I have certain things to tell you."

The next afternoon, with a few simple words of blessing, Sri Yukteswar bestowed on me the further monastic title of *Paramahansa*.[1]

"It now formally supersedes your former ride of *swami*," he said as I knelt before him. With a silent chuckle I thought of the struggle which my American students would undergo over the pronunciation of *Paramahansaji*.[2]

"My task on earth is now finished; you must carry on." Master spoke quietly, his eyes calm and gentle. My heart was palpitating in fear.

1 Literally, *param,* highest; *hansa,* swan. The *hansa* is represented in scriptural lore as the vehicle of Brahma, Supreme Spirit; as the symbol of discrimination, the white *hansa* swan is thought of as able to separate the true *soma* nectar from a mixture of milk and water. *Ham-sa* (pronounced *hong-sau*) are two sacred Sanskrit chant words possessing a vibratory connection with the incoming and outgoing breath. *Aham-Sa* is literally 'I am He.'
2 They have generally evaded the difficulty by addressing me as *sir.*

"Please send someone to take charge of our ashram at Puri," Sri Yukteswar went on. "I leave everything in your hands. You will be able to successfully sail the boat of your life and that of the organization to the divine shores."

In tears, I was embracing his feet; he rose and blessed me endearingly.

The following day I summoned from Ranchi a disciple, Swami Sebananda, and sent him to Puri to assume the hermitage duties.[3] Later my guru discussed with me the legal details of settling his estate; he was anxious to prevent the possibility of litigation by relatives, after his death, for possession of his two hermitages and other properties, which he wished to be deeded over solely for charitable purposes.

"Arrangements were recently made for Master to visit Kidderpore,[4] but he failed to go." Amulaya Babu, a brother disciple, made this remark to me one afternoon; I felt a cold wave of premonition. To my pressing inquiries, Sri Yukteswar only replied, "I shall go to Kidderpore no more." For a moment, Master trembled like a frightened child.

("Attachment to bodily residence, springing up of its own nature," Patanjali wrote,[5] "is present in slight degree even in great saints." In some of his discourses on death, my guru had been wont to add: "Just as a long-caged bird hesitates to leave its accustomed home when the door is opened.")

"Guruji," I entreated him with a sob, "don't say that! Never utter those words to me!"

Sri Yukteswar's face relaxed in a peaceful smile. Though nearing his eighty-first birthday, he looked well and strong.

Basking day by day in the sunshine of my guru's love, unspoken but keenly felt, I banished from my conscious mind the various hints he had given of his approaching passing.

"Sir, the *Kumbha Mela* is convening this month at Allahabad." I showed Master the *mela* dates in a Bengali almanac.[6]

"Do you really want to go?"

---

[3] At the Puri ashram, Swami Sebananda is still conducting a small, flourishing yoga school for boys, and meditation groups for adults. Meetings of saints and pundits also convene there periodically.

[4] A section of Calcutta.

[5] That is, springing from immemorial roots, past experiences of death. *Yoga Sutra:* II: 9.

[6] Religious *melas* are mentioned in the ancient *Mahabharata.* The Chinese traveller Hieuen Tsiang has left an account of a vast *Kumbha Mela* held in A.D. 644 at Allahabad. The largest *mela* is held every twelfth year; the next largest (*Ardha* or half) *Kumbha* occurs every sixth year. Smaller *melas* convene every third year, attracting about a million devotees. The four sacred *mela* cities are Allahabad, Hardwar, Nasik, and Ujjain.

Early Chinese travellers have left us many striking pictures of Indian society. The Chinese priest, Fa-Hsien, wrote an account of his eleven years in India during the reign of Chandragupta II (early 4th century). The Chinese author relates: "Throughout the country no one kills any living thing, nor drinks wine. . . . They do not keep pigs or fowl; there are no dealings in cattle, no butchers' shops or distilleries. Rooms with beds and mattresses, food and clothes, are provided for resident and travelling priests without fail, and this is the same in all places. The priests occupy themselves with benevolent ministrations and with chanting liturgies; or they sit in meditation." Fa-Hsien tells us the Indian people were happy and honest; capital punishment was unknown.

Not sensing Sri Yukteswar's reluctance to have me leave him, I went on, "Once you beheld the blessed sight of Babaji at an Allahabad *kumbha*. Perhaps this time I shall be fortunate enough to see him."

"I do not think you will meet him there." My guru then fell into silence, not wishing to obstruct my plans.

When I set out for Allahabad the following day with a small group, Master blessed me quietly in his usual manner. Apparently I was remaining oblivious to implications in Sri Yukteswar's attitude because the Lord wished to spare me the experience of being forced, helplessly, to witness my guru's passing. It has always happened in my life that, at the death of those dearly beloved by me, God has compassionately arranged that I be distant from the scene.[7]

Our party reached the *Kumbha Mela* on January 23, 1936. The surging crowd of nearly two million persons was an impressive sight, even an overwhelming one. The peculiar genius of the Indian people is the reverence innate in even the lowliest peasant for the worth of the Spirit, and for the monks and sadhus who have forsaken worldly ties to seek a diviner anchorage. Imposters and hypocrites there are indeed, but India respects all for the sake of the few who illumine the whole land with supernal blessings. Westerners who were viewing the vast spectacle had a unique opportunity to feel the pulse of the land, the spiritual ardour to which India owes her quenchless vitality before the blows of time.

The first day was spent by our group in sheer staring. Here were countless bathers, dipping in the holy river for remission of sins; there we saw solemn rituals of worship; yonder were devotional offerings being strewn at the dusty feet of saints; a turn of our heads, and a line of elephants, caparisoned horses and slow-paced Rajputana camels filed by, or a quaint religious parade of naked sadhus, waving scepters of gold and silver, or flags and streamers of silken velvet.

Anchorites wearing only loincloths sat quietly in little groups, their bodies besmeared with the ashes that protect them from the heat and cold. The spiritual eye was vividly represented on their foreheads by a single spot of sandalwood paste. Shaven-headed swamis appeared by the thousands, ochre-robed and carrying their bamboo staff and begging bowl. Their faces beamed with the renunciate's peace as they walked about or held philosophical discussions with disciples.

Here and there under the trees, around huge piles of burning logs, were picturesque sadhus,[8] their hair braided and massed in coils on top of their

---

7 I was not present at the deaths of my mother, elder brother Ananta, eldest sister Roma, Master, Father (who passed on at Calcutta in 1942, at the age of eighty-nine), or of several close disciples.

8 The hundreds of thousands of Indian sadhus are controlled by an executive committee of seven leaders, representing seven large sections of India. The present *mahamandaleswar* or president is Joyendra Puri. This saintly man is extremely reserved, often confining his speech to three words – Truth, Love, and Work. A sufficient conversation!

heads. Some wore beards several feet in length, curled and tied in a knot. They meditated quietly, or extended their hands in blessing to the passing throng – beggars, maharajas on elephants, women in multicoloured *saris* – their bangles and anklets tinkling, *fakirs* with thin arms held grotesquely aloft, *brahmacharis* carrying meditation elbow-props, humble sages whose solemnity hid an inner bliss. High above the din we heard the ceaseless summons of the temple bells.

On our second *mela* day my companions and I entered various ashrams and temporary huts, offering *pronams* to saintly personages. We received the blessing of the leader of the *Giri* branch of the Swami Order – a thin, ascetical monk with eyes of smiling fire. Our next visit took us to a hermitage whose guru had observed for the past nine years the vows of silence and a strict fruitarian diet. On the central dais in the ashram hall sat a blind sadhu, Prajna Chakshu,[9] profoundly learned in the *shastras* and highly revered by all sects.

After I had given a brief discourse in Hindi on *Vedanta,* our group left the peaceful hermitage to greet a near-by swami, Krishnananda, a handsome monk with rosy cheeks and impressive shoulders. Reclining near him was a tame lioness. Succumbing to the monk's spiritual charm – not, I am sure, to his powerful physique! – the jungle animal refuses all meat in favour of rice and milk. The swami has taught the tawny-haired beast to utter *Aum* in a deep, attractive growl – a cat devotee!

Our next encounter, an interview with a learned young sadhu, is well described in Mr. Wright's sparkling travel diary.

"We rode in the Ford across the very low Ganges on a creaking pontoon bridge, crawling snakelike through the crowds and over narrow, twisting lanes, passing the site on the river bank which Yoganandaji pointed out to me as the meeting place of Babaji and Sri Yukteswarji. Alighting from the car a short time later, we walked some distance through the thickening smoke of the sadhus' fires and over the slippery sands to reach a cluster of tiny, very modest mud-and-straw huts. We halted in front of one of these insignificant temporary dwellings, with a pigmy doorless entrance, the shelter of Kara Patri, a young wandering sadhu noted for his exceptional intelligence. There he sat, cross-legged on a pile of straw, his only covering – and incidentally his only possession – being an ocher cloth draped over his shoulders.

"Truly a divine face smiled at us after we had crawled on all fours into the hut and *pronamed* at the feet of this enlightened soul, while the kerosene lantern at the entrance flickered weird, dancing shadows on the thatched walls. His face, especially his eyes and perfect teeth,

9 One who sees with his *inner* intelligence.

beamed and glistened. Although I was puzzled by the Hindi, his expressions were very revealing; he was full of enthusiasm, love, spiritual glory. No one could be mistaken as to his greatness.

"Imagine the happy life of one unattached to the material world; free of the clothing problem; free of food craving, never begging, never touching cooked food except on alternate days, never carrying a begging bowl; free of all money entanglements, never handling money, never storing things away, always trusting in God; free of transportation worries, never riding in vehicles, but always walking on the banks of the sacred rivers; never remaining in one place longer than a week in order to avoid any growth of attachment.

"Such a modest soul! unusually learned in the *Vedas,* and possessing an M.A. degree and the title of *Shastri* (master of scriptures) from Benares University. A sublime feeling pervaded me as I sat at his feet; it all seemed to be an answer to my desire to see the real, the ancient India, for he is a true representative of this land of spiritual giants."

I questioned Kara Patri about his wandering life. "Don't you have any extra clothes for winter?"

"No, this is enough."

"Do you carry any books?"

"No, I teach from memory those people who wish to hear me."

"What else do you do?"

"I roam by the Ganges."

At these quiet words, I was overpowered by a yearning for the simplicity of his life. I remembered America, and all the responsibilities that lay on my shoulders.

"No, Yogananda," I thought, sadly for a moment, "in this life roaming by the Ganges is not for you."

After the sadhu had told me a few of his spiritual realizations, I shot an abrupt question.

"Are you giving these descriptions from scriptural lore, or from inward experience?"

"Half from book learning," he answered with a straightforward smile, "and half from experience."

We sat happily awhile in meditative silence. After we had left his sacred presence, I said to Mr. Wright, "He is a king sitting on a throne of golden straw."

We had our dinner that night on the *mela* grounds under the stars, eating from leaf plates pinned together with sticks. Dishwashings in India are reduced to a minimum!

Two more days of the fascinating *kumbha*; then northwest along the Yamuna banks to Agra. Once again I gazed on the Taj Mahal; in memory Jitendra stood by my side, awed by the dream in marble. Then on to the Brindaban ashram of Swami Keshabananda.

My object in seeking out Keshabananda was connected with this book. I had never forgotten Sri Yukteswar's request that I write the life of Lahiri Mahasaya. During my stay in India I was taking every opportunity of contacting direct disciples and relatives of the Yogavatar. Recording their conversations in voluminous notes, I verified facts and dates, and collected photographs, old letters, and documents. My Lahiri Mahasaya portfolio began to swell; I realized with dismay that ahead of me lay arduous labours in authorship. I prayed that I might be equal to my role as biographer of the colossal guru. Several of his disciples feared that in a written account their master might be belittled or misinterpreted.

"One can hardly do justice in cold words to the life of a divine incarnation," Panchanon Bhattacharya had once remarked to me.

Other close disciples were similarly satisfied to keep the Yogavatar hidden in their hearts as the deathless preceptor. Nevertheless, mindful of Lahiri Mahasaya's prediction about his biography, I spared no effort to secure and substantiate the facts of his outward life.

Swami Keshabananda greeted our party warmly at Brindaban in his Katayani Peeth Ashram, an imposing brick building with massive black pillars, set in a beautiful garden. He ushered us at once into a sitting room adorned with an enlargement of Lahiri Mahasaya's picture. The swami was approaching the age of ninety, but his muscular body radiated strength and health. With long hair and a snow-white beard, eyes twinkling with joy, he was a veritable patriarchal embodiment. I informed him that I wanted to mention his name in my book on India's masters.

"Please tell me about your earlier life." I smiled entreatingly; great yogis are often uncommunicative.

Keshabananda made a gesture of humility. "There is little of external moment. Practically my whole life has been spent in the Himalayan solitudes, travelling on foot from one quiet cave to another. For a while I maintained a small ashram outside Hardwar, surrounded on all sides by a grove of tall trees. It was a peaceful spot little visited by travellers, owing to the ubiquitous presence of cobras." Keshabananda chuckled. "Later a Ganges flood washed away the hermitage and cobras alike. My disciples then helped me to build this Brindaban ashram."

One of our party asked the swami how he had protected himself against the Himalayan tigers.[10]

Keshabananda shook his head. "In those high spiritual altitudes," he said, "wild beasts seldom molest the yogis. Once in the jungle I encountered a tiger face-to-face. At my sudden ejaculation, the animal was transfixed as though turned to stone." Again the swami chuckled at his memories.

"Occasionally I left my seclusion to visit my guru in Benares. He used to joke with me over my ceaseless travels in the Himalayan wilderness.

" 'You have the mark of wanderlust on your foot,' he told me once. 'I am glad that the sacred Himalayas are extensive enough to engross you.'

"Many times," Keshabananda went on, "both before and after his passing, Lahiri Mahasaya has appeared bodily before me. For him no Himalayan height is inaccessible!"

Two hours later he led us to a dining patio. I sighed in silent dismay. Another fifteen-course meal! Less than a year of Indian hospitality, and I had gained fifty pounds! Yet it would have been considered the height of rudeness to refuse any of the dishes, carefully prepared for the endless banquets in my honour. In India (nowhere else, alas!) a well-padded swami is considered a delightful sight.[11]

After dinner, Keshabananda led me to a secluded nook.

"Your arrival is not unexpected," he said. "I have a message for you."

I was surprised; no one had known of my plan to visit Keshabananda.

"While roaming last year in the northern Himalayas near Badrinarayan," the swami continued, "I lost my way. Shelter appeared in a spacious cave, which was empty, though the embers of a fire glowed in a hole in the rocky floor. Wondering about the occupant of this lonely retreat, I sat near the fire, my gaze fixed on the sunlit entrance to the cave.

" 'Keshabananda, I am glad you are here.' These words came from behind me. I turned, startled, and was dazzled to behold Babaji! The great guru had materialized himself in a recess of the cave. Overjoyed to see him again after many years, I prostrated myself at his holy feet.

" 'I called you here,' Babaji went on. 'That is why you lost your way and were led to my temporary abode in this cave. It is a long time since our last meeting; I am pleased to greet you once more.'

10 There are many methods, it appears, for outwitting a tiger. An Australian explorer, Francis Birtles, has recounted that he found the Indian jungles 'varied, beautiful, and safe.' His safety charm was flypaper. "Every night I spread a quantity of sheets around my camp and was never disturbed," he explained. "The reason is psychological. The tiger is an animal of great conscious dignity. He prowls around and challenges man until he comes to the flypaper; he then slinks away. No dignified tiger would dare face a human being after squatting down upon a sticky flypaper!"
11 After I returned to America I took off sixty-five pounds.

"The deathless master blessed me with some words of spiritual help, then added: 'I give you a message for Yogananda. He will pay you a visit on his return to India. Many matters connected with his guru and with the surviving disciples of Lahiri will keep Yogananda fully occupied. Tell him, then, that I won't see him this time, as he is eagerly hoping; but I shall see him on some other occasion.' "

I was deeply touched to receive from Keshabananda's lips this consoling promise from Babaji A certain hurt in my heart vanished; I grieved no longer that, even as Sri Yukteswar had hinted, Babaji did not appear at the *Kumbha Mela*.

Spending one night as guests of the ashram, our party set out the following afternoon for Calcutta. Riding over a bridge of the Yamuna River, we enjoyed a magnificent view of the skyline of Brindaban just as the sun set fire to the sky – a veritable furnace of Vulcan in colour, reflected below us in the still waters.

The Yamuna beach is hallowed by memories of the child Sri Krishna. Here he engaged with innocent sweetness in his *lilas* (plays) with the *gopis* (maids), exemplifying the supernal love which ever exists between a divine incarnation and his devotees. The life of Lord Krishna has been misunderstood by many Western commentators. Scriptural allegory is baffling to literal minds. A hilarious blunder by a translator will illustrate this point. The story concerns an inspired medieval saint, the cobbler Ravidas, who sang in the simple terms of his own trade of the spiritual glory hidden in all mankind:

> Under the vast vault of blue
> Lives the divinity clothed in hide.

One turns aside to hide a smile on hearing the pedestrian interpretation given to Ravidas' poem by a Western writer:

> "He afterwards built a hut, set up in it an idol which he made from
> a hide, and applied himself to its worship."

Ravidas was a brother disciple of the great Kabir. One of Ravidas' exalted chelas was the Rani of Chitor. She invited a large number of Brahmins to a feast in honour of her teacher, but they refused to eat with a lowly cobbler. As they sat down in dignified aloofness to eat their own uncontaminated meal, lo! each Brahmin found at his side the form of Ravidas. This mass vision accomplished a widespread spiritual revival in Chitor.

In a few days our little group reached Calcutta. Eager to see Sri Yukteswar, I was disappointed to hear that he had left Serampore and was now in Puri, about three hundred miles to the south.

COME TO PURI ASHRAM AT ONCE. This telegram was sent on March 8th by a brother disciple to Atul Chandra Roy Chowdhry, one of Master's chelas in Calcutta. News of the message reached my ears; anguished at its implications, I dropped to my knees and implored God that my guru's life be spared. As I was about to leave Father's home for the train, a divine voice spoke within.

"Do not go to Puri tonight. Thy prayer cannot be granted."

"Lord," I said, grief-stricken, "Thou dost not wish to engage with me in a 'tug of war' at Puri, where Thou wilt have to deny my incessant prayers for Master's life. Must he, then, depart for higher duties at Thy behest?"

In obedience to the inward command, I did not leave that night for Puri. The following evening I set out for the train; on the way, at seven o'clock, a black astral cloud suddenly covered the sky.[12] Later, while the train roared toward Puri, a vision of Sri Yukteswar appeared before me. He was sitting, very grave of countenance, with a light on each side.

"Is it all over?" I lifted my arms beseechingly.

He nodded, then slowly vanished.

As I stood on the Puri train platform the following morning, still hoping against hope, an unknown man approached me.

"Have you heard that your Master is gone?" He left me without another word; I never discovered who he was nor how he had known where to find me.

Stunned, I swayed against the platform wall, realizing that in diverse ways my guru was trying to convey to me the devastating news. Seething with rebellion, my soul was like a volcano. By the time I reached the Puri hermitage I was nearing collapse. The inner voice was tenderly repeating: "Collect yourself. Be calm."

I entered the ashram room where Master's body, unimaginably lifelike, was sitting in the lotus posture – a picture of health and loveliness. A short time before his passing, my guru had been slightly ill with fever, but before the day of his ascension into the Infinite, his body had become completely well. No matter how often I looked at his dear form I could not realize that its life had departed. His skin was smooth and soft; in his face was a beatific expression of tranquillity. He had consciously relinquished his body at the hour of mystic summoning.

"The Lion of Bengal is gone!" I cried in a daze.

I conducted the solemn rites on March 10th. Sri Yukteswar was buried[13] with the ancient rituals of the swamis in the garden of his Puri ashram. His

12 Sri Yukteswar entered *mahasamadi* at this hour – 7:00 P.M., March 09, 1936.
13 Funeral customs in India require cremation for householders; swamis and monks of other orders are not cremated, but buried. (There are occasional exceptions.) The bodies of monks are symbolically considered to have undergone cremation in the fire of wisdom at the time of taking the monastic vow. (See pg. 160)

disciples later arrived from far and near to honour their guru at a vernal equinox memorial service. The *Amrita Bazar Patrika,* leading newspaper of Calcutta, carried his picture and the following report:

The death *Bhandara* ceremony for Srimat Swami Sri Yukteswar Giri Maharaj, aged 81, took place at Puri on March 21. Many disciples came down to Puri for the rites.

One of the greatest expounders of the *Bhagavad Gita,* Swami Maharaj was a great disciple of Yogiraj Sri Shyama Charan Lahiri Mahasaya of Benares. Swami Maharaj was the founder of several Yogoda Sat-Sanga (Self Realization Fellowship) centres in India, and was the great inspiration behind the yoga movement which was carried to the West by Swami Yogananda, his principal disciple. It was Sri Yukteswarji's prophetic powers and deep realization that inspired Swami Yogananda to cross the oceans and spread in America the message of the masters of India.

His interpretations of the *Bhagavad Gita* and other scriptures testify to the depth of Sri Yukteswarji's command of the philosophy, both Eastern and Western, and remain as an eye-opener for the unity between Orient and Occident. As he believed in the unity of all religious faiths, Sri Yukteswar Maharaj established *Sadhu Sabha* (Society of Saints) with the cooperation of leaders of various sects and faiths, for the inculcation of a scientific spirit in religion. At the time of his demise he nominated Swami Yogananda his successor as the president of *Sadhu Sabha.*

India is really poorer today by the passing of such a great man. May all fortunate enough to have come near him inculcate in themselves the true spirit of India's culture and *sadhana* which was personified in him.

I returned to Calcutta. Not trusting myself as yet to go to the Serampore hermitage with its sacred memories, I summoned Prafulla, Sri Yukteswar's little disciple in Serampore, and made arrangements for him to enter the Ranchi school.

"The morning you left for the Allahabad *mela,*" Prafulla told me, "Master dropped heavily on the davenport.

" 'Yogananda is gone!' he cried. 'Yogananda is gone!' He added cryptically, 'I shall have to tell him some other way.' He sat then for hours in silence."

My days were filled with lectures, classes, interviews, and reunions with old friends. Beneath a hollow smile and a life of ceaseless activity, a stream of black brooding polluted the inner river of bliss which for so many years had meandered under the sands of all my perceptions.

"Where has that divine sage gone?" I cried silently from the depths of a tormented spirit.

No answer came.

"It is best that Master has completed his union with the Cosmic Beloved," my mind assured me. "He is eternally glowing in the dominion of deathlessness."

"Never again may you see him in the old Serampore mansion," my heart lamented. "No longer may you bring your friends to meet him, or proudly say: 'Behold, there sits India's *Jnanavatar*!' "

Mr. Wright made arrangements for our party to sail from Bombay for the West in early June. After a fortnight in May of farewell banquets and speeches at Calcutta, Miss Bletch, Mr. Wright and myself left in the Ford for Bombay. On our arrival, the ship authorities asked us to cancel our passage, as no room could be found for the Ford, which we would need again in Europe.

"Never mind," I said gloomily to Mr. Wright. "I want to return once more to Puri." I silently added, "Let my tears once again water the grave of my guru."

43. *The Resurrection of Sri Yukteswar*

"LORD KRISHNA!" The glorious form of the avatar appeared in a shimmering blaze as I sat in my room at the Regent Hotel in Bombay. Shining over the roof of a high building across the street, the ineffable vision had suddenly burst on my sight as I gazed out of my long open third-story window.

The divine figure waved to me, smiling and nodding in greeting. When I could not understand the exact message of Lord Krishna, he departed with a gesture of blessing. Wondrously uplifted, I felt that some spiritual event was presaged.

My Western voyage had, for the time being, been cancelled. I was scheduled for several public addresses in Bombay before leaving on a return visit to Bengal.

Sitting on my bed in the Bombay hotel at three o'clock in the afternoon of June 19, 1936 – one week after the vision of Krishna – I was roused from my meditation by a beatific light. Before my open and astonished eyes, the whole room was transformed into a strange world, the sunlight transmuted into supernal splendour.

Waves of rapture engulfed me as I beheld the flesh and blood form of Sri Yukteswar!

"My son!" Master spoke tenderly, on his face an angel-bewitching smile. For the first time in my life I did not kneel at his feet in greeting but instantly advanced to gather him hungrily in my arms. Moment of moments! The anguish of past months was toll I counted weightless against the torrential bliss now descending.

"Master mine, beloved of my heart, why did you leave me?" I was incoherent in an excess of joy. "Why did you let me go to the *Kumbha Mela?* How bitterly have I blamed myself for leaving you!"

"I did not want to interfere with your happy anticipation of seeing the pilgrimage spot where first I met Babaji. I left you only for a little while; am I not with you again?"

"But is it *you,* Master, the same Lion of God? Are you wearing a body like the one I buried beneath the cruel Puri sands?"

"Yes, my child, I am the same. This is a flesh and blood body. Though I see it as ethereal, to your sight it is physical. From the cosmic atoms I created an entirely new body, exactly like that cosmic-dream physical body which you laid beneath the dream-sands at Puri in your dream-world. I am in truth resurrected – not on earth but on an astral planet. Its inhabitants are better able than earthly humanity to meet my lofty standards. There you and your exalted loved ones shall someday come to be with me."

"Deathless guru, tell me more!"

Master gave a quick, mirthful chuckle. "Please, dear one," he said, "won't you relax your hold a little?"

"Only a little!" I had been embracing him with an octopus grip. I could detect the same faint, fragrant, natural odour which had been characteristic of his body before. The thrilling touch of his divine flesh still persists around the inner sides of my arms and in my palms whenever I recall those glorious hours.

"As prophets are sent on earth to help men work out their physical karma, so I have been directed by God to serve on an astral planet as a savior," Sri Yukteswar explained. "It is called *Hiranyaloka* or 'Illumined Astral Planet.' There I am aiding advanced beings to rid themselves of astral karma and thus attain liberation from astral rebirths. The dwellers on Hiranyaloka are highly developed spiritually; all of them had acquired, in their last earth-incarnation, the meditation-given power of consciously leaving their physical bodies at death. No one can enter Hiranyaloka unless he has passed on earth beyond the state of *sabikalpa samadhi* into the higher state of *nirbikalpa samadhi*.[1]

"The Hiranyaloka inhabitants have already passed through the ordinary astral spheres, where nearly all beings from earth must go at death; there they

---

1 In *sabikalpa samadhi* the devotee has spiritually progressed to a state of inward divine union, but cannot maintain his cosmic consciousness except in the immobile trance-state. By continuous meditation, he attains the superior state of *nirbikalpa samadhi*, moving freely in the world and performs his outward duties without any loss of God-realization.

worked out many seeds of their past actions in the astral worlds. None but advanced beings can perform such redemptive work effectually in the astral worlds. Then, in order to free their souls more fully from the cocoon of karmic traces lodged in their astral bodies, these higher beings were drawn by cosmic law to be reborn with new astral bodies on Hiranyaloka, the astral sun or heaven, where I have resurrected to help them. There are also highly advanced beings on Hiranyaloka who have come from the superior, subtler, causal world."

My mind was now in such perfect attunement with my guru's that he was conveying his word-pictures to me partly by speech and partly by thought-transference. I was thus quickly receiving his idea-tabloids.

"You have read in the scriptures," Master went on, "that God encased the human soul successively in three bodies – the idea, or causal body; the subtle astral body seat of man's mental and emotional natures; and the gross physical body. On earth a man is equipped with his physical senses. An astral being works with his consciousness and feelings and a body made of lifetrons.[2] A causal-bodied being remains in the blissful realm of ideas. My work is with those astral beings who are preparing to enter the causal world."

"Adorable Master, please tell me more about the astral cosmos." Though I had slightly relaxed my embrace at Sri Yukteswar's request, my arms were still around him. Treasure beyond all treasures, my guru who had laughed at death to reach me!

"There are many astral planets, teeming with astral beings," Master began. "The inhabitants use astral planes, or masses of light, to travel from one planet to another, faster than electricity and radioactive energies.

"The astral universe, made of various subtle vibrations of light and colour, is hundreds of times larger than the material cosmos. The entire physical creation hangs like a little solid basket under the huge luminous balloon of the astral sphere. Just as many physical suns and stars roam in space, so there are also countless astral solar and stellar systems. Their planets have astral suns and moons, more beautiful than the physical ones. The astral luminaries resemble the aurora borealis – the sunny astral aurora being more dazzling than the mild-rayed moon aurora. The astral day and night are longer than those of earth.

"The astral world is infinitely beautiful, clean, pure, and orderly. There are no dead plants or barren lands. The terrestrial blemishes – weeds, bacteria, insects, snakes – are absent. Unlike the variable climates and seasons of the

2 Sri Yukteswar used the word *prana;* I have translated it as lifetrons. The Hindu scriptures refer not only to the *anu*, 'atom,' and to the *paramanu*, 'beyond the atom,' finer electronic energies; but also to *prana*, 'creative lifetronic force.' Atoms and electrons are blind forces; *prana* is inherently intelligent. The pranic lifetrons in the spermatozoa and ova, for instance, guide the embryonic development according to a karmic design.

earth, the astral planets maintain the even temperature of an eternal spring, with occasional luminous white snow and rain of many-coloured lights. Astral planets abound in opal lakes and bright seas and rainbow rivers.

"The ordinary astral universe – not the subtler astral heaven of Hiranyaloka – is peopled with millions of astral beings who have come, more or less recently, from the earth, and also with myriads of fairies, mermaids, fishes, animals, goblins, gnomes, demigods and spirits, all residing on different astral planets in accordance with karmic qualifications. Various spheric mansions or vibratory regions are provided for good and evil spirits. Good ones can travel freely, but the evil spirits are confined to limited zones. In the same way that human beings live on the surface of the earth, worms inside the soil, fish in water, and birds in air, so astral beings of different grades are assigned to suitable vibratory quarters.

"Among the fallen dark angels expelled from other worlds, friction and war take place with lifetronic bombs or mental *mantric*[3] vibratory rays. These beings dwell in the gloom-drenched regions of the lower astral cosmos, working out their evil karma.

"In the vast realms above the dark astral prison, all is shining and beautiful. The astral cosmos is more naturally attuned than the earth to the divine will and plan of perfection. Every astral object is manifested primarily by the will of God, and partially by the will-call of astral beings. They possess the power of modifying or enhancing the grace and form of anything already created by the Lord. He has given His astral children the freedom and privilege of changing or improving at will the astral cosmos. On earth a solid must be transformed into liquid or other form through natural or chemical processes, but astral solids are changed into astral liquids, gases, or energy solely and instantly by the will of the inhabitants.

"The earth is dark with warfare and murder in the sea, land, and air," my guru continued, "but the astral realms know a happy harmony and equality. Astral beings dematerialize or materialize their forms at will. Flowers or fish or animals can metamorphose themselves, for a time, into astral men. All astral beings are free to assume any form, and can easily commune together. No fixed, definite, natural law hems them round – any astral tree, for example, can be successfully asked to produce an astral mango or other desired fruit, flower, or indeed any other object. Certain karmic restrictions are present, but there are no distinctions in the astral world about desirability of various forms. Everything is vibrant with God's creative light.

3 Adjective of *mantra*, chanted seed-sounds discharged by the mental gun of concentration. The *Puranas* (ancient *shastras* or treatises) describe these *mantric* wars between *devas* and *asuras* (gods and demons). An *asura* once tried to slay a *deva* with a potent chant. But his mispronunciations resulted in a boomerang and killed the demon.

"No one is born of woman; offspring are materialized by astral beings through the help of their cosmic will into specially patterned, astrally condensed forms. The recently physically disembodied being arrives in an astral family through invitation, drawn by similar mental and spiritual tendencies.

"The astral body is not subject to cold or heat or other natural conditions. The anatomy includes an astral brain, or the thousand-petaled lotus of light, and six awakened centres in the *sushumna,* or astral cerebro-spinal axis. The heart draws cosmic energy as well as light from the astral brain, and pumps it to the astral nerves and body cells, or lifetrons. Astral beings can affect their bodies by lifetronic force or by *mantric* vibrations.

"In most cases the astral body is an exact counterpart of the last physical form. Astral beings retain the same appearance which they possessed in youth in their previous earthly sojourn; occasionally an astral being chooses, like myself, to retain his old age appearance." Master, emanating the very essence of youth, chuckled merrily.

"Unlike the spacial, three-dimensional physical world cognized only by the five senses, the astral spheres are visible to the all-inclusive sixth sense – intuition," Sri Yukteswar went on. "By sheer intuitional feeling, all astral beings see, hear, smell, taste, and touch. They possess three eyes, two of which are partly closed. The third and chief astral eye, vertically placed on the forehead, is open. Astral beings have all the outer sensory organs – ears, eyes, nose, tongue, and skin – but they employ the intuitional sense to experience sensations through any part of the body; they can see through the ear, or nose, or skin. They are able to hear through the eyes or tongue, and can taste through the ears or skin, and so forth.[4]

"Man's physical body is exposed to countless dangers, and is easily hurt or maimed; the ethereal astral body may occasionally be cut or bruised but is healed at once by mere willing."

"Gurudeva, are all astral persons beautiful?"

"Beauty in the astral world is known to be a spiritual quality, and not an outward conformation," Sri Yukteswar replied. "Astral beings therefore attach little importance to facial features. They have the privilege, however, of costuming themselves at will with new, colourful, astrally materialized bodies. Just as worldly men don new array for gala events, so astral beings find occasions to bedeck themselves in specially designed forms.

"Joyous astral festivities on the higher astral planets like Hiranyaloka take place when a being is liberated from the astral world through spiritual advancement, and is therefore ready to enter the heaven of the causal world.

4 Examples of such powers are not wanting even on earth, as in the case of Helen Keller and other rare beings.

On such occasions the Invisible Heavenly Father, and the saints who are merged in Him, materialize Themselves into bodies of Their own choice and join the astral celebration. In order to please His beloved devotee, the Lord takes any desired form. If the devotee worshiped through devotion, he sees God as the Divine Mother. To Jesus, the Father-aspect of the Infinite One was appealing beyond other conceptions. The individuality with which the Creator has endowed each of His creatures makes every conceivable and inconceivable demand on the Lord's versatility!"

My guru and I laughed happily together.

"Friends of other lives easily recognize one another in the astral world," Sri Yukteswar went on in his beautiful, flutelike voice. "Rejoicing at the immortality of friendship, they realize the indestructibility of love, often doubted at the time of the sad, delusive partings of earthly life.

"The intuition of astral beings pierces through the veil and observes human activities on earth, but man cannot view the astral world unless his sixth sense is somewhat developed. Thousands of earth-dwellers have momentarily glimpsed an astral being or an astral world.[5]

"The advanced beings on Hiranyaloka remain mostly awake in ecstasy during the long astral day and night, helping to work out intricate problems of cosmic government and the redemption of prodigal sons, earthbound souls. When the Hiranyaloka beings sleep, they have occasional dreamlike astral visions. Their minds are usually engrossed in the conscious state of highest *nirbikalpa* bliss.

"Inhabitants in all parts of the astral worlds are still subject to mental agonies. The sensitive minds of the higher beings on planets like Hiranyaloka feel keen pain if any mistake is made in conduct or perception of truth. These advanced beings endeavor to attune their every act and thought with the perfection of spiritual law.

"Communication among the astral inhabitants is held entirely by astral telepathy and television; there is none of the confusion and misunderstanding of the written and spoken word which earth-dwellers must endure. Just as persons on the cinema screen appear to move and act through a series of light pictures, and do not actually breathe, so the astral beings walk and work as intelligently guided and coordinated images of light, without the necessity of drawing power from oxygen. Man depends upon solids, liquids, gases, and energy for sustenance; astral beings sustain themselves principally by cosmic light."

---

5 On earth, pure-minded children are sometimes able to see the graceful astral bodies of fairies. Through drugs or intoxicating drink, whose use is forbidden by all scriptures, a man may so derange his consciousness that he perceives the hideous forms in astral hells.

"Master mine, do astral beings eat anything?" I was drinking in his marvellous elucidations with the receptivity of all my faculties – mind, heart, soul. Superconscious perceptions of truth are permanently real and changeless, while fleeting sense experiences and impressions are never more than temporarily or relatively true, and soon lose in memory all their vividness. My guru's words were so penetratingly imprinted on the parchment of my being that at any time, by transferring my mind to the superconscious state, I can clearly relive the divine experience.

"Luminous ray-like vegetables abound in the astral soils," he answered. "The astral beings consume vegetables, and drink a nectar flowing from glorious fountains of light and from astral brooks and rivers. Just as invisible images of persons on the earth can be dug out of the ether and made visible by a television apparatus, later being dismissed again into space, so the God-created, unseen astral blueprints of vegetables and plants floating in the ether are precipitated on an astral planet by the will of its inhabitants. In the same way, from the wildest fancy of these beings, whole gardens of fragrant flowers are materialized, returning later to the etheric invisibility. Although dwellers on the heavenly planets like Hiranyaloka are almost freed from any necessity of eating, still higher is the unconditioned existence of almost completely liberated souls in the causal world, who eat nothing save the manna of bliss.

"The earth-liberated astral being meets a multitude of relatives, fathers, mothers, wives, husbands, and friends, acquired during different incarnations on earth,[6] as they appear from time to time in various parts of the astral realms. He is therefore at a loss to understand whom to love especially; he learns in this way to give a divine and equal love to all, as children and individualized expressions of God. Though the outward appearance of loved ones may have changed, more or less according to the development of new qualities in the latest life of any particular soul, the astral being employs his unerring intuition to recognize all those once dear to him in other planes of existence, and to welcome them to their new astral home. Because every atom in creation is inextinguishably dowered with individuality,[7] an astral friend will be recognized no matter what costume he may don, even as on earth an actor's identity is discoverable by close observation despite any disguise.

"The span of life in the astral world is much longer than on earth. A normal advanced astral being's average life period is from five hundred to

6 Lord Buddha was once asked why a man should love all persons equally. "Because," the great teacher replied, "in the very numerous and varied lifespans of each man, every other being has at one time or another been dear to him."

7 The eight elemental qualities which enter into all created life, from atom to man, are earth, water, fire, air, ether, motion, mind, and individuality. (*Bhagavad Gita*: VII: 4.)

one thousand years, measured in accordance with earthly standards of time. As certain redwood trees outlive most trees by millenniums, or as some yogis live several hundred years though most men die before the age of sixty, so some astral beings live much longer than the usual span of astral existence. Visitors to the astral world dwell there for a longer or shorter period in accordance with the weight of their physical karma, which draws them back to earth within a specified time.

"The astral being does not have to contend painfully with death at the time of shedding his luminous body. Many of these beings nevertheless feel slightly nervous at the thought of dropping their astral form for the subtler causal one. The astral world is free from unwilling death, disease, and old age. These three dreads are the curse of earth, where man has allowed his consciousness to identify itself almost wholly with a frail physical body requiring constant aid from air, food, and sleep in order to exist at all.

"Physical death is attended by the disappearance of breath and the disintegration of fleshly cells. Astral death consists of the dispersement of lifetrons, those manifest units of energy which constitute the life of astral beings. At physical death a being loses his consciousness of flesh and becomes aware of his subtle body in the astral world. Experiencing astral death in due time, a being thus passes from the consciousness of astral birth and death to that of physical birth and death. These recurrent cycles of astral and physical encasement are the ineluctable destiny of all unenlightened beings. Scriptural definitions of heaven and hell sometimes stir man's deeper-than-subconscious memories of his long series of experiences in the blithesome astral and disappointing terrestrial worlds."

"Beloved Master," I asked, "will you please describe more in detail the difference between rebirth on the earth and in the astral and causal spheres?"

"Man as an individualized soul is essentially causal-bodied," my guru explained. "That body is a matrix of the thirty-five *ideas* required by God as the basic or causal thought forces from which He later formed the subtle astral body of nineteen elements and the gross physical body of sixteen elements.

"The nineteen elements of the astral body are mental, emotional, and lifetronic. The nineteen components are intelligence; ego; feeling; mind (sense-consciousness); five instruments of *knowledge,* the subtle counterparts of the senses of sight, hearing, smell, taste, touch; five instruments of *action,* the mental correspondence for the executive abilities to procreate, excrete, talk, walk, and exercise manual skill; and five instruments of *life force,* those empowered to perform the crystallizing, assimilating, eliminating, metabolizing, and circulating functions of the body. This subtle astral encasement of nineteen elements survives the death of the physical body, which is made of sixteen gross metallic and nonmetallic elements.

"God thought out different ideas within Himself and projected them into dreams. Lady Cosmic Dream thus sprang out decorated in all her colossal endless ornaments of relativity.

"In thirty-five thought categories of the causal body, God elaborated all the complexities of man's nineteen astral and sixteen physical counterparts. By condensation of vibratory forces, first subtle, then gross, He produced man's astral body and finally his physical form. According to the law of relativity, by which the Prime Simplicity has become the bewildering manifold, the causal cosmos and causal body are different from the astral cosmos and astral body; the physical cosmos and physical body are likewise characteristically at variance with the other forms of creation.

The fleshly body is made of the fixed, objectified dreams of the Creator. The dualities are ever-present on earth: disease and health, pain and pleasure, loss and gain. Human beings find limitation and resistance in three-dimensional matter. When man's desire to live is severely shaken by disease or other causes, death arrives; the heavy overcoat of the flesh is temporarily shed. The soul, however, remains encased in the astral and causal bodies.[8] The adhesive force by which all three bodies are held together is desire. The power of unfulfilled desires is the root of all man's slavery.

"Physical desires are rooted in egotism and sense pleasures. The compulsion or temptation of sensory experience is more powerful than the desire-force connected with astral attachments or causal perceptions.

"Astral desires centre around enjoyment in terms of vibration. Astral beings enjoy the ethereal music of the spheres and are entranced by the sight of all creation as exhaustless expressions of changing light. The astral beings also smell, taste, and touch light. Astral desires are thus connected with an astral being's power to precipitate all objects and experiences as forms of light or as condensed thoughts or dreams.

"Causal desires are fulfilled by perception only. The nearly-free beings who are encased only in the causal body see the whole universe as realizations of the dream-ideas of God; they can materialize anything and everything in sheer thought. Causal beings therefore consider the enjoyment of physical sensations or astral delights as gross and suffocating to the soul's fine sensibilities. Causal beings work out their desires by materializing them instantly.[9] Those who find themselves covered only by the delicate veil of the causal body can bring universes into manifestation even as the Creator. Because all creation is made of the cosmic dream-texture, the soul thinly clothed in the causal has vast realizations of power.

8 Body signifies any soul-encasement, whether gross or subtle. The three bodies are cages for the Bird of Paradise.
9 Even as Babaji helped Lahiri Mahasaya to rid himself of a subconscious desire from some past life for a palace, as described in chapter 34.

"A soul, being invisible by nature, can be distinguished only by the presence of its body or bodies. The mere presence of a body signifies that its existence is made possible by unfulfilled desires.[10]

"So long as the soul of man is encased in one, two, or three body-containers, sealed tightly with the corks of ignorance and desires, he cannot merge with the sea of Spirit. When the gross physical receptacle is destroyed by the hammer of death, the other two coverings – astral and causal – still remain to prevent the soul from consciously joining the Omnipresent Life. When desirelessness is attained through wisdom, its power disintegrates the two remaining vessels. The tiny human soul emerges, free at last; it is one with the Measureless Amplitude."

I asked my divine guru to shed further light on the high and mysterious causal world.

"The causal world is indescribably subtle," he replied. "In order to understand it, one would have to possess such tremendous powers of concentration that he could close his eyes and visualize the astral cosmos and the physical cosmos in all their vastness – the luminous balloon with the solid basket – as existing in ideas only. If by this superhuman concentration one succeeded in converting or resolving the two cosmoses with all their complexities into sheer ideas, he would then reach the causal world and stand on the borderline of fusion between mind and matter. There one perceives all created things – solids, liquids, gases, electricity, energy, all beings, gods, men, animals, plants, bacteria – as forms of consciousness, just as a man can close his eyes and realize that he exists, even though his body is invisible to his physical eyes and is present only as an idea.

"Whatever a human being can do in fancy, a causal being can do in reality. The most colossal imaginative human intelligence is able, in mind only, to range from one extreme of thought to another, to skip mentally from planet to planet, or tumble endlessly down a pit of eternity, or soar rocket-like into the galaxied canopy, or scintillate like a searchlight over milky ways and the starry spaces. But beings in the causal world have a much greater freedom, and can effortlessly manifest their thoughts into instant objectivity, without any material or astral obstruction or karmic limitation.

"Causal beings realize that the physical cosmos is not primarily constructed of electrons, nor is the astral cosmos basically composed of lifetrons – both in reality are created from the minutest particles of God-

10 'And he said unto them, wheresoever the body is, thither will the eagles be gathered together.' – *Luke* 17: 37. Wherever the soul is encased in the physical body or in the astral body or in the causal body, there the eagles of desires – which prey on human sense weaknesses, or on astral and causal attachments – will also gather to keep the soul a prisoner.

thought, chopped and divided by *maya,* the law of relativity that apparently intervenes to separate creation from its Creator.

"Souls in the causal world recognize one another as individualized points of joyous Spirit; their thought-things are the only objects which surround them. Causal beings see the difference between their bodies and thoughts to be merely ideas. As a man, closing his eyes, can visualize a dazzling white light or a faint blue haze, so causal beings by thought alone are able to see, hear, feel, taste, and touch; they create anything, or dissolve it, by the power of cosmic mind.

"Both death and rebirth in the causal world are in thought. Causal-bodied beings feast only on the ambrosia of eternally new knowledge. They drink from the springs of peace, roam on the trackless soil of perceptions, swim in the ocean-endlessness of bliss. Lo! see their bright thought-bodies zoom past trillions of Spirit-created planets, fresh bubbles of universes, wisdom-stars, spectral dreams of golden nebulae, all over the skiey blue bosom of Infinity!

"Many beings remain for thousands of years in the causal cosmos. By deeper ecstasies the freed soul then withdraws itself from the little causal body and puts on the vastness of the causal cosmos. All the separate eddies of ideas, particularized waves of power, love, will, joy, peace, intuition, calmness, self-control, and concentration melt into the ever-joyous Sea of Bliss. No longer does the soul have to experience its joy as an individualized wave of consciousness, but is merged in the One Cosmic Ocean, with all its waves – eternal laughter, thrills, throbs.

"When a soul is out of the cocoon of the three bodies it escapes forever from the law of relativity and becomes the ineffable Ever-Existent.[11] Behold the butterfly of Omnipresence, its wings etched with stars and moons and suns! The soul expanded into Spirit remains alone in the region of lightless light, darkless dark, thoughtless thought, intoxicated with its ecstasy of joy in God's dream of cosmic creation."

"A free soul!" I ejaculated in awe.

"When a soul finally gets out of the three jars of bodily delusions," Master continued, "it becomes one with the Infinite without any loss of individuality. Christ had won this final freedom even before he was born as Jesus. In three stages of his past, symbolized in his earth-life as the three days of his experience of death and resurrection, he had attained the power to fully arise in Spirit.

"The undeveloped man must undergo countless earthly and astral and causal incarnations in order to emerge from his three bodies. A master

11 "Him that overcometh will I make a pillar in the temple of my God, and he shall go no more out (i.e., shall reincarnate no more). . . . To him that overcometh will I grant to sit with me in my throne, even as I also overcame, and am set down with my Father in his throne." – *Revelation* 3: 12, 21.

who achieves this final freedom may elect to return to earth as a prophet to bring other human beings back to God, or like myself he may choose to reside in the astral cosmos. There a savior assumes some of the burden of the inhabitants' karma[12] and thus helps them to terminate their cycle of reincarnation in the astral cosmos and go on permanently to the causal spheres. Or a freed soul may enter the causal world to aid its beings to shorten their span in the causal body and thus attain the Absolute Freedom."

"Resurrected One, I want to know more about the karma which forces souls to return to the three worlds." I could listen forever, I thought, to my omniscient Master. Never in his earth-life had I been able at one time to assimilate so much of his wisdom. Now for the first time I was receiving a clear, definite insight into the enigmatic interspaces on the checker-board of life and death.

"The physical karma or desires of man must be completely worked out before his permanent stay in astral worlds becomes possible," my guru elucidated in his thrilling voice. "Two kinds of beings live in the astral spheres. Those who still have earthly karma to dispose of and who must therefore reinhabit a gross physical body in order to pay their karmic debts could be classified, after physical death, as temporary visitors to the astral world rather than as permanent residents.

"Beings with unredeemed earthly karma are not permitted after astral death to go to the high causal sphere of cosmic ideas, but must shuttle to and fro from the physical and astral worlds only, conscious successively of their physical body of sixteen gross elements, and of their astral body of nineteen subtle elements. After each loss of his physical body, however, an undeveloped being from the earth remains for the most part in the deep stupor of the death-sleep and is hardly conscious of the beautiful astral sphere. After the astral rest, such a man returns to the material plane for further lessons, gradually accustoming himself, through repeated journeys, to the worlds of subtle astral texture.

"Normal or long-established residents of the astral universe, on the other hand, are those who, freed forever from all material longings, need return no more to the gross vibrations of earth. Such beings have only astral and causal karma to work out. At astral death these beings pass to the infinitely finer and more delicate causal world. Shedding the thought-form of the causal body at the end of a certain span, determined by cosmic law, these advanced beings men return to Hiranyaloka or a similar high astral planet, reborn in a new astral body to work out their unredeemed astral karma.

12 Sri Yukteswar was signifying that, even as in his earthly incarnation he had occasionally assumed the weight of disease to lighten his disciples' karma, so in the astral world his mission as a savior enabled him to take on certain astral karma of dwellers on *Hiranyaloka*, and thus hasten their evolution into the higher causal world.

"My son, you may now comprehend more fully that I am resurrected by divine decree," Sri Yukteswar continued, "as a savior of astrally reincarnating souls coming back from the causal sphere, in particular, rather than of those astral beings who are coming up from the earth. Those from the earth, if they still retain vestiges of material karma, do not rise to the very high astral planets like Hiranyaloka.

"Just as most people on earth have not learned through meditation-acquired vision to appreciate the superior joys and advantages of astral life and thus, after death, desire to return to the limited, imperfect pleasures of earth, so many astral beings, during the normal disintegration of their astral bodies, fail to picture the advanced state of spiritual joy in the causal world and, dwelling on thoughts of the more gross and gaudy astral happiness, yearn to revisit the astral paradise. Heavy astral karma must be redeemed by such beings before they can achieve after astral death a permanent stay in the causal thought-world, so thinly partitioned from the Creator.

"Only when a being has no further desires for experiences in the pleasing-to-the-eye astral cosmos, and cannot be tempted to go back there, does he remain in the causal world. Completing there the work of redeeming all causal karma or seeds of past desires, the confined soul thrusts out the last of the three corks of ignorance and, emerging from the final jar of the causal body, commingles with the Eternal.

"Now do you understand?" Master smiled so enchantingly!

"Yes, through your grace. I am speechless with joy and gratitude."

Never from song or story had I ever received such inspiring knowledge. Though the Hindu scriptures refer to the causal and astral worlds and to man's three bodies, how remote and meaningless those pages compared with the warm authenticity of my resurrected Master! For him indeed existed not a single 'undiscover'd country from whose bourn no traveller returns'![13]

"The interpenetration of man's three bodies is expressed in many ways through his threefold nature," my great guru went on. "In the wakeful state on earth a human being is conscious more or less of his three vehicles. When he is sensuously intent on tasting, smelling, touching, listening, or seeing, he is working principally through his physical body. Visualizing or willing, he is working mainly through his astral body. His causal medium finds expression when man is thinking or diving deep in introspection or meditation; the cosmical thoughts of genius come to the man who habitually contacts his causal body. In this sense an individual may be classified broadly as 'a material man,' 'an energetic man,' or 'an intellectual man.'

13 *Bourn*: destination. Shakespeare's *Hamlet* (Act III, Scene 1).

"A man identifies himself about sixteen hours daily with his physical vehicle. Then he sleeps; if he dreams, he remains in his astral body, effortlessly creating any object even as do the astral beings. If man's sleep be deep and dreamless, for several hours he is able to transfer his consciousness, or sense of *I*-ness, to the causal body; such sleep is revivifying. A dreamer is contacting his astral and not his causal body; his sleep is not fully refreshing."

I had been lovingly observing Sri Yukteswar while he gave his wondrous exposition.

"Angelic guru," I said, "your body looks exactly as it did when last I wept over it in the Puri ashram."

"O yes, my new body is a perfect copy of the old one. I materialize or dematerialize this form any time at will, much more frequently than I did while on earth. By quick dematerialization, I now travel instantly by light express from planet to planet or, indeed, from astral to causal or to physical cosmos." My divine guru smiled. "Though you move about so fast these days, I had no difficulty in finding you at Bombay!"

"O Master, I was grieving so deeply about your death!"

"Ah, wherein did I die? Isn't there some contradiction?" Sri Yukteswar's eyes were twinkling with love and amusement.

"You were only dreaming on earth; on that earth you saw my dream-body," he went on. "Later you buried that dream-image. Now my finer fleshly body – which you behold and are even now embracing rather closely! – is resurrected on another finer dream-planet of God. Someday that finer dream-body and finer dream-planet will pass away; they too are not forever. All dream-bubbles must eventually burst at a final wakeful touch. Differentiate, my son Yogananda, between dreams and Reality!"

This idea of *Vedantic*[14] resurrection struck me with wonder. I was ashamed that I had pitied Master when I had seen his lifeless body at Puri. I comprehended at last that my guru had always been fully awake in God, perceiving his own life and passing on earth, and his present resurrection, as nothing more than relativities of divine ideas in the cosmic dream.

"I have now told you, Yogananda, the truths of my life, death, and resurrection. Grieve not for me; rather broadcast everywhere the story of my resurrection from the God-dreamed earth of men to another God-dreamed planet of astrally garbed souls! New hope will be infused into the hearts of misery-mad, death-fearing dreamers of the world."

"Yes, Master!" How willingly would I share with others my joy at his resurrection!

14 Life and death as relativities of thought only. *Vedanta* says that God is the only Reality; all creation or separate existence is *maya* or illusion. This philosophy of monism is at its highest in the *Upanishad* commentaries of Shankara.

"On earth my standards were uncomfortably high, unsuited to the natures of most men. Often I scolded you more than I should have. You passed my test; your love shone through the clouds of all reprimands." He added tenderly, "I have also come today to tell you: Never again shall I wear the stern gaze of censure. I shall scold you no more."

How much I had missed the chastisements of my great guru! Each one had been a guardian angel of protection.

"Dearest Master! Rebuke me a million times – do scold me now!"

"I shall chide you no more." His divine voice was grave, yet with an undercurrent of laughter. "You and I shall smile together, so long as our two forms appear different in the *maya*-dream of God. Finally we shall merge as one in the Cosmic Beloved; our smiles shall be His smile, our unified song of joy vibrating throughout eternity to be broadcast to God-tuned souls!"

Sri Yukteswar gave me light on certain matters which I cannot reveal here. During the two hours that he spent with me in the Bombay hotel room he answered my every question. A number of world prophecies uttered by him that June day in 1936 have already come to pass.

"I leave you now, beloved one!" At these words I felt Master melting away within my encircling arms.

"My child," his voice rang out, vibrating into my very soul-firmament, "whenever you enter the door of *nirbikalpa samadhi* and call on me, I shall come to you in flesh and blood, even as today."

With this celestial promise Sri Yukteswar vanished from my sight. A cloud-voice repeated in musical thunder: "Tell all! Whosoever knows by *nirbikalpa* realization that your earth is a dream of God can come to the finer dream-created planet of Hiranyaloka, and there find me resurrected in a body exactly like my earthly one. Yogananda, tell all!"

Gone was the sorrow of parting. The pity and grief for his death, long robber of my peace, now fled in stark shame. Bliss poured forth like a fountain through endless, newly opened soul-pores. Anciently clogged with disuse, they now widened in purity at the driving flood of ecstasy. Subconscious thoughts and feelings of my past incarnations shed their karmic taints, lustrously renewed by Sri Yukteswar's divine visit.

In this chapter of my autobiography I have obeyed my guru's behest and spread the glad tiding, though they confound once more an incurious generation. Groveling, man knows well; despair is seldom alien; yet these are perversities, no part of man's true lot. The day he wills, he is set on the path to freedom. Too long has he hearkened to the dank pessimism of his 'dust-thou-art' counselors, heedless of the unconquerable soul.

I was not the only one privileged to behold the Resurrected Guru.

One of Sri Yukteswar's chelas was an aged woman, affectionately known as *Ma* (Mother), whose home was close to the Puri hermitage. Master had often stopped to chat with her during his morning walk. On the evening of March 16, 1936, Ma arrived at the ashram and asked to see her guru.

"Why, Master died a week ago!" Swami Sebananda, now in charge of the Puri hermitage, looked at her sadly.

"That's impossible!" She smiled a little. "Perhaps you are just trying to protect the guru from insistent visitors?"

"No." Sebananda recounted details of the burial. "Come," he said, "I will take you to the front garden to Sri Yukteswarji's grave."

Ma shook her head. "There is no grave for him! This morning at ten o'clock he passed in his usual walk before my door! I talked to him for several minutes in the bright outdoors.

" 'Come this evening to the ashram,' he said.

"I am here! Blessings pour on this old gray head! The deathless guru wanted me to understand in what transcendent body he had visited me this morning!"

The astounded Sebananda knelt before her.

"Ma," he said, "what a weight of grief you lift from my heart! He is risen!"

44. *With Mahatma Gandhi at Wardha*

"WELCOME TO WARDHA!" Mahadev Desai, secretary to Mahatma Gandhi, greeted Miss Bletch, Mr. Wright, and myself with these cordial words and the gift of wreaths of *khaddar* (homespun cotton). Our little group had just dismounted at the Wardha station on an early morning in August, glad to leave the dust and heat of the train. Consigning our luggage to a bullock cart, we entered an open motor car with Mr. Desai and his companions, Babasaheb Deshmukh and Dr. Pingale. A short drive over the muddy country roads brought us to *Maganvadi,* the ashram of India's political saint.

Mr. Desai led us at once to the writing room where, cross-legged, sat Mahatma Gandhi. Pen in one hand and a scrap of paper in the other, on his face a vast, winning, warm-hearted smile!

"Welcome!" he scribbled in Hindi; it was a Monday, his weekly day of silence.

Though this was our first meeting, we beamed on each other affectionately. In 1925 Mahatma Gandhi had honoured the Ranchi school by a visit, and had inscribed in its guest-book a gracious tribute.

The tiny 100-pound saint radiated physical, mental, and spiritual health. His soft brown eyes shone with intelligence, sincerity, and discrimination; this statesman has matched wits and emerged the victor in a thousand legal, social, and political battles. No other leader in the world has attained the secure niche in the hearts of his people that Gandhi occupies for India's unlettered millions. Their spontaneous tribute is his famous title – *Mahatma*, 'great soul.'[1] For them alone Gandhi confines his attire to the widely-cartooned loincloth, symbol of his oneness with the downtrodden masses who can afford no more.

"The ashram residents are wholly at your disposal; please call on them for any service." With characteristic courtesy, the Mahatma handed me this hastily-written note as Mr. Desai led our party from the writing room toward the guest house.

Our guide led us through orchards and flowering fields to a tile-roofed building with latticed windows. A front-yard well, twenty-five feet across, was used, Mr. Desai said, for watering stock; near-by stood a revolving cement wheel for threshing rice. Each of our small bedrooms proved to contain only the irreducible minimum – a bed, handmade of rope. The white-washed kitchen boasted a faucet in one corner and a fire pit for cooking in another. Simple Arcadian sounds reached our ears – the cries of crows and sparrows, the lowing of cattle, and the rap of chisels being used to chip stones.

Observing Mr. Wright's travel diary, Mr. Desai opened a page and wrote on it a list of *Satyagraha*[2] vows taken by all the Mahatma's strict followers (*satyagrahis*):

"Nonviolence; Truth; Non-Stealing; Celibacy; Non-Possession; Body-Labour; Control of the Palate; Fearlessness; Equal Respect for all Religions; *Swadeshi* (use of home manufactures); Freedom from Untouchability. These eleven should be observed as vows in a spirit of humility."

(Gandhi himself signed this page on the following day, giving the date also – August 27, 1935.)

Two hours after our arrival my companions and I were summoned to lunch. The Mahatma was already seated under the arcade of the ashram porch, across the courtyard from his study. About twenty-five barefooted *satyagrahis* were squatting before brass cups and plates. A community chorus of prayer; then a meal served from large brass pots containing *chapatis* (whole-wheat unleavened bread) sprinkled with *ghee; talsari* (boiled and diced vegetables), and a lemon jam.

The Mahatma ate *chapatis,* boiled beets, some raw vegetables, and oranges. On the side of his plate was a large lump of very bitter *neem* leaves, a notable blood cleanser. With his spoon he separated a portion and placed it on my dish. I bolted it down with water, remembering childhood days when Mother had forced me to swallow the disagreeable dose. Gandhi,

1 His family name is Mohandas Karamchand Gandhi. He never refers to himself as 'Mahatma.'
2 Translation from Sanskrit is 'holding to the truth.' *Satyagraha* is the famous nonviolence movement led by Gandhi.

however, bit by bit was eating the *neem* paste with as much relish as if it had been a delicious sweetmeat.

In this trifling incident I noted the Mahatma's ability to detach his mind from the senses at will. I recalled the famous appendectomy performed on him some years ago. Refusing anesthetics, the saint had chatted cheerfully with his disciples throughout the operation, his infectious smile revealing his unawareness of pain.

The afternoon brought an opportunity for a chat with Gandhi's noted disciple, daughter of an English admiral, Miss Madeleine Slade, now called Mira Behn.[3] Her strong, calm face lit with enthusiasm as she told me, in flawless Hindi, of her daily activities.

"Rural reconstruction work is rewarding! A group of us go every morning at five o'clock to serve the near-by villagers and teach them simple hygiene. We make it a point to clean their latrines and their mud-thatched huts. The villagers are illiterate; they cannot be educated except by example!" She laughed gaily.

I looked in admiration at this highborn Englishwoman whose true Christian humility enables her to do the scavengering work usually performed only by 'untouchables.'

"I came to India in 1925," she told me. "In this land I feel that I have 'come back home.' Now I would never be willing to return to my old life and old interests."

We discussed America for awhile. "I am always pleased and amazed," she said, "to see the deep interest in spiritual subjects exhibited by the many Americans who visit India."[4]

Mira Behn's hands were soon busy at the *charka* (spinning wheel), omnipresent in all the ashram rooms and, indeed, due to the Mahatma, omnipresent throughout rural India.

Gandhi has sound economic and cultural reasons for encouraging the revival of cottage industries, but he does not counsel a fanatical repudiation of all modern progress. Machinery, trains, automobiles, the telegraph have played important parts in his own colossal life! Fifty years of public service, in prison and out, wrestling daily with practical details and harsh realities

3 Mira Behn: Sister Mira; False and alas! malicious reports were recently circulated that Miss Slade has severed all her ties with Gandhi and forsaken her vows. Miss Slade, the Mahatma's *Satyagraha* disciple for twenty years, issued a signed statement to the *United Press*, dated Dec. 29, 1945, in which she explained that a series of baseless rumours arose after she had departed, with Gandhi's blessings, for a small site in northeastern India near the Himalayas, for the purpose of founding there her now-flourishing *Kisan Ashram* (centre for medical and agricultural aid to peasant farmers). Gandhiji plans to visit the new ashram during 1946.
4 Miss Slade reminded me of another distinguished Western woman, Miss Margaret Woodrow Wilson, eldest daughter of America's great president. I met her in New York; she was intensely interested in India. Later she went to Pondicherry, where she spent the last five years of her life, happily pursuing a path of discipline at the feet of Sri Aurobindo Ghosh. This sage (Sri Aurobindo) never speaks; he silently greets his disciples on three annual occasions only.

in the political world, have only increased his balance, open-mindedness, sanity, and humorous appreciation of the quaint human spectacle.

Our trio enjoyed a six o'clock supper as guests of Babasaheb Deshmukh. The 7:00 P.M. prayer hour found us back at the *Maganvadi* ashram, climbing to the roof where thirty *satyagrahis* were grouped in a semicircle around Gandhi. He was squatting on a straw mat, an ancient pocket watch propped up before him. The fading sun cast a last gleam over the palms and banyans; the hum of night and the crickets had started. The atmosphere was serenity itself; I was enraptured.

A solemn chant led by Mr. Desai, with responses from the group; then a *Gita* reading. The Mahatma motioned to me to give the concluding prayer. Such divine unison of thought and aspiration! A memory forever: the Wardha roof top meditation under the early stars.

Punctually at eight o'clock Gandhi ended his silence. The herculean labours of his life require him to apportion his time minutely.

"Welcome, Swamiji!" The Mahatma's greeting this time was not via paper. We had just descended from the roof to his writing room, simply furnished with square mats (no chairs), a low desk with books, papers, and a few ordinary pens (not fountain pens); a nondescript clock ticked in a corner. An all-pervasive aura of peace and devotion. Gandhi was bestowing one of his captivating, cavernous, almost toothless smiles.

"Years ago," he explained, "I started my weekly observance of a day of silence as a means for gaining time to look after my correspondence. But now those twenty-four hours have become a vital spiritual need. A periodical decree of silence is not a torture but a blessing."

I agreed wholeheartedly.[5] The Mahatma questioned me about America and Europe; we discussed India and world conditions.

"Mahadev," Gandhi said as Mr. Desai entered the room, "please make arrangements at Town Hall for Swamiji to speak there on yoga tomorrow night."

As I was bidding the Mahatma good night, he considerately handed me a bottle of citronella oil.

"The Wardha mosquitoes don't know a thing about *ahimsa*,[6] Swamiji!" he said, laughing.

The following morning our little group breakfasted early on a tasty wheat porridge with molasses and milk. At ten-thirty we were called to the ashram porch for lunch with Gandhi and the *satyagrahis*. Today the menu included brown rice, a new selection of vegetables, and cardamom seeds.

5 For years in America I had been observing periods of silence, to the consternation of callers and secretaries.
6 Harmlessness; nonviolence; the foundation rock of Gandhi's creed. He was born into a family of strict Jains, who revere *ahimsa* as the root-virtue. Jainism, a sect of Hinduism, was founded in the 6th century B.C. by Mahavira, a contemporary of Buddha. Mahavira means 'great hero'; may he look down the centuries on his heroic son Gandhi!

Noon found me strolling about the ashram grounds, on to the grazing land of a few imperturbable cows. The protection of cows is a passion with Gandhi.

"The cow to me means the entire sub-human world, extending man's sympathies beyond his own species," the Mahatma has explained. "Man through the cow is enjoined to realize his identity with all that lives. Why the ancient rishis selected the cow for apotheosis is obvious to me. The cow in India was the best compa-rison; she was the giver of plenty. Not only did she give milk, but she also made agriculture possible. The cow is a poem of pity; one reads pity in the gentle animal. She is the second mother to millions of mankind. Protection of the cow means protection of the whole dumb creation of God. The appeal of the lower order of creation is all the more forceful because it is speechless."[7]

Certain daily rituals are enjoined on the orthodox Hindu. One is *Bhuta Yajna,* an offering of food to the animal kingdom. This ceremony symbolizes man's realization of his obligations to less evolved forms of creation, instinctively tied to bodily identifications which also corrode human life, but lacking in that quality of liberating reason which is peculiar to humanity.

Bhuta Yajna thus reinforces man's readiness to succour the weak, as he in turn is comforted by countless solicitudes of higher unseen beings. Man is also under bond for rejuvenating gifts of nature, prodigal in earth, sea, and sky. The evolutionary barrier of incommunicability among nature, animals, man, and astral angels is thus overcome by offices of silent love.

Two other daily *yajnas* are *Pitri* and *Nri. Pitri Yajna* is an offering of oblations to ancestors, as a symbol of man's acknowledgment of his debt to the past, essence of whose wisdom illumines humanity today. *Nri Yajna* is an offering of food to strangers or the poor, symbol of the present responsibilities of man, his duties to contemporaries.

In the early afternoon I fulfilled a neighborly *Nri Yajna* by a visit to Gandhi's ashram for little girls. Mr. Wright accompanied me on the ten-minute drive. Tiny young flowerlike faces atop the long-stemmed colourful *saris*! At the end of a brief talk in Hindi[8] which I was giving outdoors, the skies unloosed a sudden downpour. Laughing, Mr. Wright and I climbed aboard the car and sped back to *Maganvadi* amidst sheets of driving silver. Such tropical intensity and splash!

---

7 Gandhi wrote beautifully on thousands of subjects. Of prayer he said: "It is a reminder to ourselves that we are helpless without God's support. No effort is complete without prayer, without definite recognition that the best human endeavor is of no effect if it has not God's blessing behind it. Prayer is call to humility. It is a call to self-purification, to inward search."

8 Hindi is the *lingua franca* for the whole of India. An Indo-Aryan language based largely on Sanskrit roots, Hindi is the chief vernacular of northern India. The main dialect of Western Hindi is Hindustani, written both in the *Devanagari* (Sanskrit) characters and in Arabic characters. Its subdialect, Urdu, is spoken by Moslems.

Re-entering the guest house I was struck anew by the stark simplicity and evidences of self-sacrifice which are everywhere present. The Gandhi vow of non-possession came early in his married life. Renouncing an extensive legal practice which had been yielding him an annual income of more than $20,000, the Mahatma dispersed all his wealth to the poor.

Sri Yukteswar used to poke gentle fun at the commonly inadequate conceptions of renunciation.

"A beggar cannot renounce wealth," Master would say. "If a man laments: 'My business has failed; my wife has left me; I will renounce all and enter a monastery,' to what worldly sacrifice is he referring? He did not renounce wealth and love; they renounced him!"

Saints like Gandhi, on the other hand, have made not only tangible material sacrifices, but also the more difficult renunciation of selfish motive and private goal, merging their inmost being in the stream of humanity as a whole.

The Mahatma's remarkable wife, Kasturabai, did not object when he failed to set aside any part of his wealth for the use of herself and their children. Married in early youth, Gandhi and his wife took the vow of celibacy after the birth of four sons.[9] A tranquil heroine in the intense drama that has been their life together, Kasturabai has followed her husband to prison, shared his three-week fasts, and fully borne her share of his endless responsibilities. She has paid Gandhi the following tribute:

> I thank you for having had the privilege of being your lifelong companion and helpmate. I thank you for the most perfect marriage in the world, based on *brahmacharya* (self-control) and not on sex. I thank you for having considered me your equal in your life work for India. I thank you for not being one of those husbands who spend their time in gambling, racing, women, wine, and song, tiring of their wives and children as the little boy quickly tires of his childhood toys. How thankful I am that you were not one of those husbands who devote their time to growing rich on the exploitation of the labour of others.
>
> How thankful I am that you put God and country before bribes, that you had the courage of your convictions and a complete and implicit faith in God. How thankful I am for a husband that put God and his country before me. I am grateful to you for your tolerance of me and

9 Gandhi has described his life with a devastating candour in *The Story of my Experiments with Truth* (Ahmedabad: Navajivan Press, 1927-29, 2 vol.) This autobiography has been summarized in *Mahatma Gandhi, His Own Story*, edited by C. F. Andrews, with an introduction by John Haynes Holmes (New York: Macmillan Co., 1930). Many autobiographies replete with famous names and colourful events are almost completely silent on any phase of inner analysis or development. One lays down each of these books with a certain dissatisfaction, as though saying: "Here is a man who knew many notable persons, but who never knew himself." This reaction is impossible with Gandhi's autobiography; he exposes his faults and subterfuges with an impersonal devotion to truth, rare in annals of any age.

my shortcomings of youth, when I grumbled and rebelled against the change you made in our mode of living, from so much to so little.

As a young child, I lived in your parents' home; your mother was a great and good woman; she trained me, taught me how to be a brave, courageous wife and how to keep the love and respect of her son, my future husband. As the years passed and you became India's most beloved leader, I had none of the fears that beset the wife who may be cast aside when her husband has climbed the ladder of success, as so often happens in other countries. I knew that death would still find us husband and wife.

For years Kasturabai performed the duties of treasurer of the public funds which the idolized Mahatma is able to raise by the millions. There are many humorous stories in Indian homes to the effect that husbands are nervous about their wives' wearing any jewelry to a Gandhi meeting; the Mahatma's magical tongue, pleading for the downtrodden, charms the gold bracelets and diamond necklaces right off the arms and necks of the wealthy into the collection basket!

One day the public treasurer, Kasturabai, could not account for a disbursement of four rupees. Gandhi duly published an auditing in which he inexorably pointed out his wife's four-rupee discrepancy.

I had often told this story before classes of my American students. One evening a woman in the hall had given an outraged gasp.

"Mahatma or no Mahatma," she had cried, "if he were my husband I would have given him a black eye for such an unnecessary public insult!"

After some good-humoured banter had passed between us on the subject of American wives and Hindu wives, I had gone on to a fuller explanation.

"Mrs. Gandhi considers the Mahatma not as her husband but as her guru, one who has the right to discipline her for even insignificant errors," I had pointed out. "Sometime after Kasturabai had been publicly rebuked, Gandhi was sentenced to prison on a political charge. As he was calmly bidding farewell to his wife, she fell at his feet. 'Master,' she said humbly, 'if I have ever offended you, please forgive me.' "[10]

At three o'clock that afternoon in Wardha, I betook myself, by previous appointment, to the writing room of the saint who had been able to make an unflinching disciple out of his own wife – rare miracle! Gandhi looked up with his unforgettable smile.

Kasturabai Gandhi (also called Kastur*ba*; '*ba*' for mother) died in imprisonment at Poona on February 22, 1944. The usually unemotional Gandhi wept silently. Shortly after her admirers had suggested a Memorial Fund in her honour, 125 lacs of rupees (over four million dollars) poured in from all over India. Gandhi has arranged that the fund be used for village welfare work among women and children. He reports his activities in his English weekly: *Harijan.*

"Mahatmaji," I said as I squatted beside him on the uncushioned mat, "please tell me your definition of *ahimsa*."

"The avoidance of harm to any living creature in thought or deed."

"Beautiful ideal! But the world will always ask: May one not kill a cobra to protect a child, or one's self?"

"I could not kill a cobra without violating two of my vows – fearlessness, and non-killing. I would rather try inwardly to calm the snake by vibrations of love. I cannot possibly lower my standards to suit my circumstances." With his amazing candour, Gandhi added, "I must confess that I could not carry on this conversation were I faced by a cobra!"

I remarked on several very recent Western books on diet which lay on his desk.

"Yes, diet is important in the *Satyagraha* movement – as everywhere else," he said with a chuckle. "Because I advocate complete continence for *satyagrahis,* I am always trying to find out the best diet for the celibate. One must conquer the palate before he can control the procreative instinct. Semi-starvation or unbalanced diets are not the answer. After overcoming the inward *greed* for food, a *satyagrahi* must continue to follow a rational vegetarian diet with all necessary vitamins, minerals, calories, and so forth. By inward and outward wisdom in regard to eating, the *satyagrahi's* sexual fluid is easily turned into vital energy for the whole body."

The Mahatma and I compared our knowledge of good meat-substitutes. "The avocado is excellent," I said. "There are numerous avocado groves near my centre in California."

Gandhi's face lit with interest. "I wonder if they would grow in Wardha? The *satyagrahis* would appreciate a new food."

"I will be sure to send some avocado plants from Los Angeles to Wardha."[11] I added, "Eggs are a high-protein food; are they forbidden to *satyagrahis*?"

"Not unfertilized eggs." The Mahatma laughed reminiscently. "For years I would not countenance their use; even now I personally do not eat them. One of my daughters-in-law was once dying of malnutrition; her doctor insisted on eggs. I would not agree, and advised him to give her some egg-substitute.

" 'Gandhiji,' the doctor said, 'unfertilized eggs contain no life sperm; no killing is involved.'

"I then gladly gave permission for my daughter-in-law to eat eggs; she was soon restored to health."

On the previous night Gandhi had expressed a wish to receive the *Kriya Yoga* of Lahiri Mahasaya. I was touched by the Mahatma's open-mindedness and spirit of inquiry. He is childlike in his divine quest, revealing that pure receptivity

11 I sent a shipment to Wardha, soon after my return to America. The plants, alas! died on the way, unable to withstand the rigours of the long ocean transportation.

which Jesus praised in children, " . . . of such is the kingdom of heaven."

The hour for my promised instruction had arrived; several *satyagrahis* now entered the room – Mr. Desai, Dr. Pingale, and a few others who desired the *Kriya* technique.

I first taught the little class the physical *Yogoda* exercises. The body is visualized as divided into twenty parts; the will directs energy in turn to each section. Soon everyone was vibrating before me like a human motor. It was easy to observe the rippling effect on Gandhi's twenty body parts, at all times completely exposed to view! Though very thin, he is not unpleasingly so; the skin of his body is smooth and unwrinkled.[12]

Later I initiated the group into the liberating technique of *Kriya Yoga.*

The Mahatma has reverently studied all world religions. The Jain scriptures, the Biblical New Testament, and the sociological writings of Tolstoy[13] are the three main sources of Gandhi's nonviolent convictions. He has stated his credo thus:

> I believe the Bible, the *Koran,* and the *Zend-Avesta*[14] to be as divinely inspired as the *Vedas.* I believe in the institution of Gurus, but in this age millions must go without a Guru, because it is a rare thing to find a combination of perfect purity and perfect learning. But one need not despair of ever knowing the truth of one's religion, because the fundamentals of Hinduism as of every great religion are unchangeable, and easily understood.
>
> I believe like every Hindu in God and His oneness, in rebirth and salvation. . . . I can no more describe my feeling for Hinduism than for my own wife. She moves me as no other woman in the world can. Not that she has no faults; I daresay she has many more than I see myself. But the feeling of an indissoluble bond is there. Even so I feel for and about Hinduism with all its faults and limitations. Nothing delights me so much as the music of the *Gita*, or the *Ramayana* by Tulsidas. When I fancied I was taking my last breath, the *Gita* was my solace.
>
> Hinduism is not an exclusive religion. In it there is room for the worship of all the prophets of the world.[15] It is not a missionary religion in the ordinary sense of the term. It has no doubt absorbed many tribes in its fold, but this absorption has been of an evolutionary, imperceptible

Gandhi has undergone many short and long fasts. He enjoys exceptionally good health. His books, *Diet and Diet Reform, Nature Cure*, and *Key to Health* are available from Navajivan Trust Ahamedabad, India.

Thoreau, Ruskin, and Mazzini are three other Western writers whose sociological views Gandhi has studied carefully.

The sacred scripture given to Persia about 1000 B.C. by Zoroaster.

The unique feature of Hinduism among the world religions is that it derives not from a single great founder but from the impersonal Vedic scriptures. Hinduism thus gives scope for worshipful incorporation into its fold of prophets of all ages and all lands. The Vedic scriptures regulate not only devotional practices but all important social customs, in an effort to bring man's every action into harmony with divine law.

character. Hinduism tells each man to worship God according to his own faith or *dharma*,[16] and so lives at peace with all religions.

Of Christ, Gandhi has written: "I am sure that if He were living here now among men, He would bless the lives of many who perhaps have never even heard His name . . . just as it is written: 'Not every one that saith unto me, Lord, Lord . . . but he that doeth the will of my Father.'[17] In the lesson of His own life, Jesus gave humanity the magnificent purpose and the single objective toward which we all ought to aspire. I believe that He belongs not solely to Christianity, but to the entire world, to all lands and races."

On my last evening in Wardha I addressed the meeting which had been called by Mr. Desai in Town Hall. The room was thronged to the window sills with about 400 people assembled to hear the talk on yoga. I spoke first in Hindi, then in English. Our little group returned to the ashram in time for a good-night glimpse of Gandhi, enfolded in peace and correspondence.

Night was still lingering when I rose at 5:00 A.M. Village life was already stirring; first a bullock cart by the ashram gates, then a peasant with his huge burden balanced precariously on his head. After breakfast our trio sought out Gandhi for farewell *pronams*. The saint rises at four o'clock for his morning prayer.

"Mahatmaji, good-by!" I knelt to touch his feet. "India is safe in your keeping!"

Years have rolled by since the Wardha idyll; the earth, oceans, and skies have darkened with a world at war. Alone among great leaders, Gandhi has offered a practical nonviolent alternative to armed might. To redress grievances and remove injustices, the Mahatma has employed nonviolent means which again and again have proved their effectiveness. He states his doctrine in these words:

I have found that life persists in the midst of destruction. Therefore there must be a higher law than that of destruction. Only under that law would well-ordered society be intelligible and life worth living.

If that is the law of life we must work it out in daily existence. Wherever there are wars, wherever we are confronted with an opponent, conquer by love. I have found that the certain law of love has answered in my own life as the law of destruction has never done.

In India we have had an ocular demonstration of the operation of this law on the widest scale possible. I don't claim that nonviolence has penetrated the 360,000,000 people in India, but I do claim it has

16 A comprehensive Sanskrit word for law; conformity to law or natural righteousness; duty as inherent in the circumstances in which a man finds himself at any given time. The scriptures define *dharma* as 'the natural universal laws whose observance enables man to save himself from degradation and suffering.'
17 *Matthew* 7: 21.

penetrated deeper than any other doctrine in an incredibly short time.

It takes a fairly strenuous course of training to attain a mental state of nonviolence. It is a disciplined life, like the life of a soldier. The perfect state is reached only when the mind, body, and speech are in proper coordination. Every problem would lend itself to solution if we determined to make the law of truth and nonviolence the law of life.

Just as a scientist will work wonders out of various applications of the laws of nature, a man who applies the laws of love with scientific precision can work greater wonders. Nonviolence is infinitely more wonderful and subtle than forces of nature like, for instance, electricity. The law of love is a far greater science than any modern science.

Consulting history, one may reasonably state that the problems of mankind have not been solved by the use of brute force. World War-I produced a world-chilling snowball of war karma that swelled into World War-II. Only the warmth of brotherhood can melt the present colossal snowball of war karma which may otherwise grow into World War-III. This unholy trinity will banish forever the possibility of World War-IV by a finality of atomic bombs. Use of jungle logic instead of human reason in settling disputes will restore the earth to a jungle. If brothers not in life, then brothers in violent death. It was not for such ignominy that God lovingly permitted man to discover the release of atomic energies!

War and crime never pay. The billions of dollars that went up in the smoke of explosive nothingness would have been sufficient to have made a new world, one almost free from disease and completely free from poverty. Not an earth of fear, chaos, famine, pestilence, the *danse macabre,* but one broad land of peace, of prosperity, and of widening knowledge.

The nonviolent voice of Gandhi appeals to man's highest conscience. Let nations ally themselves no longer with death, but with life; not with destruction, but with construction; not with the Annihilator, but with the creative miracles of love.

"One should forgive, under any injury," says the *Mahabharata.* "It hath been said that the continuation of species is due to man's being forgiving. Forgiveness is holiness; by forgiveness the universe is held together. Forgiveness is the might of the mighty; forgiveness is sacrifice; forgiveness is quiet of mind. Forgiveness and gentleness are the qualities of the self-possessed. They represent eternal virtue."

Nonviolence is the natural outgrowth of the law of forgiveness and love. "If loss of life becomes necessary in a righteous battle," Gandhi proclaims, "one should be prepared, like Jesus, to shed his own, not others' blood. Eventually there will be less blood spilt in the world."

Epics shall someday be written on the Indian *satyagrahis* who withstood hate with love, violence with nonviolence, who allowed themselves to be mercilessly slaughtered rather than retaliate. The result on certain historic occasions was that the armed opponents threw down their guns and fled, shamed, shaken to their depths by the sight of men who valued the life of another above their own.

"I would wait, if need be for ages," Gandhi says, "rather than seek the freedom of my country through bloody means." Never does the Mahatma forget the majestic warning: "All they that take the sword shall perish with the sword."[18] Gandhi has written:

> I call myself a nationalist, but my nationalism is as broad as the universe. It includes in its sweep all the nations of the earth.[19] My nationalism includes the well-being of the whole world. I do not want my India to rise on the ashes of other nations. I do not want India to exploit a single human being. I want India to be strong in order that she can infect the other nations also with her strength. Not so with a single nation in Europe today; they do not give strength to the others.
>
> President Wilson mentioned his beautiful fourteen points, but said: "After all, if this endeavor of ours to arrive at peace fails, we have our armaments to fall back upon." I want to reverse that position, and I say: "Our armaments have failed already. Let us now be in search of something new; let us try the force of love and God which is truth." When we have got that, we shall want nothing else.

By the Mahatma's training of thousands of true *satyagrahis* (those who have taken the eleven rigorous vows mentioned in the first part of this chapter), who in turn spread the message; by patiently educating the Indian masses to understand the spiritual and eventually material benefits of nonviolence; by arming his people with nonviolent weapons – non-cooperation with injustice, the willingness to endure indignities, prison, death itself rather than resort to arms; by enlisting world sympathy through countless examples of heroic martyrdom among *satyagrahis,* Gandhi has dramatically portrayed the practical nature of nonviolence, its solemn power to settle disputes without war.

Gandhi has already won through nonviolent means a greater number of political concessions for his land than have ever been won by any leader of any country except through bullets. Nonviolent methods for eradication of all wrongs and evils have been strikingly applied not only in the political

18 *Matthew* 26: 52, which necessarily implies the reincarnation of man. (See chapter 16). Many of life's complexities are explicable only through an understanding of the karmic law of justice.

19 'Let not a man glory in this, that he love his country; Let him rather glory in this, that he love his kind.' – *A Persian proverb.*

arena but in the delicate and complicated field of Indian social reform. Gandhi and his followers have removed many longstanding feuds between Hindus and Mohammedans; hundreds of thousands of Moslems look to the Mahatma as their leader. The untouchables have found in him their fearless and triumphant champion. "If there be a rebirth in store for me," Gandhi wrote, "I wish to be born a pariah in the midst of pariahs, because thereby I would be able to render them more effective service."

The Mahatma is indeed a 'great soul,' but it was illiterate millions who had the discernment to bestow the title. This gentle prophet is honoured in his own land. The lowly peasant has been able to rise to Gandhi's high challenge. The Mahatma wholeheartedly believes in the inherent nobility of man. The inevitable failures have never disillusioned him. "Even if the opponent plays him false twenty times," he writes, "the *satyagrahi* is ready to trust him the twenty-first time, for an implicit trust in human nature is the very essence of the creed."[20]

"Mahatmaji, you are an exceptional man. You must not expect the world to act as you do." A critic once made this observation.

"It is curious how we delude ourselves, fancying that the body can be improved, but that it is impossible to evoke the hidden powers of the soul," Gandhi replied. "I am engaged in trying to show that if I have any of those powers, I am as frail a mortal as any of us and that I never had anything extraordinary about me nor have I now. I am a simple individual liable to err like any other fellow mortal. I own, however, that I have enough humility to confess my errors and to retrace my steps. I own that I have an immovable faith in God and His goodness, and an unconsumable passion for truth and love. But is that not what every person has latent in him? If we are to make progress, we must not repeat history but make new history. We must add to the inheritance left by our ancestors. If we may make new discoveries and inventions in the phenomenal world, must we declare our bankruptcy in the spiritual domain? Is it impossible to multiply the exceptions so as to make them the rule? Must man always be brute first and man after, if at all?"[21]

) 'Then came Peter to him and said, Lord, how oft shall my brother sin against me, and I forgive him? till seven times? Jesus saith unto him, I say not unto thee, Until seven times: but, Until seventy times seven.' – *Matthew* 18: 21-22.

l Charles P. Steinmetz, the great electrical engineer, was once asked by Mr. Roger W. Babson: "What line of research will see the greatest development during the next fifty years?" "I think the greatest discovery will be made along spiritual lines," Steinmetz replied. "Here is a force which history clearly teaches has been the greatest power in the development of men. Yet we have merely been playing with it and have never seriously studied it as we have the physical forces. Someday people will learn that material things do not bring happiness and are of little use in making men and women creative and powerful. Then the scientists of the world will turn their laboratories over to the study of God and prayer and the spiritual forces which as yet have hardly been scratched. When this day comes, the world will see more advancement in one generation than it has seen in the past four."

Americans may well remember with pride the successful nonviolent experiment of William Penn in founding his 17th century colony in Pennsylvania. There were 'no forts, no soldiers, no militia, even no arms.' Amidst the savage frontier wars and the butcheries that went on between the new settlers and the Red Indians, the Quakers of Pennsylvania alone remained unmolested. "Others were slain; others were massacred; but they were safe. Not a Quaker woman suffered assault; not a Quaker child was slain, not a Quaker man was tortured." When the Quakers were finally forced to give up the government of the state, "war broke out, and some Pennsylvanians were killed. But only three Quakers were killed, three who had so far fallen from their faith as to carry weapons of defence."

"Resort to force in the Great War failed to bring tranquillity," Franklin D. Roosevelt has pointed out. "Victory and defeat were alike sterile. That lesson the world should have learned."

"The more weapons of violence, the more misery to mankind," Lao-tzu taught. "The triumph of violence ends in a festival of mourning."

"I am fighting for nothing less than world peace," Gandhi has declared. "If the Indian movement is carried to success on a nonviolent *Satyagraha* basis, it will give a new meaning to patriotism and, if I may say so in all humility, to life itself."

Before the West dismisses Gandhi's program as one of an impractical dreamer, let it first reflect on a definition of *Satyagraha* by the Master of Galilee:

"Ye have heard that it hath been said, An eye for an eye, and a tooth for a tooth: but I say unto you, That ye resist not evil:[22] but whosoever shall smite thee on thy right cheek, turn to him the other also."

Gandhi's epoch has extended, with the beautiful precision of cosmic timing, into a century already desolated and devastated by two World Wars. A divine handwriting appears on the granite wall of his life: a warning against the further shedding of blood among brothers.

* * *

22 That is, resist not evil with evil. (*Matthew* 5: 38-39)

MAHATMA GANDHI'S HANDWRITING IN HINDI

On his visit to Ranchi Mahtma Gandhi graciously wrote the foregoing lines in the guest book:
'This institution has deeply impressed my mind. I cherish high hopes that this school will further encourage the use of the spinning wheel.'

[Sep. 17, 1925 (signed) Mohandas Gandhi].

MAHATMA GANDHI IN MEMORIAM

"He was in the true sense the father of nation, and a madman has slain him. Millions and millions are mourning because the light has gone out….. The light that shone in this land was no ordinary light. For a thousand years that light will be seen in this country, and the world will see it." So spoke Prime Minister of India Jawaharlal Nehru shortly after Mahatma Gandhi had been assassinated in New Delhi on January 30, 1948.

Five months earlier, India had peacefully achieved her national independence. The work of the 78-year-old Gandhi was done; he realized that his hour was nigh. "Abha, bring me all the important papers," he said to his grandniece on the morning of the tragedy. "I must reply today. Tomorrow may never be." In numerous passages of his writings, also Gandhi gave intimation of his final destiny.

As the dying Mahatma sank slowly to the ground, three bullets in his frail and fast-worn body, he lifted his hands in the traditional Hindu gesture of greeting, silently bestowing his forgiveness. Innocent artist as he was in all the ways of his life, Gandhi became a supreme artist at the moment of his death. All the sacrifices of his selfless life had made possible that final loving gesture.

'Generations to come, it may be,' Albert Einstein wrote in a tribute to the Mahatma, 'will scarce believe that such a one as this ever in flesh and blood walked upon the earth.' A dispatch from the Vatican in Rome said: 'The assassination caused great sorrow here. Gandhi is mourned as an apostle of Christian virtues.'

Fraught with symbolic meaning are the lives of all great ones who come to earth for the accomplishment of specific righteousness. Gandhi's dramatic death in the cause of Indian unity has highlighted his message to a world torn in every continent with disunity. That message he has stated in prophetic words:

"Nonviolence has come among men and it will live. It is the harbinger of the peace of the world."

45. *The Bengali 'Joy-Permeated Mother'*

"SIR, PLEASE do not leave India without a glimpse of Nirmala Devi. Her sanctity is intense; she is known far and wide as Ananda Moyi Ma (Joy-Permeated Mother)." My niece, Amiyo Bose, gazed at me earnestly.

"Of course! I want very much to see the woman saint." I added, "I have read of her advanced state of God-realization. A little article about her appeared years ago in *East-West*."

"I have met her," Amiyo went on. "She recently visited my own little town of Jamshedpur. At the entreaty of a disciple, Ananda Moyi Ma went to the home of a dying man. She stood by his bedside; as her hand touched his forehead, his death-rattle ceased. The disease vanished at once; to the man's glad astonishment, he was well."

A few days later I heard that the Blissful Mother was staying at the home of a disciple in the Bhowanipur section of Calcutta. Mr. Wright and I set out immediately from my father's Calcutta home. As the Ford neared the Bhowanipur house, my companion and I observed an unusual street scene.

Ananda Moyi Ma was standing in an open-topped automobile, blessing a throng of about one hundred disciples. She was evidently on the point of departure. Mr. Wright parked the Ford some distance away, and accompanied me on foot toward the quiet assemblage. The woman saint glanced in our direction; she alighted from her car and walked toward us.

"Father, you have come!" With these fervent words she put her arm around my neck and her head on my shoulder. Mr. Wright, to whom I had just remarked that I did not know the saint, was hugely enjoying this extraordinary demonstration of welcome. The eyes of the one hundred chelas were also fixed with some surprise on the affectionate tableau.

I had instantly seen that the saint was in a high state of *samadhi*. Utterly oblivious to her outward garb as a woman, she knew herself as the changeless soul; from that plane she was joyously greeting another devotee of God. She led me by the hand into her automobile.

"Ananda Moyi Ma, I am delaying your journey!" I protested.

"Father, I am meeting you for the first time in this life, after ages!" she said. "Please do not leave yet."

We sat together in the rear seats of the car. The Blissful Mother soon entered the immobile ecstatic state. Her beautiful eyes glanced heavenward and, half-opened, became stilled, gazing into the near-far inner Elysium.[1] The disciples chanted gently: "Victory to Mother Divine!"

I had found many men of God-realization in India, but never before had

1 The abode of the blessed after death, in the classical mythology.

I met such an exalted woman saint. Her gentle face was burnished with the ineffable joy that had given her the name of Blissful Mother. Long black tresses lay loosely behind her unveiled head. A red dot of sandalwood paste on her forehead symbolized the spiritual eye, ever open within her. Tiny face, tiny hands, tiny feet – a contrast to her spiritual magnitude!

I put some questions to a near-by woman chela while Ananda Moyi Ma remained entranced.

"The Blissful Mother travels widely in India; in many parts she has hundreds of disciples," the chela told me. "Her courageous efforts have brought about many desirable social reforms. Although a Brahmin, the saint recognizes no caste distinctions.[2] A group of us always travel with her, looking after her comforts. We have to mother her; she takes no notice of her body. If no one gave her food, she would not eat, or make any inquiries. Even when meals are placed before her, she does not touch them. To prevent her disappearance from this world, we disciples feed her with our own hands. For days together she often stays in the divine trance, scarcely breathing, her eyes unwinking. One of her chief disciples is her husband. Many years ago, soon after their marriage, he took the vow of silence."

The chela pointed to a broad-shouldered, fine-featured man with long hair and hoary beard. He was standing quietly in the midst of the gathering, his hands folded in a disciple's reverential attitude.

Refreshed by her dip in the Infinite, Ananda Moyi Ma was now focusing her consciousness on the material world.

"Father, please tell me where you stay." Her voice was clear and melodious.

"At present, in Calcutta or Ranchi; but soon I shall be returning to America."

"America?"

"Yes. An Indian woman saint would be sincerely appreciated there by spiritual seekers. Would you like to go?"

"If Father can take me, I will go."

This reply caused her near-by disciples to start in alarm.

"Twenty or more of us always travel with the Blissful Mother," one of them told me firmly. "We could not live without her. Wherever she goes, we must go."

Reluctantly I abandoned the plan, as possessing an impractical feature of spontaneous enlargement!

"Please come at least to Ranchi, with your disciples," I said on taking leave of the saint. "As a divine child yourself, you will enjoy the little ones in my school."

"Whenever Father takes me, I will gladly go."

---

[2] I find some further facts of Ananda Moyi Ma's life, printed in *East-West*. The saint was born in 1896 in village Kheora in the Tripura District of east Bengal. Illiterate, she has yet stunned the intellectuals by her wisdom. Her verses in Sanskrit have filled scholars with wonderment. She has brought consolation to bereaved persons, and effected miraculous cures by her mere presence.

A short time later the Ranchi *Vidyalaya* was in gala array for the saint's promised visit. The youngsters looked forward to any day of festivity – no lessons, hours of music, and a feast for the climax!

"Victory! *Ananda Moyi Ma, ki jai*!" This reiterated chant from scores of enthusiastic little throats greeted the saint's party as it entered the school gates. Showers of marigolds, tinkle of cymbals, lusty blowing of conch shells and beat of the *mridanga* drum! The Blissful Mother wandered smilingly over the sunny Vidyalaya grounds, ever carrying within her the portable paradise.

"It is beautiful here," Ananda Moyi Ma said graciously as I led her into the main building. She seated herself with a childlike smile by my side. The closest of dear friends, she made one feel, yet an aura of remoteness was ever around her – the paradoxical isolation of Omnipresence.

"Please tell me something of your life."

"Father knows all about it; why repeat it?" She evidently felt that the factual history of one short incarnation was beneath notice.

I laughed, gently repeating my question.

"Father, there is little to tell." She spread her graceful hands in a deprecatory gesture. "My consciousness has never associated itself with this temporary body. Before I[3] came on this earth, Father, 'I was the same.' As a little girl, 'I was the same.' I grew into womanhood, but still 'I was the same.' When the family in which I had been born made arrangements to have this body married, 'I was the same.' And when, passion-drunk, my husband came to me and murmured endearing words, lightly touching my body, he received a violent shock, as if struck by lightning, for even then 'I was the same.'

"My husband knelt before me, folded his hands, and implored my pardon.

" 'Mother,' he said, 'because I have desecrated your bodily temple by touching it with the thought of lust – not knowing that within it dwelt not my wife but the Divine Mother – I take this solemn vow: I shall be your disciple, a celibate follower, ever caring for you in silence as a servant, never speaking to anyone again as long as I live. May I thus atone for the sin I have today committed against you, my guru.'

"Even when I quietly accepted this proposal of my husband's, 'I was the same.' And, Father, in front of you now, 'I am the same.' Ever afterward, though the dance of creation change around me in the hall of eternity, 'I shall be the same.' "

Ananda Moyi Ma sank into a deep meditative state. Her form was statue-still; she had fled to her ever-calling kingdom. The dark pools of her eyes appeared lifeless and glassy. This expression is often present when saints remove their consciousness from the physical body, which is then hardly

3 Ananda Moyi Ma does not refer to herself as 'I'; she uses humble circumlocutions like 'this body' or 'this little girl' or 'your daughter'. Nor does she refer to anyone as her 'disciple'. With impersonal wisdom she bestows equally on all human beings the divine love of the Universal Mother.

more than a piece of soulless clay. We sat together for an hour in the ecstatic trance. She returned to this world with a gay little laugh.

"Please, Ananda Moyi Ma," I said, "come with me to the garden. Mr. Wright will take some pictures."

"Of course, Father. Your will is my will." Her glorious eyes retained the unchanging divine lustre as she posed for many photographs.

Time for the feast! Ananda Moyi Ma squatted on her blanket-seat, a disciple at her elbow to feed her. Like an infant, the saint obediently swallowed the food after the chela had brought it to her lips. It was plain that the Blissful Mother did not recognize any difference between curries and sweetmeats!

As dusk approached, the saint left with her party amidst a shower of rose petals, her hands raised in blessing on the little lads. Their faces shone with the affection she had effortlessly awakened.

"Thou shalt love the Lord thy God with all thy heart, and with all thy soul, and with all thy mind, and with all thy strength:" Christ has proclaimed, "this is the first commandment."[4]

Casting aside every inferior attachment, Ananda Moyi Ma offers her sole allegiance to the Lord. Not by the hairsplitting distinctions of scholars but by the sure logic of faith, the childlike saint has solved the only problem in human life – establishment of unity with God. Man has forgotten this stark simplicity, now befogged by a million issues. Refusing a monotheistic love to God, the nations disguise their infidelity by punctilious respect before the outward shrines of charity. These humanitarian gestures are virtuous, because for a moment they divert man's attention from himself, but they do not free him from his single responsibility in life, referred to by Jesus as the first commandment. The uplifting obligation to love God is assumed with man's first breath of an air freely bestowed by his only Benefactor.[5]

On one other occasion after her Ranchi visit I had opportunity to see Ananda Moyi Ma. She stood among her disciples some months later on the Serampore station platform, waiting for the train.

"Father, I am going to the Himalayas," she told me. "Generous disciples have built me a hermitage in Dehra Dun."

As she boarded the train, I marvelled to see that whether amidst a crowd, on a train, feasting, or sitting in silence, her eyes never looked away from God. Within me I still hear her voice, an echo of measureless sweetness:

"Behold, now and always one with the Eternal, 'I am ever the same.'"

4 *Mark* 12: 30.

5 (Chap. 45) "Many feel the urge to create a new and better world. Rather than let your thoughts dwell on such matters, you should concentrate on That by the contemplation of which there is hope of perfect peace. It is man's duty to become a seeker after God or Truth" – *Ananda Moyi Ma*.

46. *The Woman Yogi who Never Eats*

"SIR, WHITHER are we bound this morning?" Mr. Wright was driving the Ford; he took his eyes off the road long enough to gaze at me with a questioning twinkle. From day to day he seldom knew what part of Bengal he would be discovering next.

"God willing," I replied devoutly, "we are on our way to see an eighth wonder of the world – a woman saint whose diet is thin air!"

"Repetition of wonders – after Therese Neumann." But Mr. Wright laughed eagerly just the same; he even accelerated the speed of the car. More extraordinary grist for his travel diary! Not one of an average tourist, that!

The Ranchi school had just been left behind us; we had risen before the sun. Besides my secretary and myself, three Bengali friends were in the party. We drank in the exhilarating air, the natural wine of the morning. Our driver guided the car warily among the early peasants and the two-wheeled carts, slowly drawn by yoked, hump-shouldered bullocks, inclined to dispute the road with a honking interloper.

"Sir, we would like to know more of the fasting saint."

"Her name is Giri Bala," I informed my companions. "I first heard about her years ago from a scholarly gentleman, Sthiti Lal Nundy. He often came to the Gurpar Road home to tutor my brother Bishnu."

" 'I know Giri Bala well,' Sthiti Babu told me. 'She employs a certain yoga technique which enables her to live without eating. I was her close neighbor in Nawabganj near Ichapur.[1] I made it a point to watch her closely; never did I find evidence that she was taking either food or drink. My interest finally mounted so high that I approached the Maharaja of Burdwan[2] and asked him to conduct an investigation. Astounded at the story, he invited her to his palace. She agreed to a test and lived for two months locked up in a small section of his home. Later she returned for a palace visit of twenty days; and then for a third test of fifteen days. The Maharaja himself told me that these three rigorous scrutinies had convinced him beyond doubt of her non-eating state.'

"This story of Sthiti Babu's has remained in my mind for over twenty-five years," I concluded. "Sometimes in America I wondered if the river of time would not swallow the *yogini*[3] before I could meet her. She must be quite aged now. I do not even know where, or if, she lives. But in a few hours we shall reach Purulia; her brother has a home there."

By ten-thirty our little group was conversing with the brother, Lambadar Dey, a lawyer of Purulia.

---

1 27 km. from Kolkata, now famous for Ordnance factories.
2 H.H.Sir Bijay Chand Mahtab, now dead. His family doubtless possesses some record of the Maharaja's three investigations of Giri Bala.
3 A woman yogi.

"Yes, my sister is living. She sometimes stays with me here, but at present she is at our family home in Biur." Lambadar Babu glanced doubtfully at the Ford. "I hardly think, Swamiji, that any automobile has ever penetrated into the interior as far as Biur. It might be best if you all resign yourselves to the ancient jolt of the bullock cart!"

As one voice our party pledged loyalty to the Pride of Detroit.

"The Ford comes from America," I told the lawyer. "It would be a shame to deprive it of an opportunity to get acquainted with the heart of Bengal!"

"May Ganesh[4] go with you!" Lambadar Babu said, laughing. He added courteously, "If you ever get there, I am sure Giri Bala will be glad to see you. She is approaching her seventies, but continues in excellent health."

"Please tell me, sir, if it is absolutely true that she eats nothing?" I looked directly into his eyes, those telltale windows of the mind.

"It is true." His gaze was open and honorable. "In more than five decades I have never seen her eat a morsel. If the world suddenly came to an end, I could not be more astonished than by the sight of my sister's taking food!"

We chuckled together over the improbability of these two cosmic events.

"Giri Bala has never sought an inaccessible solitude for her yoga practices," Lambadar Babu went on. "She has lived her entire life surrounded by her family and friends. They are all well accustomed now to her strange state. Not one of them who would not be stupefied if Giri Bala suddenly decided to eat anything! Sister is naturally retiring, as befits a Hindu widow, but our little circle in Purulia and in Biur all know that she is literally an 'exceptional' woman."

The brother's sincerity was manifest. Our little party thanked him warmly and set out toward Biur. We stopped at a street shop for curry and *luchis,* attracting a swarm of urchins who gathered round to watch Mr. Wright eating with his fingers in the simple Hindu manner.[5] Hearty appetites caused us to fortify ourselves against an afternoon which, unknown at the moment, was to prove fairly laborious.

Our way now led east through sun-baked rice fields into the Burdwan section of Bengal. On through roads lined with dense vegetation; the songs of the mynahs and the stripe-throated bulbuls streamed out from trees with huge, umbrellalike branches. A bullock cart now and then, the *rini, rini, manju, manju* squeak of its axle and iron-shod wooden wheels contrasting sharply in mind with the *swish, swish* of auto tires over the aristocratic asphalt of the cities.

"Dick, halt!" My sudden request brought a jolting protest from the Ford.

---

4 'Remover of Obstacles,' the god of good fortune.

5 Sri Yukteswar used to say: "The Lord has given us the fruits of the good earth. We like to see our food, to smell it, to taste it – the Hindu likes also to touch it!" One does not mind *hearing* it, either, if no one else is present at the meal!

"That overburdened mango tree is fairly shouting an invitation!"

The five of us dashed like children to the mango-strewn earth; the tree had benevolently shed its fruits as they had ripened.

"Full many a mango is born to lie unseen," I paraphrased, "and waste its sweetness on the stony ground."

"Nothing like this in America, Swamiji, eh?" laughed Sailesh Mazumdar, one of my Bengali students.

"No," I admitted, covered with mango juice and contentment. "How I have missed this fruit in the West! A Hindu's heaven without mangoes is inconceivable!"

I picked up a rock and downed a proud beauty hidden on the highest limb.

"Dick," I asked between bites of ambrosia, warm with the tropical sun, "are all the cameras in the car?"

"Yes, sir; in the baggage compartment."

"If Giri Bala proves to be a true saint, I want to write about her in the West. A Hindu *yogini* with such inspiring powers should not live and the unknown – like most of these mangoes."

Half an hour later I was still strolling in the sylvan peace.

"Sir," Mr. Wright remarked, "we should reach Giri Bala before the sun sets, to have enough light for photographs." He added with a grin, "The Westerners are a skeptical lot; we can't expect them to believe in the lady without any pictures!"

This bit of wisdom was indisputable; I turned my back on temptation and re-entered the car.

"You are right, Dick," I sighed as we sped along, "I sacrifice the mango paradise on the altar of Western realism. Photographs we must have!"

The road became more and more sickly: wrinkles of ruts, boils of hardened clay, the sad infirmities of old age! Our group dismounted occasionally to allow Mr. Wright to more easily manoeuvre the Ford, which the four of us pushed from behind.

"Lambodar Babu spoke truly," Sailesh acknowledged. "The car is not carrying us; we are carrying the car!"

Our climb-in, climb-out auto tedium was beguiled ever and anon by the appearance of a village, each one a scene of quaint simplicity.

"Our way twisted and turned through groves of palms among ancient, unspoiled villages nestling in the forest shade," Mr. Wright has recorded in his travel diary, under date of May 5, 1936. "Very fascinating are these clusters of thatched mud huts, decorated with one of the names of God on the door; many small, naked children innocently playing about, pausing to stare or run wildly from this big, black, bullock-less carriage tearing madly through their village. The women merely peep from the shadows, while the men lazily loll beneath the trees along the roadside, curious beneath their nonchalance. In one place, all the villagers were gaily bathing in the large tank (in their garments, changing by draping dry cloths around their bodies, dropping the wet ones). Women bearing water to their homes, in huge brass jars.

"The road led us a merry chase over mount and ridge; we bounced and tossed, dipped into small streams, detoured around an unfinished causeway, slithered across dry, sandy river beds and finally, about 5:00 P.M., we were close to our destination, Biur. This minute village in the interior of Bankura District, hidden in the protection of dense foliage, is unapproachable by travellers during the rainy season, when the streams are raging torrents and the roads serpent-like spit the mud-venom.

"Asking for a guide among a group of worshipers on their way home from a temple prayer (out in the lonely field), we were besieged by a dozen scantily clad lads who clambered on the sides of the car, eager to conduct us to Giri Bala.

"The road led toward a grove of date palms sheltering a group of mud huts, but before we had reached it, the Ford was momentarily tipped at a dangerous angle, tossed up and dropped down. The narrow trail led around trees and tank, over ridges, into holes and deep ruts. The car became anchored on a clump of bushes, then grounded on a hillock, requiring a lift of earth clods; on we proceeded, slowly and carefully; suddenly the way was stopped by a mass of brush in the middle of the cart track, necessitating a detour down a precipitous ledge into a dry tank, rescue from which demanded some scraping, adzing, and shoveling. Again and again the road seemed impassable, but the pilgrimage must go on; obliging lads fetched spades and demolished the obstacles (shades of Ganesh!) while hundreds of children and parents stared.

"Soon we were threading our way along the two ruts of antiquity, women gazing wide-eyed from their hut doors, men trailing alongside and behind us, children scampering to swell the procession. Ours was perhaps the first auto to traverse these roads; the 'bullock cart union' must be omnipotent here! What a sensation we created – a group piloted by an American and pioneering in a snorting car right into their hamlet fastness, invading the ancient privacy and sanctity!

"Halting by a narrow lane we found ourselves within a hundred feet of Giri Bala's ancestral home. We felt the thrill of fulfillment after the long road struggle crowned by a rough finish. We approached a large, two-storied building of brick and plaster, dominating the surrounding adobe huts; the house was under the process of repair, for around it was the characteristically tropical framework of bamboos.

"With feverish anticipation and suppressed rejoicing we stood before the open doors of the one blessed by the Lord's 'hungerless' touch. Constantly agape were the villagers, young and old, bare and dressed, women aloof somewhat but inquisitive too, men and boys unabashedly at our heels as they gazed on this unprecedented spectacle.

"Soon a short figure came into view in the doorway – Giri Bala! She was swathed in a cloth of dull, goldish silk; in typically Indian fashion, she drew forward modestly and hesitatingly, peering slightly from beneath the upper fold of her *swadeshi* cloth. Her eyes glistened like smouldering embers in the shadow of her head piece; we were enamoured by a most benevolent and kindly face, a face of realization and understanding, free from the taint of earthly attachment.

"Meekly she approached and silently assented to our snapping a number of pictures with our 'still' and 'movie' cameras.[6] Patiently and shyly she endured our photo techniques of posture adjustment and light arrangement. Finally we had recorded for posterity many photographs of the only woman in the world who is known to have lived without food or drink for over fifty years. (Therese Neumann, of course, has fasted since 1923.) Most motherly was Giri Bala's expression as she stood before us, completely covered in the loose-flowing cloth, nothing of her body visible but her face with its downcast eyes, her hands, and her tiny feet. A face of rare peace and innocent poise – a wide, childlike, quivering lip, a feminine nose, narrow, sparkling eyes, and a wistful smile."

Mr. Wright's impression of Giri Bala was shared by myself; spirituality enfolded her like her gently shining veil. She *pronamed* before me in the customary gesture of greeting from a householder to a monk. Her simple charm and quiet smile gave us a welcome beyond that of honeyed oratory; forgotten was our difficult, dusty trip.

The little saint seated herself cross-legged on the verandah. Though bearing the scars of age, she was not emaciated; her olive-coloured skin had remained clear and healthy in tone.

"Mother," I said in Bengali, "for over twenty-five years I have thought eagerly of this very pilgrimage! I heard about your sacred life from Sthiti Lal Nundy Babu."

She nodded in acknowledgment. "Yes, my good neighbor in Nawabganj."

"During those years I have crossed the oceans, but I never forgot my early plan to someday see you. The sublime drama that you are here playing so inconspicuously should be blazoned before a world that has long forgotten the inner food divine."

The saint lifted her eyes for a minute, smiling with serene interest.

"Baba (honoured father) knows best," she answered meekly.

I was happy that she had taken no offense; one never knows how great yogis or yoginis will react to the thought of publicity. They shun

6 Mr. Wright also took moving pictures of Sri Yukteswar during his last Winter Solstice Festival in Serampore.

it, as a rule, wishing to pursue in silence the profound soul research. An inner sanction comes to them when the proper time arrives to display their lives openly for the benefit of seeking minds.

"Mother," I went on, "please forgive me, then, for burdening you with many questions. Kindly answer only those that please you; I shall understand your silence, also."

She spread her hands in a gracious gesture. "I am glad to reply, insofar as an insignificant person like myself can give satisfactory answers."

"Oh, no, not insignificant!" I protested sincerely. "You are a great soul."

"I am the humble servant of all." She added quaintly, "I love to cook and feed people."

A strange pastime, I thought, for a non-eating saint!

"Tell me, Mother, from your own lips – do you live without food?"

"That is true." She was silent for a few moments; her next remark showed that she had been struggling with mental arithmetic. "From the age of twelve years four months down to my present age of sixty-eight – a period of over fifty-six years – I have not eaten food or taken liquids."

"Are you never tempted to eat?"

"If I felt a craving for food, I would have to eat." Simply yet regally she stated this axiomatic truth, one known too well by a world revolving around three meals a day!

"But you do eat something!" My tone held a note of remonstrance.

"Of course!" She smiled in swift understanding.

"Your nourishment derives from the finer energies of the air and sunlight,[7] and from the cosmic power which recharges your body through the medulla oblongata."

"Baba knows." Again she acquiesced, her manner soothing and unemphatic.

"Mother, please tell me about your early life. It holds a deep interest for all of India, and even for our brothers and sisters beyond the seas."

Giri Bala put aside her habitual reserve, relaxing into a conversational mood.

7 'What we eat is radiation; our food is so much quanta of energy,' Dr. George W. Crile of Cleveland told a gathering of medical men on May 17, 1933 in Memphis. This all important radiation, which releases electrical currents for the body's electrical circuit, the nervous system, is given to food by the sun's rays. Atoms, Dr. Crile says, are solar systems. Atoms are the vehicles that are filled with solar radiance as so many coiled springs. These countless atomfuls of energy are taken in as food. Once in the human body, these tense vehicles, the atoms, are discharged in the body's protoplasm, the radiance furnishing new chemical energy, new electrical currents. 'Your body is made up of such atoms,' Dr. Crile said. 'They are your muscles, brains, and sensory organs, such as the eyes and ears.'

Someday scientists will discover how man can live directly on solar energy.' 'Chlorophyll is the only substance known in nature that somehow possesses the power to act as a *sunlight trap*, ' William L. Laurence writes in the *New York Times*. 'It *catches* the energy of sunlight and stores it in the plant. Without this no life could exist. We obtain the energy we need for living from the solar energy stored in the plant-food we eat or in the flesh of the animals that eat the plants. The energy we obtain from coal or oil is solar energy trapped by the chlorophyll in plant life millions of years ago. We live by the sun through the agency of chlorophyll.'

"So be it." Her voice was low and firm. "I was born in these forest regions. My childhood was unremarkable save that I was possessed by an insatiable appetite. I had been betrothed in early years.

" 'Child,' my mother often warned me, 'try to control your greed. When the time comes for you to live among strangers in your husband's family, what will they think of you if your days are spent in nothing but eating?'

"The calamity she had foreseen came to pass. I was only twelve when I joined my husband's people in Nawabganj. My mother-in-law shamed me morning, noon, and night about my gluttonous habits. Her scoldings were a blessing in disguise, however; they roused my dormant spiritual tendencies. One morning her ridicule was merciless.

" 'I shall soon prove to you,' I said, stung to the quick, 'that I shall never touch food again as long as I live.'

"My mother-in-law laughed in derision. 'So!' she said, 'how can you live without eating, when you cannot live without overeating?'

"This remark was unanswerable! Yet an iron resolution scaffolded my spirit. In seclusion I sought my Heavenly Father.

" 'Lord,' I prayed incessantly, 'please send me a guru, one who can teach me to live by Thy light and not by food.'

"A divine ecstasy fell over me. Led by a beatific spell, I set out for the Nawabganj *ghat* on the Ganges. On the way I encountered the priest of my husband's family.

" 'Venerable sir,' I said trustingly, 'kindly tell me how to live without eating.'

"He stared at me without reply. Finally he spoke in a consoling manner. 'Child,' he said, 'come to the temple this evening; I will conduct a special *Vedic* ceremony for you.'

"This vague answer was not the one I was seeking; I continued toward the *ghat*. The morning sun pierced the waters; I purified myself in the Ganges, as though for a sacred initiation. As I left the river bank, my wet cloth around me, in the broad glare of day my master materialized himself before me!

" 'Dear little one,' he said in a voice of loving compassion, 'I am the guru sent here by God to fulfill your urgent prayer. He was deeply touched by its very unusual nature! From today you shall live by the astral light, your bodily atoms fed from the infinite current.' "

Giri Bala fell into silence. I took Mr. Wright's pencil and pad and translated into English a few items for his information.

The saint resumed the tale, her gentle voice barely audible. "The *ghat* was deserted, but my guru cast round us an aura of guarding light, that no stray bathers later disturb us. He initiated me into a *kria* technique which frees the body from dependence on the gross food of mortals. The technique includes the use of a certain *mantra*[8] and a breathing exercise more difficult than the average person could perform. No medicine or magic is involved; nothing beyond the *kria*."

In the manner of the American newspaper reporter, who had unknowingly taught me his procedure, I questioned Giri Bala on many matters which I thought would be of interest to the world. She gave me, bit by bit, the following information:

"I have never had any children: many years ago I became a widow. I sleep very little, as sleep and waking are the same to me. I meditate at night, attending to my domestic duties in the daytime. I slightly feel the change in climate from season to season. I have never been sick or experienced any disease. I feel only slight pain when accidentally injured. I have no bodily excretions. I can control my heart and breathing. I often see my guru as well as other great souls, in vision."

"Mother," I asked, "why don't you teach others the method of living without food?"

My ambitious hopes for the world's starving millions were nipped in the bud.

"No." She shook her head. "I was strictly commanded by my guru not to divulge the secret. It is not his wish to tamper with God's drama of creation. The farmers would not thank me if I taught many people to live without eating! The luscious fruits would lie uselessly on the ground. It appears that misery, starvation, and disease are whips of our karma which ultimately drive us to seek the true meaning of life."

"Mother," I said slowly, "what is the use of your having been singled out to live without eating?"

"To prove that man is Spirit." Her face lit with wisdom. "To demonstrate that by divine advancement he can gradually learn to live by the Eternal Light and not by food."[9]

The saint sank into a deep meditative state. Her gaze was directed inward; the gentle depths of her eyes became expressionless. She gave a

8 Potent vibratory chant. The literal translation of Sanskrit *mantra* is 'instrument of thought,' signifying the ideal, inaudible sounds which represent one aspect of creation; when vocalized as syllables, a *mantra* constitutes a universal terminology. The infinite powers of sound derive from AUM, the 'Word' or creative hum of the Cosmic Motor.

9 (Chap. 46) Giri Bala's yogic power comes from certain breathing exercise that affects *vishuddha chakra*, opposite the throat, controlling the fifth element, *akash* or ether, pervasive in the intra-atomic spaces of the physical cells. Concentration on this *chakra* ('wheel') enables the devotee to live by etheric energy. (Patanjali's *Yoga Sutras* III: 31)

   Therese Neumann neither lives by gross food nor practices a scientific yogic technique for non-eating. The explanation is hidden in the complexities of personal karma. Many lives of dedication to God lie behind a Neumann and a Giri Bala. Other such stigmatists are St. Lidwina of Schiedam, Blessed Elizabeth of Rent, St. Catherine of Siena, Dominica Lazarri, Blessed Angela of Foligno, and the 19th-century Louise Lateau. St. Nicholas of Flüe (Bruder Klaus, the 15th-century hermit) was an abstainer from food for 20 years.

certain sigh, the prelude to the ecstatic breathless trance. For a time she had fled to the questionless realm, the heaven of inner joy.

The tropical darkness had fallen. The light of a small kerosene lamp flickered fitfully over the faces of a score of villagers squatting silently in the shadows. The darting glowworms and distant oil lanterns of the huts wove bright eerie patterns into the velvet night. It was the painful hour of parting; a slow, tedious journey lay before our little party.

"Giri Bala," I said as the saint opened her eyes, "please give me a keepsake – a strip of one of your *saris*."

She soon returned with a piece of Benares silk, extending it in her hand as she suddenly prostrated herself on the ground.

"Mother," I said reverently, "rather let me touch your own blessed feet!"

47. *I return to the West*

"I HAVE GIVEN many yoga lessons in India and America; but I must confess that, as a Hindu, I am unusually happy to be conducting a class for English students."

My London class members laughed appreciatively; no political turmoils ever disturbed our yoga peace.

India was now a hallowed memory. It is September, 1936; I am in England to fulfill a promise, given sixteen months earlier, to lecture again in London.

England, too, is receptive to the timeless yoga message. Reporters and newsreel cameramen swarmed over my quarters at Grosvenor House. The British National Council of the World Fellowship of Faiths organized a meeting on September 29th at Whitefield's Congregational Church where I addressed the audience on the weighty subject of 'How Faith in Fellowship may Save Civilization.' The eight o'clock lectures at Caxton Hall attracted such crowds that on two nights the overflow waited in Windsor House auditorium for my second talk at nine-thirty. Yoga classes during the following weeks grew so large that Mr. Wright was obliged to arrange a transfer to another hall.

The English tenacity has admirable expression in a spiritual relationship. The London yoga students loyally organized themselves, after my departure, into a Self-Realization Fellowship centre, holding their meditation meetings weekly throughout the bitter war years.

Unforgettable weeks in England; days of sight-seeing in London, then over the beautiful countryside. Mr. Wright and I summoned the trusty Ford to visit the birthplaces and tombs of the great poets and heroes of British history.

Our little party sailed from Southampton for America in late October on the *Bremen*. The majestic Statue of Liberty in New York harbour brought a joyous emotional gulp not only to the throats of Miss Bletch and Mr. Wright, but to my own.

The Ford, a bit battered from struggles with ancient soils, was still puissant; it now took in its stride the transcontinental trip to California. In late 1936, lo! Mount Washington Centre.

The year-end holidays are celebrated annually at the Los Angeles centre with an eight-hour group meditation on December 24th (Spiritual Christmas), followed the next day by a banquet (Social Christmas). The festivities this year were augmented by the presence of dear friends and students from distant cities who had arrived to welcome home the three world travellers.

The Christmas Day feast included delicacies brought fifteen thousand miles for this glad occasion: *gucchi* mushrooms from Kashmir, canned *rasagulla* and mango pulp, *papar* biscuits, and an oil of the Indian *keora* flower which flavored our ice cream. The evening found us grouped around a huge sparkling Christmas tree, the near-by fireplace crackling with logs of aromatic cypress.

Gift-time! Presents from the earth's far corners – Palestine, Egypt, India, England, France, Italy. How laboriously had Mr. Wright counted the trunks at each foreign junction, that no pilfering hand receive the treasures intended for loved ones in America! Plaques of the sacred olive tree from the Holy Land, delicate laces and embroideries from Belgium and Holland, Persian carpets, finely woven Kashmiri shawls, everlastingly fragrant sandalwood trays from Mysore, Shiva 'bull's eye' stones from Central Provinces, old Indian coins of dynasties long fled, bejewelled vases and cups, miniatures, tapestries, temple incense and perfumes, *swadeshi* cotton prints, lacquer work, Mysore ivory carvings, Persian slippers with their inquisitive long toe, quaint old illuminated manuscripts, velvets, brocades, Gandhi caps, potteries, tiles, brass work, prayer rugs – booty of three continents!

One by one I distributed the gaily-wrapped packages from the immense pile under the tree.

"Sister Gyanamata!" I handed a long box to the saintly American lady of sweet visage and deep realization who, during my absence, had been in charge at Mt. Washington. From the paper tissues she lifted a *sari* of golden Benares silk.

"Thank you, sir; it brings the pageant of India before my eyes."

"Mr. Dickinson!" The next parcel contained a gift which I had bought in a Calcutta bazaar. "Mr. Dickinson will like this," I had thought at the time. A dearly beloved disciple, Mr. Dickinson had been present at every Christmas festivity since the 1925 founding of Mt. Washington Centre.

At this eleventh annual celebration, he was standing before me, untying the ribbons of his square little package.

"The silver cup!" Struggling with emotion, he stared at the present, a tall drinking cup. He seated himself some distance away, apparently in a daze. I smiled at him affectionately before resuming my role as Santa Claus.

The ejaculatory evening closed with a prayer to the Giver of all gifts; then a group singing of Christmas carols.

Mr. Dickinson and I were chatting together sometime later.

"Sir," he said, "please let me thank you now for the silver cup. I could not find any words on Christmas night."

"I brought the gift especially for you."

"For forty-three years I have been waiting for that silver cup! It is a long story, one I have kept hidden within me." Mr. Dickinson looked at me shyly. "The beginning was dramatic: I was drowning. My older brother had playfully pushed me into a fifteen-foot pool in a small town in Nebraska. I was only five years old then. As I was about to sink for the second time under the water, a dazzling multicoloured light appeared, filling all space. In the midst was the figure of a man with tranquil eyes and a reassuring smile. My body was sinking for the third time when one of my brother's companions bent a tall slender willow tree in such a low dip that I could grasp it with my desperate fingers. The boys lifted me to the bank and successfully gave me first-aid treatment.

"Twelve years later, a youth of seventeen, I visited Chicago with my mother. It was 1893; the great World Parliament of Religions was in session. Mother and I were walking down a main street, when again I saw the mighty flash of light. A few paces away, strolling leisurely along, was the same man I had seen years before in vision. He approached a large auditorium and vanished within the door.

" 'Mother,' I cried, 'that was the man who appeared at the time I was drowning!'

"She and I hastened into the building; the man was seated on a lecture platform. We soon learned that he was Swami Vivekananda of India.[1] After he had given a soul-stirring talk, I went forward to meet him. He smiled on me graciously, as though we were old friends. I was so young that I did not know how to give expression to my feelings, but in my heart I was hoping that he would offer to be my teacher. He read my thought.

" 'No, my son, I am not your guru.' Vivekananda gazed with his beautiful, piercing eyes deep into my own. 'Your teacher will come later. He will give you a silver cup.' After a little pause, he added, smiling, 'He will pour out to you more blessings than you are now able to hold.'

"I left Chicago in a few days," Mr. Dickinson went on, "and never saw the great Vivekananda again. But every word he had uttered was indelibly written on my inmost consciousness. Years passed; no teacher appeared. One night in 1925 I prayed deeply that the Lord would send me my guru. A few hours later, I was awakened from sleep by soft strains of melody. A band of celestial beings, carrying flutes and other instruments, came before my view. After filling the air with glorious music, the angels slowly vanished.

"The next evening I attended, one of your lectures here in Los Angeles, and knew then that my prayer had been granted."

We smiled at each other in silence.

"For eleven years now I have been your *Kriya Yoga* disciple," Mr. Dickinson continued. "Sometimes I wondered about the silver cup; I had almost persuaded myself that Vivekananda's words were only metaphorical.

But on Christmas night, as you handed me the square box by the tree, I saw, for the third time in my life, the same dazzling flash of light. In another minute I was gazing on my guru's gift which Vivekananda had foreseen for me forty-three years earlier[2] – a silver cup!"

48. *At Encinitas in California*[1]

"A SURPRISE, SIR! During your absence abroad we have had this Encinitas hermitage built; it is a 'welcome-home' gift!" Sister Gyanamata smilingly led me through a gate and up a tree-shaded walk.

I saw a building jutting out like a great white ocean liner toward the blue brine. First speechlessly, then with "Oh's!" and "Ah's!", finally with man's insufficient vocabulary of joy and gratitude, I examined the ashram – sixteen unusually large rooms, each one charmingly appointed.

The stately central hall, with immense ceiling-high windows, looks out on a united altar of grass, ocean, sky – a symphony in emerald, opal, sapphire. A mantle over the hall's huge fire-place holds the pictures of Christ, Babaji, Lahiri Mahasaya, and Sri Yukteswar; bestowing, I feel, their blessings on this tranquil Western ashram.

Directly below the hall, built into the very bluff, two solitary meditation caves confront the infinities of sky and sea. On the grounds are sun-bathing nooks, acres of orchard, a eucalypti grove, flagstone paths leading through

2 It appears that Swami Vivekananda was well aware that Yogananda was again in incarnation, and that he would go to America. Mr. Dickinson met him in Sep. 1893 – the year in which Paramahansa Yogananda was born. In 1965 Mr. Dickinson, still well and active at 89, received the title of *Yogacharya* (teacher of yoga) in a ceremony at Self-Realization Fellowship headquarters in Los Angeles. He meditated for long periods with Paramahansaji, and never missed *Kriya Yoga* practice.

Two years before his passing on June 30, 1967, Yogacharya Dickinson gave a talk to the Self-Realization Fellowship monks. He told them an interesting episode he had forgotten to mention to Paramahansaji. Yogacharya Dickinson said: "When I went up to the lecture podium in Chicago to speak to Swami Vivekananda, before I could greet the Swami he said:

" '*Young man, I want you to stay out of the water!*' "

1 A small town on Coast Highway 101, Encinitas is 100 miles south of Los Angeles, and 25 miles north of San Diego.

roses and lilies to quiet arbors, a long flight of stairs ending on an isolated beach and the vast waters! Was dream ever more concrete?

"May the good and heroic and bountiful souls of the saints come here," reads 'A Prayer for a Dwelling,' from the *Zend-Avesta,* fastened on one of the hermitage doors, "and may they go hand-in-hand with us, giving the healing virtues of their blessed gifts as widespread as the earth, as far-flung as the rivers, as high-reaching as the sun, for the furtherance of better men, for the increase of abundance and glory.

The large estate in Encinitas, California, is a gift to Self-Realization Fellowship from Mr. James J. Lynn, a faithful *Kriya Yogi* since his initiation in January 1932. An American businessmen of endless responsibilities (as head of vast oil interests and a president of the world's largest reciprocal fire-insurance exchange), Mr. Lynn nevertheless finds time daily for long and deep *Kriya Yoga* meditation. Leading thus a balanced life, he has attained in *samadhi* the grace of unshakable peace.

During my stay in India and Europe (June 1935 to October 1936), Mr. Lynn[2] had lovingly plotted with my correspondents in California to prevent any word from reaching me about the construction of the ashram in Encinitas. Astonishment, delight!

During my earlier years in America I had combed the coast of California in quest of a small site for a seaside ashram; whenever I had found a suitable location, some obstacle had invariably arisen to thwart me. Gazing now over the broad acres of Encinitas, humbly I saw the effortless fulfillment of Sri Yukteswar's long-ago prophecy: 'a hermitage by the ocean.'

A few months later, Easter of 1937, I conducted on the smooth lawns at Encinitas the first of many Sunrise Services. Like the Magi of old, several hundred students gazed in devotional awe at the daily miracle, the awakening solar fire in the eastern sky. To the west lay the inexhaustible Pacific, booming its solemn praise; in the distance a tiny white sailing boat, and the lonely flight of a seagull. 'Christ, thou art risen!' Not alone with the vernal sun, but in the eternal dawn of Spirit!

Many happy months sped by. In the peace and perfect beauty of Encinitas I was able to complete at the hermitage a long-projected work, *Cosmic Chants.* I set to English words and Western musical notation about forty songs, some original, others my adaptations of ancient melodies.

2. After Paramahansaji's passing, Mr. Lynn (Rajarsi Janakananda) served as president of Self-Realization Fellowship and Yogoda Satsanga Society of India. Of his guru Mr. Lynn said: "How heavenly is the company of a saint! Of all the things that have come to me in life, I treasure most the blessings that Paramahansaji has bestowed on me."

Mr. Lynn (b. 1892) attained *mahasamadhi* in 1955.

Included were the Shankara chant, 'No Birth, No Death'; two favourites of Sri Yukteswar's: 'Wake, Yet Wake, O my Saint!' and 'Desire, my Great Enemy'; the hoary Sanskrit 'Hymn to Brahma'; old Bengali songs, 'What Lightning Flash!' and 'They Have Heard Thy Name'; Tagore's 'Who is in my Temple?'; and a number of my compositions: 'I Will be Thine Always,' 'In the Land Beyond my Dreams,' 'Come Out of the Silent Sky,' 'Listen to my Soul Call,' 'In the Temple of Silence,' and 'Thou Art my Life.'

For a preface to the songbook I recounted my first outstanding experience with the receptivity of Westerners to the quaintly devotional airs of the East. The occasion had been a public lecture; the time, April 18, 1926; the place: Carnegie Hall in New York.

On April 17 I had confided to an American student, Mr. Alvin Hunsicker, "I am planning to ask the audience to sing an ancient Hindu chant, 'O God Beautiful!' "[3]

Mr. Hunsicker had protested that Oriental songs are alien to American understanding. What a shame if the lecture were to be marred by a commentary of over-ripe tomatoes!

I had laughingly disagreed. "Music is a universal language. Americans will not fail to feel the soul-aspiration in this lofty chant."

During the lecture Mr. Hunsicker had sat behind me on the platform, probably fearing for my safety. His doubts were groundless; not only had there been an absence of unwelcome vegetables, but for one hour and twenty-five minutes the strains of "O God Beautiful!" had sounded uninterruptedly from three thousand throats. Blasé no longer, dear New Yorkers; your hearts had soared out in a simple paean of rejoicing! Divine healings had taken place that evening among the devotees chanting with love the Lord's blessed name.

In 1941 I paid a visit to the Self-Realization Fellowship (SRF) Centre in Boston. The Boston Centre leader, Dr. M. W. Lewis, lodged me in an artistically decorated suite. "Sir," Dr. Lewis said, smiling, "during your early years in America you stayed in this city in a single room, without bath. I wanted you to know that Boston boasts some luxurious apartments!"

---

3 I translate here the words of Guru Nanak's song:
> O God beautiful! O God beautiful!
> In the forest, Thou art green,
> In the mountain, Thou an high,
> In the river, Thou art restless,
> In the ocean, Thou art grave!
> To the serviceful, Thou art service,
> To the lover, Thou art love,
> To the sorrowful, Thou art sympathy,
> To the yogi, Thou art bliss!
> O God beautiful! O God beautiful!
> At Thy feet, O I do bow!

Happy years in California sped by, filled with activity. A Self-Realization Fellowship Colony[4] in Encinitas was established in 1937. The numerous activities at the Colony give many-sided training to disciples in accordance with Self-Realization Fellowship ideals. Fruits and vegetables are grown for the use of residence of the Encinitas and Los Angeles centres.

"He hath made of one blood all nations of men."[5] 'World brotherhood' is a large term, but man must enlarge his sympathies, considering himself in the light of being a world citizen. He who truly understands that 'it is my America, my India, my Philippines, my Europe, my Africa' and so on, will never lack scope for a useful and happy life.

Though the body of Sri Yukteswar never dwelt on any soil except India's, he knew this brotherly truth:

'The world is my homeland.'

49. *The Years 1940-1951*

"WE HAVE indeed learned the value of meditation, and know that nothing can disturb our inner peace. In the last few weeks during the meetings we have heard air-raid warnings and listened to the explosion of delayed-action bombs, but our students still gather and thoroughly enjoy our beautiful service."

This brave message, written by the leader of the London Self-Realization Fellowship Centre, was one of many letters sent to me from war-ravaged England and Europe during the years that preceded America's entry into World War-II.

Dr. L. Cranmer-Byng, noted editor of *The Wisdom of the East Series* in London, wrote me in 1942 as follows:

"When I read *East-West*[1] I realised how far apart we seemed to be, apparently living in two different worlds. Beauty, order, calm, and peace come to me from Los Angeles, sailing into port as a vessel laden with the blessings and comfort of the Holy Grail to a beleaguered city.

"I see as in a dream your palm-tree grove, and the temple at Encinitas with its ocean stretches and mountain views, and above all its fellowship of spiritually minded men and women, a community comprehended in unity, absorbed in creative work, and replenished in contemplation. . . . Greetings to all the Fellowship from a common soldier, written on the watch-tower waiting for the dawn."

---

4 (Chap. 48) Now a flourishing Ashram Centre, whose buildings include the original main hermitage, ashrams for monks and nuns, dining facilities, and an attractive retreat for members and friends. A series of white pillars facing the highway side of the spacious grounds are crowned with lotuses of gold-leafed metal. In Indian art the lotus is a symbol of Cosmic Consciousness centre (*sahasrara*) in the brain, the 'thousand-petaled lotus of light.'

5 *Acts* 17: 26.

1 This magazine is now called *Self-Realization.*

A Self-Realization Fellowship Church of All Religions in Hollywood, California, was built by SRF workers and dedicated in 1942. A year later another SRF Temple was founded in San Diego, California; and, in 1947, one in Long Beach, California.

One of the most beautiful estates in the world, a floral wonderland in the Pacific Palisades section of Los Angeles, was donated in 1949 to Self-Realization Fellowship. The ten-acre site is a natural amphitheatre, surrounded by verdant hills. A large natural lake, a blue jewel in a mountain diadem, has given the estate its name of (SRF) Lake Shrine. A quaint Dutch-windmill house on the grounds contains a peaceful chapel. Near a sunken garden a large water-wheel splashes a leisurely music. Two marble statues from China adorn the site – a statue of Lord Buddha and one of Kwan Yin (the Chinese personification of the Divine Mother). A life-size statue of Christ, its serene face and flowing robes strikingly illuminated at night, stands on a hill above a waterfall. In the chapel are statues of Lord Krishna and other prophets.

A Mahatma Gandhi World Peace Memorial at the Lake Shrine was dedicated in 1950, the year that marked the thirtieth anniversary[2] of SRF in America. A portion of the Mahatma's ashes, sent from India, was enshrined in a thousand-year-old stone sarcophagus.

A Self-Realization Fellowship India Centre in Hollywood was founded in 1951. Mr. Goodwin J. Knight, Lieutenant Governor of California, and Mr. M. R. Ahuja, Consul General of India, joined me in the dedicatory services. On the site is India Hall, an auditorium seating 250 persons.

Newcomers to the various SRF centres often want further light on yoga. A question I sometimes hear is this: "Is it true, as certain organizations claim, that yoga may not be successfully studied in printed form but should be pursued only with the guidance of a nearby teacher?"

In the Atomic Age, yoga should be taught by a method of instruction such as the Self-Realization Fellowship Lessons, or the liberating science will again be restricted to a chosen few. It would indeed be a priceless boon if each student could keep by his side a guru perfected in divine wisdom; but the world is composed of many 'sinners' and few saints. How then may the multitudes be helped by yoga, if not through study in their homes of instructions written by true yogis?

The only alternative is that the 'average man' be ignored and left without yoga knowledge. Such is not God's plan for the new age. Babaji has promised to guard and guide all sincere *Kriya Yogis* in their path toward the Goal.[3] Hundreds of thousands, not dozens merely, of *Kriya Yogis* are

2 In celebrating this anniversary, I conducted a sacred rose-and-candle ceremony in Los Angeles on August 27, 1950, at which I gave *Kriya Yoga* initiation to 500 students.
3 Paramahansa Yogananda had assured his disciples worldwide that after this life he would continue to watch their spiritual progress. Since his *mahasamadhi* the truth of his beautiful promise has been amply substantiated.

needed to bring into manifestation the world of peace and plenty that awaits men when they have made the proper effort to re-establish their status as sons of the Divine Father.

The founding in the West of a Self-Realisation Fellowship organization, a 'hive for the spiritual honey,' was a duty enjoined on me by my guru Sri Yukteswar and my Mahavatar Babaji. The fulfilment of the sacred trust has not been devoid of difficulties.

"Tell me truly, Paramahansaji, has it been worth it?" This laconic question was put to me one evening by Dr. Lloyd Kennell, a leader of the temple in San Diego. I understood him to mean: "Have you been happy in America? What about the falsehoods circulated by misguided people who are anxious to prevent the spread of yoga? What about the disillusionments, the heartaches, the centre leaders who could not lead, the students who could not be taught?"

"Blessed is the man whom the Lord doth test!" I answered. "He has remembered, now and then, to put a burden on me." I thought, then, of all the faithful ones, of the love and devotion and understanding that illumines the heart of America. With slow emphasis I went on: "But my answer is yes, a thousand times yes! It *has* been worthwhile, more than ever I dreamed, to see East and West brought closer in the only lasting bond, the spiritual."

The great masters of India who have shown keen interest in the West have well understood modern conditions. They know that, until there is better assimilation in all nations of the distinctive Eastern and Western virtues, world affairs cannot improve. Each hemisphere needs the best offerings of the other.

In the course of world travel I have sadly observed much suffering.[4] In the Orient, suffering chiefly on the material plane; in the Occident, suffering chiefly on the mental or the spiritual plane.

All nations feel the painful effects of unbalanced civilizations. India, and many other Eastern lands can greatly benefit from emulation of the practical grasp of affairs, the material efficiency, of Western nations like America. The Occidental peoples, on the other hand, require a deeper understanding of the spiritual basis of life, and particularly of scientific techniques that India anciently developed for man's conscious communion with God.

---

4 That voice is round me like a bursting sea:
"And is thy earth so marred,
Shattered in shard on shard?
    Lo, all things fly thee, for thou fliest Me!
    All which I took from thee I did but take.
        Not for thy harms,
    But just that thou might'st seek it in My arms.
        All which thy child's mistake
    Fancied as lost I have stored for thee at home.
Rise, clasp My hand, and come!"

            – Francis Thompson, in *The Hound of Heaven.*

The ideal of a well-rounded civilization is not a chimerical one. For millenniums India was a land of both spiritual light and widespread material prosperity.

The poverty of the last 200 years is, in India's long history, only a passing karmic phase. A byword in the world, century after century, was 'the riches of the Indies.'[5] Abundance, material as well as spiritual, is a structural expression of *rita,* cosmic law or natural righteousness. There is no

5. The records of history present India, up until the 18th century, as the world's wealthiest nation. Incidentally, nothing in Hindu literature or tradition tends to substantiate the current Western historical theory that the early Aryans 'invaded' India from some other part of Asia or from Europe. The scholars are understandably unable to fix the starting point of this imaginary journey. The internal evidence in the *Vedas,* pointing to India as the immemorial home of the Hindus, has been presented in an unusual and very readable volume, *Rig-Vedic India,* by Abinas Chandra Das, published in 1921 by Calcutta University. Professor Das claims that emigrants from India settled in various parts of Europe and Asia, spreading the Aryan speech and folklore. The Lithuanian tongue, for example, is in many ways strikingly similar to Sanskrit. The philosopher Kant, who knew nothing of Sanskrit, was amazed at the scientific structure of the Lithuanian language. "It possesses," he said, "the key that will open all the enigmas, not only of philology but also of history".

The Bible refers to the riches of India, telling us (II *Chronicles* 9: 21,10) that the "ships of Tarshish" brought to King Solomon "gold and silver, ivory, apes, and peacocks" and a "great plenty of algum [sandalwood] trees and precious stones" from Ophir (Sopara on the Bombay coast). Megasthenes, the Greek ambassador (4th century B.C.), has left us a detailed picture of India's prosperity. Pliny (1st century A.D.) tells us that the Romans annually spent fifty million sesterces ($5,000,000) on imports from India, which was then a vast marine power.

Chinese travellers wrote vividly of the opulent Indian civilization, its widespread education and excellent government. The Chinese priest Fa-Hsien (fifth century) tells us the Indian people were happy, honest, and prosperous. See Samuel Beal's *Buddhist Records of the Western World* (India was the 'Western world' to the Chinese!), Trubner, London; and Thomas Watters' *On Yuan Chwang's Travels in India,* A.D. 629-45, Royal Asiatic Society.

Columbus, discovering the New World in the 15th century, was in reality seeking a shorter trade route to India. For centuries Europe was eager to possess the Indian exports – silks, fine cloths (of such sheerness as to deserve their descriptions: 'woven air' and 'invisible mist'), cotton prints, brocades, embroideries, rugs, cutlery, armour, ivory and ivory work, perfumes, incense, sandalwood, potteries, medicinal drugs and unguents, indigo, rice, spices, coral, gold, silver, pearls, rubies, emeralds, and diamonds.

Portuguese and Italian merchants have recorded their awe at the fabulous magnificence throughout the empire of Vijayanagar (1336-1565). The glory of its capital was described by the Arabian ambassador Razzak as "such that eye has not seen, nor has ear heard of, any place to equal it on earth".

In the 16th century, for the first time in her long history, India as a whole fell under non-Hindu rule. The Turkish Baber invaded the country in 1524 and founded a dynasty of Moslem kings. By settling in the ancient land, the new monarchs did not drain it of its riches. Weakened, however, by internal dissensions, wealthy India became the prey in the 17th century of several European nations; England finally emerged as the ruling power. India peacefully attained her independence on August 15, 1947. Like so many Indians, I have a now-it-can-be-told story. A group of young men, whom I had known in college, approached me during World War I and urged me to lead a revolutionary movement. I declined with these words: "Killing our English brothers cannot accomplish any good for India. Her freedom will not come through bullets, but through spiritual force." I then warned my friends that the arms-laden German ships, on which they were depending, would be intercepted by the British at Diamond Harbour, Bengal. The young men, however, went ahead with their plans, which proceeded to go awry in the manner I had mentioned. My friends were released from prison after a few years. Abandoning their violent convictions, several of them joined Mahatma Gandhi's ideal political movement. In the end they saw India's victory in a unique 'war' won by peace.

The sad division of the land into India and Pakistan, and the short but bloody interlude that ensued in a few parts of the country, were caused by economic factors, and not essentially by religious fanaticism (a minor reason often erroneously presented as a major one). Countless Hindus and Moslems, now as in the past, have lived side-by-side in amity. Men of both faiths, in immense numbers, became disciples of the 'creedless' master Kabir (1450-1518); and to this day he has millions of followers (*Kabir-panthis*). Under the Moslem rule of Akbar the Great, the widest possible freedom of belief prevailed throughout India. Nor is there today any serious religious disharmony amongst 95% of the simple people. The real India, the India that could understand and follow a Mahatma Gandhi, is found not in the large restless cities but in the peaceful 700,000 villages, where simple and just forms of self-government by *panchayats* (local councils) have been a feature from time immemorial. The problems that beset a newly freed India today will surely be solved in time by those great men whom India has never failed to produce.

parsimony in the Divine, nor in Its goddess of phenomena, exuberant Nature.

The Hindu scriptures teach that man is attracted to this particular earth to learn, more completely in each successive life, the infinite ways in which the Spirit may be expressed through, and be dominant over, material conditions. East and West are learning this great truth in different ways, and should gladly share with each other their discoveries. Beyond all doubt it is pleasing to the Lord when His earth-children struggle to attain a world civilization free from poverty, disease, and soul ignorance. Man's forgetfulness of his soul resources (the result of his misuse of free will)[6] is the root cause of all other forms of suffering.

The ills attributed to an anthropomorphic abstraction called 'society' may be laid more realistically at the door of Everyman.[7] Utopia must spring in the private bosom before it can flower in civic virtue, inner reforms leading naturally to outer ones. A man who has reformed himself will reform thousands.

The time-tested scriptures of the world are one in essence, inspiring man on his upward journey. One of the happiest periods of my life was spent in dictating, for *Self-Realization Magazine,* my interpretation of part of the New Testament. Fervently I implored Christ to guide me in divining the true meaning of his words, many of which have been grievously misunderstood for twenty centuries.

One night while I was engaged in silent prayer, my sitting room in the Encinitas hermitage became filled with an opal-blue light. I beheld the radiant form of the blessed Lord Jesus. A young man, he seemed, of about twenty-five with a sparse beard and moustache; his long hair, parted in the middle, was haloed by a shimmering gold.

His eyes were eternally wondrous; as I gazed, they were infinitely changing. With each divine transition in their expression, I intuitively understood the wisdom conveyed. In his glorious gaze I felt the power that upholds the myriad worlds. A Holy Grail appeared at his mouth; it came down to my lips and then returned to Jesus. After a few moments he uttered beautiful words, so personal in their nature that I keep them in my heart.

---

6.   "Freely we serve,
      Because we freely love, as in our will
      To love or not; in this we stand or fall.
      And some are fallen, to disobedience fallen,
      And so from heaven to deepest hell. O fall
      From what high state of bliss into what woe!" -- Milton, *Paradise Lost*

7. The plan of the divine *lila* or 'sportive play' by which the phenomenal worlds have come into existence is one of *reciprocity* between creature and Creator. The sole gift that man can offer to God is love; it suffices to call forth His overwhelming generosity. "Ye have robbed me, even this whole nation. Bring ye all the tithes into the storehouse, that there may be meat in mine house, and prove me now herewith, saith the Lord of hosts, if I will not open you the windows of heaven, and pour you out a blessing, that there shall not be room enough to receive it." – *Malachi* 3:9-10.

I spent much time in 1950 and 1951 at a tranquil retreat near the Mojave Desert in California. There I translated the *Bhagavad Gita* and wrote a detailed commentary[8] that presents the various paths of yoga.

Twice[9] referring explicitly to a yogic technique (the only one mentioned in the *Bhagavad Gita* and the same one that Babaji named, simply, *Kriya Yoga*), India's greatest scripture has thus offered practical as well as moral teaching. In the ocean of our dream-world, the breath is the specific storm of delusion that produces the consciousness of individual waves – the forms of men and of all other material objects.

Knowing that mere philosophical and ethical knowledge is insufficient to rouse man from his painful dream of separate existence, Lord Krishna pointed out the holy science by which the yogi may master his body and convert it, at will, into pure energy. The possibility of this yogic feat is not beyond the theoretical comprehension of modern scientists, pioneers in an Atomic Age. All matter has been proved to be reducible to energy.

The Hindu scriptures extol the yogic science because it is employable by mankind in general. The mystery of breath, it is true, has occasionally been solved without the use of formal yoga techniques, as in the cases of non-Hindu mystics who possessed transcendent powers of devotion to the Lord. Such Christian, Moslem, and other saints have indeed been observed in the breathless and motionless trance (*sabikalpa samadhi*)[10] without which no man has entered the first stages of God-perception. (After a saint has reached *nirbikalpa* or the highest *samadhi,* however, he is irrevocably established in the Lord – whether he be breathless or breathing, motionless or active.)

Brother Lawrence, the 17th-century Christian mystic, tells us how his first glimpse of God-realization came about by viewing a tree. Nearly all human beings have seen a tree; few, alas, have thereby seen the tree's Creator. Most men are utterly incapable of summoning those irresistible powers of devotion that are effortlessly possessed only by a few *ekantins*, 'single-hearted' saints found in all religious paths, whether of East or West. Yet the ordinary man[11] is not therefore shut out from the possibility of divine communion. He needs, for soul recollection, no more than the *Kriya Yoga* technique, a daily observance of the

8. The *Bhagavad Gita* is India's most beloved scripture. It contains the counsel of Lord Krishna to his disciple Arjuna: words of spiritual guidance that are timeless in their applicability by all truth-seekers. The central message of the *Gita* is that man may win emancipation through love for God, wisdom, and performance of right actions in a spirit of non-attachment.

9 *Bhagavad Gita* IV: 29 and V: 27-28.

10 See chapter 26. Among Christian mystics who have been observed in *sabikalpa samadhi* may be mentioned: St. Teresa of Avila, whose body would become so immovably fixed that the astonished nuns in the convent were unable to alter her position or to rouse her to outward consciousness.

11 The 'ordinary man' must make a spiritual start somewhere, sometime. "The journey of a thousand miles begins with one step," Lao-tzu observed. Cf. Lord Buddha: "Let no man think lightly of good, saying in his heart, 'it will not come nigh me'. By the falling of water drops a pot is filled; the wise man becomes full of good, even if he gather it little by little."

moral precepts, and an ability to cry sincerely: "Lord, I yearn to know Thee!"

The universal appeal of yoga is thus its approach to God through a daily usable scientific method, rather than through a devotional fervour that, for the average man, is beyond his emotional scope.

Various great Jain teachers of India have been called *tirthakaras*, 'ford-makers,' because they reveal the passage by which bewildered humanity may cross over and beyond the stormy seas of *samsara* (the karmic wheel – the recurrence of lives and deaths). *Samsara* (literally, 'flowing with' the phenomenal flux) induces man to take the line of least resistance. 'Whosoever therefore will be a friend of the world is the enemy of God.'[12] To become the friend of God, man must overcome the devils or evils of his own karma or actions that ever urge him to spineless acquiescence in the mayic delusions of the world. A knowledge of the iron law of karma encourages the earnest seeker to find the way of final escape from its bonds. Because the karmic slavery of human beings is rooted in the desires of *maya*-darkened minds, it is with mind control that the yogi concerns himself with. The various cloaks of karmic ignorance are laid away, and man views himself in his native essence.[13]

The mystery of life and death, whose solution is the only purpose of man's sojourn on earth, is intimately interwoven with breath. Breathlessness is deathlessness. Realising this truth, the ancient rishis of India seized on the sole clue of the breath and developed a precise and rational science of breathlessness.

Had India no other gift for the world, *Kriya Yoga* alone would suffice as a kingly offering.

The Bible contains passages which reveal that the Hebrew prophets were well aware that God has made the breath to serve as the subtle link between body and soul. *Genesis* states: 'The Lord God formed man of the dust of the ground, and breathed into his nostrils the breath of life; and man became a living soul.'[14] The human body is composed of chemical

12 *James* 4: 4.
13.   "Steadfast a lamp burns sheltered from the wind;
             Such is the likeness of the Yogi's mind
             Shut from sense-storms and burning bright to Heaven.
             When mind broods placid, soothed with holy wont;
             When Self contemplates self, and in itself
             Hath comfort; when it knows the nameless joy
             Beyond all scope of sense, revealed to soul
             Only to soul! and, knowing, wavers not,
             True to the farther Truth; when, holding this,
             It deems no other treasure comparable,
             But, harboured there, cannot be stirred or shook
             By any gravest grief, call that state 'peace,'
             That happy severance Yoga; call that man
             The perfect Yogin! "
                                        – *Bhagavad Gita* VI: 19-23 (Arnold's translation).
14 *Genesis* 2: 7

and metallic substances that are also found in the 'dust of the ground'. The flesh of man could never carry on activity nor manifest energy and motion were it not for the life currents transmitted by soul to body through the instrumentality, in unenlightened men, of the breath (gaseous energy). The life currents, operating in the human body as the fivefold *prana* or subtle life energies, are an expression of the *Aum* vibration of the omnipresent soul.

The reflection, the verisimilitude, of life that shines in the fleshly cells from the soul-source is the only cause of man's attachment to his body; obviously he would not pay solicitous homage to a clod of clay. A human being falsely identifies himself with his physical form because the life currents from the soul are breath-conveyed into the flesh with such intense power that man mistakes the effect for a cause, and idolatrously imagines the body to have life of its own.

Man's conscious state is an awareness of body and breath. His subconscious state, active in sleep, is associated with his mental, and temporary, separation from body and breath. His superconscious state is a freedom from the delusion that 'existence' depends on body and breath.[15] God lives without breath; the soul made in His image becomes conscious of itself, for the first time, only during the breathless state.

When the breath-link between soul and body is severed by evolutionary karma, the abrupt transition called 'death' ensues; the physical cells revert to their natural powerlessness. For the *Kriya Yogi,* however, the breath-link is severed at will by scientific wisdom, not by the rude intrusion of karmic necessity. Through actual experience, the yogi is already aware of his essential incorporeity, and does not require the somewhat pointed hint given by Death that man is badly advised to place his reliance on a physical body.

Life by life, each man progresses (at his own pace, be it ever so erratic) toward the goal of his own apotheosis. Death, no interruption in this onward sweep, simply offers man the more congenial environment of an astral world in which to purify his dross. 'Let not your heart be troubled. . . . In my Father's house are many mansions.'[16] It is indeed unlikely that God has exhausted His ingenuity in organizing this world, or that, in the next world, He will offer nothing more challenging to our interest than the strumming of harps.

5 'You never will enjoy the world aright till the sea itself floweth in your veins, till you are clothed with the heavens, and crowned with the stars, and perceive yourself to be the sole heir of the whole world, and more than so, because men are in it who are every one sole heirs as well as you; till you can sing and delight and rejoice in God, as misers do in gold, and kings in sceptres . . . till you are as familiar with the ways of God in all ages as with your walk and table; till you are intimately acquainted with that shady nothing out of which the world was made.' – *Thomas Traherne,* in *Centuries of Meditations.*

6 *John* 14: 1-2.

Death is not a blotting-out of existence, a final escape from life; nor is death the door to immortality. He who has fled his Self in earthly joys will not recapture it amidst the gossamer charms of an astral world. There he merely accumulates finer perceptions and more sensitive responses to the beautiful and the good, which are one. It is on the anvil of this gross earth that struggling man must hammer out the imperishable gold of spiritual identity. Bearing in his hand the hard-won golden treasure, the sole acceptable gift to greedy Death, a human being wins final freedom from the rounds of physical reincarnation.

For several years I conducted classes in Encinitas and Los Angeles on the *Yoga Sutras* of Patanjali and other profound works of Hindu philosophy.

"Why did God ever join soul and body?" a class student asked one evening. "What was His purpose in setting into initial motion this evolutionary drama of creation?" Countless other men have posed such questions; philosophers have sought, in vain, fully to answer them.

"Leave a few mysteries to explore in Eternity," Sri Yukteswar used to say with a smile. "How could man's limited reasoning powers comprehend the inconceivable motives of the Uncreated Absolute?[17] The rational faculty in man, tethered by the cause-effect principle of the phenomenal world, is baffled before the enigma of God, the Beginning-less, the Uncaused. Nevertheless, though man's reason cannot fathom the riddles of creation, every mystery will ultimately be solved for the devotee by God Himself."

He who sincerely yearns for wisdom is content to start his search by humbly mastering a few simple ABC's of the divine scheme, not demanding prematurely a precise mathematical graph of life's 'Einstein Theory'.

'No man hath seen God at any time (no mortal under 'time,' the relativities of maya,[18] can realise the Infinite); *the only begotten Son, which is in the bosom of the Father* (the reflected Christ Consciousness or outwardly projected Perfect Intelligence that, guiding all structural phenomena through *Aum* vibration, has issued forth from the 'bosom' or deeps of the Uncreated Divine in order to express the variety of Unity), *he hath declared* (subjected to form, or manifested) *him.* '[19]

"Verily, verily, I say unto you," Jesus explained, "the Son can do nothing

---

17 "For my thoughts are not your thoughts, neither are your ways my ways, saith the Lord. For as the heavens are higher than the earth, so are my ways higher than your ways, and my thoughts than your thoughts" – *Isaiah* 55: 8-9. The Author has also alluded to a verse in Dante's *Divine Comedy* which appears at the end of this Chapter (pg 367).

18 The earth's diurnal cycle, from light to darkness and vice versa, is a constant reminder to man of creation's involvement in *maya* or oppositional states. (The transitional or equilibrated periods of the day, dawn and dusk, are therefore considered auspicious for meditation.) Rending the dual-textured veil of *maya*, the yogi perceives the transcendent Unity.

19 *John* 1: 18.   20 *John* 5: 19.

of himself, but what he seeth the Father do: for what things soever he doeth, these also doeth the Son likewise."[20]

The threefold nature of God as He demonstrates Himself in the phenomenal worlds is symbolized in Hindu scriptures as Brahma the Creator, Vishnu the Preserver, and Shiva the Destroyer-Renovator. Their triune activities are ceaselessly displayed throughout vibratory creation. As the Absolute is beyond the conceptual powers of man, the devout Hindu worships It in the august embodiments of the Trinity.[21]

The universal creative-preservative-destructive aspect of God, however, is not His ultimate or even His essential nature (for cosmic creation is only His *lila*, creative sport).[22] His intrinsicality cannot be grasped even by grasping all the mysteries of the Trinity, because His outer nature, as manifested in the lawful atomic flux, merely expresses Him without revealing Him. The final nature of the Lord is known only when "the Son ascends to the Father."[23] The liberated man overpasses the vibratory realms and enters the Vibrationless Original.

All great prophets have remained silent when requested to unveil the ultimate secrets. When Pilate asked: "What is truth?"[24] Christ made no reply. The large ostentatious questions of intellectualists like Pilate seldom proceed from a burning spirit of inquiry. Such men speak rather with the empty arrogance that considers a lack of conviction about spiritual values[25] to be a sign of 'open-mindedness'.

"To this end was I born, and for this cause came I into the world, that I should bear witness unto the truth. Everyone that is of the truth heareth my voice."[26] In these few words Christ spoke volumes. A child of God 'bears witness' *by his life*. He embodies truth; if he expound it also, that is generous redundancy.

Truth is no theory, no speculative system of philosophy, no intellectual insight. Truth is exact correspondence with reality. For man, truth is unshakable knowledge of his real nature, his Self as soul. Jesus, by every act and word of his life, proved that he knew *the truth* of his being – his source in

---

1 A different conception from that of the trinitarian Reality: *Sat, Tat, Aum;* or, Father, Son, Holy Ghost. Brahma-Vishnu-Shiva represents the triune expression of God in the aspect of *Tat* or Son, the Christ Consciousness immanent (i.e. remaining or operating within a domain of reality) in vibratory creation. The *shaktis*, energies or 'consorts' of the Trinity, are symbols of *Aum* or the Holy Ghost, the sole causative force that upholds the cosmos through vibration.

2 "O Lord . . . thou has created all things, and for thy pleasure they are and were created." – *Revelation* 4: 11.

3 *John* 14: 12.   24 *John* 18: 38.

5   "Love Virtue; she alone is free;
She can teach ye how to climb
Higher than the sphery chime;
Or if Virtue feeble were,
Heaven itself would stoop to her. "
                 – Milton, *Comus*   26 *John* 18: 37.

God. Wholly identified with the omnipresent Christ Consciousness, he could say with simple finality: "Everyone that is of the truth heareth my voice."

Buddha, too, refused to shed light on the metaphysical ultimates, dryly pointing out that man's few moments on earth are best employed in perfecting the moral nature. The Chinese mystic Lao-tzu rightly taught: "He who knows, tells it not; he who tells, knows it not." The final mysteries of God are not 'open to discussion'. The decipherment of His secret code is an art that man cannot communicate to man; here the Lord alone is the Teacher.

"Be still, and know that I am God."[27] Never flaunting His omnipresence, the Lord is heard only in the immaculate silences. Reverberating throughout the universe as the creative *Aum* vibration, the Primal Sound instantly translates Itself into intelligible words for the devotee in attunement.

The divine purpose of creation, so far as man's reason can grasp it, is expounded in the *Vedas*. The rishis taught that each human being has been created by God as a soul that will uniquely manifest some special attribute of the Infinite before resuming its Absolute Identity. All men, endowed thus with a facet of Divine Individuality, are equally dear to God.

The wisdom garnered by India, the eldest brother among the nations, is a heritage of all mankind. Vedic truth, as all truth, belongs to the Lord and not to India. The rishis, whose minds were pure receptacles to receive the divine profundities of the *Vedas*, were members of the human race, born on this earth, rather than on some other, to serve humanity as a whole. Distinction by race or nation are meaningless in the realm of truth, where the only qualification is spiritual fitness to receive.

God is Love; His plan for creation can be rooted only in love. Does not that simple thought, rather than erudite reasonings, offer solace to the human heart? Every saint who has penetrated to the core of Reality has testified that a divine universal plan exists and that it is beautiful and full of joy.

To the prophet Isaiah, God revealed His intentions in these words:

"So shall my word [creative *Aum*] be that goeth forth out of my mouth: it shall not return unto me void, but it shall accomplish that which I please,[28]

27 *Psalms* 46: 10. The goal of the science of Yoga is to obtain that necessary inner stillness by which one may truly 'know God.'
28 Dante testified in *The Divine Comedy*:
> "I have been in that heaven the most illumined
> By light from Him, and seen things which to utter
> He who returns hath neither skill nor knowledge;
> For as it nears the object of its yearning
> Our intellect is overwhelmed so deeply
> It never can retrace the path it followed.
> But whatsoever of the holy kingdom
> Was in the power of memory to treasure
> Will be my theme until the song is ended."

and it shall prosper in the thing whereto I sent it. For he shall go out with joy, and be led forth with peace, the mountains and the hills shall break forth before you into singing and all the trees of the field shall clap their hands."[29]

"Ye shall go out with joy, and be led forth with peace." The men of a hard-pressed twentieth century hear longingly that wondrous promise. The full truth within it is realisable by every devotee of God who strives manfully to repossess his divine heritage.

The blessed role of Kriya Yoga in East and West has hardly more than just begun. May all men come to know that there exists a definite, scientific technique of Self-Realization for the overcoming of all human misery!

In sending loving thought-vibrations to the thousands of Kriya Yogis scattered like shining jewels over the earth. I often think gratefully:

'Lord, Thou hast given this monk a large family!'

THE END

29 *Isaiah* 55: 11-12

EPILOGUE

Paramahansa Yogananda entered *mahasamadhi* (a God-illumined and realized yogi's final and conscious exit from the body, resulting in physical death) in Los Angeles California, USA on March 7, 1952, after concluding his speech at a banquet held in the honour of the Ambassador of India.

The great master and the world teacher demonstrated the value of yoga not only in his vibrant life but in self-ordained death as well. Weeks after his passing into the ethereal world, his unchanged face shone with the divine lustre of incorruptibility. In a notarized letter sent to Self-Realization Fellowship, Mr. Harry T. Rowe, Mortuary Director of Forest Lawn Memorial-Park, Los Angeles (where the great Guru's body was temporarily placed), made the following declaration:

(Extracts): 'The absence of any visual signs of decay in the dead body of Paramahansa Yogananda offers the most extraordinary case in our experience. . . . No physical disintegration was visible in his body even after twenty days after death. . . . No mold was visible on his skin, and no visible desiccation (*i.e.* signs of drying up) took place in the bodily tissues. This state of perfect preservation of a body is, so far as we know from mortuary annals, and unparalleled one. At the time of receiving Yogananda's body, our personnel expected to observe through the glass lid of the casket, the usual progressive signs of bodily decay. Our astonishment increased as day followed day without bringing any visible change in body under observation. Yogananda's body was apparently in a phenomenal state of immutability. . . . No odor of decay emanated from his body at any time. . . .

The physical appearance of Yogananda on March 27th, just before the bronze cover of the casket was put into position, was the same as it was on March 7th. He looked on March 27th as fresh and as unravaged by decay as had looked on the night of his death. On March 27th there was no reason to say that his body had suffered any visible disintegration at all. For these reasons we state again that the case of Paramahansa Yogananda is unique in our experience.'

* *

Sri Yogananda's passing occasioned an outpouring of reverent appreciation from spiritual leaders, dignitaries, admirers, and disciples all over the world. His Holiness Swami Sivananda, founder of The Divine Life Society, wrote: 'A rare gem of inestimable value, the like of whom the world is yet to witness, His Holiness Sri Paramahansa Yogananda has been an ideal representative of the ancient sages and seers, and the glory of India.' American author and educator Dr. Wendell Thomas wrote: 'I came to [Paramahansa] Yogananda many years ago, not as a seeker or devotee, but as a writer with a sympathetic yet analytic and critical approach. Happily, I found in Yoganandaji a rare combination. While steadfast in the ancient principles of his profound faith, he had the gift of generous adaptability. . . . With his quick wit and great spirit he was well fitted to promote reconciliation and truth among the religious seekers of the world. He brought peace and joy to multitudes.'

* *

The crowded bus stand of Ranchi, the State Capital of eastern Indian state of Jharkhand, seems an unlikely place to reach the permanent abode of a Yogi and a Saint. Yet, in the noisy hubbub of blaring horns and shouting vendors, an ochre robe disappears around a particularly innocuous corner. In this intriguing contrast one follows the trail – to reach Yogoda Satsanga Ashram of the Yogoda Satsanga Society of India (YSS), a tranquil haven of peace. As the reader has seen in chapter 27, Yogoda Satsanga Society was founded by Sri Sri Paramahansa Yogananda in 1917 with an ashram and the residential school. It was shifted a year later to the Ranchi palace donated by the King of Kasimbazar, Sir Mahendra Chandra Nundy.

A visitor turns into the gate of YSS which is forever open. The marble lotus-shaped Samadhi of Paramahansa Yogananda has a tangible aura and the vibrations of this serene place are magnetic. In the soothing interior, a number of devotees sit in deep meditation before the great Master's portrait.

The concluding lines of his Autobiography then return to mind:

'Lord, Thou hast given this monk a large family.'*

If there should rise, Suddenly within the skies
Sunburst of a thousand suns, Flooding earth with beams undeemed-of,
Then might be, that Holy One's Majesty and radiance dreamed of!

– *Bhagavad Gita* XI: 12

Page 265 of this Volume

---

* "Remember," (the guru of Sri Yogananda had said) "that he who discards his worldly duties can justify himself only by assuming some kind of responsibility toward a much larger family." (See page 194).